MW00605205

DISCARD

HUMAN AGGRESSION AND VIOLENCE

HUMAN AGGRESSION AND VIOLENCE

Causes, Manifestations, and Consequences

Edited by Phillip R. Shaver and Mario Mikulincer

American Psychological Association • Washington, DC

Published by
American Psychological Association
750 First Street, NE
Washington, DC 20002
www.apa.org

To order
APA Order Department
P.O. Box 92984
Washington, DC 20090-2984
Tel: (800) 374-2721; Direct: (202) 336-5510
Fax: (202) 336-5502; TDD/TTY: (202) 336-6123
Online: www.apa.org/pubs/books
E-mail: order@apa.org

In the U.K., Europe, Africa, and the Middle East, copies may be ordered from
American Psychological Association
3 Henrietta Street
Covent Garden, London
WC2E 8LU England

Typeset in Goudy by Circle Graphics, Inc., Columbia, MD

Printer: Maple-Vail Manufacturing Group, York, PA
Cover Designer: Mercury Publishing Services, Rockville, MD

The opinions and statements published are the responsibility of the authors, and such opinions and statements do not necessarily represent the policies of the American Psychological Association.

Library of Congress Cataloging-in-Publication Data

Human aggression and violence : causes, manifestations, and consequences / edited by Phillip R. Shaver and Mario Mikulincer.
    p. cm. — (The Herzliya series on personality and social psychology)
  Includes bibliographical references and index.
  ISBN-13: 978-1-4338-0859-3 (print)
  ISBN-10: 1-4338-0859-5 (print)
  ISBN-13: 978-1-4338-0860-9 (electronic)
  ISBN-10: 1-4338-0860-9 (electronic)
1. Aggressiveness. 2. Violence. I. Shaver, Phillip R. II. Mikulincer, Mario.

  BF575.A3H867 2011
  155.2'32—dc22
                              2010005100

British Library Cataloguing-in-Publication Data

A CIP record is available from the British Library.

Printed in the United States of America
First Edition

THE HERZLIYA SERIES ON PERSONALITY
AND SOCIAL PSYCHOLOGY

Mario Mikulincer and Phillip R. Shaver, Series Editors

Series Titles

Prosocial Motives, Emotions, and Behavior: The Better Angels of Our Nature
Edited by Mario Mikulincer and Phillip R. Shaver

Human Aggression and Violence: Causes, Manifestations, and Consequences
Edited by Phillip R. Shaver and Mario Mikulincer

CONTENTS

CONTRIBUTORS

Craig A. Anderson, PhD, Department of Psychology, Iowa State University, Ames

Ximena B. Arriaga, PhD, Department of Psychological Sciences, Purdue University, West Lafayette, IN

Paul Boxer, PhD, Department of Psychology, Rutgers University, Newark, NJ

Brad J. Bushman, PhD, Department of Psychology and Institute for Social Research, University of Michigan, Ann Arbor, and VU University, Amsterdam, The Netherlands

Nicole M. Capezza, PhD, Department of Psychological Sciences, Purdue University, West Lafayette, IN

Dante Cicchetti, PhD, Institute of Child Development and Department of Psychiatry, University of Minnesota, Minneapolis

Dov Cohen, PhD, Department of Psychology, University of Illinois at Urbana–Champaign

Thomas F. Denson, PhD, School of Psychology, University of New South Wales, Sydney, Australia

C. Nathan DeWall, PhD, Department of Psychology, University of Kentucky, Lexington

Kenneth A. Dodge, PhD, Center for Child and Family Policy, Duke University, Durham, NC

John F. Dovidio, PhD, Department of Psychology, Yale University, New Haven, CT

Eric F. Dubow, PhD, Department of Psychology, Bowling Green State University, Bowling Green, OH

Donald G. Dutton, PhD, Department of Psychology, University of British Columbia, Vancouver, Canada

Eli J. Finkel, PhD, Department of Psychology, Northwestern University, Evanston, IL

Karni Ginzburg, PhD, The Bob Shapell School of Social Work, Tel Aviv University, Tel Aviv, Israel

Gail S. Goodman, PhD, Department of Psychology and Center for Public Policy Research, University of California, Davis

Eran Halperin, PhD, School of Government, Interdisciplinary Center Herzliya, Herzliya, Israel

LaTonya S. Harris, EdM, Department of Psychology and Center for Public Policy Research, University of California, Davis

Gilad Hirschberger, PhD, School of Psychology, Interdisciplinary Center Herzliya, Herzliya, Israel

L. Rowell Huesmann, PhD, Institute for Social Research, University of Michigan, Ann Arbor

Robert F. Krueger, PhD, Department of Psychology, Washington University, St. Louis, MO

Robert Kurzban, PhD, Department of Psychology, University of Pennsylvania, Philadelphia

Angela K.-y. Leung, PhD, School of Social Sciences, Singapore Management University, Singapore

Ofra Mayseless, PhD, School of Education, University of Haifa, Haifa, Israel

Michael McCullough, PhD, Department of Psychology, University of Miami, Coral Gables, FL

Mario Mikulincer, PhD, School of Psychology, Interdisciplinary Center Herzliya, Herzliya, Israel

Felicia Pratto, PhD, Department of Psychology, University of Connecticut, Storrs

Tom Pyszczynski, PhD, Department of Psychology, University of Colorado, Colorado Springs

Soo Hyun Rhee, PhD, Institute for Behavioral Genetics, University of Colorado, Boulder

Tamar Saguy, PhD, School of Psychology, Interdisciplinary Center Herzliya, Herzliya, Israel

Miri Scharf, PhD, School of Education, University of Haifa, Haifa, Israel

Michal Segev, MA, Department of Psychology, Bar-Ilan University, Ramat Gan, Israel

Aaron Sell, PhD, Department of Psychology, University of California, Santa Barbara

Phillip R. Shaver, PhD, Department of Psychology, University of California, Davis

Purnima Singh, PhD, Department of Psychology, Women's College, Aligarh Muslim University, Aligarh, India

Erica B. Slotter, MA, Department of Psychology, Northwestern University, Evanston, IL

Zahava Solomon, PhD, The Bob Shapell School of Social Work, Tel Aviv University, Tel Aviv, Israel

Benjamin A. Tabak, MSc, Department of Psychology, University of Miami, Coral Gables, FL

Jennifer L. Tackett, PhD, Department of Psychology, University of Toronto, Toronto, Canada

Nicole Tausch, PhD, Department of Psychology, Cardiff University, Cardiff, Wales, United Kingdom

Sander Thomaes, PhD, Department of Developmental Psychology, Utrecht University, Utrecht, The Netherlands

Sheree L. Toth, PhD, Mt. Hope Family Center, University of Rochester, Rochester, NY

Irwin D. Waldman, PhD, Department of Psychology, Emory University, Atlanta, GA

PREFACE

We live in a violent world. Aggression, intimidation, and cruelty are part of daily life almost everywhere. Homicides, violent robberies, gang warfare, political violence, terrorism, and international conflicts fill the daily newspapers, TV news programs, and websites. Violence ruins many marriages, damages countless children, and causes the deaths of police officers and military recruits.

Researchers and members of the general public often wonder what makes a person violent. Is it a matter of genes? Parental abuse and neglect? The media? Alcohol and drugs that impair self-control and disrupt rational problem solving? Access to guns?

Within the social and behavioral sciences, and now within the brain sciences as well, investigators agree that human aggression is complex and multifaceted and that many kinds of research are necessary to understand its causes, manifestations, and consequences. Some writers, for example, have considered aggression and violence from evolutionary and genetic perspectives and have produced solid evidence concerning the intergenerational transmission of aggression and its stability across a person's life course. Other writers have considered how parenting styles and parental modeling contribute to children's aggression; still others have focused on intergroup conflicts and warfare. Unfortunately, findings from these different perspectives are rarely integrated or effectively applied in real life.

The time is therefore right for a collaborative, creative conversation among experts on the variety of approaches to human aggression and violence. The timeliness and social relevance of the topic led us to dedicate the second volume of The Herzliya Series on Personality and Social Psychology to the psychology of aggression, violence, and their effects as viewed at different levels of analysis, from neural to societal. This series of volumes is designed to explore socially significant topics with a group of world-class researchers who are invited to visit the Interdisciplinary Center Herzliya to engage in constructively critical but collaborative conversations and then to contribute to a focused, gracefully written volume that can be shared with other members of the discipline and understood by a wide range of educated readers outside the discipline. The first volume in the series, *Prosocial Motives, Emotions, and Behavior* (published by the American Psychological Association [APA] in 2009), was dedicated to prosocial behavior. The present volume is the second in the series.

The chapter authors generously agreed to deliver lectures, participate in hours of discussion of the lectures, and then return home and prepare chapters based on these lectures and discussions. The meeting was cohosted by the two of us, and we worked together with the chapter authors to make the book as accessible, coherent, and readable as possible, so that it would be suitable for researchers and application-oriented professionals as well as university classes and the educated public. The book provides a state-of-the-art review of the major theoretical perspectives on human aggression and violence; the basic psychological processes underlying destructive behaviors; and recent research on the consequences of aggression in couple and family relationships, groups and organizations, and intergroup relations.

We are grateful to everyone who made the preparation of this volume so enjoyable and successful. We thank all of the chapter authors, an amazing group of scholars and admirable human beings who care about both their sciences and the betterment of human lives. We especially wish to thank Professor Uriel Reichmann, president of the Interdisciplinary Center Herzliya, who provided financial and staff support for an annual series of conferences on personality and social psychology. We thank the staff of the Interdisciplinary Center Herzliya—Shulli Sardes, Lior Lev-Ari, and Tsachi Ein-Dor— who handled all of the arrangements for the conference, dealt effectively with the many on-site details, and coped masterfully with the inevitable glitches and emergencies. We would also like to thank Maureen Adams, senior acquisitions editor at APA Books, for seeing the value of this book and the series in which it appears and for being a generous, thoughtful, and supportive friend during this book's preparation. Finally, we thank Tyler Aune and Katie Funk, development editor and production editor at APA Books, respectively, and copyeditor Erin O'Brien for their careful efforts.

HUMAN AGGRESSION
AND VIOLENCE

INTRODUCTION

PHILLIP R. SHAVER AND MARIO MIKULINCER

In a world riddled with greed, intimidation, and violence, there is an urgent need to understand and control these destructive forces. Within the social and behavioral sciences, and recently within genetics and neuroscience as well, there are deep and empirically supported insights into aggression and violence, but they are rarely included in a single conversation. We know more than ever about the evolutionary history and functions of aggression; several scientific disciplines have explored its genetic, developmental, interpersonal, and cultural causes. But the resulting knowledge has not been integrated and effectively applied in real life. It is time for an open, collaborative, and creative discussion among experts about the most promising perspectives on human aggression and violence, as well as ways to apply scientific insights in effective interventions.

In social psychology, *aggression* is defined as behavior performed by one person (i.e., an aggressor) with the intent of physically or psychologically harming another person who wants to avoid the harm (i.e., a victim), and *violence* is defined as an extreme, especially destructive, and cruel form of aggression (for examples and discussions of violence at the dyadic, familial, and societal levels, see Chapters 14, 16, 17, and 19–21). In psychological science, aggression and

3

violence are viewed as different from assertiveness and power. Although aggression can be used to assert one's authority and control over precious resources, there are many cases in which power can be attained without inflicting any harm to another person (for discussions of the relations among aggression, violence, and power, see Chapters 3, 4, and 13). Researchers also make distinctions between subtypes of aggression (e.g., proactive vs. reactive aggression, thoughtful vs. thoughtless aggression), but they realize that aggressive acts in the real world are often complex combinations of these subtypes that can change over time and as a function of the victim's responses (for discussions of dyadic-level effects on aggressive behavior, see Chapters 1, 2, and 20).

Historically, aggressive behavior was viewed either as the result of an inborn instinct aimed at the destruction of life (e.g., Freud's, 1920/1961, theory of the death drive) or as a learned response to the frustration of one's needs (e.g., Dollard, Doob, Miller, Mowrer, & Sears's, 1939, well-known frustration–aggression hypothesis). With the advance of psychological research, several theories of aggression and its causes have emerged. For example, *neoassociationist theory* (Berkowitz, 1993) posits that aversive events (e.g., frustration, provocation) can automatically trigger aggressive behavior, whereas a cognitive revision of this theory emphasizes that higher level cognitive processes (e.g., attributions, appraisals) moderate these automatic aggressive responses. *Social learning theory* (Bandura, 1973) proposes that people develop aggressive behavior when they observe others behaving aggressively, particularly if the others are likable, have high social status, or are rewarded for their aggressive behavior. According to *script theory* (Huesmann, 1998), individuals learn aggression-related mental representations and action plans from the wider world around them, including the mass media. *Social interaction theory* (Tedeschi & Felson, 1994) proposes that aggression is an instrumental means to achieve important goals, such as obtaining something of value or establishing a desired social identity.

Recently, Anderson and Bushman (2002) proposed a broad, integrative theory of aggression, the *general aggression model* (GAM; for a detailed discussion of this theory, see Chapter 1), encompassing the common features of previous theories of aggression. In the GAM, the causes of aggression are analyzed at two different levels of causation, distal and proximal, and within each level there are personal and situational risk factors as well as affective, motivational, and cognitive mechanisms through which the risk factors influence aggression. (These factors are discussed in detail throughout this volume.) For example, at the distal level, the GAM emphasizes genetic risk factors (see Chapters 7–9), exposure to parental aggressive behavior during childhood (Chapters 7 and 9), cultural norms and values (Chapter 10), socioeconomic risk factors, and child abuse and neglect (Chapters 13, 14, and 19). The GAM also emphasizes personality predispositions (see Chapter 5), neural mechanisms (Chapter 6), narcissism and self-esteem (Chapter 11), cognitive biases in attributions and appraisals (Chapter 9), and proximal (i.e., situational) risk factors, such as frustration, incentives, aversive stimulation, stress, alcohol and drugs, and salient opportunities for aggression. In addition, the GAM emphasizes the role of self-regulatory processes in triggering and resisting aggression (see Chapters 2, 6, and 12).

Theory and research on aggression have also informed efforts to prevent and treat aggression. The methods include reducing exposure to events that teach or reward aggressive behavior or hostile appraisals and attributions (see Chapters 7 and 9), diminishing personality and situational forces that can trigger aggression such as narcissism and alcohol abuse (see Chapters 2 and 11), strengthening prosocial virtues and action tendencies (Chapters 12 and 15), and increasing the quality of parental care and the resulting sense of emotional security (Chapters 13 and 14).

The need for understanding and reducing aggression, violence, and their destructive consequences inspired us to dedicate the second volume of *The Herzliya Series on Personality and Social Psychology* to the psychology of aggressive behavior, viewed from various levels of analysis, from the neural to the societal. We invited experts on the science of aggression and violence to explain their ideas and research findings, and encouraged them to trace the historical and theoretical background of their research and speculate about where it might lead in the future. Readers of this volume will gain a deeper and broader understanding of aggression, violence, and their social and psychological causes and effects, whether the readers are anchored in the disciplines of personality, social, and clinical psychology; the close relationships field; developmental psychology; neuroscience; or political psychology. They will also learn about methods used to study aggression and violence, and about promising psychological and social interventions that can reduce violence and deal with its destructive effects.

The volume is organized into five sections. The first, focusing on major theoretical perspectives, includes six chapters on evolutionary, neuroscientific, developmental, personality-oriented, and social psychological perspectives on aggression and violence. The second section, focusing on research into the genetic and environmental determinants of aggressive behavior, includes four chapters on the intraindividual and intrafamilial causes and correlates of aggressiveness, and the genetic, social information processing, and cultural factors that mediate the development of aggression and its transmission across generations. The third section includes five chapters dealing with psychological and social-relational processes underlying aggression and violence. The fourth section includes three chapters on the existential, emotional, and structural roots of intergroup aggression. The final section considers the consequences of aggression viewed from the perspective of its victims: the abused child, the battered romantic partner, and citizens and soldiers exposed to political violence, acts of terrorism, and wars.

In Chapter 1, Nathan DeWall and Craig Anderson present a current account of the influential GAM. They conceptualize aggression in terms of cycles—the single-episode cycle, the developmental cycle, the violence escalation cycle—and specify causes and processes, both biological and environmental, that contribute to aggressive behavior. They also discuss ways to reduce violence at the individual, community, national, and international levels. This overview of the classic research on aggression provides a foundation for the following chapters.

In Chapter 2, Erica Slotter and Eli Finkel expand on the GAM by providing a new theoretical framework, the I^3 (I-Cubed) theory, which organizes aggression risk factors into three categories: (a) instigating triggers—discrete events that arouse action tendencies conducive to aggression; (b) impelling forces—factors that increase the likelihood of an aggressive impulse following an instigating trigger; and (c) inhibiting forces—factors that increase the likelihood that aggression will be contained or held in check rather than being expressed.

In Chapter 3, Aaron Sell explains how anger and aggression may have evolved biologically to solve certain adaptive problems. Applying the methods of evolutionary psychologists' "adaptationist program" to human anger, Sell argues that anger is the output of a cognitive mechanism "designed" by natural selection to negotiate conflicts of interest, influence the weight placed by a target of anger on an angry person's interests, and cause the target of anger to treat the angry person better. Using this framework, Sell reviews recent studies of anger and aggression and shows that their findings can be explained by the process of recalibration that occurs in the mind of an anger target when his or her interaction partner becomes noticeably angry.

In Chapter 4, Phillip Shaver, Michal Segev, and Mario Mikulincer consider an attachment-theoretical perspective on aggression. Attachment theory parses human motivation into several life domains and considers the biological function of the behavioral systems that evolved to solve adaptive problems within each of these domains. Shaver et al. propose that a "power" behavioral system evolved to encourage the attainment and maintenance of dominance and influence in social relations. They describe a new Power Behavioral System Scale that measures hyperactivation and deactivation of the power system, and present new research findings concerning how these two dimensions provide a framework for understanding individual differences in aggressive behavior.

In Chapter 5, Jennifer Tackett and Robert Krueger present a personality trait perspective on aggression, showing how aggression is situated within current models of personality and psychopathology. They review research on stable individual differences in aggressive tendencies and the associations of these tendencies with other personality constructs and with "externalizing" (e.g., aggressive or antisocial) forms of psychopathology. Tackett and Krueger explain the current state of theory and research concerning how genetic and environmental factors combine to influence aggression while emphasizing that genetic factors are best understood in relation to particular environmental contexts.

In Chapter 6, Thomas Denson moves to the neural level of analysis and considers how some of the processes discussed by other chapter authors are manifested in the brain. He shows that the limbic system and the dorsal anterior cingulate are involved in the arousal of anger, and that regions associated with emotion regulation are involved in rumination and displaced aggression (i.e., harming people who are not responsible for the aggressor's problems). In addition, neural regions involved in reward processing are active during acts of aggression, helping to explain the difficulty of down-regulating aggression. Many provocative exciting ideas for future research are proposed in this chapter.

The second section of the volume begins with a chapter by Rowell Huesmann, Eric Dubow, and Paul Boxer (Chapter 7), who consider the prevalence of aggressiveness from childhood to adulthood and the extent to which this trait is transmitted across generations. They also provide a road map for understanding the relative importance of genetic factors, continuity in environments, and social learning processes in determining within-individual and cross-generational forms of continuity in aggression. Huesmann et al. propose a model that includes all of these factors and then apply it to data from a three-generation longitudinal study.

In Chapter 8, Soo Hyun Rhee and Irwin Waldman explore genetic influences on aggression and compare the patterns and magnitudes of genetic and environmental influences on different forms of aggression. On the basis of a meta-analysis of twin and adoption studies of antisocial behavior in general, and of specific forms of aggressive behavior in particular, Rhee and Waldman conclude that aggression is partially attributable to genes and that the heritability of aggression and antisocial behavior depends on the type of aggression assessed, the assessment method, and the age and sex of the people under study.

In Chapter 9, Kenneth Dodge presents his well-researched social information processing model of aggression. Dodge argues that (a) aggression-related social information processing patterns (e.g., hypervigilance to threat cues, hostile attributional biases) are influenced by genetic and environmental factors, (b) these patterns account for the effects of genetic and environmental factors on aggression, and (c) interventions to alter processing patterns can prevent aggressive behavior. Dodge evaluates his model with data from the ongoing longitudinal Child Development Project. His work has important implications for the design of interventions to impede the development of aggressive and violent behavior.

In Chapter 10, Dov Cohen and Angela Leung combine an individual-differences approach with a cultural perspective on variations in aggressive behavior. They describe three kinds of cultures, those of honor, dignity, and face, and consider within-culture variations in the extent to which individuals position themselves in alignment with the dominant value system of their culture. They review recent studies of people from honor, dignity, and face cultures, showing that both within- and between-culture forms of variation are important in explaining a person's propensity to behave aggressively.

The third section of the volume begins with Sander Thomaes and Brad Bushman's chapter (Chapter 11) on the relations among narcissism, self-esteem, and aggression. In the first section of the chapter, the authors present evidence against the familiar hypothesis that low self-esteem leads to aggression. In the second section, they argue that aggressive individuals are typically self-absorbed, believing they are better than others and overestimating their own valuable qualities; in other words, they are narcissistic. Thomaes and Bushman review recent findings showing that the combination of narcissism and insult leads to exceptionally high levels of aggression. Their work is important for designers of school programs that foster self-views that deter aggression.

In Chapter 12, Michael McCullough, Robert Kurzban, and Benjamin Tabak discuss the adaptive functions of the evolved mechanisms underlying humans' capacities for revenge and forgiveness. They argue against characterizations of revenge as something "gone wrong" in human nature, and against characterizations of forgiveness as an "antidote" for the "poison" of revenge. They review evidence suggesting that both revenge and forgiveness are behavioral adaptations that helped our human ancestors solve prevalent social problems. McCullough et al. enumerate the selection pressures that probably gave rise to both revenge and forgiveness and describe the psychological processes that activate these processes in contemporary humans.

Chapters 13 (by Mario Mikulincer & Phillip Shaver) and Chapter 14 (by Donald Dutton) use attachment theory to conceptualize the psychodynamic mechanisms and interpersonal processes that underlie functional and dysfunctional forms of aggression. We have included two chapters about this perspective because there are two different lines of work combining attachment theory with (a) personality and social psychological research on social motives, emotions, cognitions, and behavior (covered by Mikulincer & Shaver) and (b) issues in clinical and forensic psychology (covered by Dutton). In the first of these chapters (Chapter 13), Mikulincer and Shaver focus on attachment insecurities in adulthood and their effects on human aggression. They review research on the links between these insecurities and anger, domestic violence, antisocial behavior, and intergroup hostility. They also consider the main goal of human aggression—to maintain power and dominance—and present exploratory research on the influence of attachment-related processes on cognition and action when a person's sense of power is experimentally enhanced.

Dutton (in Chapter 14) focuses on the clinical implications of attachment theory and argues that violence toward relationship partners (i.e., domestic violence) or oneself (e.g., self-cutting or suicide) can be caused by attachment-related threats (e.g., threats of separation, rejection, or abandonment). Dutton also discusses *symbolic attachment*, the promise of reunion with and high praise from loved ones after death, and considers its role in religion-based aggression, military violence, and other forms of violence against members of outgroups.

In Chapter 15, Ofra Mayseless and Miri Scharf discuss the importance of respect in social relationships as a buffer against aggression. They consider various definitions of respect and draw distinctions between respect and other emotions or attitudes thought to be buffers against aggression, such as trust, empathy, and acceptance. They review studies that illuminate the role of respect in reducing aggression in unequal relationships, such as the respect shown by parents for their children and by children for their parents, and the respect shown by teachers for their students and by students for their teachers. The chapter provides important insights into the role of respect in interventions aimed at reducing aggression in homes and schools.

In the first chapter in the fourth section of the volume (see Chapter 16), Gilad Hirschberger and Tom Pyszczynski provide an existential perspective on intergroup aggression. Expanding terror management theory, the authors argue that basic existential fears and awareness of one's own mortality affect the extent to which people rely on aggression and violence to solve intergroup conflicts. They review studies from their own and other laboratories showing that experimentally increasing death awareness increases support for violent actions against enemies. Hirschberger and Pyszczynski also review evidence regarding contextual factors that inhibit the effects of existential concerns on the escalation of violence. The chapter ends with an integrative model showing how patriotism, vengeance, and pacifism are all rooted in basic existential concerns.

In Chapter 17, Eran Halperin probes the emotional roots of intergroup aggression—anger and hatred—and reveals their different and interactive roles. Equipped with an integration of theories from social psychology and the field of conflict resolution, Halperin reviews studies focused mainly on the Israeli–Palestinian conflict, showing that neither anger nor hatred alone is sufficient to arouse intergroup violence. Instead, only the co-occurrence of these two emotions incites large-scale aggression. The optimistic message of this chapter is that the link between anger and escalating cycles of violence is avoidable if hatred is reduced or contained.

Tamar Saguy, Nicole Tausch, John Dovidio, Felicia Pratto, and Purnima Singh explore in Chapter 18 ways of reducing intergroup aggression while discounting the basic premise of *contact theory*, which proposes that intergroup aggression can be reduced by bringing members of opposing groups together under conditions that stress commonalities. Instead, Saguy et al. focus on power-related dynamics and review findings from both laboratory and real-world studies showing that stressing commonalities between strong and weak groups can create tension rather than harmony. The authors show that well-intentioned interventions aimed at reducing intergroup hostility may paradoxically reduce the likelihood of reconciliation.

The final section of the volume deals with the consequences of aggression viewed from the perspectives of its victims. In Chapter 19, Sheree Toth, LaTonya Harris, Gail Goodman, and Dante Cicchetti discuss the long-term consequences of aggression against children (child abuse and maltreatment). The authors focus on emotion regulation, attachment insecurity, and mental health, as well as effects of maltreatment on memories of abusive experiences and events. They suggest policies and practices that can benefit children, adolescents, and adults who were abused, neglected, or maltreated during infancy and childhood. They also suggest practices that may increase the accuracy of such people's memories and reports in forensic contexts.

In Chapter 20, Ximena Arriaga and Nicole Capezza focus on intimate partner violence and consider the paradox of being a victim of a partner's aggression while still being committed to the aggressive partner and the troubled relationship. Using the frameworks of interdependence theory and cognitive consistency theories, Arriaga and Capezza explain how committed victims of partner aggression justify or downplay their partner's destructive acts. These authors then present findings from several studies showing that a victim's well-being and the maintenance of the victim's relationship are sometimes at odds. The chapter emphasizes the need for special interventions to protect the victims of relational aggression.

In Chapter 21, Zahava Solomon and Karni Ginzburg discuss the long-term pathogenic consequences of exposure to political violence, acts of terror, and warfare. Using life in Israel as an example of recurrent and prolonged exposure to military and political violence, Solomon and Ginzburg review findings from 3-decade longitudinal studies of (a) veterans of the First Lebanon War in 1982 and (b) ex-POWs from the Yom Kippur War in 1973. The studies reveal that for many soldiers and civilians the war does not end when the shooting stops but continues to plague them in diverse and complicated ways. In some cases, the violence is brought home from the battlefield and adversely affects families and civil society.

As can be seen from these brief thumbnail sketches, the chapters in this volume cover a broad array of ideas and research on aggression and violence, their detrimental effects, and interventions to dampen or eliminate these harmful effects. The book is realistic, recognizing that aggression arises partly from human evolution, genes, and natural interpersonal and intergroup conflict and is therefore not likely to be completely eliminated. But the book is also hopeful, showing that scientific insight and a variety of research-based interventions can reduce the development, expression, and detrimental consequences of aggression and violence. The authors have provided a commendable service to readers by writing clearly and compellingly about their areas of expertise, discussing their ideas in person with each other at a vibrant and creative series of meetings in Israel, and cross-referencing their chapters to help readers pursue useful connections. Together they offer a deep, mature portrait of human aggression and violence and suggest concrete ways in which it can be reduced in future generations.

REFERENCES

Anderson, C. A., & Bushman, B. J. (2002). Human aggression. *Annual Review of Psychology, 53,* 27–51. doi:10.1146/annurev.psych.53.100901.135231

Bandura, A. (1973). *Aggression: A social learning analysis.* Englewood Cliffs, NJ: Prentice-Hall.

Berkowitz, L. (1993). *Aggression: Its causes, consequences, and control.* New York, NY: McGraw-Hill.

Dollard, J., Doob, L., Miller, N. E., Mowrer, O. H., & Sears, R. R. (1939). *Frustration and aggression.* New Haven, CT: Yale University Press. doi:10.1037/10022-000

Freud, S. (1961). *Beyond the pleasure principle* (J. Strachey, Ed. & Trans.). New York, NY: Norton. (Original work published 1920) doi:10.1037/11189-000

Huesmann, L. R. (1998). The role of social information processing and cognitive schema in the acquisition and maintenance of habitual aggressive behavior. In R. G. Geen & E. Donnerstein (Eds.), *Human aggression: Theories, research, and implications for social policy* (pp. 73–109). San Diego, CA: Academic Press.

Tedeschi, J. T., & Felson, R. B. (1994). *Violence, aggression, and coercive actions.* Washington, DC: American Psychological Association. doi:10.1037/10160-000

I

MAJOR THEORETICAL
PERSPECTIVES

1

THE GENERAL AGGRESSION MODEL

C. NATHAN DeWALL AND CRAIG A. ANDERSON

Marwan Abu Ubeida contradicts general stereotypes of would-be mass murderers. He had a privileged upbringing, is deeply religious, and shows none of the signs of psychopathology typically used to identify violent people. Yet he has an insatiable drive to kill as many people as he can. Marwan is an Iraqi suicide bomber. When asked what will happen in the last moments of his life, Marwan outlined a two-step process (Ghosh, 2005). First, he will ask Allah to bless his holy mission with a high rate of American casualties. Second, he will ask for a pure soul that is suitable to see Allah and his mujahideen brothers who are already in paradise. Marwan's final wishes are both chilling and puzzling, suggesting, as they do, that Allah will approve and assist Marwan's murder of many Americans. How does such a privileged youth become a suicide bomber?

Further puzzlement comes from the behavior of Lynndie England. She joined the American National Guard not to inflict pain on others but to provide a means to pay for her education. She has a son toward whom she behaves with love and kindness. As a guard in the Abu Ghraib prison in Iraq, however, she wreaked havoc on Iraqi prisoners through the use of cruel and humiliating torture practices. Her acts gained worldwide attention through the publication of pictures showing her apparent glee over inflicting pain and humiliation on naked, shackled prisoners. In interviews, Lynndie deflected responsibility for her actions, noting that she was merely following orders from superiors and seeking the approval of a fellow soldier with whom she was in love. What leads a person such as Lynndie England to perform such aggressive acts?

Scholars, politicians, and the general public are often perplexed not only by aggressive acts committed by individuals but also by aggression between groups large and small. The escalating conflict between Israelis and Palestinians, for example, has claimed the lives of thousands of people, including many unarmed civilians. Both Israeli and Palestinian leaders have offered logical suggestions for ways to end the conflict, and other governments have done the same. Yet the end of the conflict is nowhere in sight. The dispute appears intractable (see Chapters 16 and 17). On December 29, 2008, Israel launched a major military offensive designed to stop Hamas militants from firing missiles into the Jewish state. Over 1,000 people died, with more than 4,500 additional people wounded. After the assault ended, the Hamas rockets continued to land in southern Israel. Why does the Israeli–Palestinian conflict continue to escalate despite recurrent efforts to end it peacefully?

The purpose of this chapter is to demonstrate how the general aggression model (GAM; Anderson & Bushman, 2002; Anderson & Huesmann, 2003) helps to answer these perplexing questions (and many others) regarding the causes and conditions of aggression and violence. The GAM is a dynamic, social–cognitive, developmental model that provides an integrative framework for domain-specific aggression theories. It includes situational, personological, and biological variables. The GAM draws heavily on social–cognitive and social learning theories that have been developed over the past 40 years by social, personality, cognitive, and developmental psychologists (e.g., Bandura, 1977; Berkowitz, 1989; Crick & Dodge, 1994; Dodge, 1980; Huesmann, 1988; Mischel, 1973; Mischel & Shoda, 1995; Chapters 7 and 9, this volume). These perspectives paved the way for understanding the learning and developmental processes involved in shaping aggressive behavior and understanding how aggression operates under the control of intrapsychological processes aimed at overriding impulses to remain in agreement with standards for appropriate behavior (see Chapter 2, this volume).

The chapter is organized into seven sections. First, we offer definitions of antisocial, aggressive, and violent behavior. Second, we provide a brief description of the GAM. Third, we discuss the dynamic process by which personological and situational factors establish and sustain aggression: the *violence escalation cycle*. Fourth, we use the GAM to understand how seemingly ordinary citizens become terrorists, suicide bombers, torturers, and other doers of aggression and violence. Fifth, we discuss the implications of the GAM for aggression between groups of people. Sixth, we apply the GAM to show how certain government actions designed to promote peace can increase aggression and violent behavior. Seventh, we discuss useful suggestions based on the GAM regarding ways to reduce aggression and violence.

ANTISOCIAL BEHAVIOR, AGGRESSION, AND VIOLENCE

Much has changed since the Mesolithic period, during which human evolution presumably formed many of our current innate tendencies. Agriculture now dominates people's access to food, allowing people to settle in communities instead of hunting and gathering in nomadic groups. Cultural progress enables people to depend on others for food, clothing, and shelter instead of having to provide for themselves. Technological advances provide people with the means to travel easily and to transmit knowledge to each other quickly. Despite these revolutionary changes in human lives, aggression and violence remain important topics in modern society, just as they must have been to our evolutionary ancestors.

Archeological and historical evidence indicates that aggression and violence were prevalent among our hunter/gatherer ancestors 25,000 years ago. Aggression and violence was widespread among Greek, Egyptian, and Roman societies 2,000 to 3,000 years ago. Just as modern citizens of the world ingest violent media, ancient Romans had their own form of "media violence" in which gladiators inflicted physical injury and death on each other in the presence of thousands of viewers. Aggression and violence continue to be widespread. In short, they remain ubiquitous parts of human life. Before we can understand the causes and conditions of aggression and violence, it is necessary to discuss what we mean when we say that a person or group acts antisocially, aggressively, or violently.

Antisocial Behavior

Antisocial behavior refers to any action that violates personal or cultural standards for appropriate behavior. Antisocial behavior often involves aggression and violence, but not always. In societies with norms prohibiting physical violence between romantic partners, punching, kicking, or biting one's spouse would be considered antisocial behavior. Littering, lying, and stealing also represent antisocial behaviors, although none of these behaviors involves physical aggression or violence. People with antisocial personality disorder (Hare, 1996) often engage in aggressive and violent actions, but they also violate standards for appropriate behavior in nonaggressive ways such as cheating, stealing, and breaking other laws. Thus, antisocial behavior can involve aggression, violence, or any other type of response that defies cultural standards for desirable behavior. This chapter focuses primarily on aggressive and violent behavior.

Aggression and Violence

Aggression refers to behavior carried out with the proximal (i.e., immediate) intention to inflict harm on another person who is motivated to avoid the harm (e.g., Anderson & Bushman, 2002; Baron & Richardson, 1994). Harmful behavior that is accidental or an incidental by-product of helpful actions is not aggressive. From a social psychological perspective, *violence* usually refers to the most severe types of physical aggression, those that are likely to cause serious bodily injury. Occasionally, researchers in this domain use "emotional" or "psychological" violence to indicate severe forms of nonphysical aggression. All acts of violence fit our definition of aggression, but not all aggressive acts are violent. By our definition, violent actions need not involve illegal behavior. Note, however, that other behavioral sciences (e.g., criminology) define violence in somewhat different ways, such as by requiring the act to be illegal (Neuilly, 2007).

GENERAL AGGRESSION MODEL

Several dichotomous distinctions among various forms of aggression have been proposed. Although these distinctions (i.e., proactive vs. reactive, instrumental vs. hostile, impulsive vs. premeditated) have yielded important insights, we argue for a more flexible understanding of aggression based on a knowledge structure approach (Bushman & Anderson, 2001). We also argue that different forms of aggression can be distinguished in terms of proximate and ultimate goals (Anderson & Bushman, 2002). Furthermore, we can characterize any aggressive behavior according to four dimensions, each of which fits well with research on the development, use, and automatization of knowledge structures. Any aggressive act (i.e., proximal intent to harm, target motivated to avoid the act) can be characterized along each of the following dimensions: degree of hostile or agitated affect present, automaticity, degree to which the primary (i.e., ultimate) goal is to harm the victim versus benefit the perpetrator, and degree to which consequences are considered. Because many aggressive acts involve mixed motivations or are sensitive to specific consequences, considering aggression along these four dimensions rather than relying on dichotomous category systems provides researchers with a better means of understanding aggression and of creating useful interventions (Anderson & Bushman, 2002; Anderson & Huesmann, 2003).

Basic Model

The GAM takes into account how aggression depends on cognitive factors within the individual. Aggression depends on how an individual perceives and interprets his or her environment and the people therein, expectations regarding the likelihood of various outcomes, knowledge and beliefs about how people typically respond in certain situations, and how much people believe they have the abilities to respond to a variety of events (see Chapters 7 and 9). By understanding these cognitions, researchers have a basis for understanding both within-person and situation-specific stability in aggression because people show similarity in how they respond to similar events over time, and because situations frequently impose realistic demands that limit the number of options regarding how people can construe the situation. Furthermore, such social–cognitive models also account for variability in aggression across time, people, and contexts, as different knowledge structures develop and change, and as different situational contexts prime different knowledge structures.

The GAM also focuses heavily on how the development and use of knowledge structures influence both early (e.g., basic visual perception) and downstream (e.g., judgments, decisions behaviors) psychological processes (e.g., Bargh, 1996; Fiske & Taylor, 1991; Wegner & Bargh, 1998). People develop knowledge structures from their experience. Within the context of aggression, knowledge structures can influence toward whom a person directs visual attention as a function of possible threat, affective responses to provocation or cues linked to aggression in memory, attributions regarding the causes of a provocateur's behavior, judgments regarding the costs and benefits of various behavioral options, memory for people who do and do not represent potential threat, and actual behavior directed toward a target.

Of particular interest are findings showing that through repeated practice and exposure, complex judgments and choices become automatized, requiring little or no mental energy or conscious awareness (Bargh & Pietromonaco, 1982). A "shoot first, ask questions later" mentality may result from learning through repeated experience or cultural teachings that members of various groups represent threats and therefore should be perceived as dangerous even in neutral or ambiguous situations. For example, repeated experience and cultural teachings that African Americans are likely to be hostile and pose a physical threat have been shown to affect decisions to shoot unarmed African American crime suspects—decisions made by both college student research participants (Correll, Park, Judd, & Wittenbrink, 2002) and police officers (Plant & Peruche, 2005). The effect that knowledge structures can have on violence was demonstrated in the tragic incident of Amadou Diallo, an African American man who was shot 19 times by New York City police officers as he reached for his wallet (Cooper, 1999). Thus, knowledge structures set the stage for understanding how people identify objects, people, and complex social events as relevant or irrelevant to aggression; how beliefs about specific people (e.g., Osama bin Laden) or groups (e.g., Nazis, Hutus) shape perceptions of relevance to aggression; and how people use behavioral scripts to guide their behavior under various circumstances (e.g., responding with retaliation to an insult when that insult increases hostile affect).

Single Episode Cycle

At the most basic level, the GAM focuses primarily on how aggression unfolds within one cycle of an ongoing social interaction. At this level the model emphasizes three main issues: person and situation inputs, present internal state (i.e., cognition, arousal, affect), and outcomes of appraisal and decision-making processes (see Anderson & Bushman, 2002, Figure 2).

Person and Situation Inputs

The GAM considers both situation and person factors—relatively enduring traits, motivations, attitudes, beliefs, and other chronic knowledge structures and less enduring cognitive, affective, and arousal states that arise in particular contexts (see Chapters 2, 7, and 9). Person and situation inputs are proximate causes in that they provide the most direct guiding force behind aggression behavior, although the behavior may also serve an ultimate goal (see Tooby & Cosmides, 1992). Social psychologists have identified a variety of situational factors that promote aggressive behavior, such as provocation, exposure to weapons, a hot environment, unpleasant odors, loud noises, violent media, and physical pain (for a review, see Anderson & Bushman, 2002). Examples of person factors known to increase aggression are hostile attribution bias, narcissism, being male, and a host of beliefs, attitudes, values, and behavioral scripts (see Chapters 2, 5, 9, 10, 11, 13, and 14, this volume).

Situation and person factors are not mutually exclusive. Some situational factors give rise to states that closely resemble person variables; for example, social rejection or playing violent video games can strengthen hostile cognitive biases (Bushman & Anderson, 2002; DeWall, Twenge, Gitter, & Baumeister, 2009). In addition, situational variables often interact with person variables to predict aggression. In response to provocation, for example, narcissistic people tend to behave quite aggressively, whereas narcissists do not show high levels of aggression in response to praise (Bushman & Baumeister, 1998; Chapter 11, this volume). Similarly, exposure to hunting and assault weapons influences the mental accessibility of hostile cognitions and aggressive behavior differently according to whether people have developed knowledge structures through experience to certain kinds of weapons (e.g., hunters compared with people who have less differentiated knowledge about types of weapons; Bartholow, Carnagey, & Anderson, 2005).

Internal States

Person and situation variables influence aggression through the internal states they create. That is, internal states serve as mechanisms underlying the relationship between person and situation variables and outcomes of appraisal and decision-making processes. Affect, arousal, and cognition represent the three most significant internal states. A specific person variable (e.g., high trait hostility) or situational variable (e.g., viewing violent media) may influence one, two, or all three types of internal states. Violent media, for example, affect all three states. Moreover, the three internal states can influence each other.

Outcomes

A large body of literature within social psychology suggests that complex information processes can involve reliance on the automatic system or the controlled system (Smith & Lazarus, 1993). In the GAM (see Anderson & Bushman, 2002, Figure 3), the third stage includes complex appraisal and decision processes that range from automatic to heavily controlled (Strack & Deutsch, 2004; Chapter 6, this volume). Therefore, inputs (Stage 1) affect internal states (Stage 2), which in turn influence appraisal and decision processes (Stage 3). The appraisal and decision processes include automatic processes referred to as *immediate appraisal* and more controlled processes referred to as *reappraisal*. Based on the outcomes of immediate appraisal or reappraisal processes, people are impelled to act in either thoughtful or impulsive ways. These actions enter a feedback loop that becomes part of the input for the next episode.

Immediate appraisals depend heavily on the automatic system and influence affective, goal, and intention information. Appraising environmental threat, for example, occurs effortlessly and without conscious awareness (e.g., Öhman, Lundqvist, & Esteves, 2001). This immediate appraisal process may include fear and anger-related affect, goals related to aggression, and the formation of intentions to carry out aggression-related acts. Person and situation inputs guide immediate appraisals in ways that are congruent with a person's social learning history (i.e., personality) and current psychological and physiological state. Because immediate appraisal is effortless and requires few resources, some aggressive acts occur so fast that it may seem that appraisal has not even occurred, and indeed some behavioral scripts may be so closely linked to the perception of a particular stimulus that the behavioral response is functionally a part of perceiving the stimulus.

Reappraisal processes, in contrast, depend on whether people have adequate resources and whether the immediate appraisal is judged (automatically) to be both important and unsatisfactory. A growing body of literature suggests, for example, that the ability to override unwanted impulses depends on a limited energy resource that becomes depleted after prior exertion (Gailliot et al., 2007; Chapter 2, this volume). If a person has recently engaged in an act involving the expenditure of self-regulatory energy, that person will be less likely to engage in reappraisal (DeWall, Baumeister, Stillman, & Gailliot, 2007; Finkel, DeWall, Slotter, Oaten, & Foshee, 2009; Chapter 6, this volume). Likewise, if a person's immediate appraisal indicates that the probable outcome is either satisfying or unimportant, then the person will be less likely to engage in reappraisal. Other resource limitations, such as time and cognitive capacity, may also preclude reappraisal.

Thus, aggression results from the proximate convergence of situations and personological inputs. Situations can impel or inhibit aggression, whereas personological factors enhance or diminish a person's propensity to behave aggressively. These situational and personological inputs activate affective, arousal, and cognitive internal states, which in turn influence aggression by means of appraisal and decision processes. Once the individual has performed the impulsive or thoughtful action, the behavior feeds back to the situation and personological inputs to guide the next episodic cycle.

Aggression Before and After the Single Episode Cycle

Is the GAM stuck in the present? At first glance, the GAM appears to focus most of its attention on how current internal states determine aggression, neglecting the importance of the past and future. However, the personological input factors bring the past to the present in the form of knowledge structures and well-rehearsed cognitive and affective processes that have been influenced by biological factors (e.g., genes, hormones) and past history (see Anderson & Bushman, 2002, Figure 4).

Similarly, the GAM details how the present influences and is influenced by the future through the knowledge structures used to perceive, react, and learn. The present influences the future in at least two different ways: by changing the person's relatively enduring beliefs, attitudes, expectations (i.e., personality) and by changing the person's social environment (i.e., the attitudes, beliefs, expectations other people have of the person). Chronic exposure to violent media, for example, can increase aggressive attitudes, beliefs, expectations of others as hostile, and desensitization to future violence (Anderson, Carnagey, & Eubanks, 2003; Bartholow, Bushman, & Sestir, 2006; Carnagey, Anderson, & Bushman, 2007). The present is influenced by the future through the person's beliefs and expectations about how others will act, their goals, and other plans. Thus, the GAM focuses on internal states as they relate to what people bring with them to the present episode from the past and also shows how the present episode can influence future personological and situational factors that will influence future internal states and subsequent appraisal and decision processes that guide aggression. It even provides a simple process by which personality influences situations.

VIOLENCE ESCALATION CYCLE

Most incidents involving aggression and violence occur after a series of conflict-based interactions in which the two parties trade retaliatory behaviors back and forth in an escalating cycle. Such escalating cycles include what some refer to as "ordinary" violent crimes between individuals (e.g., assault and murder) and between larger groups and nations. Figure 1.1 illustrates the violence escalation cycle.

The violence escalation cycle begins with an initial triggering event that may be serious or relatively benign. The triggering event can influence any kind of dyad, including two people, two groups, two religions, or two nations. Whereas person or group A considers retaliation to the event to be justified and relatively mild, person or group B considers the retaliation to be unjustified and severe, leading to retaliation toward person or group A. The cycle persists through several iterations of violent actions in which one unit perceives its retaliation to be appropriate and justified, whereas the second unit perceives it to be inappropriate and exaggerated (see similar analyses in Chapters 10 and 12).

Consider an example of the violence escalation cycle within the context of street gangs. Members of gang A venture to a part of town normally considered to be gang B's turf. Gang B perceives this lack of respect for gang boundaries as an affront to their power and influence. As a result, members of gang B retaliate in a manner that they perceive to be both justified and relatively mild: They destroy several cars belonging to gang A's leaders and assault several members of gang A who try to stop the destruction of the cars. Gang B's retaliation therefore becomes gang A's provocation, leading them to shoot and kill several members of gang B. The escalation cycle continues over the course of several weeks or months, with dozens of members of both gangs experiencing serious physical injury or death. Real-world examples of the violence escalation cycle abound in contemporary society. The Israeli–Palestinian conflict and the "preemptive" war on Iraq by the United States are examples of violence escalation cycles.

Why do violence escalations persist? We propose three reasons. First, violence often produces violence as a result of faulty attributions. Whereas neutral third parties can make accurate causal inferences regarding violence between two parties, the parties themselves usually cannot. In a version of the *fundamental attribution error*, people tend to explain the causes of others' behaviors as due to dispositions and their own behavior as due to situational

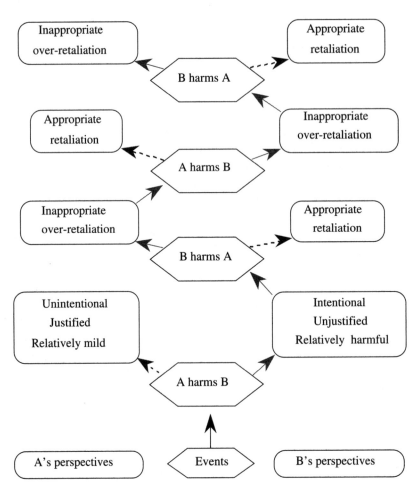

Figure 1.1. Violence escalation cycle. Adapted from "Creating Your Own Hostile Environment: A Laboratory Examination of Trait Aggression and the Violence Escalation Cycle," by C. A. Anderson, K. E. Buckley, and N. L. Carnagey, 2008, *Personality and Social Psychology Bulletin, 34,* pp. 462–473. Copyright 2008 by Sage. Adapted with permission.

forces (Anderson, Krull, & Weiner, 1996); people become caught in a web in which members perceive the other party as acting out of malice or evil and perceive their own behavior as appropriate responses to the situation at hand. Outgroup homogeneity effects may also prevent members of both parties from making accurate attributions. U.S. citizens, for example, may perceive all members of the Islamic faith as jihadists, when in reality this term represents a minority of Muslims. Second, retaliation often exceeds prior levels of aggression. A push turns into a punch, a punch turns into shooting someone, shooting one person turns into shooting many people, and so on. Such escalation is often an attempt to signal to the other side that it should back down (see Chapters 3 and 12, this volume). Third, increased levels of retaliatory violence stem from perspective biases in which the most recent perpetrator views the harmful behavior as appropriate and justified, whereas the most recent victim perceives the perpetrator's act as an inappropriate overreaction.

The violence escalation cycle corresponds to the GAM's assertion that personological and situational factors can influence each other in a dynamic manner. Social psychology frequently demonstrates that powerful situational factors can override personality traits. But personality traits (including beliefs, attitudes, and insecurities) sometimes dramatically influence the situation (see Chapters 4 and 5). People who characteristically perceive the world as hostile and who resolve conflict through the use of aggression can turn a situation that involves potentially mild conflict into a severely hostile one that gives rises to escalating violence (Anderson, Buckley, & Carnagey, 2008; Chapters 11, 13, and 14, this volume).

USING THE GENERAL AGGRESSION MODEL TO UNDERSTAND HOW PERPETRATORS OF VIOLENCE ARE CREATED

Scholars have often approached violence from two different perspectives, one focusing on the development of aberrant individuals who become violent criminals, the other focusing on how large segments of a population become involved in "institutionalized" violence. The habitual violent offender is the prototype of the former, whereas various genocidal events (e.g., the Holocaust, Rwanda) are exemplars of the latter. Other forms of aggression do not fit this dichotomy so well. For example, some "terrorists," such as Oklahoma City bomber Timothy McVeigh, do not seem to fit either. Larger and more persistent terrorist groups seem more institutional (e.g., Irish Republican Army, Hamas), but labeling such groups as "terrorist organizations" is to some extent more of a political statement than an objective description. From the standpoint of understanding how individuals become involved in violence against others, it may be best to avoid the political labels whenever possible, and focus research (and intervention) efforts on understanding the precursors.

A lot is known about the precursors of violence, and in our view the GAM can be used to organize them all. One point to keep in mind, however, is that the GAM is intended to provide an overarching general view of aggression. It is not a compendium of specific factors and microprocesses that are unique to each specific type of aggression and violence.

Social psychologists have long been interested in understanding how "ordinary" people can carry out horrific acts of aggression and violence. Stanley Milgram's (1963) obedience to authority studies and Haney, Banks, and

Zimbardo's (1973) simulation of prison conditions shocked researchers and laypersons by showing how easy it is to create a situation in which people will behave aggressively toward strangers. The terrorist attacks on the World Trade Center and the Pentagon on September 11, 2001; the proliferation of suicide bombers in the Middle East; and recent instances of waterboarding and other brutal tactics used by members of the U.S. military continue to raise the question: How are terrorists, suicide bombers, and torturers created?

Subsequent chapters in this volume provide many more specific details about the precursors of specific categories of violence. Many can be summarized in a few statements. Many precursors can be seen as factors that promote the development of individuals who are capable of and predisposed to use aggression and violence to solve conflicts (e.g., Chapters 4, 5, and 7). Other precursors are immediate situational factors (in the case of individual violence) or the current social milieu, serving in some cases as triggers (i.e., precipitating causes) or as factors that support ongoing violence (e.g., Chapters 9 and 16).

Beliefs, attitudes, and expectations supportive of violence must come from somewhere. And they do. If you want to create people who are predisposed to aggression and violence, begin by depriving them of resources necessary to meet basic needs—physical, emotional, psychological, and social. Provide them with multiple examples of aggression and violence, examples in which such behavior appears to work. Desensitize them to the images, sounds, smells, and, in general, to the horrors of violence by exposing them to these stimuli, both live and in electronic media form. Then provide them with a belief system that serves to dehumanize potential targets, that justifies on moral grounds any and all forms of attacks on potential targets, and that minimizes negative consequences to oneself and one's social group while maximizing positive consequences in the near future and/or in an afterlife. Finally, if you want specific forms of violence to emerge, provide training (i.e., the behavioral scripts) in those specific forms of violence. Link these violence scripts to the social support system and the belief systems that you have already provided, and you will have a group of people who are quite prepared to behave violently. Put these people into the right situation, and the desired violence will occur (Miller, 2004).

IMPLICATIONS OF THE GENERAL AGGRESSION MODEL FOR AGGRESSION BETWEEN GROUPS OF PEOPLE

The GAM makes specific predictions about aggression not only between two people but also between groups of people large (e.g., nations) and small (e.g., two or more people with a defined identity and common goal). The majority of evidence supporting GAM, however, is derived from correlational, experimental, and longitudinal research on the aggressive behavior of individuals. Increasing the number of people involved in an episode changes features of the situation in the same manner as other situational inputs (e.g., hot ambient temperatures, violent media), which in turn influences current internal states and subsequent appraisal and decision processes.

In a recent review, Meier, Hinsz, and Heimerdinger (2007) argued that groups commit and receive more aggression than individuals. Although the aggression literature is dominated by research on aggression between individuals, the available evidence on aggression between small groups supports this view (Jaffe, Shapir, & Yinon, 1981; Meier & Hinsz, 2004; Wildschut, Pinter, Vevea, Insko, & Schopler, 2003). The findings suggest that group size functions as a situational factor that produces increased levels of aggressive behavior from both the initial perpetrator and the initial target.

According to the GAM, heightened aggression between groups (relative to individuals) results from increased levels of aggressive affect, arousal, or cognition. Indeed, expecting to interact with an unfriendly group increases hostile expectations (Hoyle, Pinkley, & Insko, 1989), and the presence of others increases arousal (Zajonc, 1965). Finally, terror management theory suggests additional ways in which groups will become more embedded in escalating cycles of violence (Chapter 16, this volume).

GOVERNMENT ACTIONS AND THEIR IMPACT ON AGGRESSION AND VIOLENCE

Most, if not all, known human societies have governmental structures. Governments have many functions, one of which is to protect citizens against aggression and violence from perpetrators within and outside the society. Despite the good intentions behind many government actions, governmental efforts to reduce aggression and violence often fail. Even worse, some governmental actions designed to reduce aggression and violence actually increase them. The GAM helps to explain why governmental programs designed to reduce aggression and violence often fail or even enhance the likelihood that people will respond to the program by behaving more aggressively and violently.

War offers an example of how government actions can affect aggression and violence. Wars begin as a result of one or more events that affect two or more nations, frequently by causing some harm or injustice to one or both parties. Often, the precipitating events involve disputes over resources, including not only traditional natural resources (e.g., land, water) but psychological ones as well (e.g., access to religious sites, traditional homeland boundaries; Avalos, 2005). One nation responds in a manner that its citizens believe is justified, whereas the other nation perceives the action to be unjustified and overly harsh. An escalating cycle of violence between nations ensues, with each retaliation growing more violent. Over time, these governmental actions cause citizens of each nation to develop aggression-relevant knowledge structures regarding the enemy. Citizens develop and display more aggressive personalities, which influence their construal and reaction to situations and which change the nature of situations they will encounter in the future. As a result, it is difficult for citizens to understand how their nation's actions can be considered "evil" by members of the enemy nation and how the enemy nation can feel justified in its retaliatory actions.

Consider how two ongoing conflicts—the U.S. War on Terrorism in Afghanistan and Iraq and the Israeli–Palestinian conflict—fit the GAM's explanation of how governmental action can influence aggression and violence. The U.S. War on Terrorism in Afghanistan and the war in Iraq are, in large part, governmental responses to the terrorist attacks on the United States on September 11, 2001, by members of al-Qaeda. Many U.S. citizens perceive the actions taken by the United States as justified responses to the terrorist attacks, but these same U.S. citizens appear baffled that Arab groups and other members of the Gulf region perceive U.S. governmental actions as evil or at least unjustified overreactions. There is also evidence that the 9/11 attacks changed aggression-related knowledge structures in a manner consistent with the GAM. After the 9/11 attacks, college students showed increased positive attitudes toward war and more aggressive personalities (Carnagey & Anderson, 2007). The increased aggressive attitudes about the war and the increase in trait physical aggression persisted even a year after the terrorist attacks. These findings provide at least indirect evidence that the U.S. government's actions in Afghanistan and Iraq affected attitudes toward war and aggressive personality traits. The broader implication is that the U.S. government's actions created not only hostile attitudes toward Arabs and Muslims among U.S. citizens but also had the unplanned effect of pushing many people who suffered from the U.S. military actions to join terrorist factions to retaliate against what they perceived as unwarranted and harsh attacks on their nations. The U.S. War on Terrorism may therefore have created more U.S. enemies than it killed.

The Israeli–Palestinian conflict grew out of violent outbreaks between Israeli and Arab residents of the region alternately called Israel or Palestine, a strip of land that Jews claim as their birthright and Palestinians claim as their own. Persistent fighting between Israelis and Palestinians over the course of the past 60 years shows little sign of waning (see Chapters 16, 17, and 21). Although most members of each group perceive their own leaders' actions as justified, they have difficulty understanding how members of the enemy group perceive their government's actions as justified. The leaders of both groups acknowledge that their actions aimed at reducing intergroup violence may actually increase the level of violence between the groups. For example, Israel's top generals and intelligence officers have admitted that their military actions in response to Palestinian suicide bombings have had the effect of creating additional Palestinian terrorist cells (Moore, 2003). Thus, the GAM provides a useful framework for understanding how governmental actions can produce an escalating cycle of violence between groups and even nations.

These two examples illustrate another key point about escalatory violence. When the two parties in a conflict have vastly different resources, their forms of violence and of escalation will vary. Al-Qaeda cannot launch a conventional war against the West, so its attacks include unconventional forms of violence, such as roadside or suicide bombings. Similarly, the Palestinians cannot win a conventional war with Israel, so they resort to terrorist tactics.

USING THE GENERAL AGGRESSION MODEL TO REDUCE AGGRESSION AND VIOLENCE

Thus far, we have dwelled on how the GAM can help to describe, predict, and explain aggressive behavior. The GAM can also help researchers, government officials, and laypersons understand how to control or prevent aggression. The most likely points for intervention will vary from case to case, but several stand out. In the case of groups or individuals already in conflict, the first step should be to stop the violence cycle. Interventions by third parties may be necessary. A second step should be to ensure that people's basic needs are met. A third step would be to address people's symbolic needs (e.g., by giving them access to religious sites).

Longer term interventions should focus on reducing the risk factors that cause individuals to be predisposed to aggression. This is likely to be most effective in the case of individuals who have not already become aggression-prone, either in general or specifically toward an enemy outgroup. Thus, one must provide for the healthy development of children, both physical and psychological. This includes the learning of basic attitudes, beliefs, and values that foster positive social interactions—even with outgroups—and encourage nonviolent problem solving.

Although retraining people who are already violence prone is more difficult, research in the violent crime domain has found that intensive interventions with high-risk youth can be highly successful (U.S. Department of Health and Human Services, 2001). This is a different conclusion from the one that most scholars and public policy makers in the United States held as recently as the late 1980s and early 1990s.

CONCLUSIONS

In summary, the GAM integrates several domain-specific theories of human aggression to form a general understanding of why people behave aggressively. It identifies a wide range of factors that influence the development of aggressive tendencies over time. It explains how highly aggressive contexts are created and maintained through violence escalation cycles. It clarifies why government actions designed to bring about peace often fail, creating even more violent conflict. And perhaps most important, it offers possible solutions for preventing and reducing aggression and violence both between individuals and groups.

REFERENCES

Anderson, C. A., Buckley, K. E., & Carnagey, N. L. (2008). Creating your own hostile environment: A laboratory examination of trait aggression and the violence escalation cycle. *Personality and Social Psychology Bulletin, 34,* 462–473. doi:10.1177/0146167207311282

Anderson, C. A., & Bushman, B. J. (2002). Human aggression. *Annual Review of Psychology, 53,* 27–51. doi:10.1146/annurev.psych.53.100901.135231

Anderson, C. A., Carnagey, N. L., & Eubanks, J. (2003). Exposure to violent media: The effects of songs with violent lyrics on aggressive thoughts and feelings. *Journal of Personality and Social Psychology, 84,* 960–971. doi:10.1037/0022-3514.84.5.960

Anderson, C. A., & Huesmann, L. R. (2003). Human aggression: A social–cognitive view. In M. A. Hogg & J. Cooper (Eds.), *Handbook of social psychology* (pp. 296–323). London, England: Sage.

Anderson, C. A., Krull, D. S., & Weiner, B. (1996). Explanations: Processes and consequences. In E. T. Higgins & A. W. Kruglanski (Eds.), *Social psychology: Handbook of basic principles* (pp. 271–296). New York, NY: Guilford Press.

Avalos, H. (2005). *Fighting words: The origins of religious violence.* Buffalo, NY: Prometheus Books.

Bandura, A. (1977). *Social learning theory.* New York, NY: Prentice Hall.

Bargh, J. A. (1996). Automaticity in social psychology. In E. T. Higgins & A. W. Kruglanski (Eds.), *Social psychology: Handbook of basic principles* (pp. 169–183). New York, NY: Guilford Press.

Bargh, J. A., & Pietromonaco, P. (1982). Automatic information processing and social perception: The influence of trait information presented outside of conscious awareness on impression formation. *Journal of Personality and Social Psychology, 43,* 437–449. doi:10.1037/0022-3514.43.3.437

Baron, R. A., & Richardson, D. R. (1994). *Human aggression* (2nd ed.). New York, NY: Plenum Press.

Bartholow, B. D., Bushman, B. J., & Sestir, M. A. (2006). Chronic violent video game exposure and desensitization: Behavioral and event-related brain potential data. *Journal of Experimental Social Psychology, 42,* 532–539. doi:10.1016/j.jesp.2005.08.006

Berkowitz, L. (1989). Frustration–aggression hypothesis: Examination and reformulation. *Psychological Bulletin, 106,* 59–73. doi:10.1037/0033-2909.106.1.59

Bushman, B. J., & Anderson, C. A. (2001). Is it time to pull the plug on the hostile versus instrumental aggression dichotomy? *Psychological Review, 108,* 273–279. doi:10.1037/0033-295X.108.1.273

Bushman, B. J., & Anderson, C. A. (2002). Violent video games and hostile expectations: A test of the general aggression model. *Personality and Social Psychology Bulletin, 28,* 1679–1686. doi:10.1177/014616702237649

Bushman, B. J., & Baumeister, R. F. (1998). Threatened egotism, narcissism, self-esteem, and direct and displaced aggression: Does self-love or self-hate lead to violence? *Journal of Personality and Social Psychology, 75,* 219–229. doi:10.1037/0022-3514.75.1.219

Carnagey, N. L., & Anderson, C. A. (2005). The effects of reward and punishment in violent video games on aggressive affect, cognition, and behavior. *Psychological Science, 16,* 882–889. doi:10.1111/j.1467-9280.2005.01632.x

Carnagey, N. L., & Anderson, C. A. (2007). Changes in attitudes towards war and violence after September 11, 2001. *Aggressive Behavior, 33,* 118–129. doi:10.1002/ab.20173

Carnagey, N. L., Anderson, C. A., & Bushman, B. J. (2007). The effect of video game violence on physiological desensitization to real-life violence. *Journal of Experimental Social Psychology, 43,* 489–496. doi:10.1016/j.jesp.2006.05.003

Cooper, M. (1999, February 5). Officers in Bronx fire 41 shots, and an unarmed man is killed. *The New York Times.* Retrieved from http://www.nytimes.com/1999/02/05/nyregion/officers-in-bronx-fire-41-shots-and-an-unarmed-man-is-killed.html

Correll, J., Park, B., Judd, C. M., & Wittenbrink, B. (2002). The police officer's dilemma: Using ethnicity to disambiguate potentially threatening individuals. *Journal of Personality and Social Psychology, 83,* 1314–1329. doi:10.1037/0022-3514.83.6.1314

Crick, N. R., & Dodge, K. A. (1994). A review and reformulation of social information processing mechanisms in children's adjustment. *Psychological Bulletin, 115,* 74–101. doi:10.1037/0033-2909.115.1.74

DeWall, C. N., Baumeister, R. F., Stillman, T. F., & Gailliot, M. T. (2007). Violence restrained: Effects of self-regulatory capacity and its depletion on aggressive behavior. *Journal of Experimental Social Psychology, 43,* 62–76. doi:10.1016/j.jesp.2005.12.005

DeWall, C. N., Twenge, J. M., Gitter, S. A., & Baumeister, R. F. (2009). It's the thought that counts: The role of hostile cognition in shaping aggressive responses to social exclusion. *Journal of Personality and Social Psychology, 96*, 45–59. doi: 10.1037/a0013196

Dodge, K. A. (1980). Social cognition and children's aggressive behavior. *Child Development, 51*, 162–170. doi:10.2307/1129603

Finkel, E. J., DeWall, C. N., Slotter, E. B., Oaten, M., & Foshee, V. A. (2009). Self-regulatory failure and intimate partner violence perpetration. *Journal of Personality and Social Psychology, 97*, 483–499. doi:10.1037/a0015433

Fiske, S. T., & Taylor, S. E. (1991). *Social cognition* (2nd ed.). New York, NY: McGraw-Hill.

Gailliot, M. T., Baumeister, R. F., DeWall, C. N., Maner, J. K., Plant, E. A., Tice, D. M., . . . Schmeichel, B. J. (2007). Self-control relies on glucose as a limited energy source: Willpower is more than a metaphor. *Journal of Personality and Social Psychology, 92*, 325–336. doi:10.1037/0022-3514.92.2.325

Ghosh, B. (2005, June 28). Inside the mind of an Iraqi suicide bomber. *Time*. Retrieved from http://www.time.com/time/magazine/article/0,9171,1077288,00.html

Haney, C., Banks, W. C., & Zimbardo, P. G. (1973). Interpersonal dynamics in a simulated prison. *International Journal of Criminology and Penology, 1*, 69–97.

Hare, R. D. (1996). Psychopathy: A clinical construct whose time has come. *Criminal Justice and Behavior, 23*, 25–54. doi:10.1177/0093854896023001004

Hoyle, R. H., Pinkley, R. L., & Insko, C. A. (1989). Perceptions of social behavior: Evidence of differing expectations for interpersonal and intergroup interaction. *Personality and Social Psychology Bulletin, 15*, 365–376. doi:10.1177/0146167289153007

Huesmann, L. R. (1988). An information processing model for the development of aggression. *Aggressive Behavior, 14*, 13–24. doi:10.1002/1098-2337(1988)14:1<13::AID-AB2480140104>3.0.CO;2-J

Jaffe, Y., Shapir, N., & Yinon, Y. (1981). Aggression and its escalation. *Journal of Cross-Cultural Psychology, 12*, 21–36. doi:10.1177/0022022181121002

Meier, B. P., & Hinsz, V. B. (2004). A comparison of human aggression committed by groups and individuals: An interindividual–intergroup discontinuity. *Journal of Experimental Social Psychology, 40*, 551–559. doi:10.1016/j.jesp.2003.11.002

Meier, B. P., Hinsz, V. B., & Heimerdinger, S. R. (2007). A framework for explaining aggression involving groups. *Social and Personality Psychology Compass, 1*, 298–312. doi:10.1111/j.1751-9004.2007.00015.x

Milgram, S. (1963). Behavioral study of obedience. *Journal of Abnormal and Social Psychology, 67*, 371–378. doi:10.1037/h0040525

Miller, A. (Ed.). (2004). *The social psychology of good and evil* (pp. 168–192). New York, NY: Guilford Press.

Mischel, W. (1973). Toward a cognitive social learning reconceptualization of personality. *Psychological Review, 80*, 252–283. doi:10.1037/h0035002

Mischel, W., & Shoda, Y. (1995). A cognitive–affective system theory of personality: Reconceptualizing situations, dispositions, dynamics, and invariance in personality structure. *Psychological Review, 102,* 246–268. doi:10.1037/0033-295X.102.2.246

Moore, M. (2003, October 31). Top Israeli officer says tactics are backfiring. *The Washington Post,* p. A1.

Neuilly, M.-A. (2007). When murder is not enough: Toward a new definition of community violence. *Aggression and Violent Behavior, 12,* 598–610. doi:10.1016/j.avb.2007.02.004

Öhman, A., Lundqvist, D., & Esteves, F. (2001). The face in the crowd effect: An anger superiority effect with schematic stimuli. *Journal of Personality and Social Psychology, 80,* 381–396.

Plant, E. A., & Peruche, B. M. (2005). The consequences of race for police officers' responses to criminal suspects. *Psychological Science, 16,* 180–183. doi:10.1111/j.0956-7976.2005.00800.x

Smith, C. A., & Lazarus, R. S. (1993). Appraisal components, core relational themes, and the emotions. *Cognition and Emotion, 7,* 233–269. doi:10.1080/02699939308409189

Strack, F., & Deutsch, R. (2004). Reflective and impulsive determinants of social behavior. *Personality and Social Psychology Review, 8,* 220–247. doi:10.1207/s15327957pspr0803_1

Tooby, J., & Cosmides, L. (1992). The psychological foundations of culture. In J. Barkow, L. Cosmides, & J. Tooby (Eds.), *The adapted mind* (pp. 19–136). New York, NY: Oxford University Press.

U.S. Department of Health and Human Services. (2001). *Youth violence: A report of the Surgeon General.* Rockville, MD: Author.

Wegner, D. M., & Bargh, J. A. (1998). Control and automaticity in social life. In D. T. Gilbert, S. T. Fiske, & G. Lindzey (Eds.), *The handbook of social psychology* (4th ed., Vol. 1, pp. 446–496). New York, NY: McGraw-Hill.

Wildschut, T., Pinter, B., Vevea, J. L., Insko, C. A., & Schopler, J. (2003). Beyond the group mind: A quantitative review of the interindividual–intergroup discontinuity effect. *Psychological Bulletin, 129,* 698–722. doi:10.1037/0033-2909.129.5.698

Zajonc, R. B. (1965, July 16). Social facilitation. *Science, 149,* 269–274. doi:10.1126/science.149.3681.269

2

I³ THEORY: INSTIGATING, IMPELLING, AND INHIBITING FACTORS IN AGGRESSION

ERICA B. SLOTTER AND ELI J. FINKEL

Interpersonal aggression is prevalent and disturbing. This chapter presents a metatheoretical perspective, *I³ theory*, that seeks (a) to impose theoretical coherence on the massive number of established risk factors for aggression and (b) to use the tools of statistical (and conceptual) moderation to gain new insights into the processes by which a previously nonaggressive interaction escalates into an aggressive one (see Finkel, 2007, 2008). I³ theory (pronounced "I-cubed theory") does not advance one key variable (or even a specific set of key variables) as the root cause of aggression. Rather, it seeks to present an organizational structure for understanding both (a) the process by which a given risk factor promotes aggression and (b) how multiple risk factors interrelate to aggravate or mitigate the aggression-promoting tendencies of each. As detailed in this chapter, I³ theory suggests that scholars can predict whether an individual will behave aggressively in a given situation by examining the main and interactive effects of the instigating triggers, impelling forces, and inhibiting forces at play.

Scholars have advanced a broad range of theories to understand *aggression*, which in this chapter refers to any behavior carried out with the primary proximal goal of inflicting physical harm on a target who is motivated to avoid being harmed (Baron & Richardson, 1994). (We do not examine in this chapter other forms of aggression, such as verbal, relational, or sexual aggression.) Craig Anderson and colleagues have sought to integrate many of these theories into a broad metatheory called the *general aggression model* (GAM; Anderson & Bushman, 2002; see Chapter 1, this volume). As with I³ theory, the GAM focuses less on a particular variable or process than on general classes of aggression risk factors and processes. The GAM consists of three main foci. The first emphasizes person and situation *inputs*, or risk factors, for aggression. *Person inputs* include personality traits, gender, beliefs, attitudes, values, long-term goals, and scripts; *situation inputs* include aggressive cues (e.g., presence of guns), provocation, frustration, pain and discomfort, drugs, and incentives (determined by a cost/benefit analysis). The second focus is the interconnected affective, arousal, and cognitive *routes*, or mechanisms, through which the inputs influence aggressive behavior. *Affective routes* include mood and emotion and expressive motor tendencies; *arousal routes* include the strengthening of a dominant action tendency or certain misattribution processes; *cognitive routes* include hostile thoughts and scripts. Finally, the third focus is the *outcomes* of the underlying appraisal and decision processes. Individuals are likely to act impulsively when they lack the resources and motivation to alter their immediate appraisal of the situation. If they possess the resources and motivation, however, they may reappraise the situation and act in a more thoughtful fashion.

I³ THEORY

I³ theory, which is a process-oriented metatheory designed to identify the circumstances under which a nonaggressive interaction can become an aggressive one, has different emphases from the general aggression model. For example, although both metatheories seek to integrate extant theories of aggression into a broad, coherent model, I³ theory incorporates recent research on self-regulation as a core emphasis of the model, and it specifies the novel ways in which aggression risk factors interact to predict aggressive behavior.

The theory begins by posing three questions. First, does at least one individual in the interaction experience strong instigating triggers toward aggression? Second, does that individual experience strong impelling forces toward aggression? Third, does that individual experience weak forces to inhibit or override the aggressive impulses? Each affirmative answer increases the likelihood of aggressive behavior via both a main effect and interactive effects with variables relevant to one or both of the other questions. Whereas the strength of impelling forces is determined by the collective power of the variables that cause the individual to experience an urge to aggress in response to a given instigating trigger, the strength of inhibiting forces is determined by the collective power of the variables that cause the individual to override this aggressive urge.

In addition to these three initial questions, I^3 theory poses a fourth: How do effects of variables in one category (i.e., instigating triggers, impelling forces, or inhibiting forces) interact with effects of one or more variables from the other categories to predict aggressive behavior? As presented in Table 2.1, answering these four questions enables scholars to identify seven key I^3 theory effects. Figure 2.1 (which builds on work by Fals-Stewart, Leonard, & Birchler, 2005) illustrates how these seven effects can work together to increase or decrease the likelihood of aggressive behavior.

I^3 theory diverges from the aggression theories mentioned earlier in its central emphasis on inhibitory processes. The theory recognizes the importance of instigating triggers and impelling forces, but it argues that such factors cause individuals to enact aggressive behavior only when their collective power is stronger than the collective power of inhibitory processes. Although other theories address the importance of inhibitory processes in aggression (e.g., Chapters 1, 6, 9, and 15), the emphasis on such processes gains new prominence with I^3 theory.

Instigating Triggers

The first stage of I^3 theory concerns the presence of one or more *instigating triggers*, which are discrete situational events or circumstances that induce rudimentary action tendencies toward physical aggression. As illustrated at the lower left of Figure 2.1, impelling and inhibiting forces are irrelevant when instigating triggers are absent. Even the world's angriest, least controlled person is not aggressive all the time; some situational variable (even if it only serves to activate a long-standing goal or grievance) is required before the person becomes aggressive. Aversive events can trigger (via automatic associative networks or cognitive appraisal processes) hostile cognitive, affective, physiological, and even motor tendencies that prime the individual to aggress (Berkowitz, 1993; Chapters 1 and 9, this volume). I^3 theory suggests that certain events can also trigger aggressive tendencies driven by instrumental goals (e.g., having an individual offer you money to beat up his enemy).

Instigating triggers fall into one of two categories: dyadic and third-party. *Dyadic triggers* refer to events or circumstances that the potentially aggressive individual perceives as having originated in the target. Examples include direct provocation (Bettencourt & Miller, 1996), goal obstruction (Dollard, Doob, Miller, Mowrer, & Sears, 1939), and social rejection (Leary, Twenge, & Quinlivan, 2006). *Third-party triggers* refer to events or circumstances that the potentially aggressive individual perceives as having originated in somebody other than the target. The same kinds of triggers that lead

TABLE 2.1
I³ Theory of Aggression: The Seven Effects

I³ Effect (#)	I³ Effect (Stage)	I³ Effect (Description)	Example	Citation for example
1	Stage 1	Instigating Trigger Main Effect	Social Rejection	Twenge et al., 2001
2	Stage 2	Impelling Forces Main Effect	Testosterone	Dabbs et al., 1987
3	Stage 3	Inhibiting Forces Main Effect	Self-Regulatory Strength	DeWall et al., 2007
4	Stage 1 × Stage 2	Instigating Trigger × Impelling Forces Interaction Effect	Ego Threat × Narcissism	Bushman & Baumeister, 1998
5	Stage 1 × Stage 3	Instigating Trigger × Inhibiting Forces Interaction Effect	Provocation × Self-Regulatory Strength	Finkel et al., 2009
6	Stage 2 × Stage 3	Impelling Forces × Inhibiting Forces Interaction Effect	Physical Proclivity × Negative Outcome Expectancies	Finkel & Foshee, 2009
7	Stage 1 × Stage 2 × Stage 3	Instigating Trigger × Impelling Forces × Inhibiting Forces Interaction Effect	[No Known Example]	[No Known Example]

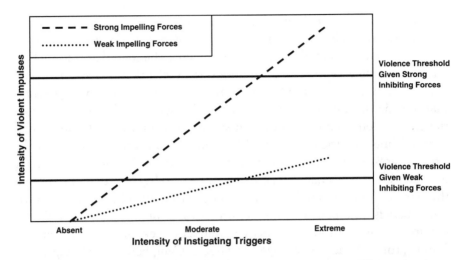

Figure 2.1. How the three components of I³ theory interrelate to predict aggressive behavior. For ease of illustration, impelling forces and inhibiting forces are depicted as if they are binary—either weak or strong. In reality, the intensity of each type of force varies continuously from weak to strong.

to a rudimentary action tendency to aggress against the provocateur can also lead to this tendency with respect to a third party. For example, an individual who feels provoked or rejected may experience an instigation to aggress not only against the source of the provocation or rejection but also (or alternately) toward another target whom the potential perpetrator believes would make a more acceptable or desirable target (e.g., somebody who is less likely to fight back).

Impelling Forces

The second stage of I³ theory concerns risk factors that determine the strength of the aggressive impulse experienced by the individual, through main effects and through interactions with instigating triggers. In some situations, individuals may effortlessly shrug off (or perhaps not even notice; see Chapter 9) an instigating trigger, experiencing virtually no impulse toward aggression. In others, individuals may react strongly to a trigger, experiencing a powerful impulse toward aggression. *Impelling forces* refer to factors that increase the likelihood that individuals will experience an aggressive impulse in response to an instigating trigger. Individuals tend to experience more powerful aggressive impulses when impelling forces are strong than when they are weak (see dashed vs. dotted lines in Figure 2.1), especially to the degree that the instigating trigger is severe.

Impelling forces fall into one of four categories: evolutionary and cultural, personal, dyadic, and situational. *Evolutionary and cultural impellors* refer to features of the potentially aggressive individual's biological or cultural heritage, including evolutionary adaptations and social norms (see Chapters 3 and 10). Examples include adaptations resulting from evolutionary pressures that provided ancestral men and women with a survival advantage for experiencing violent impulses in certain situations (Lorenz, 1966) and social norms delineating the extent to which certain instigating triggers provoke strong aggressive impulses (Nisbett & Cohen, 1996). *Personal impellors* refer to relatively stable characteristics of a given individual that differ from those of many other individuals, including personality characteristics, attitudes, beliefs, interpersonal interaction styles, or biological factors. Examples include dispositional hostility (Norlander & Eckhardt, 2005; Chapters 5 and 8, this volume), narcissism (Twenge & Campbell, 2003; Chapter 11, this volume), and testosterone (Dabbs, Frady, Carr, & Besch, 1987; Van Goozen, Frijda, & Van de Poll, 1994). *Dyadic impellors* refer to characteristics of the relationship between the potential aggressor and the potential target. Examples include dissatisfaction with the amount of power one has in a relationship (Ronfeldt, Kimerling, & Arias, 1998), target-specific jealousy (Dutton, van Ginkel, & Landolt, 1996; Holtzworth-Munroe, Stuart, & Hutchinson, 1997), and feelings of vulnerability or insecurity in the relationship (Carney & Buttell, 2005; Holtzworth-Munroe et al., 1997; Chapters 13 and 14, this volume). Finally, *situational impellors* refer to momentarily activated cognitive, affective, or physiological experiences. Examples include uncomfortable temperatures (Anderson, Anderson, Dorr, DeNeve, & Flanagan, 2000), physical pain (Berkowitz, 1998), and exposure to violent media (Anderson & Bushman, 2001; Anderson, Carnagey, & Eubanks, 2003).

Inhibiting Forces

The third stage of I³ theory concerns risk factors that determine whether individuals will override the aggressive impulses that emerge from the instigating triggers, impelling factors, and their interaction. In some situations, individuals succumb to these impulses, engaging in aggressive behavior. In others, individuals override them in favor of nonviolent behavior. *Inhibiting forces* refer to factors that increase the likelihood that individuals will override aggressive impulses rather than acting on them. Inhibiting factors collectively determine the threshold above which aggressive impulses will manifest themselves in aggressive behavior. If the inhibiting forces are weak (i.e., the lower horizontal line in Figure 2.1), then aggressive impulses need not be especially strong to result in aggressive behavior. If the inhibiting forces are strong (i.e., the upper horizontal line in Figure 2.1), then aggressive impulses must be strong to result in aggressive behavior.

As with impelling forces, inhibiting forces fall into one of four categories: evolutionary and cultural, personal, dyadic, and situational. Examples of *evolutionary and cultural inhibitors* include adaptations resulting from evolutionary pressures that provided ancestral men and women with a survival advantage for overriding aggressive impulses in certain situations (Baumeister, 2005; Chapter 3, this volume) and social norms or institutions that decrease the likelihood that individuals will act on aggressive impulses (Guerra, Huesmann, & Spindler, 2003; Sampson, Raudenbush, & Earls, 1997; Chapter 10, this volume). Examples of *personal inhibitors* include dispositional self-control (Finkel, DeWall, Slotter, Oaten, & Foshee, 2009), executive functioning (Giancola, 2000; Chapter 6, this volume), and beliefs that enacting aggressive behavior will lead to poor outcomes for the self (Slaby & Guerra, 1988). Examples of *dyadic inhibitors* include partner empathy or perspective taking (Richardson, Green, & Lago, 1998; Van Baardewijk, Stegge, Bushman, & Vermeiren, in press), relationship commitment (Gaertner & Foshee, 1999; Slotter, Finkel, & Bodenhausen, 2009), and relative physical size (Archer & Benson, 2008; Felson, 1996; Chapter 3, this volume). Finally, examples of *situational inhibitors* include sobriety (i.e., vs. alcohol intoxication; Bushman & Cooper, 1990; Denson et al., 2008), nondepleted self-regulatory resources (DeWall, Baumeister, Stillman, & Gailliot, 2007; Finkel et al., 2009; Chapter 6, this volume), and plentiful cognitive processing time (Finkel et al., 2009).

Reviewing the Aggression Literature From the Perspective of I³ Theory

One purpose of I³ theory is to provide a coherent framework for categorizing aggression risk factors and examining the interplay among them. To illustrate how I³ theory can accomplish these goals, we review key findings in the aggression literature through its lens, with a particular emphasis on interaction effects. This review is illustrative rather than exhaustive.

I³ theory encompasses seven key effects: three main effects (i.e., instigating triggers, impelling forces, and inhibiting forces), three two-way interaction effects (i.e., instigating triggers × impelling forces, instigating triggers × inhibiting forces, and impelling forces × inhibiting forces), and one three-way interaction effect (instigating triggers × impelling forces × inhibiting forces). Table 2.1 lists these seven effects and provides an example of each. We discuss examples of these effects in turn.

1. An Illustrative Main Effect of Instigating Triggers: Social Rejection

As shown in the first row of Table 2.1, an illustrative instigating trigger is *social rejection*, which refers to a class of interpersonal processes in which individuals feel rejected, excluded, or ostracized. Diverse lines of evidence demonstrate that individuals who experience social rejection are more aggressive than individuals who do not (Leary et al., 2006). In one study, participants who had been unanimously rejected by a group of fellow participants administered substantially louder, more painful sound blasts to an unknown stranger than did participants who had been unanimously accepted (Twenge, Baumeister, Tice, & Stucke, 2001, Study 5). In this study, social rejection served as a displaced instigating trigger because the target of the aggression was not a member of the group who had previously rejected the participant. Another study, which provided an in-depth analysis of all well-documented school shootings in the United States between 1995 and 2001, yielded compatible conclusions, with acute or chronic rejection preceding the shootings in 87% of the cases (Leary, Kowalski, Smith, & Phillips, 2003).

2. An Illustrative Main Effect of Impelling Forces: Testosterone

As shown in the second row of Table 2.1, an illustrative impelling force is the androgen *testosterone*. Although testosterone is higher in men than in women, its level predicts aggression in both sexes (Archer, Birring, & Wu, 1998; Dabbs & Hargrove, 1997; see Sapolsky, 1998). In a study of male prison inmates, testosterone levels correlated positively with crime severity; indeed, nine of the 11 inmates with the lowest testosterone levels had committed nonviolent crimes, whereas 10 of the 11 inmates with the highest testosterone levels had committed violent crimes (Dabbs et al., 1987). In another study, female-to-male transsexuals became considerably more aggressive in the first 3 months of androgen injections (Van Goozen, Cohen-Kettenis, Gooren, Frijda, & Van de Poll, 1995).

3. An Illustrative Main Effect of Inhibiting Forces: Self-Regulatory Strength

As shown in the third row of Table 2.1, an illustrative inhibiting factor is *self-regulatory strength*, which refers to the psychological resource that undergirds willful acts of self-regulation. According to the strength model of self-regulation (Baumeister, Gailliot, DeWall, & Oaten, 2006), all such acts depend on a unitary resource that resembles a muscle. The strength of this resource can be temporarily diminished by self-regulatory exertions (leading to a state of "ego depletion"), just as holding a heavy weight fatigues a muscle in the short term but it also can be bolstered over time by adherence to a self-regulatory bolstering "regimen," just as a consistent weight-lifting regimen strengthens a muscle over time. In one study, hungry participants who had, moments earlier, exerted self-regulation by resisting the temptation to eat an indulgent food (a donut; high ego depletion condition) were more aggressive toward a same-sex provoking interaction partner (forcing this partner to eat a snack with plentiful hot sauce despite his or her distaste for spicy foods) than were participants who had previously resisted eating a less tempting food (radishes; low ego depletion condition), even though participants in the two conditions did not differ in how angry they were in response to the provocation (DeWall et al., 2007, Study 1).

Complementing this evidence that short-term self-regulatory exertions can deplete self-regulatory resources and thereby predict elevated aggression is evidence that longer term self-regulatory exertion regimens can bolster self-regulatory strength and thereby predict reduced aggression. A recent study demonstrated that individuals who had adhered to a 2-week self-regulatory strength-bolstering regimen declined significantly from before to after the regimen in their aggressive tendencies toward their romantic partner (Finkel et al., 2009, Study 5). In this study, participants who deliberately regulated either their physical behavior (e.g., brushing their teeth with their non-dominant hand) or their verbal behavior (e.g., making sure not to begin sentences with "I") reported a reduced likelihood of being physically aggressive in response to various partner provocations (e.g., "I walk in and catch my partner having sex with someone"), whereas participants in a no-intervention condition exhibited no change from pretest to posttest.

4. An Illustrative Instigating Trigger × Impelling Forces Interaction Effect: Ego Threat × Narcissism

We now turn from I³ theory's three main effects to its three two-way interaction effects. As shown in the fourth row of Table 2.1, an illustrative instigating trigger × impelling forces interaction effect is *ego threat × narcissism*. Although many scholars have suggested that low self-esteem causes aggression, others have increasingly argued that a form of high self-esteem is frequently more likely to do so. In particular, individuals whose self-views are not only favorable but also unstable, inflated, or uncertain are especially prone toward aggressive behavior when their favorable self-views are socially threatened (Baumeister, Smart, & Boden, 1996; Chapter 11, this volume). One series of studies demonstrated that participants who had experienced an ego threat in the form of insulting feedback about an essay they had written (an instigating trigger) were more aggressive toward the same-sex provocateur (subjecting him or her to painfully loud noise blasts) than were participants who had not experienced an ego threat (Bushman & Baumeister, 1998). The key finding, however, was that this main effect of ego threat was substantially larger for participants who were high in narcissism (an impelling factor) than for participants who were low in narcissism.

Additional research has examined how self-views moderate the link between other instigating triggers (aside from insults) and aggression. One study demonstrated that the link between social rejection and displaced aggression (painful noise blasts) was substantially stronger for individuals who were high in narcissism than for those who were low in narcissism (Twenge & Campbell, 2003, Study 4), and another demonstrated that the link between social rejection and aggression (aversive hot sauce) was substantially stronger for individuals who were high in rejection sensitivity (those who anxiously expect, readily perceive, and overreact to rejection) than for those who were low in rejection sensitivity (Ayduk, Gyurak, & Luerssen, 2008).

5. An Illustrative Instigating Trigger × Inhibiting Forces Interaction Effect: Provocation × Self-Regulatory Strength

As shown in the fifth row of Table 2.1, an illustrative instigating trigger × inhibiting forces interaction effect is *provocation × self-regulatory strength*. As discussed previously, both provocation and self-regulatory strength predict aggression via main effects. Recent studies confirm the I³ theory prediction that incorporating their interaction effect yields a richer story (e.g., Chapter 6). Two recent experiments, one in which the aggression was directed at strangers (aversive sound blasts; DeWall et al., 2007, Study 2) and one in which the aggression was directed at one's romantic partner (forcing him or her to maintain body poses for painfully long durations; Finkel et al., 2009, Study 4), demonstrated that participants were especially aggressive when they experienced both provocation (in the form of insulting feedback) and ego depletion.

Another example of an instigating trigger × inhibiting forces interaction effect is *provocation severity × frontal lobe functioning* (Lau, Pihl, & Peterson, 1995). In this study, participants were preselected if they were in the upper or lower quartile on frontal-lobe-based cognitive functioning, which underlies the ability to control one's impulses (Hecaen & Albert, 1978). Consistent with I³ theory, participants were more aggressive (administering painful electric shocks) to the degree that the opponent had previously provoked them severely rather than mildly (i.e., had administered painful electric shocks to them), but this provocation main effect was substantially stronger among individuals with weak rather than strong frontal lobe functioning (Lau et al., 1995).

Yet another example of an instigating trigger × inhibiting forces interaction effect is *provocation salience × alcohol consumption* (Densen et al., 2008). In this study, participants who had just consumed four alcoholic or placebo beverages were provoked in either a salient or a subtle way and then had the opportunity to aggress against their provocateur by determining for how long the provocateur would have to keep his or her hand immersed in iced water. Participants were more aggressive in the salient provocation condition than in the subtle provocation condition, and this effect was significantly stronger in the alcohol than in the placebo condition.

A final example of an instigating trigger × inhibiting forces interaction effect is *provocation level × relationship commitment* within the context of an ongoing romantic relationship (Slotter et al., 2009). In these studies, participants were more aggressive toward their romantic partner after he or she had provoked them, and this provocation main effect was especially strong among participants who were low in relationship commitment. Extending work suggesting that commitment promotes prorelationship behaviors in other conflictual relationship domains, such as forgiveness (Finkel, Rusbult, Kumashiro, & Hannon, 2002), it appears that individuals who are highly committed to their romantic relationships are able to override aggressive impulses when their partner provokes them.

6. An Illustrative Impelling Forces × Inhibiting Forces Interaction Effect: Physical Proclivity × Negative Outcome Expectancies

As shown in the sixth row of Table 2.1, an illustrative impelling forces × inhibiting forces interaction effect is *physical proclivity × negative outcome expectancies*. Individuals vary in the degree to which they prefer physical versus cognitive tasks, and a relative preference for the former predicts increased tendencies toward aggression and criminal behavior (Gottfredson & Hirschi, 1990). Individuals also vary in the degree to which they believe that engaging in aggressive behavior will cause them to experience negative outcomes, such as physical harm or social derision, and stronger beliefs in this causal link predict decreased tendencies toward aggression (Slaby & Guerra, 1988). One recent study examined whether physical proclivity (an impelling factor) interacts with negative outcome expectancies (an inhibiting factor) to predict aggression toward a romantic partner (Finkel & Foshee, 2009). Results revealed a strong positive association of physical proclivity with self-reported aggressive behavior over the previous year, but only when negative outcome expectancies were low. It seems that the tendencies to prefer physical to cognitive tasks predicts greater aggression among individuals whose aggression is not restrained by beliefs that being aggressive will bring about negative effects for them, but not among individuals whose aggression is so restrained.

7. Instigating Triggers × Impelling Forces × Inhibiting Forces Interaction Effects: A Null Set

Although the three main effects and the three two-way interaction effects reviewed previously are key components of I³ theory, the instigating triggers × impelling forces × inhibiting forces three-way interaction effect represents the most important component of the theory. Indeed, the theory suggests that all three of the preceding two-way interaction effects are moderated by third variables from whichever category is not represented in that two-way interaction.

Testing for such a three-way interaction would not be difficult. For example, it would be easy to examine (a) whether the ego threat × narcissism (instigating trigger × impelling factor) interaction effect is moderated by an inhibiting factor (e.g., self-regulatory strength, alcohol consumption, strong relationship commitment), (b) whether the provocation × self-regulation strength (instigating trigger × inhibiting factor) interaction effect is moderated by an impelling factor (e.g., testosterone, physical proclivity, dispositional anger), and (c) whether the physical proclivity × negative outcome expectancy (impelling factor × inhibiting factor) interaction effect is moderated by an instigating trigger (e.g., social rejection, ego threat, provocation). Testing for such interaction effects is an important direction for future research.

DISCUSSION

I³ theory seeks (a) to impose enhanced theoretical coherence on the vast array of aggression risk factors by identifying how each of them increases the likelihood of aggression (via instigating triggers, impelling forces, and/or inhibiting forces) and (b) to examine the manner in which risk factors from one category interact with those from one or both of the other categories to predict aggressive behavior. In the preceding section (also see Table 2.1 and Figure 2.1), we reviewed specific examples of how certain risk factors fit into I³ theory and how they interface with variables from the other I³ theory categories.

One important direction for future research, aside from providing the first tests of I³ theory's instigating trigger × impelling factor × inhibiting factor three-way interaction effect, will be to develop and hone empirical procedures for classifying a given risk factor into an I³ theory category (instigating trigger, impelling forces, and/or inhibiting forces) or perhaps into more than one category if a given variable both increases aggressive impulses and decreases restraint. In this chapter, we have relied on theory to determine, for example, (a) that social rejection, ego threat, and provocation are instigating triggers; (b) that testosterone, narcissism, and physical proclivity are impelling factors; and (c) that self-regulatory strength, lack of alcohol consumption, and negative outcome expectancies are inhibiting factors. One limitation of this approach is that existing theory is in many cases not sufficiently developed vis-à-vis the I³ theory parameters to allow for definitive classification. For example, we are reasonably confident that dispositional self-control predicts reduced aggression in large part by raising the inhibition threshold (see the horizontal lines in Figure 2.1), thereby increasing the likelihood that individuals will override aggressive impulses. That said, perhaps such dispositional self-control also predicts reduced aggression in part by reducing impelling forces, thereby decreasing the strength of the aggressive impulse in the first place.

How might scholars use empirical procedures to determine whether a given variable promotes aggression by increasing aggressive impulses or by decreasing restraint? One promising approach is to adapt recent developments in process dissociation paradigms used by social cognition researchers. Scholars have recently modeled behavior on laboratory tasks to discern the degree to which participants exhibit certain automatic tendencies (e.g., toward prejudice or discrimination) and also controlled tendencies that override these automatic tendencies (Payne, 2001; Sherman et al., 2008; see also Jacoby, 1991). After developing empirical procedures for distinguishing impulses toward aggressive behavior from self-controlled processes that override those impulses, scholars will be able to examine the association of a given risk factor with both (a) individuals' tendencies to experience impulses to aggress and (b) their tendencies to override those impulses (Chapter 6, this volume). We predict that variables such as testosterone, narcissism, and physical proclivity will correlate positively with the automatic aggressive tendencies identified by these process dissociation procedures and negligibly with the controlled tendencies that override these automatic tendencies. In contrast, we predict that variables such as self-regulatory strength, sobriety, and negative outcome expectancies will correlate negligibly with the automatic aggressive tendencies identified by these process dissociation procedures and positively with the controlled tendencies that override these automatic tendencies.

Once scholars determine (using theoretical tools, empirical tools, or both) which risk factors function by strengthening aggressive impulses and which function by weakening behavioral inhibition processes, I³ theory may hold promise for interventions designed to reduce aggressive behavior. For example, the theory highlights the importance of inhibitory factors (especially self-regulation) in predicting aggressive behavior, and scholars have suggested that interventions designed to help individuals override their impulses are likely to be more effective than interventions designed to prevent them from experiencing those impulses in the first place (e.g., Baumeister, 2005). To the degree that such scholars are correct, interventions designed to strengthen inhibitory forces may turn out to be more effective on average than interventions designed to weaken impelling forces. Early research inspired by I³ theory suggests that inhibition-relevant interventions at the dispositional level (e.g., building self-regulatory strength via bolstering regimens), relational level (e.g., strengthening relationship commitment), and situational level (e.g., having participants wait 10 seconds before responding to a provocation) can reduce aggressive behavior (Finkel et al., 2009; Slotter et al., 2009; see Finkel et al., 2002, for evidence that relationship commitment is amenable to experimental manipulation). And, as discussed earlier, distal inhibitory factors such as prevalent social norms also seem to influence aggressive behavior (Guerra et al., 2003; Sampson, Raudenbush, & Earls, 1997; Chapter 10, this volume), which hints at the possibility that large-scale social interventions could potentially reduce aggression at the societal level.

In conclusion, I³ theory is an attempt to categorize aggression risk factors into instigating triggers, impelling factors, and/or inhibiting factors and to identify the interplay among variables across categories (see Figure 2.1). To the degree that extant theory provides good reason to believe that particular risk factors fit relatively neatly into one of the I³ theory categories, the theory provides an immediately accessible agenda for future research, oriented less toward identifying additional risk factors than toward identifying (a) the processes by which risk factors, considered in isolation, increase aggression and (b) the manner in which they interact to do so. In the long run, I³ theory can inform interventions designed to help individuals manage their aggressive impulses in a constructive manner. Indeed, scholarship may well progress to the point where interventions can be tailored to the specific inhibiting risk factors most relevant to a given person, perhaps reducing one individual's aggression by bolstering self-regulatory strength and reducing another individual's aggression by bolstering empathy. Such tailored interventions, which would require valid assessment instruments, hold particular promise for reducing the prevalence and severity of interpersonal aggression.

REFERENCES

Anderson, C. A., Anderson, K. B., Dorr, N., DeNeve, K. M., & Flanagan, M. (2000). Temperature and aggression. *Advances in Experimental Social Psychology, 32,* 63–133. doi:10.1016/S0065-2601(00)80004-0

Anderson, C. A., & Bushman, B. J. (2001). Effects of violent video games on aggressive behavior, aggressive cognition, aggressive affect, physiological arousal, and prosocial behavior: A meta-analytic review of the scientific literature. *Psychological Science, 12,* 353–359. doi:10.1111/1467-9280.00366

Anderson, C. A., & Bushman, B. J. (2002). Human aggression. *Annual Review of Psychology, 53,* 27–51. doi:10.1146/annurev.psych.53.100901.135231

Anderson, C. A., Carnagey, N. L., & Eubanks, J. (2003). Exposure to violent media: The effects of songs with violent lyrics on aggressive thoughts and feelings. *Journal of Personality and Social Psychology, 84,* 960–971. doi:10.1037/0022-3514.84.5.960

Archer, J., & Benson, D. (2008). Physical aggression as a function of perceived fighting ability and provocation: An experimental investigation. *Aggressive Behavior, 34,* 9–24. doi:10.1002/ab.20179

Archer, J., Birring, S. S., & Wu, F. C. W. (1998). The association between testosterone and aggression among young men: Empirical findings and a meta-analysis.

Aggressive Behavior, 24, 411–420. doi:10.1002/(SICI)1098-2337(1998)24:6<411:: AID-AB2>3.0.CO;2-9

Ayduk, O., Gyurak, A., & Luerssen, A. (2008). Individual differences in the rejection–aggression link in the hot sauce paradigm: The case of rejection sensitivity. *Journal of Experimental Social Psychology, 44,* 775–782. doi:10.1016/ j.jesp.2007.07.004

Baron, R. A., & Richardson, D. R. (1994). *Human aggression* (2nd ed.). New York, NY: Plenum Press.

Baumeister, R. F. (2005). *The cultural animal: Human nature, meaning, and social life.* New York, NY: Oxford University Press.

Baumeister, R. F., Gailliot, M., DeWall, C. N., & Oaten, M. (2006). Self-regulation and personality: How interventions increase regulatory success, and how depletion moderates the effects of trait on behavior. *Journal of Personality, 74,* 1773–1802. doi:10.1111/j.1467-6494.2006.00428.x

Baumeister, R. F., Smart, L., & Boden, J. M. (1996). Relation of threatened egotism to violence and aggression: The dark side of high self-esteem. *Psychological Review, 103,* 5–33. doi:10.1037/0033-295X.103.1.5

Berkowitz, L. (1993). *Aggression: Its causes, consequences, and control.* New York, NY: McGraw-Hill.

Berkowitz, L. (1998). Affective aggression: The role of stress, pain, and negative affect. In R. G. Geen & E. Donnerstein (Eds.), *Human aggression: Theories, research, and implications for social policy* (pp. 49–72). San Diego, CA: Academic Press.

Bettencourt, B. A., & Miller, N. (1996). Gender differences in aggression as a function of provocation: A meta-analysis. *Psychological Bulletin, 119,* 422–447. doi:10.1037/0033-2909.119.3.422

Bushman, B. J., & Baumeister, R. F. (1998). Threatened egotism, narcissism, self-esteem, and direct or displaced aggression: Does self-love of self-hate lead to violence? *Journal of Personality and Social Psychology, 75,* 219–229. doi:10.1037/ 0022-3514.75.1.219

Bushman, B. J., & Cooper, H. M. (1990). Alcohol and human aggression: An integrative research review. *Psychological Bulletin, 107,* 341–354. doi:10.1037/ 0033-2909.107.3.341

Carney, M. M., & Buttell, F. P. (2006). Exploring the relevance of attachment theory as a dependent variable in the treatment of women mandated into treatment for domestic violence offenses. *Journal of Offender Rehabilitation, 41,* 33–61. doi:10.1300/J076v41n04_02

Dabbs, J. M., Jr., Frady, R. L., Carr, T. S., & Besch, N. F. (1987). Saliva testosterone and criminal violence in young adult prison inmates. *Psychosomatic Medicine, 49,* 174–182.

Dabbs, J. M., Jr., & Hargrove, M. F. (1997). Age, testosterone, and behavior among female prison inmates. *Psychosomatic Medicine, 59,* 477–480.

Denson, T. F., Aviles, F. E., Pollock, V. E., Earleywince, M., Vasquez, E. A., & Miller, N. (2008). The effects of alcohol and the salience of aggressive cues on triggered displaced aggression. *Aggressive Behavior, 34,* 25–33. doi:10.1002/ab.20177

DeWall, C. N., Baumeister, R. F., Stillman, R. G., & Gailliot, M. T. (2007). Violence restrained: Effects of self-regulation and its depletion on aggression. *Journal of Experimental Social Psychology, 43,* 62–76. doi:10.1016/j.jesp.2005.12.005

Dollard, J., Doob, L. W., Miller, N. E., Mowrer, O. H., & Sears, R. R. (1939). *Frustration and aggression.* New Haven, CT: Yale University Press. doi:10.1037/10022-000

Dutton, D. G., van Ginkel, C., & Landolt, M. (1996). Jealousy, intrusiveness, and intimate abusiveness. *Journal of Family Violence, 11,* 411–423. doi:10.1007/BF02333425

Fals-Stewart, W., Leonard, K. E., & Birchler, G. R. (2005). The occurrence of male-to-female intimate partner violence on days of men's drinking: The moderating effects of antisocial personality disorder. *Journal of Consulting and Clinical Psychology, 73,* 239–248. doi:10.1037/0022-006X.73.2.239

Felson, R. B. (1996). Big people hit little people: Sex differences in physical power and interpersonal violence. *Criminology, 34,* 433–452. doi:10.1111/j.1745-9125.1996.tb01214.x

Finkel, E. J. (2007). Impelling and inhibiting forces in the perpetration of intimate partner violence. *Review of General Psychology, 11,* 193–207. doi:10.1037/1089-2680.11.2.193

Finkel, E. J. (2008). Intimate partner violence perpetration: Insights from the science of self-regulation. In J. P. Forgas & J. Fitness (Eds.), *Social relationships: Cognitive, affective, and motivational processes* (pp. 271–288). New York, NY: Psychology Press.

Finkel, E. J., DeWall, C. N., Slotter, E., B., Oaten, M., & Foshee, V. A. (2009). Self-regulatory failure and intimate partner violence perpetration. *Journal of Personality and Social Psychology, 97,* 483–499. doi:10.1037/a0015433

Finkel, E. J., & Foshee, V. A. (2009). *Impelling and inhibiting forces in the perpetration of intimate partner violence.* Unpublished manuscript, Northwestern University, Evanston, IL.

Finkel, E. J., Rusbult, C. E., Kumashiro, M., & Hannon, P. A. (2002). Dealing with betrayal in close relationships: Does commitment promote forgiveness? *Journal of Personality and Social Psychology, 82,* 956–974. doi:10.1037/0022-3514.82.6.956

Gaertner, L., & Foshee, V. (1999). Commitment and the perpetration of relationship violence. *Personal Relationships, 6,* 227–239. doi:10.1111/j.1475-6811.1999.tb00189.x

Giancola, P. R. (2000). Executive functioning: A conceptual framework for alcohol-related aggression. *Experimental and Clinical Psychopharmacology, 8,* 576–597. doi:10.1037/1064-1297.8.4.576

Gottfredson, M. R., & Hirschi, T. (1990). *A general theory of crime*. Stanford, CA: Stanford University Press.

Guerra, N. G., Huesmann, L. R., & Spindler, A. (2003). Community violence exposure, social cognition, and aggression among urban elementary school children. *Child Development, 74*, 1561–1576. doi:10.1111/1467-8624.00623

Hecaen, H., & Albert, M. L. (1978). *Human neuropsychology*. New York, NY: Wiley.

Holtzworth-Munroe, A., Stuart, G. L., & Hutchinson, G. (1997). Violent versus nonviolent husbands: Differences in attachment patterns, dependency, and jealousy. *Journal of Family Psychology, 11*, 314–331. doi:10.1037/0893-3200.11.3.314

Jacoby, L. L. (1991). A process dissociation framework: Separating automatic from intentional uses of memory. *Journal of Memory and Language, 30*, 513–541. doi:10.1016/0749-596X(91)90025-F

Lau, M. A., Pihl, R. O., & Peterson, J. B. (1995). Provocation, acute alcohol intoxication, cognitive performance, and aggression. *Journal of Abnormal Psychology, 104*, 150–155. doi:10.1037/0021-843X.104.1.150

Leary, M. R., Kowalski, R. M., Smith, L., & Phillips, S. (2003). Teasing, rejection, and violence: Case studies of the school shootings. *Aggressive Behavior, 29*, 202–214. doi:10.1002/ab.10061

Leary, M. R., Twenge, J. M., & Quinlivan, E. (2006). Interpersonal rejection as a determinant of anger and aggression. *Personality and Social Psychology Review, 10*, 111–132. doi:10.1207/s15327957pspr1002_2

Lorenz, K. (1966). *On aggression*. San Diego, CA: Harcourt, Brace & World.

Nisbett, R. E., & Cohen, D. (1996). *Culture of honor: The psychology of violence in the South*. Boulder, CO: Westview Press.

Norlander, B., & Eckhardt, C. (2005). Anger, hostility, and male perpetrators of intimate partner violence: A meta-analytic review. *Clinical Psychology Review, 25*, 119–152. doi:10.1016/j.cpr.2004.10.001

Payne, B. K. (2001). Prejudice and perception: The role of automatic and controlled processes in misperceiving a weapon. *Journal of Personality and Social Psychology, 81*, 181–192. doi:10.1037/0022-3514.81.2.181

Richardson, D. R., Green, L. R., & Lago, T. (1998). The relationship between perspective-taking and nonaggressive responding in the face of an attack. *Journal of Personality, 66*, 235–256. doi:10.1111/1467-6494.00011

Ronfeldt, H. M., Kimerling, R., & Arias, I. (1998). Satisfaction with relationship power and the perpetration of dating violence. *Journal of Marriage and the Family, 60*, 70–78. doi:10.2307/353442

Sampson, R. J., Raudenbush, S. W., & Earls, F. (1997, August 15). Neighborhoods and violent crime: A multilevel study of collective efficacy. *Science, 277*, 918–924. doi:10.1126/science.277.5328.918

Sapolsky, R. M. (1998). *The trouble with testosterone and other essays on the biology of the human predicament*. New York, NY: Scribner.

Sherman, J. W., Gowronski, B., Gonsalkorale, K., Hugenberg, K., Allen, T. J., & Groom, C. J. (2008). The self-regulation of automatic associations and behavioral impulses. *Psychological Review, 115*, 314–335. doi:10.1037/0033-295X.115.2.314

Slaby, R. G., & Guerra, N. G. (1988). Cognitive mediators of aggression in adolescent offenders: I. Assessment. *Developmental Psychology, 24*, 580–588. doi:10.1037/0012-1649.24.4.580

Slotter, E. B., Finkel, E. J., & Bodenhausen, G. V. (2009). *Provocation and commitment in intimate partner violence.* Unpublished manuscript, Northwestern University, Evanston, IL.

Twenge, J. M., Baumeister, R. F., Tice, D. M., & Stucke, T. J. (2001). If you can't join them, beat them: Effects of social exclusion on aggressive behavior. *Journal of Personality and Social Psychology, 81*, 1058–1069. doi:10.1037/0022-3514.81.6.1058

Twenge, J. M., & Campbell, W. K. (2003). Isn't it fun to get the respect we deserve? Narcissism, social rejection, and aggression. *Personality and Social Psychology Bulletin, 29*, 261–272. doi:10.1177/0146167202239051

Van Baardewijk, Y., Stegge, H., Bushman, B. J., & Vermeiren, R. (in press). "I feel your pain" (but only when I am forced to focus on it): Psychopathy, distress, and aggressive behavior. *Journal of Child Psychology and Psychiatry, and Allied Disciplines.*

Van Goozen, S. H. M., Cohen-Kettenis, P. T., Gooren, L. J. G., Frijda, N. H., & Van de Poll, N. E. (1995). Gender differences in behaviour: Activating effects of cross-sex hormones. *Psychoneuroendocrinology, 20*, 343–363. doi:10.1016/0306-4530(94)00076-X

Van Goozen, S., Frijda, N., & Van de Poll, N. (1994). Anger and aggression in women: Influence of sports choice and testosterone administration. *Aggressive Behavior, 20*, 213–222. doi:10.1002/1098-2337(1994)20:3<213::AID-AB2480200308>3.0.CO;2-4

3

APPLYING ADAPTATIONISM
TO HUMAN ANGER:
THE RECALIBRATIONAL THEORY

AARON SELL

In the late 1960s and early 1970s, evolutionary biology underwent a scientific revolution in which poorly defined models of evolutionary change were replaced with a theoretically rigorous program of research that integrated the major findings of evolutionary biology, animal behavior, and genetics. This integration included a method, known as the *adaptationist program*, for identifying and describing design in organisms, a method that matches the engineering requirements inherent in adaptive problems to features in the organism that are designed to solve those problems.

In this chapter, I apply the methods of the adaptationist program to human anger. The resultant theory, called the *recalibrational theory*, states that anger is the output of a cognitive mechanism designed by natural selection to negotiate conflicts of interest. The causes of anger, the behavior it produces, the factors that mitigate it, and its effects on physiology, perception, and cognition can be explained by reference to this adaptive function.

In brief, the recalibrational theory states that anger is a system designed by natural selection to recalibrate the weight another individual places on the angry person's interests so that they become less likely to impose costs or deny benefits to the angry individual. Anger deploys two main strategies to convince the target to treat the angry individual better: (a) toward those with whom the angry individual has a cooperative relationship, he or she may withhold benefits; and (b) toward those who have little incentive to value the cooperation of the angry individual, anger can mobilize aggression. This latter option is responsible for a great deal of human aggression and is close in design and function to aggression against conspecifics in other animals.

EVOLUTIONARY BIOLOGY OF CONFLICT

Natural selection is the only process shown capable of creating complex functional design in organisms (Williams, 1966). Evolutionary psychology is an approach to psychology that uses analyses of selection pressures to discover and understand the cognitive machinery designed by those selection pressures. The closer the fit between the logic of the selection pressures and the known features of the mechanism under study, the more confident one can be about the proposed function of the mechanism, the accuracy of the posited selection pressures, and any future predictions derived from the model. Therefore, a thorough examination of both the selection pressures and the proposed cognitive mechanism are necessary for a theoretically sound computational model of any organic mechanism designed by natural selection. An analysis of the selection pressures inherent in conflicts of interest and the major features of human anger fit together well, making a strong case that human anger was designed by natural selection to regulate conflicts of interest.

Selection Pressures Inherent in Conflicts of Interest

By virtue of their common design, organisms of the same species tend to exploit the same resources in their environment. For example, they tend to mate with members of the same species, eat the same foods, and seek to occupy the same territories. Selection pressures to gain increased access to finite resources will naturally produce organisms that are designed to compete for those resources. Excluding kin, and assuming there are no reciprocal consequences, natural selection will design one organism to attempt to gain resources with no regard for the destructive effects of their activities on competitors.

But animals should be sensitive to the cost–benefit structure of aggressive competition. An examination of the selection pressures involved in conflicts of interest led evolutionary biologists to two key variables that animals respond to when deciding whether to engage in aggression to secure a benefit. The first of these is the relative value of the contested resource to the individual organisms (i.e., who needs it more). This variable determines an organism's *fitness budget* (i.e., the maximum cost an organism is willing to incur to attain the resource). If a food item is worth 10 fitness units to an organism, then he or she should be willing to accept up to 9 units in cost to attain it. Therefore, animals that value a contested resource more will fight longer and harder for it. The second factor animals respond to when deciding whether to fight for a contested resource is the relative fighting ability of the organisms (Hammerstein & Parker, 1982; Maynard Smith & Parker, 1976). Contestants that are better able to impose costs will deplete their competitor's fitness budgets earlier and win the conflict. If these two selection pressures, relative formidability and relative valuation, have been active in the design of animal brains, then we would expect to see animals respond in adaptive ways to assessments of these two variables.

Five converging lines of evidence demonstrate that animals have been designed to respond adaptively to the selection pressures inherent in conflicts of interest as modeled by evolutionary biologists.

- Animals are designed such that relative formidability partially determines the resolution of resource conflicts. The advantage of being the more formidable competitor has been noted in species as distantly related as the sea anemone (Brace & Pavey, 1978), African buffalo (Sinclair, 1977), and crayfish (Hazlett, Rubenstein, & Ritschoff, 1975). A particularly dramatic example was found by Petrie (1984), who studied territory size in the moorhen (*Gallinula chloropus*). He found that relative male weight was a perfect predictor (Spearman correlation coefficient of 1.0) of territory size. (For more examples, see Archer, 1988.)
- Animals are designed such that the relative valuation of the contested resource partially determines the resolution of resource conflicts. Animals that have been deprived of food for a longer time tend to win contests over food. This effect has been replicated with chimpanzees (Nowlis, 1941), crayfish (Hazlett et al., 1975), bald eagles (Hansen, 1986), and dark-eyed juncos (Cristol, 1992), among other species. The effect is not limited to differential valuation of food; it has also been found for differential value of mating opportunities, nesting sites, feeding sites, and spiderwebs (for a review, see Enquist & Leimar, 1983; for a particularly clear example, see Austad, 1983).
- Animals are designed to assess relative formidability and the relative value of the conflict. Because the costs of aggression can be avoided if animals know in advance who will win, animals will be selected to assess cues that predict who is likely to win and to respond appropriately. A variety of species are designed not only to calculate their competitor's fighting ability but also to broadcast their own. Several species of birds and lizards have

evolved physical signals of fighting ability (i.e., badges) that track, quite accurately, the organism's fighting ability (Rohwer & Rohwer, 1978). These badges would be worthless if competitors did not use the signals to compute the animals' formidability. Furthermore, the existence of dominance hierarchies in many species indicates the ability of animals to measure their relative formidability. (For a review of the nonprimate animal literature, see Huntingford & Turner, 1987; for primate examples, see Smuts, Cheney, Seyfarth, Wrangham, & Struhsaker, 1987.)

- Animals are designed to demonstrate formidability to lower the costs of conflict. Two organisms can minimize the cost of conflict if the eventual loser can recognize that it will lose. If a type of animal aggression is designed to demonstrate relative formidability, these conflicts should follow a general pattern of escalation in which lower-cost demonstrations (which are probably less accurate) are exchanged before higher-cost demonstrations or nonritualistic, "no holds barred" combat ensues. Large discrepancies in formidability should be evident even in cases where demonstrations of formidability are somewhat inaccurate. For example, tail beating in male cichlid fish (i.e., shaking one's tail at an opponent so that waves hit him) is an indicator of body size and strength that is presumed to be less predictive than mouth-locked wrestling (during which fish lock mouths and vigorously shake each other), but mouth-locked wrestling is more costly in terms of energy and probability of injury. This pattern of escalation, a model of which is called the *sequential assessment game* (Enquist & Leimar, 1983), has been observed in numerous and distally related species, including cichlid fish (Enquist, Leimar, Ljungberg, Mallner, & Segerdahl, 1990), bowl and doily spiders (Austad, 1983), African buffalo (Sinclair, 1977), red deer (Clutton-Brock & Albon, 1979), and pigs (Jensen & Yngvesson, 1998).

- Species in which animals typically engage in repeated interactions will maintain an internal representation of relative formidability that governs conflicts of interest without individuals needing to reestablish formidability through competitive interactions. The internal storage of relative formidability is indicated by what are called *dominance hierarchies*, which have been noted in many social species, including dark-eyed juncos (Cristol, 1992), chickens (Guhl, 1956), hyenas (Owens & Owens, 1996), and every social monkey and ape (Smuts et al., 1987). Although dominance hierarchies are talked about as if they were features of a community, it is important to remember that the information about one's position compared with other group members is stored within individual brains.

Constructing a Cognitive Model of Human Anger

Human conflicts of interest often look different from nonhuman animal resource competition largely because of humans' ability to mentally represent conflicts of interests. A dung fly can fight with a competitor over a piece of food, but a human can fight over whether someone should have gotten a piece of food or even whether someone should have agreed with someone else who wanted to give a piece of food to a third party, and so on. Most human conflicts of interest do not involve tangible material resources but instead involve conflicts over courses of action (retrospective and prospective), exchanges of information, social alliances, and other abstract cost–benefit tradeoffs between individuals. The logic of the selection pressures and the role of relative valuation and relative formidability, however, are the same.

An analysis of human conflicts and the selection pressures surrounding conflicts of interest argues for the existence of an internal variable similar to that which underlies dominance hierarchies in nonhuman animals, which regulates decisions about cost–benefit interactions in humans. This has been called a *welfare tradeoff ratio* (Tooby, Cosmides, Sell, Liberman, & Sznycer, 2008; Sell, Tooby, & Cosmides, 2009).

WELFARE TRADEOFF RATIOS

It is posited that humans internally represent a threshold for acceptable cost–benefit transactions, a welfare tradeoff ratio (WTR), for every individual they interact with. For an agent, X, the WTR with respect to agent Y defines the cost–benefit ratio below which X will give Y the resource and above which X will attempt to take the resource. This is represented mathematically as

$$v(X) > v(Y) * \text{WTRxy}$$

In other words, the WTR X has toward Y (WTRxy) indicates how much weight X puts on Y's interests when making decisions that affect them both. For example, if X's WTR toward Y is .5, then X will give up a resource worth 5 to himself if Y values it at more than 10. WTRs are theorized to be the computational elements underlying folk notions such as love, respect, and deference.

An individual will have different WTRs for different individuals. For example, a person might be willing to ruin a stranger's sweater to dress a pet's wound but unwilling to ruin a work supervisor's sweater for that same purpose, because the WTR he or she has with respect to the supervisor is higher than toward a stranger.

Given mutual human dependence, the costs of contests, and the nature of kin and friendship, natural selection is predicted to have designed humans such that WTRs will be set higher based on numerous factors related to another's ability to enforce his or her own welfare. One set of factors is related to the ability to enforce WTRs by threatening to inflict harm; these factors include, for example, greater physical strength and more coalitional support. WTRs set primarily by the threat of force will be consulted, presumably, only when there is some possibility that the individual will be present to defend his or her interests. This is entirely analogous to the relative formidability that is known to affect conflicts of interest in nonhuman animals. Another set of factors that set WTRs is related to the ability to defend one's welfare by threatening to withdraw the benefits of cooperation. These include, for example, the person's status as a frequent and dependable reciprocation partner, his or her status as a friend who has a stake in one's welfare (Tooby & Cosmides, 1996), or his or her possession of special abilities that can be deployed to benefit others.

There are at least two kinds of WTRs that govern cost–benefit transactions in different contexts: (a) *monitored WTRs*, which define the threshold of cost–benefit transactions when both parties are present or otherwise capable of defending their interests; and (b) *intrinsic WTRs*, which define the threshold of cost–benefit transactions when the other individual is not present or is unable to defend his or her interests. Presumably, intrinsic WTRs allowed individuals to partition cost–benefit transactions adaptively in a world where the welfare of other individuals was of adaptive significance for oneself.

Though the full selection pressure analysis of intrinsic WTRs is beyond the scope of this chapter, a quick starting point would be as follows: A subset of individuals in one's social world can improve one's welfare as a result of their existence, social power, and well-being (e.g., a devoted friend, a caretaker of one's children, a generous acquaintance). Benefits given to them, even without their knowledge, will correspond to benefits to oneself.

RECALIBRATIONAL THEORY OF ANGER: HUMAN ANGER IS AN
ADAPTATION TO RAISE ANOTHER'S WELFARE TRADEOFF
RATIO WITH RESPECT TO ONESELF

I propose that a large and well-bounded subset of phenomena that people refer to when they use the word *anger* can be understood as the output of a highly sophisticated, complex, reliably developing computational system, instantiated in neural tissue and designed by natural selection, that is deployed as a negotiation tool to resolve present and future conflicts of interest in the angered individual's favor. The anger system does this by initiating behaviors that (a) recalibrate the target's estimates of the costs and benefits of actions to the target and to the angered individual and (b) raise the target's WTR toward the angered individual, so the target takes that individual's welfare more into account in the present, the future, or both. The two main negotiation strategies deployed to recalibrate the target's WTR are (a) threatening to inflict costs (or actually doing so) and (b) threatening to withdraw cooperation (or actually doing so).

Causes of Human Anger

Anger should be triggered when one individual interprets the actions of the target as indicating that the target's WTR toward the individual is lower than the accepted level. WTRs are theorized to be used when making cost–benefit decisions—indeed, that is their hypothesized function—but they may also be used by other cognitive programs, such as memory storage related to particular individuals (e.g., we may remember our niece's birthday but not our mailman's birthday), frequency of consideration (e.g., one thinks daily about a spouse but may forget about old friends for weeks at a time), inherent pleasure in being around an individual, the weight placed on the veracity of another's beliefs, one's willingness to seek advice or share secrets, and vicarious WTR toward friends of friends. Because WTRs are used by so many cognitive systems, there is predicted to be a plethora of computationally distinct ways of triggering anger, each with its own blend of behavioral responses dependent on how the WTR was indicated (see examples that follow).

Theoretically, the clearest indication of a low WTR is the target's willingness to take actions that impose a large cost on the angry individual in order for the target to receive a small benefit. Holding other variables constant, anger is more likely to be activated over a cost–benefit transaction as (a) the cost imposed on the individual increases, (b) the benefit reaped as a result of that cost decreases, and (c) characteristics of the instigator and the angry individual indicate that it is possible for the angry individual to force the other to use a higher WTR than was indicated by the cost–benefit transaction imposed.

Behavioral Responses Generated by Anger

The primary functions of anger are to raise the magnitude of the WTR of an individual who has demonstrated a lower WTR than is acceptable to the angry individual and/or to recalibrate that individual's estimates of the magnitude of the costs imposed and benefits received. WTRs in the target should be open to modification when this will allow the target to avoid being harmed or having cooperation withdrawn—more precisely, in circumstances that predicted ancestrally that these two negative outcomes were likely.

Thus, when the anger system is triggered by evidence that the target's WTR toward the angry individual is too low, it should motivate him or her to make credible threats or demonstrate qualities that would make such threats credible, if issued. WTRs are hypothesized to be set partly by relative formidability, as is the case with many other animals. Thus if an individual is showing evidence of a low WTR, it could be the result of an underestimation of one's willingness or ability to use force and could be recalibrated by a demonstration of said force. As with nonhuman animals, formidability should be demonstrated starting with low-cost, presumably less accurate, demonstrations of physical strength and escalated as needed to more accurate and dangerous demonstrations of strength.

The theory also predicts that anger should be designed to manipulate the target's estimates of the magnitude of costs and benefits inherent in the transaction. To the extent that you can increase another's perception of a cost he or she imposed on you, you can decrease the probability that the individual will impose such a cost on you again. The same is true of reducing another's perception of the benefit he or she received.

KNOWN FEATURES OF ANGER

Given the breadth of data collected on human anger, the first step when proposing a new theory must be to determine its consistency with empirical findings that have been shown to be both large in effect and robust across studies. It should be noted that although I did my best to choose the following data sets on the basis of their effect sizes, reliability, and cross-cultural documentation, I am not providing a complete review of the anger literature.

Feature 1: Anger Frequently Results From the Imposition of Costs

Individuals tend to get angry when costs are imposed on them. Most important, the magnitude of the anger response is positively correlated with the magnitude of the cost. Empirical studies that varied the magnitude of the cost have confirmed this relationship across a host of different cost types, such as the voltage of electric shocks (O'Leary & Dengerink, 1973), severity of insults (Taylor, 1967), seriousness of a crime (Blumstein & Cohen, 1980), and monetary payoffs in economic games (Fehr & Gaechter, 2000).

Feature 2: Intentionality Increases the Likelihood of Anger

When a cost is imposed without prior knowledge on behalf of the imposer, there is much less anger and retaliation than if the cost was knowingly imposed (see Epstein & Taylor, 1967). Theories that posit intentionality have used different definitions. For example, Heider (1958) defined *intention* as a plan that guides action, Kaufmann (1970) defined an *aggressive action* as one that is known by the actor to have a nonzero chance of inflicting harm on the target, and Tedeschi and Felson (1994) defined an *intentional action* as one "performed with the expectation that it will produce a proximate outcome of value to the actor" (p. 164).

Intentionality, not being directly observable, is a category the human mind uses to classify types of actions and thus must be discovered and explored rather than defined as a given, objective feature of the world. A theory of intentionality will have to specify, at a minimum, what information must be known for something to qualify as intentional. For example, if someone plans to hit you with a toy ball and expects that you will enjoy this as part of a game but you become angry when hit because you did not want to play, should the person's act be viewed as intentional? Heider's (1958) definition cannot answer this question. Kaufmann's (1970) definition would result in the act being judged as not intentional. Tedeschi and Felson's (1994) definition would classify the act as intentional.

Feature 3: Apologies Mitigate Anger

The most reliable way to reduce anger, according to the empirical literature, is to apologize (Riordan, Marlin, & Kellogg, 1983). The content of apologies varies, and a great deal of empirical work remains to be done on distinguishing "real" from "false" apologies and discovering why angry individuals are so sensitive to the difference (see Holtgraves, 1989).

Feature 4: Anger and Aggression Are Often Used by Males to Restore "Face"

Violent and homicidal aggressive acts are most common among young men across cultures and time periods (Daly & Wilson, 1988). These acts are largely the result of insults and attempts to save face or attain status by fighting. This account of violent aggression among males has been noted, to some extent independently, by criminologists (Luckenbill, 1977), social psychologists (Berg & Fox, 1947; see also Chapter 10, this volume; Felson, 1982), and evolutionary psychologists (Daly & Wilson, 1988). Most impressively, a host of cultural anthropologists have documented the positive association between fighting ability and status in nonpolice societies, including the Yanamamo of Venezuela (Chagnon, 1983), the Dani of Highland New Guinea (Sargent, 1974), the Montenegrins of Eastern Europe (Boehm, 1984), the Inuit (Balikci, 1970), the Jivaro Indians of the western Amazon (Karsten, 1935), and American gangs (Toch, 1969). In each of those societies, threats to one's face or status are often the trigger for violent episodes between young men.

Feature 5: Personal Insults Are One of the Most Reliable Causes of Anger

Though not usually the object of study, personal insults have been used in aggression research for 40 years and have (in most cases) been shown to be sufficient causes of anger (Geen, 1968). In nonlaboratory cases of aggression, it has been found that personal insults almost always precede homicides (Berg & Fox, 1947; Luckenbill, 1977; Toch, 1969) and assaults (Felson, 1982).

Feature 6: Anger Results in an Exchange of Argument

The most common response to an anger-inducing event in naturally occurring situations is to engage in an argument. Averill (1982) established this fact with an influential study of a large sample of adults.

Feature 7: Anger Has Both Cross-Culturally Universal Features and Neurophysiological Locality

The anger expression is universal across individuals and cultures, including cultures with no historical contact with the West (Ekman, 1973). It has been demonstrated in 6-month-old infants (Stenberg & Campos, 1990) and in congenitally blind children (Galati, Sini, Schmidt, & Tinti, 2003). Physiological changes accompanying anger have been found to be similar across cultures (Rime & Giovannini, 1986). Subjects from a broad European sample reported that anger felt unpleasant and warm and was frequently associated with muscular tension. These response patterns were different from those of other emotions.

Behavioral responses that result from anger are also similar across European countries. Specifically, anger often leads to vocal changes involving increased volume and sometimes trembling; it also leads to changes in movement quality, clenched fists, and increased hand movement (Shaver, Schwartz, Kirson, & O'Connor, 1987; Wallbott, Ricci-Bitti, & Baenninger-Huber, 1986). Furthermore, Scherer and colleagues categorized vocal expressions of emotion and showed that when a person is angry, fundamental frequency (roughly, pitch) often increases in mean and variability (Banse & Scherer, 1996). This pattern is also distinct from those of other emotions.

The antecedents of anger have also been shown to be cross-culturally similar. Recall the cross-cultural data on aggression being driven by insults to one's face reviewed in feature 4. Wallbott and Scherer (1986) noted similar antecedents of anger in a broad range of European countries.

Finally, there have been numerous studies of parts of the brain that are differentially activated by anger, showing that its neural underpinnings are similar across individuals and species and that they are distinct from those of other emotions (see also Chapter 6). Panksepp (2000) theorized, based on brain imaging and lesion studies, that anger relies mostly on the medial amygdala, bed nucleus of stria terminalis, and the medial and perifornical hypothalamus. The anger/rage system is moderated primarily by acetylcholine and glutamate in ways that connect the amygdala and periaqueductal gray with the hypothalamus (Siegel & Schubert, 1995). Finally, a recent meta-analysis confirmed that testosterone tracks individual differences in tendencies toward anger and aggression with an effect size of .4 (Cohen's d; Archer, 2006; see also Chapter 2, this volume).

HOW DOES THE RECALIBRATIONAL THEORY ACCOUNT FOR FEATURES OF ANGER?

The recalibrational theory accounts well for the major features of anger and provides testable predictions that promise to more fully elaborate the computational and functional structure of each feature. These explanations are discussed briefly next.

Feature 1: Cost Imposition

The recalibrational theory predicts that the cause of anger is not negative affect but the indication that another person holds a low WTR with respect to oneself. A common indication of such a WTR is the imposition of a cost that is too large given the benefit the offender received. Holding the magnitude of the benefit constant, the larger the cost one is willing to impose, the more likely anger is to be triggered. Likewise, holding the cost constant and the more the other person benefits by imposing that cost, the less angry one will be (Sell, 2006).

Feature 2: Intentionality

Intentionality judgments, in the context of anger, can be thought of as the outputs of a cognitive mechanism that determines whether a WTR was engaged when a cost was imposed. This predicts that anger-relevant intentionality requires knowledge of the magnitude of the imposed cost, the magnitude of the benefit received, and the identity of the individual on whom the cost was imposed. Each of these three components has been shown to affect anger in the predicted direction (Sell, 2006).

Feature 3: Apologies

The recalibrational theory suggests that apologies are explicit acknowledgements of either (a) a past discrepant WTR that has been recalibrated upward or (b) a misperception or accident on behalf of the target of anger that led them to commit an act that does not reflect their true WTR toward the angry individual. The contents of WTR-recalibrated apologies (Type 1) are predicted to contain statements that translate into the following cognitive grammar: "I will demonstrate a more favorable welfare tradeoff ratio with respect to you, such that I will no longer impose costs of that magnitude on you for benefits of that magnitude." This kind of claim may be best validated by restitution or by indicating a willingness to incur a cost to repay the angry individual. The content of Type 2 apologies should contain statements about the magnitude of perceived costs and benefits; for example, "I didn't realize that would hurt you so badly; I thought I had a good reason for doing that, but I was wrong."

Feature 4: Role of Face and Status

Perceptions of formidability play a part in the setting of WTRs, particularly for males (Sell et al., 2009; Sell, Tooby, & Cosmides, 2009). As such, the recalibrational theory predicts that demonstrations of physical strength in humans should involve the same procedures as strength contests in non-human animals, such as signals of challenge, escalating conflicts that start with low levels of violence (e.g., pushing contests, staring contests) and move either to more violent demonstrations (e.g., wrestling, punching, weaponry) or to signals of surrender that end the violence. These patterns fit the data on homicide quite well (Luckenbill, 1977).

Feature 5: Insults

The recalibrational theory predicts that anger-inducing insults can be understood as attempts to directly indicate a low WTR with respect to another individual and perhaps as attempts to influence others to hold lower WTRs with respect to the insulted individual. Insults should, psychologically, translate to the form, "I do not value your interests highly." More proximately, insults can be declarations of a deficit in a variable that is used to determine one's WTR toward that individual. One such variable, for males at least, is physical strength (Sell, Tooby, & Cosmides, 2009). Fitting the theory, many insults applied disproportionately to men target insufficient masculinity or strength (e.g., wimp, wuss, nerd, girly-man, pussy, weakling; Harris, 1993; Preston & Stanley, 1987). Although beyond the scope of this analysis, it seems likely that other insults fit into categories that make a man socially powerful or not, such as his intent to cooperate (e.g., asshole, prick, bastard [colloquial meaning]), his being unable or unwilling to function as a reliable cooperator or being otherwise unworthy of having others take his interests into account (e.g., punk, white trash, bum), or his competence (e.g., idiot, fool, loser).

Insulting beliefs are a kind of implied insult that is often mistakenly revealed. For example, imagine a professor who offers to help her student with a simple math problem. The student may be angry and insulted because he believes the professor thinks he is stupid. This is a different kind of insult, but it causes anger because it reveals that a trait used to set WTRs (in this case intelligence) is being underestimated and presumably results in the professor holding a lower WTR toward the student.

Feature 6: Arguments

The recalibrational theory predicts two primary functions of arguments: (a) to recalibrate the target's WTR, raising it so the target's decisions will take the angered person's welfare more fully into account; and (b) to recalibrate the target's perception of the cost–benefit transaction that caused anger. When WTRs are largely based on relative fighting ability, one would predict arguments about aggressive potential, for example, "I could kick your ass" or "My dad could beat up your dad!" When one has an expectation of inherent value (e.g., with friends, kin, and others with whom long-term cooperation would be mutually beneficial), the theory predicts that statements of relative friendship quality would be used to boost another's intrinsic WTR toward oneself. For example, "I wouldn't do that to you" or "Remember when your mother was sick and I took notes for you in all your classes."

Secondary functions of arguments may include (a) gathering information to determine the magnitude of the offender's WTR, such as the magnitudes of the values involved in the cost–benefit exchange (e.g., "Why did you do that?"); the offender's knowledge of the magnitude of the cost, benefit, and victim identity (e.g., "Do you know how much that hurt?" "Do you know who you're messing with?"); the offender's perception of his or her WTR with respect to you (e.g., "I thought we were friends"); and other variables that are used to set WTRs; and (b) testing the boundaries of one's WTR with respect to the other and vice versa (e.g., verbal bullying).

Feature 7: Universality

In contrast to many other theories, the recalibrational theory clearly predicts that anger is an adaptation designed by natural selection and that its basic computational structure should be universal across cultures and should share a phylogenetic relationship with structures in closely related nonhuman animals, residing in similarly localized brain areas. Furthermore, like nonhuman animals, humans should use signals of aggressive intent based on enhanced features of formidability (e.g., facial and vocal expressions), physiological preparedness for aggression if necessary, and a structured functional set of causes and behavioral responses that are similar across cultures.

CONCLUSION: HOW TO ACCOUNT FOR COMPLEX DESIGN

Social science has had difficulty accounting for complex features of human behavior largely because it has ignored the one known cause of complex functional design in organisms: natural selection (Tooby & Cosmides, 1992). Without functional theories capable of generating testable predictions about many different aspects of the domain of study, researchers have had two choices: (a) retreat into smaller data sets that can be predicted and cogently summarized by one or two main effects or (b) posit intuitive concepts to account for a great range of data but remain computationally intractable and pliable enough to account for shifting data sets.

The alternative to computationally vague theories, or theories that are specific but restricted to smaller data sets, are computationally specific, functional theories that posit many testable hypotheses based on a simple model of selection pressures and the logical extensions of them given what is known about human evolutionary history and the design of other animals. Natural selection is the only process shown to be capable of organizing and designing organisms. It is the only process that could have designed anger, and thus any functional design in the anger system (including facial expressions, vocalizations, physiological changes, recalibrational learning mechanisms, and behavioral responses) can be explained only as a computational system designed to address the selection pressures that created anger. If one prefers to theorize that anger is the result of learning, natural selection is the only process that could have designed the learning mechanism responsible for learning anger.

The selection pressures described in this chapter may or may not be the ones most responsible for the functional structure of human anger, although they have had great early success in making predictions and explaining many of the most reliable and significant features of anger. Ultimately, the recalibrational theory will be judged by its ability to generate computationally specific explanations capable of organizing and explaining features of anger that have been intractable to intuitive theories and by its ability to make novel predictions that lead to large, reliable effects. If it fails, the alternative must be another computationally specific functional theory that is consistent with evolutionary biology. The data set on anger is now too large to be described by simple learning mechanisms and too detailed to be accounted for by theories that do not computationally specify their primary components.

REFERENCES

Archer, J. (1988). *The behavioral biology of aggression*. Cambridge, England: Cambridge University Press.

Archer, J. (2006). Testosterone and human aggression: An evaluation of the challenge hypothesis. *Neuroscience and Biobehavioral Reviews, 30*, 319–345. doi:10.1016/j.neubiorev.2004.12.007

Austad, S. (1983). A game theoretical interpretation of male combat in the bowl and doily spider. *Animal Behaviour, 31*, 59–73. doi:10.1016/S0003-3472(83)80173-0

Averill, J. (1982). *Anger and aggression: An essay on emotion*. New York, NY: Springer-Verlag.

Balikci, A. (1970). *The Netsilik Eskimo*. Garden City, NY: The Natural History Press.

Banse, R., & Scherer, K. (1996). Acoustic profiles in vocal emotion expression. *Journal of Personality and Social Psychology, 70*, 614–636. doi:10.1037/0022-3514.70.3.614

Berg, I., & Fox, V. (1947). Factors in homicides committed by 200 males. *Journal of Social Psychology, 26*, 109–119.

Blumstein, A., & Cohen, J. (1980). Sentencing of convicted offenders: An analysis of the public's view. *Law & Society Review, 14*, 223–261. doi:10.2307/3053313

Boehm, C. (1984). *Blood revenge: The anthropology of feuding in Montenegro and other tribal societies*. Lawrence, KS: University Press of Kansas.

Brace, R., & Pavey, J. (1978). Size-dependent dominance hierarchy in the anemone *Actinia equine. Nature, 273*, 752–753. doi:10.1038/273752a0

Chagnon, N. (1983). *Yanomamo: The fierce people* (3rd ed.). New York, NY: Holt, Rinehart & Winston.

Clutton-Brock, T., & Albon, S. (1979). The roaring of red deer and the evolution of honest advertisement. *Behaviour, 69*, 145–170. doi:10.1163/156853979X00449

Cristol, D. (1992). Food deprivation influences dominance status in dark-eyed juncos, *Junco hyemalis. Animal Behaviour, 43*, 117–124. doi:10.1016/S0003-3472(05)80077-6

Daly, M., & Wilson, M. (1988). *Homicide*. New York, NY: Aldine de Gruyter.

Ekman, P. (1973). Cross-cultural studies of facial expression. In P. Ekman (Ed.), *Darwin and facial expression: A century of research in review* (pp. 169–222). New York, NY: Academic Press.

Enquist, M., & Leimar, O. (1983). Evolution of fighting behaviour: Decision rules and assessment of relative strength. *Journal of Theoretical Biology, 102,* 387–410. doi:10.1016/0022-5193(83)90376-4

Enquist, M., Leimar, O., Ljungberg, T., Mallner, Y., & Segerdahl, N. (1990). A test of the sequential assessment game: Fighting in the cichlid fish *Nannacara anomala. Animal Behaviour, 40,* 1–14. doi:10.1016/S0003-3472(05)80660-8

Epstein, S., & Taylor, S. (1967). Instigation to aggression as a function of degree of defeat and perceived aggressive intent of the opponent. *Journal of Personality, 35,* 265–-289.

Fehr, E., & Gaechter, S. (2000). Cooperation and punishment in public goods experiments. *The American Economic Review, 90,* 980–994.

Felson, R. B. (1982). Impression management and the escalation of aggression and violence. *Social Psychology Quarterly, 45,* 245–254. doi:10.2307/3033920

Galati, D., Sini, B., Schmidt, S., & Tinti, C. (2003). Spontaneous facial expressions in congenitally blind and sighted children aged 8–11. *Journal of Visual Impairment & Blindness, 97,* 418–428.

Geen, R. (1968). Effects of frustration, attack and prior training in aggressiveness upon aggressive behavior. *Journal of Personality and Social Psychology, 9,* 316–321. doi:10.1037/h0026054

Guhl, A. M. (1956, February). The social order of chickens. *Scientific American, 194*(2), 42–46.

Hammerstein, P., & Parker, G. A. (1982). The asymmetric war of attrition. *Journal of Theoretical Biology, 96,* 647–682. doi:10.1016/0022-5193(82)90235-1

Hansen, A. J. (1986). Fighting behavior in bald eagles: A test of game theory. *Ecology, 67,* 787–797. doi:10.2307/1937701

Harris, M. B. (1993). How provoking: What makes men and women angry? *Aggressive Behavior, 19,* 199–211. doi:10.1002/1098-2337(1993)19:3<199::AID-AB2480190305>3.0.CO;2-D

Hazlett, B. A., Rubenstein, D. & Rittschoff, D. (1975). Starvation, aggression and energy reserves in the crayfish *Orconectes virilis. Crustaceana, 28,* 11–16. doi:10.1163/156854075X00801

Heider, F. (1958). *The psychology of interpersonal relations.* New York, NY: Wiley. doi:10.1037/10628-000

Holtgraves, T. (1989). The form and function of remedial moves: Reported use, psychological reality, and perceived effectiveness. *Journal of Language and Social Psychology, 8,* 1–16. doi:10.1177/0261927X8900800101

Huntingford, F. A., & Turner, A. K. (1987). *Animal conflict.* New York, NY: Chapman & Hall.

Jensen, P., & Yngvesson, J. (1998). Aggression between unacquainted pigs: Sequential assessment and effects of familiarity and weight. *Applied Animal Behaviour Science, 58,* 49–61. doi:10.1016/S0168-1591(97)00097-X

Karsten, R. (1935). *The head-hunters of western Amazonus*. Helsingfors, Finland: Societas Scientiarum Fennica.

Kaufmann, H. (1970). *Aggression and altruism*. New York, NY: Holt, Rinehart & Winston.

Luckenbill, D. (1977). Criminal homicide as a situated transaction. *Social Problems, 25*, 176–186. doi:10.1525/sp.1977.25.2.03a00050

Maynard Smith, J., & Parker, G. A. (1976). The logic of asymmetric contests. *Animal Behaviour, 24*, 159–175. doi:10.1016/S0003-3472(76)80110-8

Nowlis, V. (1941). The relation of degree of hunger to competitive interaction in chimpanzee. *Journal of Comparative Psychology, 32*, 91–115. doi:10.1037/h0063065

O'Leary, M., & Dengerink, H. (1973). Aggression as a function of the intensity and pattern of attack. *Journal of Research in Personality, 7*, 61–70. doi:10.1016/0092-6566(73)90032-9

Owens, D., & Owens, M. (1996). Social dominance and reproductive patterns in brown hyaenas, *Hyaena brunnea*, of the central Kalahari Desert. *Animal Behaviour, 51*, 535–551. doi:10.1006/anbe.1996.0058

Panksepp, J. (2000). Emotions as natural kinds within the mammalian brain. In M. Lewis & J. Haviland-Jones (Eds.), *Handbook of emotions* (2nd ed., pp. 137–156). New York, NY: Guilford Press.

Petrie, M. (1984). Territory size in the moorhen (*Gallinula chloropus*): An outcome of RHP asymmetry between neighbours. *Animal Behaviour, 32*, 861–870. doi:10.1016/S0003-3472(84)80163-3

Preston, K., & Stanley, K. (1987). "What's the worst thing . . . ?": Gender-directed insults. *Sex Roles, 17*, 209–219. doi:10.1007/BF00287626

Rime, B., & Giovannini, D. (1986). The physiological patterns of reported emotional states. In K. Scherer, H. Wallbott, & A. Summerfield (Eds.), *Experiencing emotion: A cross-cultural study* (pp. 84–97). Cambridge, England: Cambridge University Press.

Riordan, C., Marlin, N., & Kellogg, R. (1983). The effectiveness of accounts following transgression. *Social Psychology Quarterly, 46*, 213–219. doi:10.2307/3033792

Rohwer, S., & Rohwer, F. (1978). Status signaling in Harris sparrows: Experimental deceptions achieved. *Animal Behaviour, 26*, 1012–1022. doi:10.1016/0003-3472(78)90090-8

Sargent, W. (1974). *People of the valley*. New York, NY: Random House.

Sell, A. (2006). Regulating welfare tradeoff ratios: Three tests of an evolutionary-computational model of human anger. *Dissertation Abstracts International: Section B. Sciences and Engineering, 66*(8-B), 4516.

Sell, A., Cosmides, L., Tooby, J., Sznycer, D., von Rueden, C., & Gurven, M. (2009). Human adaptations for the visual assessment of strength and fighting ability from the body and face. *Proceedings of the Royal Society B. Biological Sciences, 276*, 575–584. doi:10.1098/rspb.2008.1177

Sell, A., Tooby, J., & Cosmides, L. (2009). Formidability and the logic of human anger. *Proceedings of the National Academy of Science, 106*(35), 15073–15078.

Shaver, P. R., Schwartz, J., Kirson, D., & O'Connor, C. (1987). Emotion knowledge: Further exploration of a prototype approach. *Journal of Personality and Social Psychology, 52*, 1061–1086. doi:10.1037/0022-3514.52.6.1061

Siegel, A., & Schubert, K. (1995). Neurotransmitters regulating feline aggressive behavior. *Reviews in the Neurosciences, 6*, 47–61.

Sinclair, A. (1977). *The African buffalo.* Chicago, IL: University of Chicago Press.

Smuts, B., Cheney, D., Seyfarth, R., Wrangham, R., & Struhsaker, T. (1987). *Primate societies.* Chicago, IL: University of Chicago Press.

Stenberg, C. R., & Campos, J. J. (1990). The development of anger expression in infancy. In N. Stein, B. Leventhal, & T. Trabasso (Eds.), *Psychological and biological approaches to emotion* (pp. 247–282). Hillsdale, NJ: Erlbaum.

Taylor, S. P. (1967). Aggressive behavior and physiological arousal as a function of provocation and tendency to inhibit aggression. *Journal of Personality, 35*, 297–310. doi:10.1111/j.1467-6494.1967.tb01430.x

Tedeschi, J., & Felson, R. (1994). *Violence, aggression, and coercive actions.* Washington, DC: American Psychological Association. doi:10.1037/10160-000

Toch, H. (1969). *Violent men.* Chicago, IL: Aldine.

Tooby, J., & Cosmides, L. (1992). The psychological foundations of culture. In J. Barkow, L. Cosmides, & J. Tooby (Eds.), *The adapted mind: Evolutionary psychology and the generation of culture* (pp. 19–136). New York, NY: Oxford University Press.

Tooby, J., & Cosmides, L. (1996). Friendship and the banker's paradox: Other pathways to the evolution of adaptations for altruism. *Proceedings of the British Academy, 88*, 119–143.

Tooby, J., Cosmides, L., Sell, A., Liberman, D., & Sznycer, D. (2008). Internal regulatory variables and the design of human motivation: A computational and evolutionary approach. In A. J. Elliot (Ed.), *Handbook of approach and avoidance motivation* (pp. 251–271). New York, NY: Psychology Press.

Wallbott, H., Ricci-Bitti, P., & Baenninger-Huber, E. (1986). Nonverbal reactions to emotional experiences. In K. Scherer, H. Wallbott, & A. Summerfield (Eds.), *Experiencing emotion: A cross-cultural study* (pp. 98–116). Cambridge, England: Cambridge University Press.

Wallbott, H., & Scherer, K. (1986). The antecedents of emotional experiences. In K. Scherer, H. Wallbott, & A. Summerfield (Eds.), *Experiencing emotion: A cross-cultural study* (pp. 69–83). Cambridge, England: Cambridge University Press.

Williams, G. (1966). *Adaptation and natural selection.* Princeton, NJ: Princeton University Press.

4

A BEHAVIORAL SYSTEMS PERSPECTIVE ON POWER AND AGGRESSION

PHILLIP R. SHAVER, MICHAL SEGEV, AND MARIO MIKULINCER

Attachment theory (Bowlby, 1982) has proven to be unique among psychodynamic theories in stimulating a large, coherent body of empirical research (Cassidy & Shaver, 2008). Beginning with a focus on the importance for personality development of a child's early relationships with primary caregivers, Bowlby (1982) developed a theory of mental processes and social behavior that has affected multiple domains of psychological research, including developmental, social, and clinical psychology. The theory has been successful partly because Bowlby retained some of the most valuable contributions of prior psychoanalytic theorists (e.g., unconscious mental processes, self-protective defenses, lasting effects of early social experiences) while adding many important insights and research findings from cognitive psychology, primate ethology, and community psychiatry. Along the way, Bowlby made several important contributions to psychoanalytic motivation theory, as we explain in this chapter, but we are especially interested here in something he largely left out: Freud's focus on aggression.

For various reasons, Bowlby (1982) wanted to move away from Freud's (1920/1961) emphasis on sexual and aggressive instincts or drives. It seemed misleading to conceptualize human infants' seeking of intimate contact with caregivers as inherently sexual (a mistake Freud may have made because he

71

was struck early in his career by the number of his patients who had been sexually abused—or, as he called it, "seduced"—by adults). It also seemed that infant anger was a reaction to unreliable or frightening parental behavior, not a primary motivational force in its own right (see Chapters 13 and 14, this volume). In other respects, Bowlby's emphasis on what he called *behavioral systems*—that is, functional patterns of motivated behavior that evolved over evolutionary time because they contributed to human survival and successful reproduction— was laudable. It has been one of his ideas that has encouraged behavioral measurement of attachment-related phenomena (e.g., Ainsworth, Blehar, Waters, & Wall, 1978), something that earlier psychoanalytic theories did not do. The purpose of the present chapter is to begin exploring the possibility that it would be worthwhile to supplement attachment theory with a hypothesized behavioral system concerned with power or assertive influence. When this system goes awry, one result might be dysfunctional anger and aggression.

In the following section of the chapter, we briefly explain the behavioral system construct and describe some of the behavioral systems that Bowlby (1982) proposed (e.g., attachment, exploration, caregiving). We then propose a power or assertion behavioral system and show that individual differences in the functioning of this system can be measured with self-report scales such as the ones we have used in the past to measure attachment and caregiving orientations. We describe the development of the Power Behavioral System Scale (PBSS), which measures hyperactivation and deactivation of the power behavioral system. We then show how these two tendencies relate to other measures of power, anger, and aggression, as well as measures of key personality traits, attachment insecurities, subjective well-being, and social functioning. We also present preliminary evidence concerning the extent to which the new power system subscales predict individual differences in actual aggressive behavior.

THE BEHAVIORAL SYSTEM CONCEPT

In his trilogy on attachment theory, *Attachment and Loss*, Bowlby (1973, 1980, 1982), a psychoanalyst, conceptualized personality and social development in terms of behavioral systems, a concept borrowed from ethology that Bowlby believed could usefully replace Freud's (1920/1961) notion of sexual and aggressive, or life and death, instincts. A behavioral system is a species-universal neural program that governs the choice, activation, and termination of behavioral sequences in ways that Bowlby (1982) thought had increased the likelihood of survival and reproductive success in human evolutionary history. He imagined different behavioral systems that served separate functions, systems he called, for example, the *attachment system*, the *exploration system*, and the *caregiving system*.

Each system was viewed as having a major aim or goal, for example, attaining a sense of safety and security, curiously exploring and learning about one's environment, and promoting others' (especially loved ones') safety and welfare. Each system was thought to include a repertoire of interchangeable, functionally equivalent behaviors that constitute the *primary strategy* used by the system to attain its goal (e.g., maintaining proximity to a protective attachment figure in times of need). These sets of behaviors or behavioral tendencies were thought to be "activated" automatically by stimuli or situations that made a particular goal salient (e.g., loud noises that signaled danger and aroused a need for protection) and were "deactivated" or "terminated" by other stimuli that signaled goal attainment.

Inasmuch as each behavioral system presumably evolved because it increased the likelihood of coping successfully with environmental demands, it is easy to understand why its optimal functioning in today's human beings is important for mental health, social adjustment, and a satisfying life. Consider, for example, the *attachment behavioral system*. It is activated by perceived threats and dangers, which cause a person to seek proximity to another person who is viewed as a "safe haven" and "secure base" (Bowlby, 1982). Successfully attaining proximity, protection, and emotional comfort from such an "attachment figure" results in what Sroufe and Waters (1977) called *felt security*. Moreover, following repeated experiences of successfully attaining protection and support, a person develops positive mental representations of self and others that become an inherent part of the attachment system's operation. Hundreds of empirical studies provide compelling evidence for the benefits of attachment security in childhood and adulthood (for a review, see Mikulincer & Shaver, 2007).

Bowlby (1982) believed that the strategies associated with each behavioral system undergo experience-based development. People learn to alter the parameters or settings of their behavioral systems to fit pervasive contextual demands, and in the process they form reliable expectations about available access routes and likely barriers to goal attainment. These expectations, which Bowlby (1973) called *internal working models*, become part of a behavioral system's neural wiring; their systematic and prolonged effects are observable as individual differences in cognitive processes, emotional reactions, emotion-regulation strategies, and personality traits.

Changes in behavioral strategies can be characterized in terms of hyperactivation or deactivation of the relevant behavioral system (e.g., Cassidy & Kobak, 1988; Mikulincer & Shaver, 2007). *Hyperactivating strategies* intensify the primary strategy of the system to influence other people to respond in accordance with the system's goals (e.g., to provide adequate emotional support). These strategies keep a behavioral system chronically and intensely activated until its goal is achieved. They are learned in social environments that place a person on a partial reinforcement schedule for noisily and successfully persisting. (The reinforcement schedule is partial because other people's responses to it are unreliable and unpredictable.) Unfortunately, although hyperactivation is sometimes successful, it is also accompanied by heightened agitation and distress, which often upsets interaction partners by seeming overly intrusive, demanding, and controlling.

In contrast, *deactivating strategies* involve down-regulation of a behavioral system to reduce the frustration and anguish of repeatedly unsuccessful efforts to attain the system's goal. These strategies develop in the presence of people who disapprove of or punish the system's primary strategy (e.g., crying, reaching, clinging). This disapproval or punishment suggests that one can expect better outcomes if the primary strategy of a particular behavioral system is blocked or suppressed, which unfortunately means that the system's goal is not often fully attained. The problem with deactivating strategies is that they require a narrowing of experience and the relative absence of many of life's rewards (e.g., shared intimacy). By suppressing what would, in other circumstances, be normal behavior, deactivating strategies prevent a person from realizing that there are other social relationships or social environments in which the system's primary strategy would be effective.

DEFINING THE POWER OR ASSERTION BEHAVIORAL SYSTEM

In previous work (e.g., Mikulincer & Shaver, 2007; Shaver, Mikulincer, & Shemesh-Iron, 2010) we have shown that stable individual differences in hyperactivation and deactivation of the attachment system and the caregiving system (both of which were proposed by Bowlby, 1982) can be measured and that they are associated in theoretically predicted ways with other psychological and behavioral processes. In the present chapter we propose, more speculatively, that human beings are born with the rudiments of a behavioral system the aim of which is to acquire and control material and social resources (e.g., food, shelter, social status, sexual mates) that contribute to survival and reproductive success. We propose further that these innate behavioral strategies, as they emerge in development, are organized by an evolved and generally adaptive *power or assertion behavioral system,* which for the sake of simplicity we will call the *power system.* This system presumably evolved because it contributes to the propagation of one's genes in a competitive social environment. According to this fitness logic, the proliferation of a person's genes depends on his or her ability to acquire and control precious resources and to cope effectively with people and events that threaten resource control (see Chapter 3, this volume).

In personality and social psychology, having a *sense of power* (analogous to felt security in the attachment domain) is defined as perceiving that one has control over valuable resources and outcomes within a particular situation (e.g., Keltner, Gruenfeld, & Anderson, 2003). Because resources are finite and people compete to acquire and control them, this definition implies that people who have a sense of power also have control over others' access to resources and can influence their behavior (see Chapter 3, this volume). This reasoning led Keltner et al. (2003) to define *power* as "an individual's relative capacity to modify others' states by providing or withholding resources or administering punishments" (p. 265). Another implication of this definition is that power often involves freedom and independence from others' influence when seeking desired resources. Galinsky, Magee, Gruenfeld, Whitson, and Liljenquist (2008) stated, "Power, it could also be said, is the capacity to be uninfluenced by others. Without power, one's outcomes are constrained by others" (p. 1451).

Before conceptualizing the normative components and operations of the power behavioral system, we should distinguish power from aggression. From an evolutionary standpoint, human aggression is a "fight" mechanism (e.g., Buss & Shackelford, 1997). It presumably evolved in many animal species because it facilitates control over precious resources, which makes it natural to equate aggression with power. We emphasize, however, that there definitely are aggressive acts whose sole purpose is to damage or destroy someone or something else, and there are many cases in which one's sense of power can be restored simply by asserting one's position and authority (see Chapter 3, this volume). We would like to consider the possibility that the power system is not "designed" primarily to attack and destroy, but to gain, maintain, or restore one's sense of power without necessarily damaging one's own social ties or equanimity.

Normative Parameters of the Power System

We propose that the main goal of the power system is to remove threats and obstacles that interfere with a person's sense of power. In other words, the power system seeks to maintain a stable inner sense of power and to restore this sense when one perceives that others are attempting to constrain one's access to valuable resources or influence one's behavior in a particular situation. This does not imply that people seek power simply for power's sake. Rather, following Bowlby's (1982) contention that attachment security (i.e., felt security) provides a solid foundation for exploration, we propose that power facilitates the smooth functioning of other behavioral systems, such as exploration, affiliation, caregiving, and sex. With a sense of power, people can more easily explore and master their environment; help and get along with other people without worrying about being influenced, exploited, or constrained; and have sex with desirable partners and produce offspring to carry one's genes into future generations.

The proposed power behavioral system is likely to be activated in one of two kinds of situations: (a) when a person competes for access to valuable resources and (b) when other people constrain one's access to resources or attempt to influence one's attitudes and actions. In either case, people are motivated to protect or restore their sense of power when they appraise an event or social interaction as a threat to their power, not when they simply encounter someone who has a certain objective status or acts in a particular way. That is, the power system is not typically activated if a person detects no threat to his or her sense of power. By the same token, a person can inappropriately appraise something as a threat even in the absence of another person's explicit signaling of competition, provocation, or superiority (see Chapter 9).

Once a person's power system is activated (appropriately or not), he or she calls on a repertoire of behaviors aimed at protecting or restoring a sense of power. This repertoire, which reflects the system's primary strategy, includes behaviors meant to maintain what Parker (1974) called *resource-holding power*, behaviors such as asserting one's dominance, authority, and competence to deal with the situation; expressing confidence in one's strengths, attitudes, and opinions; deterring others from competing for or exerting control over one's resources; and verbally or physically attacking (or threatening to attack) others until power is restored (e.g., Gilbert, 1989; see also Chapter 3, this volume). Beyond these basic strategies that can be observed in most animal species, Gilbert (1989) also proposed that humans can protect or restore their sense of power by using what he called *social attention-holding* strategies, efforts to emphasize one's attractiveness and social value or display one's special talents, skills, and other positive attributes.

Activating these strategies is often accompanied by physiological arousal and, often, a feeling of anger, which in our view is an emotional signature of power-system activation. According to Lazarus (1991), the core relational theme of anger is "a demeaning offense against me and mine" (p. 222), an assault on or threat to one's identity or other important personal goals and possessions. Shaver, Schwartz, Kirson, and O'Connor (1987) viewed anger as a signal that control over an important resource is being threatened illegitimately and that some assertive action needs be taken to reduce or eliminate the threat, repair the damage, or prevent further assaults. In the second volume of his *Attachment and Loss* trilogy, Bowlby (1973) argued that anger is a protest response against a partner's signs of unavailability, detachment, or rejection. Viewed from our conception of power, these signs indicate that one lacks the power to obtain needed resources, such as affection and support, and that one is dependent on others' unreliable responsiveness.

When the power system, like other behavioral systems, works properly, it contributes greatly to one's subjective well-being and social adaptation (Keltner et al., 2003). Moreover, it encourages what Higgins (1998) called a *promotion focus*—a motivational orientation that facilitates goal pursuit and realization of aspirations—because powerful people expect positive outcomes from their efforts and relatively little interference from others. Research shows that people with a sense of power devote attention to rewards and goal pursuit, have more frequent positive emotions, and experience fewer threat-related thoughts and emotions (for reviews, see Keltner et al., 2003; Chapter 13, this volume).

Individual Differences in the Activation and Functioning of the Power System

Although we assume that everyone is born with the potential to develop a stable sense of power, the functioning of the power system can be impaired by experiencing repeated failures to obtain desired outcomes, remove threats, and overcome obstacles. Such failures may result from physical illnesses that prevent the effective use of the power system's primary strategies. They may also result from social arrangements that preclude or constrain competition; frustrate attempts to acquire needed resources; severely punish assertiveness, anger, aggression, or other resource-holding power strategies; or demand submission or self-abasement. Such conditions may arouse anxiety about asserting oneself, serious doubts about one's power and influence, and a loss of confidence in one's abilities to maintain or restore power when power is desirable.

As with the other behavioral systems, failures of the power system can result in one or both of two nonoptimal (i.e., secondary) power strategies: hyperactivation or deactivation of the power system. *Hyperactivated power-oriented behavior* involves a substantial increase in efforts to restore a sense of power despite adverse circumstances and doubts and anxieties that arise when one experiences repeated and unpredictable failures. Hyperactivation is fueled by two motives: an excessive urge to gain power and an extreme fear of failure in the use of resource-holding power strategies. This combination results in chronic activation of the power system, even when there is no imminent threat or actual damage to one's power; an indiscriminate urge to assert power over others; frequent anger and hostility toward others (who are viewed as potential rivals); and a proclivity to attack others following minimal or ambiguous signs of competition or provocation. In an extreme form, it can lead to flagrant vindictiveness and destructive, even murderous, behavior. Hyperactivation is also characterized by a tendency to misinterpret social situations as threatening or hostile (i.e., a hostile attribution bias; see Chapter 9).

Deactivation, in contrast, involves terminating or "shutting off" the power system, thereby giving up on the possibility of using the system's primary strategies to defend against threats and damages to one's sense of power. Deactivation is evident in submissiveness, self-abasement, and the absence of resource-holding power strategies, even in the presence of clear-cut, explicit assault or provocation, to the point of experiencing substantial physical or psychological harm as a result. Deactivation also involves a tendency to avoid situations that call for activation of the power system and assertion of one's rights and opinions: competitions, arguments, disputes, and interpersonal conflicts. It is important to note, however, that such deactivation does not necessarily involve reduced sensitivity to threats. In fact, powerless people are often highly sensitive to threat-related cues, prone to ruminate about threats, and experience negative emotions because of perceived threats and injustices (for a review, see Keltner et al., 2003). In other words, deactivation is not a peaceful or calm state; it is characterized by a blend of worries, doubts, and defenses against the pain and frustration of "losing" or dodging a "fight."

A review of self-report measures of beliefs, attitudes, and feelings related to power and aggression led us to conclude that no instrument had been explicitly designed to assess the two nonoptimal power strategies, activation and deactivation. We did gain insights from examining existing scales, however. We concluded, for example, that Buss and Perry's (1992) Aggression Questionnaire, which assesses several aspects of trait aggression (e.g., physical aggression, verbal aggression), taps hyperactivated power, an extreme and chronic proclivity to engage in hostile aggression. This scale, however, does not distinguish people with an optimally functioning power system from those who deactivate their power system, because neither kind of person typically relies on hostile aggression as a way to deal with competitions, arguments, or conflicts. Similarly, low scores on Rathus's (1973) Assertiveness Questionnaire might indicate power-system deactivation. However, this scale fails to distinguish people with an optimally functioning power system from those who hyperactivate the system, because both groups are capable of asserting opinions (although often by different means).

There are also scales that measure a sense of power or dominance (e.g., Gough, 1964), but they fail to distinguish between people who hyperactivate or deactivate their power systems because both groups experience doubts and worries about the extent to which they have power over resources. One measure that taps constructs similar to the ones we are proposing here is the Inventory of Interpersonal Problems (Horowitz, Rosenberg, Baer, Ureno, & Villasenor, 1988). It includes two subscales that describe forms of hyperactivation—*overly autocratic* (e.g., "I try to control other people too much") and *overly competitive* (e.g., "I fight with other people too much")—and two subscales that describe forms of deactivation—*overly subassertive* (e.g., "It is hard for me to be assertive with another person") and *overly exploitable* (e.g., "I let other people take advantage of me too much"). Despite these useful near-approximations to the measures we were seeking, we decided to create a new measure that, like the Caregiving System Scale (Shaver et al., 2010) and the Experiences in Close Relationships Inventory (ECR; Brennan, Clark, & Shaver, 1998) that is used to measure insecure attachment, would be specifically designed to assess hyperactivating and deactivating power strategies. (These scales are all part of an overall effort to create a theory and set of measures to cover all major human behavioral systems related to social behavior.) Here, we present data from the first stage of this research program: the construction of a self-report Power Behavioral System Scale (PBSS) to assess individual differences in hyperactivation and deactivation of the power system.

ASSESSING HYPERACTIVATION AND DEACTIVATION OF THE POWER SYSTEM

In the first stage of scale development, we constructed a pool of 50 items that might index the two secondary power-system strategies. In writing the items we attempted to capture the various cognitive, emotional, motivational, and behavioral aspects of hyperactivated and deactivated power strategies described in the present chapter. For example, the 25 items designed to assess hyperactivation focused on the urgent and exaggerated need for power and control over resources and other people, frequent bouts of anger and aggression, and anxieties and worries about being defeated in competitions and disputes. The 25 items designed to assess deactivation of the system focused on attempts to avoid behavioral assertions of power and authority as well as feelings of uneasiness with competition and disputes.

The instructions asked respondents to think about situations in which they had a disagreement or conflict with another person or group and to rate the extent to which each item was or was not self-descriptive. Hence, the PBSS measures a person's general, overall orientation to power rather than the exertion of power in a particular situation or relationship, although the items could easily be adapted to assess domain-specific or partner-specific power strategies, as is sometimes done with the ECR when measuring attachment insecurities.

Factor Structure

Our initial 50-item scale was administered to a sample of 292 Israeli undergraduates (185 women and 88 men). Item and factor analyses indicated that the items did assess the two secondary power-system strategies: hyperactivating and deactivating. Based on these analyses, we chose the 14 most representative items from each factor (i.e., the ones that loaded highest on the intended factor and lowest on the other factor), keeping in mind our goal of representing various aspects of hyperactivation and deactivation. We then administered the new 28-item scale to 362 Israeli undergraduates (211 women and 151 men) and conducted a new factor analysis. As expected, the analysis yielded the intended two factors, which accounted for 52% of the variance. The 14 deactivation items loaded higher than .40 on the first factor (28% of explained variance). Here are examples of these items: "I tend to relinquish important goals if their attainment requires confronting other people"; "I tend to avoid attacking, even if it's a matter of self-defense"; "I'd rather let others win an argument, even when I know I'm right"; and "I'd rather not show people I'm angry, even when my anger is justified." The 14 hyperactivation items loaded higher than .40 on the second factor (24%). The following are examples: "I feel anxious in situations where I have little control over other people and their actions"; "In an argument or disagreement, my strong desire to fight back makes it difficult for me to consider other possible responses"; "It's hard for me to stop arguing, even when the other person has conceded"; and "When somebody hurts me, I'm flooded with thoughts of revenge." Cronbach alphas were .85 for the hyperactivation items and .90 for deactivation items. (Similar results were obtained in a replication study conducted in English at the University of California, Davis.)

As intended, the correlation between the hyperactivation and deactivation scores was not statistically significant, $r(360) = .07$. That is, hyperactivation and deactivation are orthogonal strategies, and the two scales form a two-dimensional space in which different power orientations can be represented.

Stability Over Time and Across Reporters and Measure Type

In a new sample of 97 Israeli undergraduates, we administered the PBSS twice, in sessions separated by 4 months, and found adequate test–retest reliability (.74 and .79, respectively, for the hyperactivation and deactivation scales). For another sample of 82 Israeli undergraduates, we asked two relatives, friends, or romantic partners of each participant to use the PBSS items to describe the participant. Significant correlations were found between self-reports and partner-reports regarding both the hyperactivation and deactivation dimensions, with rs ranging from .46 to .54. These findings imply that the PBSS measures, in part, behavioral tendencies that can be observed by relationship partners.

Convergent Validity

In eight additional samples of Israeli undergraduates (with ns ranging from 120 to 178), we examined the convergent validity of the PBSS scores. First, we examined associations between the PBSS and preexisting self-report measures tapping various aspects of aggression: the Aggression Questionnaire (Buss & Perry, 1992), a measure of violence risk (Plutchik & Van Praag, 1990), and the Abuse within Intimate Relationships Scale (Borjesson, Aarons, & Dunn, 2003). The hyperactivation score was associated with reports of physical aggression, verbal aggression, anger, and hostility; risk of violent behavior; and abusive behavior in intimate relationship, with rs ranging from .27 to .46, all $ps < .01$. The deactivation score was not significantly associated with these measures. As expected, aggressive, violent, and abusive behaviors can be viewed as manifestations of hyperactivated power, but they do not differentiate between people scoring low or high on the deactivation dimension. Stated differently, aggression and violence are not default strategies for gaining power but seem to develop from repeated failure to control resources that eventually results in hyperactivation of the power system.

Second, we examined associations between the PBSS and preexisting self-report measures of various aspects of anger arousal and expression: the Anger Expression Scale (Spielberger, Jacobs, Russell, & Crane, 1983), the Trait subscale of the State–Trait Anger Scale (Spielberger, 1983), the Multidimensional Anger Inventory (Siegel, 1986), and the Anger Rumination Scale (Sukhodolsky, Golub, & Cronwell, 2001). In line with our theoretical analysis, hyperactivation was associated with trait anger, anger externalization, anger arousal, hostile outlook, rumination on anger-related thoughts, and problems in controlling anger expression, with rs ranging from .31 to .58, all $ps < .01$. The deactivation score was not significantly associated with most of these signs of anger, with the exception of a positive association with anger internalization, $r(176) = .37, p < .05$. This finding suggests that an angry state of mind is still active despite deactivation of the power system and that anger-related feelings are directed toward the self rather than other people.

Third, we examined associations between the PBSS and preexisting self-report measures of power, dominance, and assertiveness: the Dominance and Abasement scales of the Personality Research Form (Jackson, 1984), and the Dominance and Submissiveness scales of the Revised Interpersonal Adjective Scales (Wiggins, Trapnell, & Phillips, 1988). As expected, both hyperactivation and deactivation were associated with lower scores on scales measuring feelings of dominance and power (rs ranging from $-.33$ to $-.42$, all $ps < .01$), implying that these orientations may be alternative ways of coping with lack of power. In addition, deactivation but not hyperactivation was associated with measures of submissiveness and self-abasement, with rs ranging from .30 to .65, all $ps < .01$. These findings indicate that people who score high on deactivation of the power system suppress their own needs and desires while deferring to others.

Fourth, we examined associations between the PBSS and preexisting self-report measures of interpersonal conflicts and reactions to others' transgressions: the Styles of Handling Interpersonal Conflict Scale (Rahim, 1983) and the Transgression-Related Interpersonal Motivations Inventory (McCullough & Hoyt, 2002). As expected, hyperactivation was associated with more aggressive and conflict-escalating behavior during conflicts and greater vengeance and less forgiveness following others' transgressions, with rs ranging from .29 to .51, all $ps < .01$. Correlations for the deactivation scale were also compatible with our theoretical analysis: Deactivation was associated with avoidance and giving up during interpersonal conflicts and a tendency to withdraw in response to interpersonal transgressions, with rs ranging from .22 to .56, all $ps < .01$.

Discriminant and Construct Validity

In the eight participant samples we also considered the discriminant and construct validity of the PBSS scores. Participants completed the Crowne-Marlowe Social Desirability Scale (Crowne & Marlowe, 1964), the Big Five Inventory (John & Srivastava, 1999), and the ECR (Brennan et al., 1998). The two PBSS scores were not associated with social desirability, $rs < .05$, but they were correlated in theoretically expected ways with other personality constructs. Hyperactivation was associated with emotional instability (i.e., neuroticism), social avoidance and unpleasantness (i.e., low agreeableness), and both attachment anxiety and avoidance, with rs ranging from .26 to .54, $p < .01$. Deactivation was significantly associated with introversion and high levels of neuroticism, agreeableness, and attachment anxiety, with rs ranging from .22 to .37, all $ps < .01$. These correlations were only moderate in size, suggesting that the PBSS scores are not simply redundant with attachment insecurities or with broad personality traits. That is, we believe that the PBSS measures something unique to the power system that is not measured precisely by the other scales.

Whereas people who deactivate the power system tend to be introverted but agreeable, those who hyperactivate the system tend to be quarrelsome and socially unpleasant. However, despite these differences, people scoring high on either hyperactivation or deactivation of the power system share emotional instability (i.e., neuroticism) and worries about being loved, accepted, and esteemed by others (i.e., anxious attachment). That is, even the external façade of agreeableness, submissiveness, and passivity that characterizes power deactivation tends to be accompanied by inner emotionality, including attachment-related anxieties (for a broader analysis of dispositional influences on aggression, see Chapter 5).

In the eight samples, we also examined the extent to which hyper- and deactivated forms of power are associated with regulatory deficits and social skill deficits. Power hyperactivation was associated with deficits in emotion-regulation, self-regulation, and social skills. The deficits were reflected in lower scores on scales measuring self-control (Tangney, Baumeister, & Boone, 2004), negative mood regulation (Catanzaro & Mearns, 1990), and social skills (Buhrmester, Furman, Wittenberg, & Reis, 1988), with rs ranging from $-.38$ to $-.55$, all $ps < .01$. As expected, hyperactivation was also correlated with two of the interpersonal problems measured by Horowitz et al.'s (1988) Inventory of Interpersonal Problems (IIP): being overly autocratic and overly competitive, with rs of .44 and .47, $ps < .01$. Although deactivation was not associated with problems in self-control, it was associated with lower scores on negative mood regulation and social skills, with rs ranging from $-.42$ to $-.50$, all $ps < .01$. As expected, deactivation was also associated with two kinds of IIP interpersonal problems: being overly subassertive and overly exploitable, with rs of .58 and .52, $ps < .01$.

Taken together, these correlations imply that people who either hyperactivate or deactivate their power system have a difficult time regulating their negative emotions and lack the social skills that promote effective social interactions. However, whereas those who hyperactivate the power system have problems with self-control and have difficulties in being overly aggressive and competitive (see also Chapters 2 and 6), those who deactivate the system have problems related to subassertiveness.

Beneficial Correlates of Optimal Functioning of the Power System

In conceptualizing the power system, we assumed that optimal functioning of the system enhances a person's self-esteem and sense of well-being. If hyperactivation and deactivation interfere with optimal system functioning, our scales should be inversely correlated with measures of positive psychological states. In assessments of the eight participant samples, we included measures of self-esteem (Rosenberg, 1979), self-mastery (Pearlin, Menaghan, Lieberman, & Mullan, 1981), optimism (Scheier & Carver, 1985), and psychological well-being (Veit & Ware, 1983). As expected, both hyperactivation and deactivation were associated with lower self-esteem, mastery, optimism, and psychological well-being, with rs ranging from $-.23$ to $-.46$ for hyperactivation and from $-.22$ to $-.48$ for deactivation, all $ps < .01$.

Predicting Actual Behavior

In an additional study, we gathered preliminary data examining the predictive validity of the PBSS with respect to actual behavior during a couple conflict in the laboratory. Both members of 100 young Israeli heterosexual couples who had been dating for less than 5 months completed the PBSS, the ECR, and the Big Five Inventory, and then were invited to a laboratory session in which they were asked to discuss a major unresolved problem in their relationship. Each couple was videotaped while discussing this problem. Two independent judges who were unaware of participants' scores on the other measures rated the extent to which each member of the couple displayed signs of anger, hostility, and distress, and the extent to which they attacked their partner, deferred submissively to their partner, and reached a joint solution to the problem.

As expected, participants who scored higher on power hyperactivation were rated by judges as displaying more anger, hostility, and distress, and as executing more attacks on their partner, with rs ranging from .33 to .46, $ps < .01$. In contrast, participants who scored higher on power deactivation were rated by judges as displaying more distress, but not anger or hostility, and more submissive behavior, with rs of .49 and .42, $ps < .01$. In addition, both hyperactivation and deactivation scores were associated with problems in finding a solution to the relationship problem, with rs of $-.32$ and $-.27$, $ps < .01$. It is important that these associations were unique to the PBSS and were not explained by attachment insecurities or the Big Five personality trait scores. These findings indicate that conflict resolution between members of dating couples is impeded by either deactivation or hyperactivation of the power system.

CONCLUSIONS

The new concepts of power-system hyperactivation and deactivation fit well with the rest of attachment theory and make increased sense of many of the power, aggression, and anger measures that were already available in the literature. Our new scales, although still preliminary, seem promising in efficiently assessing power system hyperactivation and deactivation as orthogonal dimensions. As is the case in the attachment and caregiving domains outlined by attachment theory, both hyperactivation and deactivation, which are viewed as secondary strategies that come into play when a system's primary strategy fails to work, are associated with nonoptimal outcomes in adult relationships. The new concepts and scales fit well in our overall conception of social motivation based on the behavioral system construct. Their addition to attachment theory may allow us to recover an important component of

Freud's psychoanalytic theory that was deemphasized and almost omitted from Bowlby's theory.

REFERENCES

Ainsworth, M. D. S., Blehar, M. C., Waters, E., & Wall, S. (1978). *Patterns of attachment: Assessed in the Strange Situation and at home*. Hillsdale, NJ: Erlbaum.

Borjesson, W. I., Aarons, G. A., & Dunn, M. E. (2003). Development and confirmatory factor analysis of the Abuse within Intimate Relationship Scale. *Journal of Interpersonal Violence, 18*, 295–309. doi:10.1177/0886260502250089

Bowlby, J. (1973). *Attachment and loss: Vol. 2. Separation: Anxiety and anger*. New York, NY: Basic Books.

Bowlby, J. (1980). *Attachment and loss: Vol. 3. Sadness and depression*. New York, NY: Basic Books.

Bowlby, J. (1982). *Attachment and loss: Vol. 1. Attachment* (2nd ed.). New York, NY: Basic Books.

Brennan, K. A., Clark, C. L., & Shaver, P. R. (1998). Self-report measurement of adult attachment: An integrative overview. In J. A. Simpson & W. S. Rholes (Eds.), *Attachment theory and close relationships* (pp. 46–76). New York, NY: Guilford Press.

Buhrmester, D., Furman, W., Wittenberg, M. T., & Reis, H. T. (1988). Five domains of interpersonal competence in peer relationships. *Journal of Personality and Social Psychology, 55*, 991–1008. doi:10.1037/0022-3514.55.6.991

Buss, A. H., & Perry, M. (1992). The Aggression Questionnaire. *Journal of Personality and Social Psychology, 63*, 452–459. doi:10.1037/0022-3514.63.3.452

Buss, D. M., & Shackelford, T. K. (1997). Human aggression in evolutionary psychological perspective. *Clinical Psychology Review, 17*, 605–619. doi:10.1016/S0272-7358(97)00037-8

Cassidy, J., & Kobak, R. R. (1988). Avoidance and its relationship with other defensive processes. In J. Belsky & T. Nezworski (Eds.), *Clinical implications of attachment* (pp. 300–323). Hillsdale, NJ: Erlbaum.

Cassidy, J., & Shaver, P. R. (Eds.). (2008). *Handbook of attachment: Theory, research, and clinical applications* (2nd ed.). New York, NY: Guilford Press.

Catanzaro, S. J., & Mearns, J. (1990). Measuring generalized expectancies for negative mood regulation: Initial scale development and implications. *Journal of Personality Assessment, 54*, 546–563. doi:10.1207/s15327752jpa5403&4_11

Crowne, D. P., & Marlowe, D. (1964). *The approval motive: Studies in evaluative dependence*. New York, NY: Wiley.

Freud, S. (1961). *Beyond the pleasure principle* (J. Strachey, Trans.). New York, NY: Norton. (Original work published 1920)

Galinsky, A. D., Magee, J. C., Gruenfeld, D. H., Whitson, J. A., & Liljenquist, K. A. (2008). Power reduces the press of the situation: Implications for creativity, conformity, and dissonance. *Journal of Personality and Social Psychology, 95,* 1450–1466. doi:10.1037/a0012633

Gilbert, P. (1989). *Human nature and suffering.* Hove, England: Erlbaum.

Gough, H. G. (1964). *California Psychological Inventory manual.* Palo Alto, CA: Consulting Psychologists Press.

Higgins, E. T. (1998). Promotion and prevention: Regulatory focus as a motivational principle. In M. P. Zanna (Ed.), *Advances in experimental social psychology* (Vol. 30, pp. 1–46). New York, NY: Academic Press.

Horowitz, L. M., Rosenberg, S. E., Baer, B. A., Ureno, G., & Villasenor, L. (1988). Inventory of Interpersonal Problems: Psychometric properties and clinical applications. *Journal of Consulting and Clinical Psychology, 56,* 885–892. doi:10.1037/0022-006X.56.6.885

Jackson, D. N. (1984). *Personality Research Form manual.* Port Huron, MI: Research Psychologists Press.

John, O. P., & Srivastava, S. (1999). The Big Five trait taxonomy: History, measurement, and theoretical perspectives. In O. P. John & L. A. Pervin (Eds.), *Handbook of personality: Theory and research* (2nd ed., pp. 102–138). New York, NY: Guilford Press.

Keltner, D., Gruenfeld, D. H., & Anderson, C. (2003). Power, approach, and inhibition. *Psychological Review, 110,* 265–284. doi:10.1037/0033-295X.110.2.265

Lazarus, R. S. (1991). *Emotion and adaptation.* New York, NY: Oxford University Press.

McCullough, M. E., & Hoyt, W. T. (2002). Transgression-related motivational dispositions: Personality substrates of forgiveness and their links to the Big Five. *Personality and Social Psychology Bulletin, 28,* 1556–1573. doi:10.1177/014616702237583

Mikulincer, M., & Shaver, P. R. (2007). *Attachment in adulthood: Structure, dynamics, and change.* New York, NY: Guilford Press.

Parker, G. A. (1974). Assessment strategy and the evolution of fighting behavior. *Journal of Theoretical Biology, 47,* 223–243. doi:10.1016/0022-5193(74)90111-8

Pearlin, L. I., Menaghan, E. G., Lieberman, M. E., & Mullan, J. T. (1981). The stress process. *Journal of Health and Social Behavior, 22,* 337–356. doi:10.2307/2136676

Plutchik, R., & Van Praag, H. M. (1990). A self-report measure of violence risk. *Comprehensive Psychiatry, 31,* 450–456. doi:10.1016/0010-440X(90)90031-M

Rahim, M. A. (1983). A measure of styles of handling interpersonal conflict. *Academy of Management Journal, 26,* 368–376. doi:10.2307/255985

Rathus, S. A. (1973). A 30-item schedule for assessing assertive behavior. *Behavior Therapy, 4,* 398–406. doi:10.1016/S0005-7894(73)80120-0

Rosenberg, M. (1979). *Conceiving the self.* New York, NY: Basic Books.

Scheier, M. F., & Carver, C. S. (1985). Optimism, coping, and health: Assessment and implications of generalized outcome expectancies. *Health Psychology, 4,* 219–247. doi:10.1037/0278-6133.4.3.219

Shaver, P. R., Mikulincer, M., & Shemesh-Iron, M. (2010). A behavioral systems perspective on prosocial behavior. In M. Mikulincer & P. R. Shaver (Eds.), *Prosocial motives, emotions, and behavior: The better angels of our nature* (pp. 73–91). Washington, DC: American Psychological Association. doi:10.1037/12061-004

Shaver, P. R., Schwartz, J., Kirson, D., & O'Connor, C. (1987). Emotion knowledge: Further exploration of a prototype approach. *Journal of Personality and Social Psychology, 52,* 1061–1086. doi:10.1037/0022-3514.52.6.1061

Siegel, J. M. (1986). The Multidimensional Anger Inventory. *Journal of Personality and Social Psychology, 51,* 191–200. doi:10.1037/0022-3514.51.1.191

Sroufe, L. A., & Waters, E. (1977). Attachment as an organizational construct. *Child Development, 48,* 1184–1199. doi:10.2307/1128475

Sukhodolsky, D. G., Golub, A., & Cronwell, E. N. (2001). Development and validation of the anger rumination scale. *Personality and Individual Differences, 31,* 689–700. doi:10.1016/S0191-8869(00)00171-9

Tangney, J. P., Baumeister, R. F., & Boone, A. L. (2004). High self-control predicts good adjustment, less pathology, better grades, and interpersonal success. *Journal of Personality, 72,* 271–324. doi:10.1111/j.0022-3506.2004.00263.x

Veit, C. T., & Ware, J. E. (1983). The structure of psychological stress and well being in general populations. *Journal of Consulting and Clinical Psychology, 51,* 730–742. doi:10.1037/0022-006X.51.5.730

Wiggins, J. S., Trapnell, P., & Phillips, N. (1988). Psychometric and geometric characteristics of the revised interpersonal adjective scales (IAS-R). *Multivariate Behavioral Research, 23,* 517–530. doi:10.1207/s15327906mbr2304_8

5

DISPOSITIONAL INFLUENCES ON HUMAN AGGRESSION

JENNIFER L. TACKETT AND ROBERT F. KRUEGER

People differ in their propensity to engage in aggressive behavior. The primary goal of this chapter is to review recent research on stable individual differences in aggressive tendencies. A secondary goal is to consider how these tendencies arise, that is, how genetic and environmental factors combine to create individual differences in aggression. We begin by considering how aggressive tendencies fit with other personality constructs and how aggression is situated within prominent structural models of personality. We then extend this understanding to encompass a broader range of more pathological externalizing or disinhibitory tendencies, describing how aggressive tendencies fit with other forms of externalizing behavior. We conclude by reviewing specific genetic and environmental factors that shape externalizing and aggressive tendencies.

THE TRAIT APPROACH IN PERSONALITY PSYCHOLOGY

The most common approach to examining enduring human dispositions is personality trait theory. *Traits* are typically conceptualized as pervasive and enduring characteristics that can be used to predict future behavior. The most widely accepted trait model is the *five-factor model* (FFM; e.g., Goldberg, 1993). The FFM is a taxonomy of higher order, broadly defined personality traits that include Neuroticism, Extraversion, Conscientiousness, Agreeableness, and Openness to Experience. *Neuroticism* is defined by the experience of negative moods and emotions, such as anxiety, dysphoria, and low self-esteem. *Extraversion* encompasses positive emotions as well as behaviors such as sociability and assertiveness. *Conscientiousness* includes abilities to organize and inhibit behavioral tendencies. *Agreeableness* includes affiliation and altruism conceptualized as the opposites of interpersonal irritability and antagonism. *Openness to Experience* includes intellectual curiosity as well as imagination and fantasy.

The FFM is replicable across languages and cultures, making it a useful general framework for characterizing major individual differences. In addition, recent research has demonstrated empirical connections between various higher order personality trait models, which provides a better understanding of interrelationships among them (Markon, Krueger, & Watson, 2005). There is much less agreement about the structure of lower order personality traits (e.g., the *facets* of the five major traits assessed with the commonly used personality instrument, the NEO–PI–R measure of the traits anxiety, excitement-seeking, trust, openness to feelings, and self-discipline; for details, see Costa & McCrae, 1992), even though lower order traits are useful for distinguishing among specific behavioral outcomes (e.g., Reynolds & Clark, 2001).

Researchers have more recently addressed questions regarding the potential applicability of the FFM across the life span, including childhood (e.g., Halverson et al., 2003). Structural analyses of trait measures suitable for children have found empirical relations among higher order trait models that parallel those found in adults (Tackett, Krueger, Iacono, & McGue, 2008), allowing comparison across studies using different trait models. Scores on the five trait factors change systematically across the adult years (Srivastava, John, Gosling, & Potter, 2003), but individual differences on the factors generally remain quite stable (e.g., McCrae & Costa, 1990).

THE EXTERNALIZING SPECTRUM: CONNECTING AGGRESSION WITH OTHER FORMS OF MALADAPTIVE DISINHIBITION

In parallel with research on trait models of normal personality, such as the FFM, investigators have attempted to find the empirical structure of the mental disorders described in standard psychiatric classification systems. Although mental disorders have traditionally been conceptualized as discrete and categorical, extensive evidence suggests that many disorders are better conceived of in terms of continuous dimensions (Helzer, Kraemer, & Krueger, 2006). In addition, putatively separate disorders tend to blend into each other, a phenomenon traditionally conceptualized in terms of comorbidity (i.e., the co-occurrence of separate disorders). This phenomenon can be better understood in terms of dimensionally organized *spectrums of psychopathology* (Krueger & Markon, 2006).

Psychopathology spectrums bear conceptual similarities to higher order personality traits, both of which can be organized in a multidimensional space. This resemblance is empirical as well as conceptual. Especially relevant to this chapter, forms of psychopathology that involve aggression can be viewed in terms of a broad spectrum that has generally been labeled *externalizing* disorders. Aggressive personality dispositions also fall within this spectrum (Krueger, Markon, Patrick, Benning, & Kramer, 2007). The externalizing spectrum encompasses disinhibitory personality traits such as impulsivity and aggression, as well as clinical disorders such as antisocial personality disorder and illicit substance dependence. In FFM terms, the externalizing spectrum is closely aligned with a combination of disagreeableness and low conscientiousness, domains that are associated with a higher order domain of disinhibition (Markon et al., 2005). That is, FFM disagreeableness and low conscientiousness are correlated with each other, giving rise to a broader personality trait domain of disinhibition. Stated somewhat differently, disinhibition (a combination of disagreeableness and low conscientiousness) appears to be the personality-trait core of aggressive and externalizing behavioral tendencies (see also Chapters 1, 2, and 6, this volume).

The Structure of the Externalizing Spectrum in Adults

We recently sought to develop an empirical model of individual differences in externalizing tendencies, including diverse forms of aggression (Krueger et al., 2007). To do this, we created 23 novel facet-level measures of various externalizing tendencies. The 23 facets cover a variety of specific individual-difference variables, ranging from those more traditionally characterized as *personality* (e.g., problematic impulsivity) to those more traditionally characterized as *psychopathology* or *behavior problems* (e.g., drug problems). Research participants completed self-report questionnaires containing the items, and then the items were pruned and refined based on psychometric analyses of the results. Both factor and cluster analyses of the item-level data were used to isolate specific, narrow-band facets of the broader externalizing spectrum.

With specific facets in hand, we then used item response theory (IRT) analyses to ensure that the items indexing a specific facet also covered a range of individual differences within that facet. IRT models are suited to this task because they parameterize the location of items along a specific dimension. The goal was to ensure that the items were appropriately arrayed to cover a wide range of the dimension. Items were then deleted or revised, and additional items written, to improve our ability to measure facets of externalizing tendencies well, across their entire range (for additional methodological details, see Krueger et al., 2007). Three specific facets of aggression were identified in the course of this scale development project: relational, physical, and destructive aggression. In addition to these three facets of aggression, 20 additional facets of externalizing were identified (for a complete list, see Krueger et al., 2007, Table 2). These additional facets cover a range of content, including deficient empathy; a tendency to externalize blame (i.e., to blame others for one's own problems); alienation from others in the interpersonal environment; problems with alcohol, marijuana, and "harder" substances; difficulties controlling impulses; behavior that would be grounds for arrest (e.g., theft and fraud); dishonesty; irresponsibility; rebelliousness; a tendency to prefer exciting but potentially unsafe activities to safer but more boring activities; and proneness to boredom.

Structural Analysis of the 23 Facets of the Externalizing Spectrum in Adults

Exploratory analyses of the 23 facets of the externalizing spectrum suggested that three factors could account for the relations among the 23 facets: (a) a broad, general factor (i.e., overall externalizing tendencies, indicated by all of the scales to a nontrivial extent but most strongly indicated by irresponsible and impulsive tendencies); (b) a narrower factor encompassing callous aggression (indicated primarily by the three aggression facets and a facet indexing lack of empathy); and (c) a narrower factor encompassing use of and problems with substances (indicated primarily by the alcohol, marijuana, and "hard drug" facets).

Following these exploratory analyses, we compared the fit of three confirmatory models: (a) a one-factor model, where all 23 scales were indicators of one and only one general externalizing factor; (b) a *higher order* model, where the two narrower factors (callous aggression and substance use/problems) load directly on the 23 facet scales, and the general externalizing factor, in turn, loads on callous aggression and substance use/problems; and (c) a *bifactor* structural model (also known as a *hierarchical* model; Yung, Thissen, & McLeod, 1999) of the three factors (i.e., general externalizing, callous aggression, substance use/problems), where all indicators load on the general factor, and indicators of callous aggression and substance use/problems also load on their respective narrower factors, but the factors are modeled as uncorrelated.

The contrast between the higher order and bifactor models pertains to the ways in which relations among the general, broad externalizing factor and the narrower callous aggression and substance use/problems factors are modeled. In the higher order model, the general, broad externalizing factor is indicated indirectly via loadings of the narrower callous aggression and substance use/ problems factors, which are at an intermediate level between the 23 primary facets and the general, broad externalizing factor. By contrast, in the bifactor model, all 23 primary facets load directly on the general, broad externalizing factor, and specific subsets of scales also load directly on the narrower factors.

Multiple fit indices converged to indicate a superior fit for the bifactor model over the higher order model (Krueger et al., 2007). This finding had intriguing implications for the meaning of individual differences in aggressive tendencies, as indexed by the three aggression facet scales (i.e., relational, physical, destructive). These implications were revealed by considering the structure of the bifactor model (i.e., three mutually uncorrelated factors) along with the relative magnitudes of the loadings of the aggression scales on those factors. Relational aggression was a stronger indicator of the callous–aggressive factor than of the general externalizing factor, physical aggression was more closely linked to overall externalizing than to callous aggression, and destructive aggression loaded similarly on overall externalizing and callous aggression (albeit higher on overall externalizing).

The general conclusion is that there are multiple pathways to aggressive outcomes. Specific aggressive outcomes can emerge because a person's impulses are unconstrained in general (i.e., via the general externalizing factor) or because a person is unusually callous and aggressive (i.e., via the callous–aggressive factor, which is uncorrelated with general externalizing, this pathway applying in particular to relational aggression). As described earlier, evidence in favor of this multiple-pathways conceptualization derives from the superior fit of the bifactor model, when compared with the two other models (i.e., the one factor model and higher order model). In the bifactor model, the factors are mutually uncorrelated. Hence, the factors can be interpreted as independent, multiple pathways to a specific outcome such as relational aggression because relational aggression loaded notably on both factors, that is, variation in relational aggressive tendencies can be traced to at least two, independent, underlying processes.

The Externalizing Spectrum in Children and Adolescents

Research examining associations between the domains of personality and psychopathology in childhood and adolescence has produced results that are largely consistent with findings for adults, although these younger age groups are less often studied in the personality literature. Aggressive and externalizing behaviors in children are related primarily to disinhibitory dispositions (i.e., disagreeableness and low conscientiousness; Lahey & Waldman, 2003; Nigg, 2006; Tackett, 2006), although much of this research has been correlational in nature, precluding a deeper understanding of the development of associations between personality and psychopathology over time (Tackett, 2006).

The longitudinal research that does exist pertaining to connections between personality and externalizing behaviors has generally been conducted within a vulnerability, or risk, framework, which postulates that personality or temperament serves as a risk factor for the development of later disorders. An alternative framework is the spectrum or common cause model, which conceptualizes personality and externalizing psychopathology as dimensionally related and as sharing core etiologic factors. One issue in this literature is that longitudinal studies that fail to measure potentially shared causal factors cannot disentangle evidence for a vulnerability model from evidence for a spectrum model (Tackett, 2006).

Externalizing disorders in younger age groups have their own disorder categories in the *Diagnostic and Statistical Manual of Mental Disorders* (4th ed., text rev., American Psychiatric Association, 2000). They include oppositional defiant disorder, conduct disorder, and attention-deficit/hyperactivity disorder (ADHD). Other potential externalizing behaviors in early adolescence include precocious sexual behavior and early substance use. Some behaviors, such as relational aggression (i.e., using social power and social exclusion to aggress against one's victims), are still relatively new as forms of pathological aggression and are not yet incorporated into the childhood externalizing disorders framework (e.g., Tackett, Waldman, & Lahey, 2009), although relational aggression was included as a key facet when we developed the aforementioned model of adult externalizing behaviors (Krueger et al., 2007).

One important task for future research is to identify both common and unique personality correlates that provide a more comprehensive picture of the hierarchical nature of externalizing behavior problems (Tackett, 2010). For example, relational aggression appears to have personality correlates similar to those of other externalizing behaviors: lower conscientiousness and agreeableness (Schell & Tackett, 2010). This finding suggests that we should connect relational aggression to a broader externalizing spectrum, as we did in the studies of adults described earlier (Krueger et al., 2007). This work is currently limited by the lack of strong empirical studies of the structure of the personality, temperament, and disorder measures used in studies of children and adolescents.

As noted previously, lower order personality traits may be especially useful in predicting aggressive and externalizing behaviors (e.g., Paunonen & Ashton, 2001; Reynolds & Clark, 2001), but the structure of these traits in childhood and adolescence is also not well studied (Shiner, 1998; Tackett et al., 2008). Recently proposed models of childhood personality traits offer possible lower order facets for further investigation (Halverson et al., 2003), as do common models of temperament (e.g., Rothbart, Ahadi, Hershey, & Fisher, 2001). As mentioned previously, lower order traits reflect more narrowly defined characteristics (e.g., warmth) than do more broadly defined higher order traits (e.g., extraversion). A few theoretical reviews have begun to compare and integrate proposed lower order trait structures in different models (e.g., Halverson et al., 2003; Shiner & Caspi, 2003), which provides an important starting point for future empirical work.

An additional place to look for relevant lower order traits is the research literature on such narrowly defined personality characteristics as callous–unemotional traits, which are related to conduct problems (e.g., Frick, Cornell, Barry, Bodin, & Dane, 2003). Callous–unemotional characteristics reflect remorselessness and a lack of empathy. Frick and colleagues have begun to integrate callous–unemotional traits into broader personality and temperament models, which have identified consistent connections with the broader externalizing work by highlighting the importance of negative emotionality and effortful control (Frick & Sheffield-Morris, 2004) and low levels of agreeableness and conscientiousness (Essau, Sasagawa, & Frick, 2006). One useful approach might be to use the 23-facet model developed by Krueger et al. (2007) for adults and extend it downward to see whether it applies to children and adolescents. Some parallels already seem clear. For example, callousness figures prominently as a narrow-band factor in the Krueger et al. (2007) model, as it does in the thinking of Frick and his colleagues.

INTEGRATING ENVIRONMENTAL AND SITUATIONAL FACTORS

A diathesis–stress perspective (i.e., a perspective in which a vulnerability combines with stressful experiences) can be applied to conceptualizing personality's influence on the development of externalizing problems. In fact, examining person-by-situation interactions is already a flourishing approach to personality research (for a recent review, see Funder, 2008) and is useful for understanding aggressive and externalizing tendencies (see Chapters 1, 7, 8, and 9, this volume). Personality traits are substantially influenced by genetic factors and this general finding appears to be largely consistent across the life span.

In addition to stability, of course, there is evidence for personality change. It is important to adopt a dynamic perspective on the influences of personality on behavioral outcomes that includes both stability and change and considers environmental factors that can impinge on a person at different points in development. For example, although early research demonstrated connections between trait impulsivity, negative affect, and increased risk of suicidal behaviors (Caspi, Moffitt, Newman, & Silva, 1996), recent research suggests that this is particularly important early in life, with the strength of association declining across the life span (McGirr et al., 2008). Similarly, research suggests that early-onset conduct problems are more likely to be influenced by dispositional factors than those that arise later in development (Lahey & Waldman, 2003; Moffitt, 2003).

Personality can be an important moderator of individual responses to a particular kind of situation, including aggressive responses. For example, individuals low in Conscientiousness are more likely to engage in aggressive behavior in the face of anger-provoking stimuli than individuals who are high in Conscientiousness (Jensen-Campbell, Knack, Waldrip, & Campbell, 2007). That is, the experience of angry affect alone does not determine a person's responses, because self-regulatory capacities act on the affective experience to differentiate individual responses. This is consistent with temperament models that differentiate approach/positive emotionality and avoidance/negative emotionality from self-regulatory traits that are considered superordinate in these models (e.g., Ahadi & Rothbart, 1994; Carver, Johnson, & Joormann, 2008; Clark, 2005).

Psychobiological factors such as hormones, genes, and cortical activity also play an important role in explaining connections between personality traits and externalizing behaviors (see Chapter 6; see also Chapter 8 and 9). For example, low serotonergic functioning is associated with personality traits such as hostility and impulsivity as well as aggressive behavior (e.g., Carver et al., 2008). This connection has been illuminated by molecular genetic investigations of the short allele of the serotonin 5-HTTLPR polymorphism (Carver et al., 2008; see also Chapter 8, this volume). Electroencephalograph (EEG) studies of brain processes have also shed light on associations between personality variables and externalizing behaviors. For example, reduced amplitude of the P300 event-related potential measured by EEG during a visual oddball task has been linked to both externalizing behaviors and trait impulsivity (Iacono, Malone, & McGue, 2003). This research provides a possible endophenotype, or marker, for genetic risk of externalizing behavior (Hicks et al., 2007).

It is also possible that psychobiological risk factors increase response strength to external stimuli, leading to differential expressions of aggression and antisocial behavior (Hay, 2007). Such processes can be properly investigated only with research designs that include measures of both person and situation variables (for a taxonomy of such interactions, see Chapter 2, this volume). For example, adolescents with early-onset conduct disorder (compared with controls and adolescents with ADHD) show increased left-sided amygdala activation when presented with negative pictures (Herpertz et al., 2008). In related work, individuals with high levels of trait anger (compared with individuals lower in trait anger) show increased left frontal activation in response to anger-provoking pictures (Harmon-Jones, 2007). These findings suggest psychobiological predispositions that influence reactivity to negative or threatening situations.

GENETIC RESEARCH ON EXTERNALIZING PHENOMENA

In recent years, genetic research on externalizing syndromes and behaviors has focused on exploring the coherence of these syndromes as elements within a broader spectrum, following from the phenotypic work described earlier in this chapter. Genetic effects on different externalizing syndromes are mostly common across these syndromes, but there are also specific genetic effects on substance-dependence syndromes that are not shared with other externalizing syndromes (Kendler, Prescott, Myers, & Neale, 2003; Krueger et al., 2002; Young, Stallings, Corley, Krauter, & Hewitt, 2000). This makes a great deal of physiological sense: It is reasonable for dependence on substances to be traceable to both genetic effects unique to substances (presumably reflecting substance metabolism) and more general effects, presumably reflecting disinhibited personality traits such as disagreeableness and lack of conscientiousness. Note the similarity of these findings to the model proposed by Krueger et al. (2007) and described earlier, where drug problems were affected by a specific factor, beyond the effect of the general externalizing factor. The heritability of general externalizing tendencies is quite substantial, around 80%, suggesting that this general factor would be a good target for gene-hunting studies.

Along these lines, Dick et al. (2008) recently conducted molecular genetic research on alcohol dependence, antisocial personality disorder, conduct disorder, drug dependence, novelty seeing, sensation seeking, and a general externalizing tendency linking these syndromes. The strength of genetic linkage was stronger for the externalizing component than for the individual syndromes. In particular, a region on Chromosome 7 appeared to contribute to general risk, transcending specific externalizing syndromes (cf. Stallings et al., 2005).

Going beyond linkage, Dick and her colleagues also studied single nucleotide polymorphisms (SNPs) in the CHRM2 gene. CHRM2 had been associated with alcohol dependence in previous research and has been associated with risk of alcohol dependence combined with drug dependence, making it an appealing potential candidate gene for studies focused on general externalizing tendencies. In Dick et al.'s (2008) study, general externalizing, as compared with the other syndromes, was most strongly associated with with SNPs in CHRM2.

With regard to Gene × Environment interactions, both twin studies and molecular genetic studies suggest that environmental effects are critical in shaping the expression of genetic risk of externalizing behavior (see Chapter 8). Statistical indexes such as heritability (the overall magnitude of genetic influence on a phenotype) are typically estimated for an entire population. For example, the 80% heritability of externalizing behavior is an estimate that applies to an entire population, without regard to various subgroups within that population. Refining these general estimates with subgroup information is one way to pursue Gene × Environment interaction effects, because genetic effects may be moderated by measurable environmental variables associated with population subgroups.

An example is a recent study by Legrand, Keyes, McGue, Iacono, and Krueger (2008). A sample of 17-year-old twins assessed on diverse externalizing syndromes was divided into those living in rural areas and those living in urban areas. In urban areas, genetic influences predominated, but in rural areas, shared environmental effects (environmental effects making people similar within families) predominated. This suggests that the previously described 80% heritability masks interesting and potentially important subgroup differences.

In the domain of molecular genetic studies, Caspi et al. (2002) examined how childhood maltreatment interacted with a gene coding for MAO-A (monoamine oxidase-A, an enzyme that metabolizes major neurotransmitters) in predicting antisocial behavior in a birth cohort of males. These investigators found that the effect of childhood maltreatment on antisocial behavior was moderated by MAO-A genotype. The genetic polymorphism that predicts high MAO-A activity had a protective effect, such that men with this genotype were protected from the measured deleterious effects of childhood maltreatment. Although there are exceptions, this finding has proven to be generally replicable (Kim-Cohen et al., 2006).

SUMMARY AND CONCLUSIONS

The hierarchical trait model provides a compelling way to conceptualize stable dispositional characteristics that differentiate individuals. Such hierarchical models have been integrated with structural dimensions of psychopathology, including externalizing behaviors such as aggression and violence (Krueger et al., 2007). Studies aimed at the higher order trait level have implicated primarily disinhibitory traits such as disagreeableness and a lack of conscientiousness in connection with aggression measured from early childhood through adulthood (Blonigen & Krueger, 2007; Tackett, 2006). Lower order personality traits may offer increased predictive validity over higher order traits, particularly for specific behavioral outcomes such as physical aggression and violence. Research linking lower order traits to externalizing behaviors is much less common, but extant research implicates alienation in adults (Blonigen & Krueger, 2007) and callous–unemotional traits in children (Frick et al., 2003).

Much of our recent work has been conducted within the externalizing spectrum framework (Krueger et al., 2007; Tackett, 2010), which posits dimensional relations among correlated personality traits and externalizing behaviors. This approach has been fruitful in identifying factors common to the broader externalizing domain as well as specific factors differentiating types of externalizing behaviors (Krueger et al., 2002, 2007; Tackett, Krueger, Sawyer, & Graetz, 2003; Tackett, Krueger, Iacono, & McGue, 2005; Tackett et al., 2009). Indeed, as work on molecular genetic linkage and Gene × Environment interactions progresses, it is possible that the spectrum approach will be helpful in the search for specific genes and relevant environmental stressors (Dick et al., 2008).

Nevertheless, limitations to a full understanding of personality connections to externalizing behaviors remain. There is not yet a clear picture of the life span trajectory of the externalizing spectrum (Tackett, 2010). For example, some disorders typically conceptualized as externalizing syndromes in childhood do not have officially recognized analogs in adult disorder typologies (e.g., ADHD, oppositional defiant disorder). Other behaviors, such as relational aggression, which are often viewed as externalizing (e.g., Baker, Jacobson, Raine, Lozano, & Bezdjian, 2007; Krueger et al., 2007), are not yet clearly identified as pathological behaviors in younger age groups (Tackett et al., 2009). In addition, pathways from early temperamental traits to adult personality traits have not been fully articulated, limiting our ability to provide a complete life span perspective.

As psychopathology research moves toward a broad person × environment perspective, it presents an opportunity for integration with developmental approaches, which have often emphasized environmental influences on specific behavioral outcomes (Jenkins, 2008). Epigenetic approaches, which focus on the role of gene expression, are also becoming increasingly salient to psychopathology researchers. Methodological advances in epigenetics offer new opportunities for integrating complex personality and psychopathology phenotypes (Kaminsky et al., 2008; Mill & Petronis, 2007). They highlight the need to focus on particular developmental periods and processes and on better measurement of potential environmental influences.

REFERENCES

Ahadi, S. A., & Rothbart, M. K. (1994). Temperament, development, and the Big Five. In C. F. Halverson, Jr., G. A. Kohnstamm, & R. P. Martin (Eds.), *The developing structure of temperament and personality from infancy to adulthood* (pp. 189–207). Hillsdale, NJ: Erlbaum.

American Psychiatric Association. (2000). *Diagnostic and statistical manual of mental disorders* (4th ed., text rev.). Washington, DC: Author.

Baker, L. A., Jacobson, K. C., Raine, A., Lozano, D. I., & Bezdjian, S. (2007). Genetic and environmental bases of childhood antisocial behavior: A multi-informant twin study. *Journal of Abnormal Psychology, 116*, 219–235. doi:10.1037/0021-843X.116.2.219

Blonigen, D. M., & Krueger, R. F. (2007). Personality and violence: The unifying role of structural models of personality. In I. Waldman, D. J. Flannery, & A. T. Vazsonyi (Eds.), *The Cambridge handbook of violent behavior* (pp. 288–305). Cambridge, England: Cambridge University Press.

Carver, C. S., Johnson, S. L., & Joormann, J. (2008). Serotonergic function, two-mode models of self-regulation, and vulnerability to depression: What depression has in common with impulsive aggression. *Psychological Bulletin, 134*, 912–943. doi:10.1037/a0013740

Caspi, A., McClay, J., Moffitt, T., E., Mill, J., Martin, J., Craig, I. W., Taylor, A., & Poulton, R. (2002, August). Role of genotype in the cycle of violence in maltreated children. *Science, 297*, 851–854. doi:10.1126/science.1072290

Caspi, A., Moffitt, T. E., Newman, D. L., & Silva, P. A. (1996). Behavioral observations at age 3 years predict adult psychiatric disorders. *Archives of General Psychiatry, 53*, 1033–1039.

Clark, L. A. (2005). Temperament as a unifying basis for personality and psychopathology. *Journal of Abnormal Psychology, 114*, 505–521. doi:10.1037/0021-843X.114.4.505

Costa, P. T., Jr., & McCrae, R. R. (1992). *NEO PI-R professional manual.* Odessa, FL: Psychological Assessment Resources.

Dick, D. M., Aliev, F., Wang, J. C., Grucza, R. A., Schuckit, M., Kuperman, S., ...Goate, A. (2008). Using dimensional models of externalizing psychopathology to aid in gene identification. *Archives of General Psychiatry, 65*, 310–318.

Essau, C. A., Sasagawa, S., & Frick, P. J. (2006). Callous-unemotional traits in a community sample of adolescents. *Assessment, 13*, 454–469. doi:10.1177/1073191106287354

Frick, P. J., Cornell, A. H., Barry, C. T., Bodin, S. D., & Dane, H. E. (2003). Callous-unemotional traits and conduct problems in the prediction of conduct problem severity, aggression, and self-report of delinquency. *Journal of Abnormal Child Psychology, 31*, 457–470. doi:10.1023/A:1023899703866

Frick, P. J., & Sheffield-Morris, A. (2004). Temperament and developmental pathways to conduct problems. *Journal of Clinical Child and Adolescent Psychology, 33*, 54–68. doi:10.1207/S15374424JCCP3301_6

Funder, D. C. (2008). Persons, situations, and person–situation interactions. In O. P. John, R. W. Robins, & L. A. Pervin (Eds.), *Handbook of personality: Theory and research* (3rd ed., pp. 568–580). New York, NY: Guilford Press.

Goldberg, L. R. (1993). The structure of phenotypic personality traits. *American Psychologist, 48,* 26–34. doi:10.1037/0003-066X.48.1.26

Halverson, C. F., Havill, V. L., Deal, J., Baker, S. R., Victor, J. B., Pavlopoulos, V., . . . Wen, L. (2003). Personality structure as derived from parental ratings of free descriptions of children: The Inventory of Child Individual Differences. *Journal of Personality, 71,* 995–1026. doi:10.1111/1467-6494.7106005

Harmon-Jones, E. (2007). Trait anger predicts relative left frontal cortical activation to anger-inducing stimuli. *International Journal of Psychophysiology, 66,* 154–160. doi:10.1016/j.ijpsycho.2007.03.020

Hay, D. F. (2007). The gradual emergence of sex differences in aggression: Alternative hypotheses. *Psychological Medicine, 37,* 1527–1537. doi:10.1017/S0033291707000165

Helzer, J. E., Kraemer, H. C., & Krueger, R. F. (2006). The feasibility and need for dimensional psychiatric diagnoses. *Psychological Medicine, 36,* 1671–1680. doi:10.1017/S003329170600821X

Herpertz, S. C., Huebner, T., Marx, I., Vloet, T. D., Fink, G. R., Stoecker, T., . . . Herpertz-Dahlmann, B. (2008). Emotional processing in male adolescents with childhood-onset conduct disorder. *Journal of Child Psychology and Psychiatry, and Allied Disciplines, 49,* 781–791. doi:10.1111/j.1469-7610.2008.01905.x

Hicks, B. M., Bernat, E., Malone, S. M., Iacono, W. G., Patrick, C. J., Krueger, R. F., & McGue, M. (2007). Genes mediate the association between P3 amplitude and externalizing disorders. *Psychophysiology, 44,* 98–105. doi:10.1111/j.1469-8986.2006.00471.x

Iacono, W. G., Malone, S. M., & McGue, M. (2003). Substance use disorders, externalizing psychopathology, and event-related potential amplitude. *International Journal of Psychophysiology, 48,* 147–178. doi:10.1016/S0167-8760(03)00052-7

Jenkins, J. (2008). Psychosocial adversity and resilience. In M. Rutter, D. Bishop, D. Pine, S. Scott, J. Stevenson, E. Taylor, & A. Thapar (Eds.), *Rutter's handbook of child and adolescent psychiatry* (5th ed., pp. 377–391). Oxford, England: Blackwell. doi:10.1002/9781444300895.ch25

Jensen-Campbell, L. A., Knack, J. M., Waldrip, A. M., & Campbell, S. D. (2007). Do Big Five personality traits associated with self-control influence the regulation of anger and aggression? *Journal of Research in Personality, 41,* 403–424. doi:10.1016/j.jrp.2006.05.001

Kaminsky, Z., Petronis, A., Wang, S. C., Levine, B., Ghaffar, O., Floden, D., & Feinstein, A. (2008). Epigenetics of personality traits: An illustrative study of identical twins discordant for risk-taking behavior. *Twin Research and Human Genetics, 11,* 1–11. doi:10.1375/twin.11.1.1

Kendler, K. S., Prescott, C. A., Myers, J., & Neale, M. C. (2003). The structure of genetic and environmental risk factors for common psychiatric and substance use disorders in men and women. *Archives of General Psychiatry, 60,* 929–937. doi:10.1001/archpsyc.60.9.929

Kim-Cohen, J., Caspi, A., Taylor, A., Williams, B., Newcombe, R., Craig, I. W., & Moffitt, T. E. (2006). MAO-A, maltreatment, and gene–environment interaction predicting children's mental health: New evidence and a meta-analysis. *Molecular Psychiatry, 11*, 903–913. doi:10.1038/sj.mp.4001851

Krueger, R. F., Hicks, B. M., Patrick, C. J., Carlson, S. R., Iacono, W. G., & McGue, M. (2002). Etiologic connections among substance dependence, antisocial behavior, and personality: Modeling the externalizing spectrum. *Journal of Abnormal Psychology, 111*, 411–424. doi:10.1037/0021-843X.111.3.411

Krueger, R. F., & Markon, K. E. (2006). Reinterpreting comorbidity: A model-based approach to understanding and classifying psychopathology. *Annual Review of Clinical Psychology, 2*, 111–133. doi:10.1146/annurev.clinpsy.2.022305.095213

Krueger, R. F., Markon, K. E., Patrick, C. J., Benning, S. D., & Kramer, M. (2007). Linking antisocial behavior, substance use, and personality: An integrative quantitative model of the adult externalizing spectrum. *Journal of Abnormal Psychology, 116*, 645–666. doi:10.1037/0021-843X.116.4.645

Lahey, B. B., & Waldman, I. D. (2003). A developmental propensity model of the origins of conduct problems during childhood and adolescence. In B. B. Lahey, T. E. Moffitt, & A. Caspi (Eds.), *Causes of conduct disorder and juvenile delinquency* (pp. 76–117). New York, NY: Guilford Press.

Legrand, L. N., Keyes, M., McGue, M., Iacono, W. G., & Krueger, R. F. (2008). Rural residency reduces the genetic influence on adolescent substance-use and rule-breaking behavior. *Psychological Medicine, 38*, 1341–1350. doi:10.1017/S0033291707001596

Markon, K. E., Krueger, R. F., & Watson, D. (2005). Delineating the structure of normal and abnormal personality: An integrative hierarchical approach. *Journal of Personality and Social Psychology, 88*, 139–157. doi:10.1037/0022-3514.88.1.139

McCrae, R. R., & Costa, P. T. (1990). *Personality in adulthood.* New York, NY: Guilford Press.

McGirr, A., Renaud, J., Bureau, A., Seguin, M., Lesage, A., & Turecki, G. (2008). Impulsive-aggressive behaviours and completed suicide across the life cycle: A predisposition for younger age of suicide. *Psychological Medicine, 38*, 407–417. doi:10.1017/S0033291707001419

Mill, J., & Petronis, A. (2007). Molecular studies of major depressive disorder: The epigenetic perspective. *Molecular Psychiatry, 12*, 799–814. doi:10.1038/sj.mp.4001992

Moffitt, T. E. (2003). Life-course-persistent and adolescence-limited antisocial behavior: A 10-year research review and a research agenda. In B. B. Lahey, T. E. Moffitt, & A. Caspi (Eds.), *Causes of conduct disorder and juvenile delinquency* (pp. 49–75). New York, NY: Guilford Press.

Nigg, J. T. (2006). Temperament and developmental psychopathology. *Journal of Child Psychology and Psychiatry, and Allied Disciplines, 47*, 395–422. doi:10.1111/j.1469-7610.2006.01612.x

Paunonen, S. V., & Ashton, M. C. (2001). Big Five factors and facets and the prediction of behavior. *Journal of Personality and Social Psychology, 81*, 524–539. doi:10.1037/0022-3514.81.3.524

Reynolds, S. K., & Clark, L. A. (2001). Predicting dimensions of personality disorder from domains and facets of the five-factor model. *Journal of Personality, 69*, 199–222. doi:10.1111/1467-6494.00142

Rothbart, M. K., Ahadi, S. A., Hershey, K. L., & Fisher, P. (2001). Investigations of temperament at 3 to 7 years: The Children's Behavior Questionnaire. *Child Development, 72*, 1394–1408. doi:10.1111/1467-8624.00355

Saudino, K. J., Plomin, R., & DeFries, J. C. (1996). Tester-rated temperament at 14, 20, and 24 months: Environmental change and genetic continuity. *The British Journal of Developmental Psychology, 14*, 129–144.

Schell, G. C., & Tackett, J. L. (2009). *Agency and communion as indicators of personality in middle childhood.* Manuscript submitted for publication.

Shiner, R. L. (1998). How shall we speak of children's personalities in middle childhood? A preliminary taxonomy. *Psychological Bulletin, 124*, 308–332. doi:10.1037/0033-2909.124.3.308

Shiner, R., & Caspi, A. (2003). Personality differences in childhood and adolescence: Measurement, development, and consequences. *Journal of Child Psychology and Psychiatry, and Allied Disciplines, 44*, 2–32. doi:10.1111/1469-7610.00101

Srivastava, S., John, O. P., Gosling, S. D., & Potter, J. (2003). Development of personality in early and middle adulthood: Set like plaster or persistent change? *Journal of Personality and Social Psychology, 84*, 1041–1053. doi:10.1037/0022-3514.84.5.1041

Stallings, M. C., Corley, R. P., Dennehey, B., Hewitt, J. K., Krauter, K. S., Lessem, J. M., . . . Crowley, T. J. (2005). A genome-wide search for quantitative trait loci that influence antisocial substance dependence in adolescence. *Archives of General Psychiatry, 62*, 1042–1051. doi:10.1001/archpsyc.62.9.1042

Tackett, J. L. (2006). Evaluating models of the personality–psychopathology relationship in children and adolescents. *Clinical Psychology Review, 26*, 584–599. doi:10.1016/j.cpr.2006.04.003

Tackett, J. L. (2010). *Toward a developmentally integrated externalizing spectrum in DSM–V.* Manuscript submitted for publication.

Tackett, J. L., Krueger, R. F., Iacono, W. G., & McGue, M. (2005). Symptom-based subfactors of DSM-defined conduct disorder: Evidence for etiologic distinctions. *Journal of Abnormal Psychology, 114*, 483–487. doi:10.1037/0021-843X.114.3.483

Tackett, J. L., Krueger, R. F., Iacono, W. G., & McGue, M. (2008). Personality in middle childhood: A hierarchical structure and longitudinal connections with personality in late adolescence. *Journal of Research in Personality, 42*, 1456–1462. doi:10.1016/j.jrp.2008.06.005

Tackett, J. L., Krueger, R. F., Sawyer, M. G., & Graetz, B. W. (2003). Subfactors of DSM–IV conduct disorder: Evidence and connections with syndromes from the

Child Behavior Checklist. *Journal of Abnormal Child Psychology, 31*, 647–654. doi:10.1023/A:1026214324287

Tackett, J. L., Waldman, I., & Lahey, B. B. (2009). Etiology and measurement of relational aggression: A multi-informant behavior genetic investigation. *Journal of Abnormal Psychology, 118*, 722–733.

Young, S. E., Stallings, M. C., Corley, R. P., Krauter, K. S., & Hewitt, J. K. (2000). Genetic and environmental influences on behavioral disinhibition. *American Journal of Medical Genetics. Part B, Neuropsychiatric Genetics, 96*, 684–695. doi:10.1002/1096-8628(20001009)96:5<684::AID-AJMG16>3.0.CO;2-G

Yung, Y., Thissen, D., & McLeod, L. D. (1999). On the relationship between the higher order factor model and the hierarchical factor model. *Psychometrika, 64*, 113–128. doi:10.1007/BF02294531

6

A SOCIAL NEUROSCIENCE PERSPECTIVE ON THE NEUROBIOLOGICAL BASES OF AGGRESSION

THOMAS F. DENSON

The discovery of brain regions and mental processes that contribute to aggressive behavior has long been a significant concern in psychology. Although much progress has been made, identification of the underlying neural mechanisms remains elusive (Davidson, Putnam, & Larson, 2000). It is thought that neural functioning mediates aggressive behavior by biasing mental processes toward aggressive responses to social situations (Raine, 2008). Relying on advances in the emerging field of social neuroscience, this chapter reviews research that has increased our understanding of the neural mechanisms associated with human aggression. This review contains a brief discussion of relevant brain anatomy, followed by a review of structural and functional brain abnormalities in highly aggressive populations. Next, I discuss the application of a recent social neuroscience dual-process model, the X- and C-systems model, to the study of anger and aggression. This is followed by a discussion of social neuroscience research that is consistent with social psychological theory. Finally, I discuss the role played by top-down executive control in determining aggressive behavior.

This chapter was supported by the Australian Research Council's *Discovery Projects* funding scheme (DP0985182). Thank you to Ajay Satpute for comments on an earlier draft of this chapter.

ANATOMY

Reviews of anger and aggression converge on the importance of the pre-frontal cortex (PFC) underlying these phenomena (Davidson et al., 2000; Raine, 2008; Siever, 2008). Indeed, the PFC is broadly involved in the regulation and control of affect and behavior. Within the PFC, four regions are particularly relevant to aggressive behavior. The dorsolateral PFC is involved in planning and behavioral control. The ventral PFC, which encompasses the ventromedial PFC, ventrolateral PFC, and the orbitofrontal cortex, is involved in emotion regulation. The dorsal region of medial PFC (mPFC) is involved in introspection and the awareness of emotion as well as emotion regulation. Finally, the dorsal anterior cingulate cortex (dACC) is involved in the detection of conflict and triggering activity in top-down control regions (see Figure 6.1).

In terms of neurotransmitter involvement, converging evidence suggests that serotonin has a prominent role in facilitating and inhibiting anger and hostile aggression via $5\text{-}HT_2$ receptors in the PFC (Davidson et al., 2000; Siever, 2008; see also Chapter 8, this volume). Because a detailed discussion of neurotransmitter modulation is beyond the scope of this chapter, the purpose here is to review the most current research on brain regions implicated in anger and aggression.

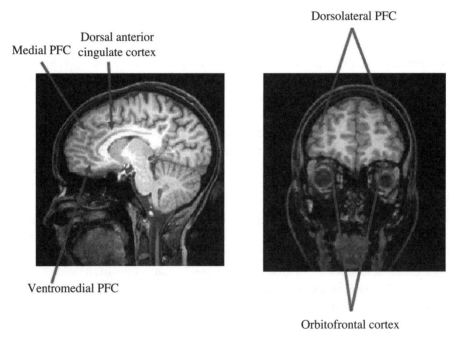

Figure 6.1. Brain regions implicated in anger and aggression. PFC = prefrontal cortex.

EVIDENCE FROM ABNORMAL POPULATIONS

Early examinations of patients with brain lesions revealed that abnormalities in the PFC were associated with aggressive and antisocial behavior. The classic case of Phineas Gage, who suffered trauma to his orbitofrontal cortex, is illustrative of the dramatic within-person change from agreeable and conscientious to hostile and antagonistic that is associated with trauma to this region. A fairly large study of 279 Vietnam War veterans with brain lesions revealed that those who suffered injury to the orbitofrontal cortex and mPFC were more irritable, hostile, and aggressive than control participants (Grafman et al., 1996).

More recent neuroimaging studies have examined structural differences in groups of individuals known to be highly aggressive compared with less aggressive matched controls. Several studies have identified prefrontal structural differences in the brains of aggressive individuals, such as violent offenders and psychopaths, relative to matched controls (for reviews, see Raine, 2008; Yang, Glenn, & Raine, 2008). For instance, individuals with antisocial personality disorder have an 11% to 14% deficit in prefrontal gray matter relative to normal controls, substance-dependent individuals, and individuals with other psychiatric disorders (Raine, Lencz, Bihrle, LaCasse, & Colletti, 2000).

These differences are not limited to brain structure. Numerous studies document functional impairment in frontal and limbic regions such as the ventral PFC, dorsolateral PFC, mPFC, anterior cingulate cortex (ACC), posterior cingulate cortex (PCC), hippocampus, and amygdala (Raine, 2008; Raine & Yang, 2008). For instance, a positron emission tomography (PET) study reported reduced glucose metabolism in the PFC in a group of murderers compared with a matched control group (Raine, Buchsbaum, & LaCasse, 1997). Another study found that when processing emotional versus neutral words, criminal psychopaths show less activation in the lateral PFC, ACC, PCC, and amygdala than noncriminal psychopaths and normal controls (Kiehl et al., 2001). In summary, violence-prone groups show deficits in the structure and functioning of key brain regions involved in emotion regulation and behavioral control. Although these data are correlational, presumably these abnormalities reduce the ability to regulate and control angry feelings and aggressive behavior.

A SOCIAL NEUROSCIENCE FRAMEWORK: THE X- AND C-SYSTEMS

Although research on abnormally aggressive individuals is instructive, most social and personality psychologists are primarily interested in the normal spectrum of human behavior. Indeed, decades of social psychological and personality research demonstrate that we are all capable of behaving aggressively under certain circumstances and that some individuals within the normal range tend to be more aggressive than others across a variety of contexts (e.g., Anderson & Bushman, 2002; see also Chapters 1, 2, and 7, this volume). Social neuroscience is an emerging field that examines the neural correlates of social psychological phenomena. Because functional neuroimaging technology, especially functional magnetic resonance imaging (fMRI), is relatively widely available, we are now able to examine neural processes in normal individuals using experimental methods drawn from social and cognitive psychology. Tools such as fMRI enable us to explore previously unquantifiable aspects of human functioning that are directly relevant to social psychological questions.

In an effort to integrate findings from the rapidly expanding field of social neuroscience, Lieberman and colleagues (Lieberman, 2007; Lieberman, Gaunt, Gilbert, & Trope, 2002; Satpute & Lieberman, 2006) proposed a dual-process framework known as the X- and C-systems model. The X component of the model, which we likely share with other animals, represents our continuous stream of current experience (Lieberman et al., 2002, p. 204). The X stands for the *x* in reflexive. The X-system is phylogenetically older than the C-system, operates quickly, supports spontaneous processes, and engages in parallel processing. Brain regions that make up the X-system are the ventromedial PFC, dACC, amygdala, basal ganglia, and lateral temporal cortex. Social psychological phenomena associated with this region include implicit prejudice, emotional pain resulting from social rejection, and intuition-based self-knowledge (see Lieberman, 2007).

In contrast with the X-system, the C-system underlies reflective and control processes. The C stands for the *c* in reflective. The C-system is phylogenetically newer than the X-system, operates slowly, is associated with volitional processes, uses serial processing (i.e., not parallel processing), and involves abstract thought (Lieberman, 2007). We experience activity in the C-system during reflective thought. Thus, current experience is the result of the X-system, whereas reflecting on this experience is supported by the C-system. The C-system often becomes active when the X-system detects a problem. Brain regions that make up the C-system include the lateral and mPFC, lateral and medial parietal cortex, medial temporal lobe, and ventrolateral PFC. Social psychological phenomena associated with the C-system include explicit attitudes, reflecting on current experiences, impulse control, reappraising emotional events, and moral reasoning (see Lane, Fink, Chau, & Dolan, 1997; Lieberman, 2007; MacDonald, 2008). Although research on anger and aggression was not considered in Lieberman's (2007) review, the X- and C-systems provide a valuable framework for discussing the neural bases of anger and aggression. Specifically, many of the processes associated with the X- and C-systems are relevant for understanding aggressive behavior.

SOCIAL NEUROSCIENCE RESEARCH
ON ANGER AND AGGRESSION

In this section, I review research conducted primarily with normal individuals. Specifically, I review social neuroscience research relevant to anger, angry rumination, cognitive neoassociation theory, social learning, media influences, and aggressive behavior.

Anger

Most functional imaging studies of anger in nonclinical samples have exposed participants to angry faces or asked them to recall and reexperience anger-inducing events. Two recent meta-analyses of nine PET and fMRI studies revealed that some of the most prominent areas of frontal and limbic brain reactivity were the mPFC, ventromedial PFC, ACC, PCC, lateral PFC, and thalamus (Murphy, Nimmo-Smith, & Lawrence, 2003; Phan, Wager, Taylor, & Liberzon, 2002). It is interesting that whereas the amygdala has a prominent role in fear, it was not implicated in these studies of angry faces and memories (Phan et al., 2002).

My colleagues and I recently examined the neural correlates of anger more directly by exposing participants to an interpersonal insult (Denson, Pedersen, Ronquillo, & Nandy, 2009). Anderson and Bushman (2002) described such a provocation as "perhaps the most important single cause of human aggression" (p. 37). In this fMRI study, participants were asked to complete difficult anagrams and state the answer aloud or say "no answer" if they did not know the answer. Following two polite prompts to speak louder, the experimenter then insulted participants by saying in an irritated and condescending voice, "Look, this is the third time I've had to say this! Can't you follow directions?" We found that, relative to baseline, participants showed increased activation in many of the same regions active during exposure to angry faces and autobiographical recall of anger experiences. Moreover, we found that a component of the X-system, the dACC, played a special role in the subjective experience of anger. Specifically, self-reported anger was correlated with dACC activation ($r = .56$). Activity in the dACC was also correlated with scores on the Buss and Perry (1992) Aggression Questionnaire, a measure of general trait anger, hostility, and aggression ($r = .61$). Consistent with the claim that the dACC is involved in the subjective experience of anger, individuals who have had portions of the ACC removed demonstrate decreased anger (Cohen et al., 2000).

Angry Rumination

Reflective processes also play a role in anger and aggression. Regions of the C-system that have been implicated in anger and aggression include the lateral PFC, mPFC, and medial parietal cortex. As noted earlier, following provocation, participants demonstrated increased activity in regions of the C-system as well as the X-system. One important reflective process that can influence aggressive behavior is the way one regulates emotions. One particularly pernicious form of emotion regulation is angry rumination. Immersive rumination on anger-inducing experiences increases anger, aggression, cardiovascular arousal, and cortisol levels (Bushman, 2002; Bushman, Bonacci, Pedersen, Vasquez, & Miller, 2005; Denson, Fabiansson, Creswell, & Pedersen, 2009; Denson, Pedersen, & Miller, 2006; Ray, Wilhelm, & Gross, 2008; Rusting & Nolen-Hoeksema, 1998).

In addition to these negative consequences of angry rumination, our recent research demonstrates that angry rumination also increases activity in parts of the C-system (Denson, Pedersen, et al., 2009). In the second part of the experiment described earlier, following the provocation, participants were asked to engage in a "memory task," which served as a rumination manipulation. Using a modified within-participants rumination task from prior research (Bushman et al., 2005; Denson et al., 2006; Rusting & Nolen-Hoeksema, 1998), during the rumination task participants were asked to think about what had occurred in the experiment so far, who they interacted with, and their current mood. During the distraction period, participants were asked to think about neutral events. Relative to distraction, rumination increased activity in regions of the C-system such as medial and lateral PFC, insula, precuneus, and PCC. Furthermore, self-reported rumination was correlated with activity in the mPFC ($r = .42$), as were scores on the Displaced Aggression Questionnaire, an individual difference measure of trait displaced aggression (Denson et al., 2006). The relationship between the mPFC and the displaced aggression measure was likely due to the fact that when provoked, individuals high in trait displaced aggression tend to ruminate about the event rather than immediately retaliate against the provocateur.

We expected that the mPFC would be especially relevant to angry rumination because it supports many of the reflective processes at work during rumination. For example, the mPFC is activated during tasks that require the self-awareness of emotions and self-relevant cognition (Lane et al., 1997; Lieberman, 2007; Ochsner et al., 2004). This region is also active when monitoring one's emotional state, reflecting on feelings, and reappraising emotional responses to distressing stimuli (Amodio & Frith, 2006; Ochsner et al., 2004; Ochsner, Bunge, Gross, & Gabrieli, 2002). Furthermore, Ray et al. (2005) reported that when participants were asked to decrease their negative affective responses to aversive photographs, a composite measure of trait rumination was correlated with mPFC activity.

Cognitive Neoassociation Theory

As previously noted, my colleagues and I found that activity in the dACC was linearly related to self-reported anger following provocation (Denson, Pedersen, et al., 2009). The dACC is of social psychological interest because it is involved in at least two additional negative emotional states that have been shown to increase aggression. This is relevant because a core tenet of Berkowitz's (1993) cognitive neoassociationistic model of aggression states that any form of negative affect can increase aggression. A large body of evidence supports Berkowitz's supposition. For example, physical pain and social rejection both increase aggression and activation in the dACC (Berkowitz, Cochran, & Embree, 1981; Eisenberger, Liberman, & Williams, 2003; Rainville, Duncan, Price, Carrier, & Bushnell, 1997; Twenge, Baumeister, Tice, & Stucke, 2001). These and the anger findings converge to suggest the existence of a common neural mechanism underlying the process Berkowitz proposed, although the mediating role of dACC activation between anger, pain, social rejection, and actual aggressive behavior remains to be investigated. Future neuroimaging research examining additional aversive stimuli known to increase aggression, such as noxious odors and heat, might demonstrate increased activity in the dACC as well.

Social Learning, Media Violence, and Script Theory

According to social learning perspectives on aggression, individuals learn how and when to behave aggressively by observing others either in person or vicariously in the media (Bandura, 1973). A tremendous amount of research supports this notion (e.g., Anderson et al., 2003). Expanding on social learning theory, Huesmann (1998) proposed that individuals learn behavioral scripts from aggressive media exposure. Scripts are closely connected concepts in memory that can become strengthened by rehearsal and chronic exposure to violent media. When activated, such scripts can increase the likelihood of aggressive behavior (see Chapter 7, this volume).

Only a handful of social neuroscience studies have examined neural responses during exposure to violent media (for a review, see Carnagey, Anderson, & Bartholow, 2007). In one study, in an attempt to identify children most responsive to violent media, children who showed heart rate acceleration to violent media on a pretest were exposed to violent (i.e., boxing) and nonviolent (i.e., animal) scenes while functional images were acquired (Murray et al., 2006). The strongest activity was located in the right PCC and the right precuneus (in the medial parietal cortex). Because of its role in memory, these authors speculated that activity in the PCC might correspond to the activation of stored aggressive scripts. This is consistent with our research showing that the PCC was active during angry rumination, because the revenge planning that occurs during angry rumination likely involves the activation of aggressive scripts (Denson, Pedersen, et al., 2009). Indeed, factor analytic work indicates that angry rumination involves rehearsing acts of revenge (Caprara, 1986; Denson et al., 2006; Sukhodolsky, Golub, & Cromwell, 2001).

Two additional studies found that violent media influence brain activity in what is thought to be a maladaptive manner. Specifically, in an investigation of the hypothesis that chronic exposure to violent media desensitizes individuals to aggressive content, one study examined the P300 component of the event-related brain potential in people who played relatively high levels of aggressive video games and those who played aggressive video games less often (Bartholow, Bushman, & Sestir, 2006). When exposed to violent images in the laboratory, chronic exposure to violent video games was associated with decreased P300 amplitude to violent images but not to negative or neutral images. These findings support the notion that violent video game play can desensitize basic neural responses to violent stimuli. Furthermore, the P300 deficit predicted increased aggression as assessed by choosing to deliver loud noise blasts to a fictitious participant. Although electroencephalogram methods do not allow for precise localization of brain processes, presumably the automatic response of the P300 reflects activity in the X-system, suggesting that chronic exposure to media violence can alter even quite rudimentary information processing such that individuals with high levels of exposure actually experience violent media differently than those low in exposure.

An fMRI study investigated brain activity during actual violent video game play (Weber, Ritterfeld, & Mathiak, 2006). In a sophisticated frame-by-frame analysis of violent game play, these authors demonstrated that activity in the dACC preceded suppression in the rostral ACC (rACC), which is involved in affective information processing, and in the amygdala during aggressive "search and destroy" sequences. Recall that the dACC is associated with the subjective experience of anger (Denson, Pedersen, et al., 2009). This suppression of the rACC by the dACC when committing acts of video game violence suggests that the dACC overrides affective input from the rACC. Consistent with the suppression function of the dACC, when participants were in danger, under attack, or using a weapon, the dACC was more active than when participants were passive or safe.

Aggressive Behavior

Only two neuroimaging studies have investigated brain activity during actual acts of aggression. The first such fMRI study examined brain activity in

14 men high and low in psychopathy during their performance in a Taylor (1967) aggression paradigm that was modified such that participants could see a fictitious participant receive the allocated bursts of physically painful pressure to their hand (Lotze, Veit, Anders, & Birbaumer, 2007). Of primary interest, activity in the mPFC was positively correlated with the intensity of pain participants chose to have administered to the confederate. This latter finding is consistent with the role of the mPFC in angry rumination, emotion regulation, attributions, and theory of mind (e.g., Amodio & Frith, 2006; Denson, Pedersen, et al., 2009; Harris, Todorov, & Fiske, 2005; Ochsner et al., 2002).

A second study of normal young adults used a modified white-noise Taylor (1967) paradigm in which the decision phase (i.e., deciding what noise level to choose) and the outcome phase (i.e., the aggressive act) were analyzed separately (Krämer, Jansma, Tempelmann, & Münte, 2007). Furthermore, participants were given the opportunity to aggress against highly provocative and less provocative bogus participants as well as against a computer. This allowed the authors to identify the neural mechanisms specifically associated with aggression rather than social interaction per se. Under high provocation, the dACC and mPFC were active during the decision phase, suggesting the presence of anger and rumination (e.g., Denson, Pedersen, et al., 2009).

Perhaps the most intriguing result of this study is that a component of the reward system—the dorsal striatum—was activated during the decision phase in which participants chose the level at which to blast the highly provocative participant with noise. This finding, which the authors called the "sweetness of revenge" (Krämer, Jansma, Tempelmann, & Münte, 2007, p. 209), suggests that aggression can be inherently rewarding, and thereby provides a neural basis that might partially explain why it is difficult to reduce retaliatory aggressive behavior. During the outcome phase, activation in another region of the reward system, the ventral striatum, was also observed. However, the authors concluded that this was most likely due to relief derived from the successful avoidance of the noise blast.

In summary, the brain regions associated with anger, angry rumination, and actual aggressive behavior, as well as issues addressed by cognitive theories of aggression and media violence, involve elements of both the X- and C-systems. The concept of a dual system harkens back to the days of Freud, who posited an innate form of destruction motivation (i.e., Thanatos) emanating from the id that resists control by the ego and superego. This notion of conflict between primitive aggressive urges and control of these urges remains with us today (see Chapter 2). However, the X- and C-systems framework differs markedly from Freud's notion of destructive drives. The X- and C- systems are compatible. When the situation calls for it, the C-system intervenes. For example, when someone cuts us off on the freeway while making an obscene gesture, the dACC sounds the neural alarm and snaps us out of our placid stream of experience. Our subsequent behavior, aggressive or otherwise, will depend on a number of factors, one of which is the activation in top-down control regions of the brain. I discuss this in more detail later.

ROLE OF TOP-DOWN CONTROL AND EMOTION REGULATION MECHANISMS

For the aggressor, aggressive behavior can have positive consequences (e.g., self-defense, achievement of dominance) and negative consequences (e.g., developing a bad reputation, instigating retaliation, and even being killed). Evolutionary theorists argue that in our ancestral past, aggression was a risky strategy, but when successfully executed, aggression likely increased reproductive success (e.g., MacDonald, 2008; see also Chapters 3 and 4, this volume). Although he did not use the X- and C-system framework, in a review of the literature on effortful control, MacDonald (2008) argued that a conscious system located in the PFC (C-system) allows humans to inhibit prepotent impulses toward aggression stemming primarily from limbic structures (X-system). When the X-system cannot solve a problem, it calls on the C-system. It is the C-system that allows individuals to make "explicit appraisals of costs and benefits" (MacDonald, p. 1014) that are "only . . . available through explicit processing" (MacDonald, p. 1015). These explicit appraisals play a key role in determining whether aggression will or will not occur, and it is precisely these appraisals that distinguish human aggression from the purely reflexive aggression observed in other animals.

The general aggression model (GAM; Anderson & Bushman, 2002; see also Chapter 1, this volume) highlights the importance of the explicit decision-making process. According to the GAM, appraisals and decision-making processes precede thoughtful or impulsive action. One key implication of the GAM and other models of effortful control is that individual differences in impairment of self-control should be related to aggression and impulsivity in general. Indeed, individual differences in trait aggression, executive functioning, and impulsivity are interrelated (MacDonald, 2008). Moreover, temporary experimental impairment in self-control increases aggression (DeWall, Baumeister, Stillman, & Gailliot, 2007; Stucke & Baumeister, 2006; see also Chapter 2, this volume). Acute alcohol intoxication has similar effects, likely via altered activity in the dorsolateral PFC (Dao-Castellana et al., 1998).

In the modern world, aggression is still risky. One might even argue that the negative consequences (e.g., imprisonment, legal fees, social rejection) are typically a more likely outcome following aggression than any positive consequences. Thus, the ability to effectively weigh the costs and benefits of aggression is critical (see Chapter 3). This is not to say that the C-system flawlessly functions in our best interest. Indeed, in modern society we still find that most aggressive acts are impulsive acts. For example, the majority of homicides and other aggressive crimes occur when people are provoked and angry and either explicitly decide to aggress or are simply unable to resist the motivation to behave aggressively. Thus, the immediate cause of many acts of aggression is often a loss of self-control (DeWall et al., 2007).

Substantial neuropsychological and imaging research indicates that the PFC is the seat of self-control (Banfield, Wyland, Macrae, Munte, & Heatherton, 2004), and integral parts of the circuit that underlie self-control are the dACC, dorsolateral PFC, and mPFC (Cohen, Botvinick, & Carter, 2000). The neural substrates of emotion regulation include the medial, ventrolateral PFC, and ventromedial PFC. The lateral and medial regions of the PFC share rich connectivity with cortical and limbic structures such as the dACC and ventromedial PFC and have been implicated in emotion regulation and behavioral control (Inzlicht & Gutsell, 2007). Accordingly, Davidson et al. (2000) proposed that impaired functioning of an emotion regulation circuit involving the dACC, ventromedial PFC, and the dorsolateral PFC predisposes individuals to aggressive behavior. Indeed, engaging in self-control or completing neuropsychological measures that rely on inhibitory ability recruits the dACC and dorsolateral PFC (Botvinick, Braver, Barch, Carter, & Cohen, 2001; Richeson et al., 2003). As noted previously, both provocation and subsequent angry rumination recruit neural regions underlying executive control and emotion regulation mechanisms (Denson, Pedersen, et al., 2009).

Part of the anger and aggression circuit, the dACC, has been dubbed a "neural alarm system" because of its role in detecting conflict (Eisenberger & Lieberman, 2004; Kross, Egner, Ochsner, Hirsch, & Downey, 2007). In the presence of unjustified wrongdoing, there is likely a conflict between how people feel they should be treated and how they were actually treated (see Chapter 3, this volume). This is consistent with the associations of the dACC with self-reported social distress and anger following ostracism and provocation (Denson, Pedersen, et al., 2009; Eisenberger et al., 2003). Because there are costs and benefits to aggression, there is also likely to be a conflict between motivation to aggress and motivation not to aggress. As Krämer et al. (2007) suggested, when a person is unjustly wronged, it is likely that the dACC initiates regulatory behavior via activity in the dorsolateral PFC.

There is some evidence to suggest that exposure to media violence impairs top-down control mechanisms. Mathews et al. (2005) examined adolescents who had been diagnosed with a disruptive behavior disorder, including aggressive features, and matched controls who had either high or low levels of exposure to media violence. During neuroimaging, participants completed the Stroop task, which typically activates the dACC and dorsolateral PFC. The aggressive group demonstrated decreased activity, and this activation was not different from that in the normal adolescents who had been exposed to high levels of media violence. Only the normal adolescents with low levels of exposure to media violence demonstrated the typical pattern of lateral PFC and dACC activity during the Stroop task.

CONCLUSION AND FUTURE DIRECTIONS

The evidence reviewed here implicates a network of neural regions that underlie anger, angry rumination, aggression, and media violence. Activity in these regions and the processes that they support are consistent with social psychological models of aggression, such as cognitive neoassociation theory, script theory, and the GAM. The hostile aggression circuit described here implicates limbic and top-down prefrontal regions, which support both reflective and reflexive processes. Anger, pain, and social rejection are mediated by activity in the dACC, whereas angry rumination is mediated by the mPFC. There is also evidence that high levels of exposure to media violence are associated with abnormal functioning in the aggression circuit. Furthermore, during actual acts of aggression, neural regions involved in reward processing are active. This finding partially explains the difficulty associated with effectively reducing aggression.

Much work remains to be done. For instance, because alcohol is involved in a large number of aggressive acts, neuroimaging research investigating the pathways by which alcohol influences reactions to provocation seems worthwhile. Future research could also investigate genetic markers that might influence neural reactivity to provocation such as the MAOA polymorphism. Additional work could also investigate the connection between neural activity, other systems (e.g., cardiovascular, endocrine), and actual aggressive behavior in more detail. Furthermore, one might also examine the effects of interventions known to reduce aggression (e.g., distraction, self-control training) on long-term changes in neural reactivity. By grounding social psychological theory in brain processes, future research will expand our understanding of situational and personological influences on aggressive behavior.

REFERENCES

Amodio, D. M., & Frith, C. D. (2006). Meeting of minds: The medial frontal cortex and social cognition. *Nature Reviews. Neuroscience, 7,* 268–277. doi:10.1038/nrn1884

Anderson, C. A., Berkowitz, L., Donnerstein, E., Huesmann, L. R., Johnson, J. D., Linz, D., . . . Wartella, E. (2003). The influence of media violence on youth. *Psychological Science in the Public Interest, 4,* 81–110.

Anderson, C. A., & Bushman, B. J. (2002). Human aggression. *Annual Review of Psychology, 53,* 27–51. doi:10.1146/annurev.psych.53.100901.135231

Bandura, A. (1973). *A social learning analysis.* Englewood Cliffs, NJ: Prentice-Hall.

Banfield, J. F., Wyland, C. L., Macrae, C. N., Munte, T. F., & Heatherton, T. F. (2004). The cognitive neuroscience of self-regulation. In R. F. Baumeister & K. D. Vohs (Eds.), *Handbook of self-regulation* (pp. 62–83). New York, NY: Guilford Press.

Bartholow, B. D., Bushman, B. J., & Sestir, M. A. (2006). Chronic violent video game exposure and desensitization to violence: Behavioral and event-related brain potential data. *Journal of Experimental Social Psychology, 42,* 532–539. doi:10.1016/j.jesp.2005.08.006

Berkowitz, L. (1993). *Aggression: Its causes, consequences, and control.* New York, NY: McGraw-Hill.

Berkowitz, L., Cochran, S., & Embree, M. C. (1981). Physical pain and the goal of aversively stimulated aggression. *Journal of Personality and Social Psychology, 40,* 687–700. doi:10.1037/0022-3514.40.4.687

Botvinick, M. M., Braver, T. S., Barch, D. M., Carter, C. S., & Cohen, J. D. (2001). Conflict monitoring and cognitive control. *Psychological Review, 108,* 624–652. doi:10.1037/0033-295X.108.3.624

Bushman, B. J. (2002). Does venting anger feed or extinguish the flame? Catharsis, rumination, distraction, anger, and aggressive responding. *Personality and Social Psychology Bulletin, 28,* 724–731. doi:10.1177/0146167202289002

Bushman, B. J., Bonacci, A. M., Pedersen, W. C., Vasquez, E. A., & Miller, N. (2005). Chewing on it can chew you up: Effects of rumination on triggered displaced aggression. *Journal of Personality and Social Psychology, 88,* 969–983. doi:10.1037/0022-3514.88.6.969

Buss, A. H., & Perry, M. (1992). The Aggression Questionnaire. *Journal of Personality and Social Psychology, 63,* 452–459. doi:10.1037/0022-3514.63.3.452

Caprara, G. V. (1986). Indicators of aggression: The Dissipation–Rumination Scale. *Personality and Individual Differences, 7,* 763–769. doi:10.1016/0191-8869(86)90074-7

Carnagey, N. L., Anderson, C. A., & Bartholow, B. D. (2007). Media violence and social neuroscience: New questions and new opportunities. *Current Directions in Psychological Science, 16,* 178–182. doi:10.1111/j.1467-8721.2007.00499.x

Cohen, J. D., Botvinick, M., & Carter, C. S. (2000). Anterior cingulate and prefrontal cortex: Who's in control? *Nature Neuroscience, 3,* 421–423. doi:10.1038/74783

Cohen, R. A., Paul, R., Zawacki, T. M., Moser, D. J., Sweet, L., & Wilkinson, H. (2001). Emotional and personality changes following cingulotomy. *Emotion, 1,* 38–50. doi:10.1037/1528-3542.1.1.38

Dao-Castellana, M. H., Samson, Y., Legault, F., Martinot, J. L., Aubin, H. J., Crouzel, C., . . . Syrota, A. (1998). Frontal dysfunction in neurologically normal chronic alcoholic subjects: Metabolic and neuropsychological findings. *Psychological Medicine, 28,* 1039–1048. doi:10.1017/S0033291798006849

Davidson, R. J., Putnam, K. M., & Larson, C. L. (2000, July). Dysfunction in the neural circuitry of emotion regulation: A possible prelude to violence. *Science, 289*, 591–594. doi:10.1126/science.289.5479.591

Denson, T. F., Fabiansson, E. C., Creswell, J. D., & Pedersen, W. C. (2009). Experimental effects of rumination styles on salivary cortisol responses. *Motivation and Emotion, 33*, 42–48. doi:10.1007/s11031-008-9114-0

Denson, T. F., Pedersen, W. C., & Miller, N. (2006). The Displaced Aggression Questionnaire. *Journal of Personality and Social Psychology, 90*, 1032–1051. doi:10.1037/0022-3514.90.6.1032

Denson, T. F., Pedersen, W. C., Ronquillo, J., & Nandy, A. S. (2009). The angry brain: Neural correlates of anger, angry rumination, and aggressive personality. *Journal of Cognitive Neuroscience, 21*, 734–744. doi:10.1162/jocn.2009.21051

DeWall, C. N., Baumeister, R. F., Stillman, T. F., & Gailliot, M. T. (2007). Violence restrained: Effects of self-regulation and its depletion on aggression. *Journal of Experimental Social Psychology, 43*, 62–76. doi:10.1016/j.jesp.2005.12.005

Eisenberger, N. I., & Lieberman, M. D. (2004). Why rejection hurts: A common neural alarm system for physical and social pain. *Trends in Cognitive Sciences, 8*, 294–300. doi:10.1016/j.tics.2004.05.010

Eisenberger, N. I., Liberman, M. D., & Williams, K. D. (2003, October). Does rejection hurt? An fMRI study of social exclusion. *Science, 302*, 290–292. doi:10.1126/science.1089134

Grafman, J., Schwab, K., Warden, D., Pridgen, A., Brown, H. R., & Salazar, A. M. (1996). Frontal lobe injuries, violence, and aggression: A report of the Vietnam Head Injury Study. *Neurology, 46*, 1231–1238.

Harris, L. T., Todorov, A., & Fiske, S. T. (2005). Attributions on the brain: Neuroimaging dispositional inferences, beyond theory of mind. *NeuroImage, 28*, 763–769. doi:10.1016/j.neuroimage.2005.05.021

Huesmann, L. R. (1998). The role of social information processing and cognitive schema in the acquisition and maintenance of habitual aggressive behavior. In R. G. Geen & E. Donnerstein (Eds.), *Human aggression: Theories, research, and implications for social policy* (pp. 73–109). San Diego, CA: Academic Press.

Inzlicht, M., & Gutsell, J. N. (2007). Running on empty: Neural signals for self-control failure. *Psychological Science, 18*, 933–937. doi:10.1111/j.1467-9280.2007.02004.x

Kiehl, K. A., Smith, A. M., Hare, R. D., Mendrek, A., Forster, B. B., Brink, J., & Liddle, P. F. (2001). Limbic abnormalities in affective processing by criminal psychopaths as revealed by functional magnetic resonance imaging. *Biological Psychiatry, 50*, 677–684. doi:10.1016/S0006-3223(01)01222-7

Krämer, U. M., Jansma, H., Tempelmann, C., & Münte, T. F. (2007). Tit-for-tat: The neural basis of reactive aggression. *NeuroImage, 38*, 203–211. doi:10.1016/j.neuroimage.2007.07.029

Kross, E., Egner, T., Ochsner, K., Hirsch, J., & Downey, G. (2007). Neural dynamics of rejection sensitivity. *Journal of Cognitive Neuroscience, 19*, 945–956. doi:10.1162/jocn.2007.19.6.945

Lane, R. D., Fink, G. R., Chau, P. M.-L., & Dolan, R. J. (1997). Neural activation during selective attention to subjective emotional responses. *Neuroreport, 8,* 3969–3972. doi:10.1097/00001756-199712220-00024

Lieberman, M. D. (2007). Social cognitive neuroscience: A review of core processes. *Annual Review of Psychology, 58,* 259–289. doi:10.1146/annurev.psych.58.110405.085654

Lieberman, M. D., Gaunt, R., Gilbert, D. T., & Trope, Y. (2002). Reflexion and reflection: A social cognitive neuroscience approach to attributional inference. *Advances in Experimental Social Psychology, 34,* 199–249. doi:10.1016/S0065-2601(02)80006-5

Lotze, M., Veit, R., Anders, S., & Birbaumer, N. (2007). Evidence for a different role of the ventral and dorsal medial PFC for social reactive aggression: An interactive fMRI study. *NeuroImage, 34,* 470–478. doi:10.1016/j.neuroimage.2006.09.028

MacDonald, K. B. (2008). Effortful control, explicit processing, and the regulation of human evolved predispositions. *Psychological Review, 115,* 1012–1031. doi:10.1037/a0013327

Mathews, V. P., Kronenberger, W. G., Want, Y., Lurito, J. T., Lowe, M. J., & Dunn, D. W. (2005). Media violence exposure and frontal lobe activation measure by functional magnetic resonance imaging in aggressive and nonaggressive adolescents. *Journal of Computer Assisted Tomography, 29,* 287–292. doi:10.1097/01.rct.0000162822.46958.33

Murphy, F. C., Nimmo-Smith, I., & Lawrence, A. D. (2003). Functional neuroanatomy of emotions: A meta-analysis. *Cognitive, Affective, & Behavioral Neuroscience, 3,* 207–233. doi:10.3758/CABN.3.3.207

Murray, J. P., Liotti, M., Ingmundson, P. T., Mayberg, H. S., Pu, Y., Zamarripa, F., . . . Fox, P. T. (2006). Children's brain activations while viewing televised violence revealed by fMRI. *Media Psychology, 8,* 25–37. doi:10.1207/S1532785XMEP0801_3

Ochsner, K. N., Bunge, S. A., Gross, J. J., & Gabrieli, J. D. E. (2002). Rethinking feelings: An fMRI study of the cognitive regulation of emotion. *Journal of Cognitive Neuroscience, 14,* 1215–1229. doi:10.1162/089892902760807212

Ochsner, K. N., Knierim, K., Ludlow, D. H., Hanelin, J., Ramachandran, T., Glover, G., & Mackey, S. C. (2004). Reflection upon feelings: An fMRI study of neural systems supporting the attribution of emotion to self and other. *Journal of Cognitive Neuroscience, 16,* 1746–1772. doi:10.1162/0898929042947829

Phan, K. L., Wager, T., Taylor, S. F., & Liberzon, I. (2002). Functional neuroanatomy of emotion: A meta-analysis of emotion activation studies in PET and fMRI. *NeuroImage, 16,* 331–348. doi:10.1006/nimg.2002.1087

Raine, A. (2008). From genes to brain to antisocial behaviour. *Current Directions in Psychological Science, 17,* 323–328. doi:10.1111/j.1467-8721.2008.00599.x

Raine, A., Buchsbaum, M., & LaCasse, L. (1997). Brain abnormalities in murderers indicated by positron emission tomography. *Biological Psychiatry, 42,* 495–508. doi:10.1016/S0006-3223(96)00362-9

Raine, A., Lencz, T., Bihrle, S., LaCasse, L., & Colletti, P. (2000). Reduced prefrontal gray matter volume and reduced autonomic activity in antisocial personality disorder. *Archives of General Psychiatry, 57,* 119–127. doi:10.1001/archpsyc.57.2.119

Raine, A., & Yang, Y. (2008). Neural foundations to moral reasoning and antisocial behaviour. *Social Cognitive and Affective Neuroscience, 1,* 203–213.

Rainville, P., Duncan, G. H., Price, D. D., Carrier, B., & Bushnell, M. C. (1997, August). Pain affect encoded in human anterior cingulate but not somatosensory cortex. *Science, 277,* 968–971. doi:10.1126/science.277.5328.968

Ray, R. D., Ochsner, K. N., Cooper, J. C., Roberston, E. R., Gabrieli, J. D. E., & Gross, J. J. (2005). Individual differences in trait rumination and the neural systems supporting cognitive reappraisal. *Cognitive, Affective, & Behavioral Neuroscience, 5,* 156–168. doi:10.3758/CABN.5.2.156

Ray, R. D., Wilhelm, F. H., & Gross, J. J. (2008). All in the mind's eye? Anger rumination and reappraisal. *Journal of Personality and Social Psychology, 94,* 133–145. doi:10.1037/0022-3514.94.1.133

Richeson, J. A., Baird, A. A., Gordon, H. L., Heatherton, T. F., Wyland, C. L., Trawalter, S., & Shelton, J. N. (2003). An fMRI investigation of the impact of interracial contact on executive function. *Nature Neuroscience, 6,* 1323–1328. doi:10.1038/nn1156

Rusting, C. L., & Nolen-Hoeksema, S. (1998). Regulating responses to anger: Effects of rumination and distraction on angry mood. *Journal of Personality and Social Psychology, 74,* 790–803. doi:10.1037/0022-3514.74.3.790

Satpute, A. B., & Lieberman, M. D. (2006). Integrating automatic and controlled processes into neurocognitive models of social cognition. *Brain Research, 1079,* 86–97. doi:10.1016/j.brainres.2006.01.005

Siever, L. J. (2008). Neurobiology of aggression and violence. *The American Journal of Psychiatry, 165,* 429–442. doi:10.1176/appi.ajp.2008.07111774

Stucke, T. S., & Baumeister, R. F. (2006). Ego depletion and aggressive behavior: Is the inhibition of aggression a limited resource? *European Journal of Social Psychology, 36,* 1–13. doi:10.1002/ejsp.285

Sukhodolsky, D. G., Golub, A., & Cromwell, E. N. (2001). Development and validation of the Anger Rumination Scale. *Personality and Individual Differences, 31,* 689–700. doi:10.1016/S0191-8869(00)00171-9

Taylor, S. P. (1967). Aggressive behavior and physiological arousal as a function of provocation and the tendency to inhibit aggression. *Journal of Personality, 35,* 297–310. doi:10.1111/j.1467-6494.1967.tb01430.x

Twenge, J. M., Baumeister, R. F., Tice, D. M., & Stucke, T. S. (2001). If you can't join them, beat them: Effects of social exclusion on aggressive behavior. *Journal of Personality and Social Psychology, 81,* 1058–1069. doi:10.1037/0022-3514.81.6.1058

Weber, R., Ritterfeld, U., & Mathiak, K. (2006). Does playing violent video games induce aggression? Empirical evidence of a functional magnetic resonance imaging study. *Media Psychology, 8,* 39–60. doi:10.1207/S1532785XMEP0801_4

II

GENETIC AND ENVIRONMENTAL DETERMINANTS

7

THE TRANSMISSION OF AGGRESSIVENESS ACROSS GENERATIONS: BIOLOGICAL, CONTEXTUAL, AND SOCIAL LEARNING PROCESSES

L. ROWELL HUESMANN, ERIC F. DUBOW, AND PAUL BOXER

In this chapter, we present a theoretical perspective for examining the cross-generational transmission of aggressive or nonaggressive behavior. We begin by reviewing the evidence that there is substantial continuity of aggression within a generation across the life span. We note that this continuity is due as much to the continuity of unaggressiveness as to the continuity of aggressiveness. We then turn to examining the empirical evidence concerning the cross-generational continuity of aggression. We note that although a number of studies suggest such continuity, a number of methodological issues have not been resolved by most of the studies to date. Most notably, the number of prospective cross-generational life-span studies is still small. We then present a social–cognitive model that has evolved to explain aggressive behavior and its continuity in the life span, and we discuss how this model can be applied to understanding cross-generational continuity within a broader framework that explains such continuity as a product of four processes: genetic predispositions

This research was supported in part by grants from the National Institute of Mental Health and the National Institute of Child Health and Human Development. The authors wish to acknowledge the contributions of Leonard Eron, Monroe Lefkowitz, and Leopold Walder to the Columbia County Longitudinal Study.

interacting with environmental factors, continuities or discontinuities in environments, observational learning processes with a focus on parents as models, and conditioning processes with a focus on parents as the conditioners. Finally, we present some data from a 40-year, three-generational longitudinal study that shows that children's aggressiveness after they grow up is predicted by their parents' own childhood aggressiveness and their parents' aggressiveness when the children were young or adults but not by their parents' adolescent aggressiveness. It is shown that continuity of aggression within the life span plus transmission between generations during the critical childhood period of the second generation can adequately explain the cross-generational relations. These findings are consistent with intergenerational transmission through genetic and biological predispositions and learning processes during the childhood years.

WITHIN-PERSON CONTINUITY OF AGGRESSIVE BEHAVIOR ACROSS THE LIFE SPAN

One of the most consistently asked questions of prospective, longitudinal data is whether personality traits, behaviors, or other aspects of psychosocial functioning remain stable over the life course. The continuity of intellectual ability from childhood to adulthood is substantial, with correlations typically in the moderate range (about .50). Research, including our own, on the development of aggression suggests that adult aggression and antisocial behavior are also statistically predictable from childhood aggression and antisocial behavior (Farrington, 2003; Farrington, Ttofi, & Coid, 2009; Huesmann, Dubow, & Boxer, 2009; Huesmann, Eron, Lefkowitz, & Walder, 1984; Kokko, Pulkkinen, Huesmann, Dubow, & Boxer, 2009; Loeber & Dishion, 1983; Moffitt, 1993; Olweus, 1979; Pulkkinen, Lyyra, & Kokko, 2009).

Our most recent estimates are based on analyses of data from the Columbia County Longitudinal Study, a study of a cohort of 856 eight-year-olds first evaluated in 1960 and then reevaluated at age 19 in 1970 to 1971, at age 30 in 1982, and at age 48 in 2000. Their parents were also interviewed in 1960, and 525 of their children were interviewed in 2000, providing data on three generations. We call the main sample the Generation 2 (G2) sample, and they have provided 40 years of data on continuity of aggression across the life span. When the continuity coefficients for 40 years are estimated with structural equation models that control for measurement error and method variance (see Huesmann et al., 2009), we obtain coefficients of .50 for males and .42 for females. These approach the continuity of intellectual ability. The consequences of such continuity can be serious. As Kokko et al. (2009) recently showed with data from Finland and the United States, early aggressiveness is more predictive of physical aggression and lack of self-control in later middle adulthood than it is of verbal aggression.

It is worth noting that the continuity correlations over time are due as much to low aggressive children staying low on aggression throughout life as they are to high aggressive children staying high on aggression throughout life (Huesmann et al., 2009). To demonstrate this fact, we grouped participants based on age-8 peer-nominated aggression into "high" and "low" categories using both median and one-third splits and examined how many stayed in the same category over 40 years. For the full sample, 37% (52 of 141) of individuals who were low in third grade stayed low through late adolescence (i.e., age 19), through young adulthood (i.e., age 30), and into middle adulthood (i.e., age 48) on the composite measure of aggression. Of individuals who were high in third grade, 35% (i.e., 31 of 89) stayed high through adolescence and into middle adulthood. In other words, continuity was as much due to low aggressives staying low as to high aggressives staying high. When we inspected these patterns by gender, interesting differences became evident. For males, 38% of those who were low in childhood stayed low through age 48. Similarly, 36% of females who were low in childhood stayed low into middle adulthood. However, the differences were striking with regard to those classified as high on aggression. Among males, 47% of those who were high in childhood stayed high into middle adulthood, whereas for females, only 18% who were high in childhood continued to be high into middle adulthood (χ [1] = 14.97, $p < .001$).

These results open the possibility that differential socialization of males and females places more pressure on females to reduce their aggression than it does on males. Early aggressiveness may also have more lasting serious consequences for males. For example, Huesmann, Eron, and Dubow (2002) found that early aggressiveness was the most important predictor of males being arrested by the time they were 30 years old, in comparison with a large variety of contextual and personal variables assessed in the Columbia County Longitudinal Study. The standardized odds ratio for age-8 aggression in predicting "ever arrested by age 30" was highly significant: 1.45, $p < .01$.

Of course, even continuity coefficients as large as .5 and odds ratios approaching 1.5 still mean that a substantial portion of adult aggressive and criminal behavior is not predictable from childhood aggressive behavior and is probably related to context (Broidy et al., 2003; Sameroff, Seifer, Baldwin, & Baldwin, 1993). In addition, it seems to be only aggressive and antisocial behavior that emerges early in life that has lasting negative consequences. As Moffitt (1993) suggested and a number of recent studies confirmed, some aggressive and antisocial behavior often emerges in adolescence and is relatively short lived. This kind of aggression seems to have few long-term negative consequences, whereas life course persistent aggression that begins in early childhood has lasting detrimental consequences (Bergman & Andershed, 2009; Farrington et al., 2009; Huesmann et al., 2009; Pulkkinen et al., 2009).

Similar findings regarding continuity have been reported in studies of other indicators of adjustment over time. For example, Helson, Jones, and Kwan (2002) demonstrated quadratic changes in various indicators of personality functioning from early to late adulthood: Certain attributes such as dominance and independence peaked in middle adulthood. In her influential island of Kauai prospective study, Werner (2002) summarized long-term outcomes for children and adolescents with behavior disorders: By age 40, only one third of those males and one fifth of those females exhibited continuing difficulties (e.g., financial, marital, substance use). However, far less is known about the degree of continuity of positive psychosocial adjustment from childhood to adulthood, although this appears to be an emergent concern of longitudinal researchers. As an example, with data from the Jyväsklyä Longitudinal Study, Pulkkinen and her colleagues demonstrated that prosocial behavior in childhood predicted greater self-esteem and subjective well-being and shorter lived periods of unemployment in adulthood (Kokko & Pulkkinen, 2000; Pulkkinen, Nygren, & Kokko, 2002). Flouri and Buchanan (2002) showed that good family relationships in childhood led to better marital adjustment in adulthood.

RECENT STUDIES OF INTERGENERATIONAL CONTINUITY OF AGGRESSION

The discovery of strong continuity of aggression across the life course has stimulated interest in the continuity of aggression and antisocial behavior across generations. Although many studies have investigated parent–child relations statically (i.e., cross-sectionally), longitudinal cross-generational investigations of continuity and discontinuity in personality, behavior, and adjustment are relatively few and are limited primarily to examining contemporaneous or retrospective links between parent and child behavior. Several discussions of the intergenerational transmission of aggression have been published in the child development literature over the past decade (e.g., Constantino, 1996; MacEwen, 1994). Those reviews indicated that most relevant studies have used self-report, retrospective questionnaire data obtained from two generations. However, response bias problems cloud the interpretation of such findings. Three studies in a 1998 special issue of *Developmental Psychology* did use prospective methodology and multiple methods of measuring aggression (Cairns, Cairns, Xie, Leung, & Hearne, 1998; Capaldi & Clark, 1998;

Serbin et al., 1998), and all reported modest to moderate cross-generational continuity. But those studies included only two generations.

More recently, four studies on cross-generational consistencies in parenting and in aggressive and antisocial behavior were published in a special issue of the *Journal of Abnormal Child Psychology* (Capaldi, Pears, Patterson, & Owen, 2003; Conger, Neppl, Kim, & Scaramella, 2003; Hops, Davis, Leve, & Sheever, 2003; Thornberry, Freeman-Gallant, Lizotte, Krohn, & Smith, 2003; see also Smith & Farrington, 2004). All four studies measured parenting by two generations (G1 and G2) and aggressive behavior in two generations (G2 and G3). Two of the four studies found significant intergenerational continuity of aggression. The two that did not report such continuity had the smallest sample sizes. All four studies also reported intergenerational continuity for some parenting factors relevant to aggression (e.g., negative affect in parent–child interactions, consistency of discipline). The results also suggested that child aggression mediates some of the continuity of parenting as well as parenting mediating some of the continuity of aggression. For example, Thornberry et al. (2003), using self-report questionnaire data, found a chain of relations for males from G1 parenting to G2 aggression to G2 parenting to G3 aggression. For females, the pattern was similar, although the link from G1 parenting to G2 aggression was not significant. Conger et al. (2003), using observational data, found both that G1 observed parenting had direct effects on G2 observed aggression and that G2 observed parenting had direct effects on G3 observed aggression. Hops et al. (2003), also using observations of parenting, obtained a fully mediated path from G1 parenting, to G2 aggression, to G2 parenting, and finally to G3 aggression. Capaldi et al. (2003) reported findings similar to those of the other studies, with an important methodological distinction: the use of multiple informants and sources of data, moving beyond the parent and child observational and questionnaire data used in the other studies to include teacher reports and archival records.

A plausible conclusion that can be drawn from these similar results in the four studies is that parenting behavior and aggressive behavior seem to have reciprocal influences on each other. Within generations, aggression in youth is often followed by aggression-promoting parenting. Aggression-promoting parenting, in turn, seems to contribute to aggression in offspring. However, this conclusion might be attenuated by important considerations related to the theory on which these cross-generational investigations are based. In spite of increasing empirical attention, the processes by which patterns of positive or negative adjustment are transmitted from parents to children are not yet well understood or firmly established, and more research is needed to explicate cross-generational links and the theory explaining such links (Dubow, Huesmann, & Boxer, 2003; Rutter, 1998; Shaw, 2003).

PSYCHOLOGICAL PROCESSES INVOLVED
IN AGGRESSIVE BEHAVIOR

To begin with, to talk theoretically about the cross-generational transmission of aggression, we need a model for the psychological processes through which predisposing personal factors and precipitating situational factors interact to determine whether a person behaves aggressively. The model needs to include a representation of the enduring psychological structures that control and influence these processes. Such a model has been provided by Huesmann (1998) in a unified information-processing model for social problem solving. According to this model that integrates previous theorizing of Huesmann (1988), Bandura (1977), Dodge (1982), and Anderson (Anderson & Huesmann, 2003), an individual's emotional state and encoded schemas about the world interact with situational cues to lead the individual to make attributions about the situation. These attributions change the individual's emotional state and prime the activation of scripts for behaving. The scripts are filtered through a set of normative beliefs about appropriateness until a script is accepted and followed.

Within this model, the long-term determinants of aggressiveness include (a) encoded cognitions represented by schemas about the world, (b) scripts for behavior, and (c) normative beliefs for filtering scripts, along with (d) the individual's emotional predispositions. More specifically, hostile attributional biases (e.g., "People are mean"; Dodge, 1982; see also Chapter 9, this volume) occur when hostility is emphasized by the "world schema" that an individual has acquired. Attributions influence emotions and the type of script an individual will retrieve to deal with a social situation. Scripts (Huesmann, 1998) can be viewed as cognitive programs that have been acquired over time and are stored in a person's memory and are used as guides for behavior and social problem solving. Not all scripts that occur to the child will be used. Before acting out the script, the child reevaluates the appropriateness of the script in light of existing internalized social norms—called *normative beliefs* (Huesmann, 1998; Huesmann & Guerra, 1997)—and examines the likely consequences of the script. These normative beliefs and expectations about outcome must also have been acquired over time.

Our focus on cognitive-information processes does not mean that emotions are unimportant. We view emotion regulation as an important influence on aggressive behavior that influences attributions, script selection, and evaluation of scripts. Emotion regulation has held a place of prominence in the study of behavioral development for some time, particularly with regard to developmental psychopathology (e.g., Cicchetti, Ackerman, & Izard, 1995; Frick & Morris, 2004).

Processes for the Intergenerational Transmission of Aggression

Given this model, how can a tendency to behave in a characteristic manner (e.g., aggressively or nonaggressively) be transmitted from one person (e.g., a parent) to another (e.g., the parent's child)? Our position is that there are four major processes by which this may occur that need to be considered: (a) through the transmission of genes that influence social behavior, (b) by changes parents make in the child's environment or through continuity in the parent's and child's environment, (c) through children observing parents' behaviors, and (d) through conditioning of the children's behavior in which the parent participates.

Genetic Influences on Aggression

Genetic influences are well established empirically (see Chapter 8). Individual differences in emotional arousal, neurotransmitter levels, perceptual biases, and other characteristics relevant to aggression seem to be influenced by genes. The evidence for a heritable predisposition to aggression from twin and adoption studies is impressive (Cloninger & Gottesman, 1987; Deater-Deckard & Plomin, 1999; Mednick, Gabrielli, & Hutchings, 1984). Miles and Carey (1997) performed a meta-analysis of 24 genetically informative studies that included twin and adoption designs and found significant heritability estimates (in the .4 range) for self-report measures of aggression. In addition, a variety of adoption studies have revealed relations between children's aggressiveness or antisocial behavior and the aggressive or antisocial behavior of both their natural and adoptive parents.

However, these seem to be predisposing influences rather than deterministic influences. Estimates from behavior genetic analyses of low shared environmental variance depend on unlikely assumptions of genes being uncorrelated, noninteracting, and not influencing the environment of the individual. The weight of evidence suggests, rather, that biosocial interactions between genes and the environment are likely influences.

Recent studies are beginning to go beyond global estimates of the relative influences of genetic differences in accounting for phenotypic differences to look for the specific genes responsible (e.g., Chapter 8). Strategies based on genome scans have proved disappointing in the search for loci that influence behavioral phenotypes, but investigations of polymorphisms of candidate genes have been surprisingly productive. Although methods are still developing for statistical discrimination of reliable signals from noise when many candidate genes are studied, effects of monoamine oxidase (MAO) and serotonin promoters have been confirmed and others are under study (for a review, see Munafò et al., 2003). Studies by Caspi and colleagues (2002, 2003) have indicated that there are important childhood contextual–genetic interactions in the expression of social behavior. For example, those authors found that a gene that causes slightly lower MAO increases risk of aggression only in a child who is exposed to high amounts of stress during childhood and adolescence. Similarly, the perinatal environment is known to affect the risk of aggressive behavior (Raine, Brennan, & Mednick, 1995). Whatever their source, a variety of individual differences in neurophysiology, neurotransmitters, hormones, and heart rate correlate with individual differences in early aggressiveness (Knoblich & King, 1992; Olweus, Mattsson, Schaling, & Loew, 1988; Raine & Jones, 1987).

Intergenerational Environmental Continuity and Change and Their Influences on Continuity and Change in Aggression

Many environmental influences on risk and resilience for aggression and violence have been identified. These include stress, poverty, abuse, parental rejection, peer behaviors, and religion, to name a few. To the extent that such environments are passed from parent to child, one can expect cross-generational continuity. To the extent that such environments change from parent to child, one can expect cross-generational discontinuity.

A major question in developmental research concerns how changes over time in the social contexts people inhabit affect development (Higgins & Parsons, 1983; Huesmann, Dubow, Eron, & Boxer, 2006; Sameroff, 1983). One needs to understand whether the degree of continuity in positive and negative adjustment over time and across generations is related to the degree of continuity in contextual factors. Is there continuity in parenting practices from what a current parent experienced in interactions with his or her parents to what the parent delivers to his or her child? Does continuity or change in socioeconomic status promote continuity or change in aggression? Many children have to cope with family changes: Their parents might divorce, get into trouble with the law, or lose their jobs. Evidence suggests that the stress engendered by such changes is a risk factor for children's socioemotional development (Caspi et al., 2002), thus increasing the likelihood of negative changes that might have long-term consequences. Our hypothesis is that similar discontinuities of a positive nature (e.g., a substantial improvement in the family's financial situation, a significant improvement in the child's academic performance) can turn trajectories of psychosocial adjustment upward toward greater success, achievement, and life satisfaction.

A second question in developmental research concerns the timing of exposure to contextual influences. What contexts at what points during childhood are most predictive of later outcomes? For example, Duncan (2002) found that poverty experienced during the early childhood years had the strongest effects on the number of years of education the child attained by early adulthood. This suggests that the environment in which the parent lives and the child develops would be more important than the parent's own early environment.

A third issue of great relevance is the extent to which the larger historical context surrounding individual development influences the trajectories taken by cohorts embedded in those circumstances. As an example, what is the differential impact of being an adolescent in a society that is at war as compared with the same society experiencing relative peace, and how might the institution of selective or compulsory service magnify that impact?

These issues lead to a fourth broad contextual concern: major life transitions or turning points in individual development (Rönkä, Oravala, & Pulkkinen, 2002; Rutter, 1996). *Turning points* are positive or negative events, over which the individual may or may not have control, which significantly alter the life trajectory. According to Rutter (1996), an event can be a turning point only if it leads to an enduring, long-term modification of the trajectory. Thus, turning points cannot be assessed contemporaneously for their impact. Longitudinal data are necessary because often individuals do not recognize turning points in their lives until some time has passed and the individual has understood the importance and meaningfulness of the event.

Children Observing Parents' Behaviors

The observation of parents' behaviors by children can be expected to influence social behavior in general and aggressive behavior in particular, and this can occur through two quite different processes: short-term stimulating processes and long-term learning processes. These processes operate more generally to make the child imitate anything he or she observes, including aggressive acts by others (Huesmann & Kirwil, 2007).

In the short run, when children see their parents behave aggressively, schemas, scripts, and normative beliefs associated with aggression are primed in the children's minds. In addition, emotions associated with the behavior are aroused in the child (e.g., anger may be stimulated). These processes alone can lead to short-term increases in the risk of aggressive behavior. In addition, however, because children generally identify with their parents, they are likely to mimic behaviors almost immediately. All of these short-term stimulating processes make it likely that a child will behave aggressively after observing his or her parents behaving aggressively.

However, the more important observational processes for the intergenerational transmission of aggression are probably long-term observational learning processes involving parent and child. As mentioned earlier, children generally identify strongly with their parents. Consequently, they tend to encode into their repertoire of scripts the scripts they see their parents using, they tend to adopt the world schemas they perceive their parents to be holding, and they tend to accept the normative beliefs of their parents about the appropriateness of social behavior. For a long time, children's imitation of parents' behaviors was thought to be a relatively low-level childish form of behavior. "But recent work across a variety of sciences argues that imitation is a rare ability fundamentally linked to characteristically human forms of intelligence, in particular to language, culture, and the ability to understand other minds" (Hurley & Chater, 2005, p. 1). Imitation of parents' behaviors appears to be innate and occurs automatically in young primate infants (Meltzoff & Moore, 1983). Specific mirror neurons seem to organize imitation in primate brains (Gallese, Fadiga, Fogassi, & Rizzolatti, 1996). However, recent work suggests that imitation goes far beyond the copying of specific sequences of behaviors to the encoding of social cognitions fundamental to the control of social behavior (Meltzoff, 2007).

These observational learning processes are also involved in the development of emotion regulation. Eisenberg, Cumberland, and Spinrad (1998) described three processes by which emotion socialization leads to social competence. First, through everyday family interactions, children display a wide range of both positive and negative emotions, thus providing parents with numerous opportunities to react in both positive (e.g., encouraging) and negative (e.g., punishing) ways. Second, when parents discuss various aspects of emotion (e.g., causes and consequences, emotional experience and regulation) with their children, they serve as models for understanding and coping with emotion. A child who receives a high degree of emotion knowledge from his or her parents should be better equipped to contend with emotionally charged events. Third, family emotional expressivity relates in important ways to children's social competence. Through observation, children can learn positive (e.g., smiling) or negative (e.g., yelling) modes of expressing emotions, as well as heuristics for interpreting the emotions of others. This model of emotion socialization suggests individual and cross-generational continuity of emotional regulation and, in turn, social behaviors, as well as taking into account potential moderating influences of contextual or individual factors.

Conditioning of Children's Behaviors to Be Similar to or Different from Parents

Of course, observational learning is not the only learning process crucial to intergenerational transmission of aggressive tendencies. As Patterson (1986) demonstrated, parents may unintentionally condition their children operantly to behave aggressively. Through coercive family interactions, they may unintentionally reinforce their children for behaving aggressively. They may also deliberately and directly reinforce their children for being aggressive if the parents believe aggression is appropriate.

Parents who harshly punish and abuse their children may also classically condition them to experience anger responses to stimuli that might seem benign to others (e.g., persons of authority). They may classically condition alienation from society in this way and make appropriate socialization of the child by others in the child's environment difficult.

Analysis of Intergenerational Continuity in the Columbia County Longitudinal Study

The first analyses of the four waves of data spanning three generations from the Columbia County Longitudinal Study suggest that genetic and dispositional processes, learning processes operating during the child-rearing years, and environmental continuities may all contribute to cross-generational continuity of aggressiveness. The sample we used in these analyses consists of 349 of the 551 G3 offspring who were interviewed when their G3 parent was 48 years old. The 349 represent one child of each G2 subject interviewed— the youngest child for subjects with more than one child (in 202 families two children were interviewed). The ages of the G3 sample at the time of the interview ranged from 6 to 33, with a median age of 18.

In these analyses, we assessed aggression in the G2 generation with the same composite measure we developed to assess continuity of aggression across the life span in the G2 generation. The indicators we used in that analysis of four waves of G2 data were peer nominations at age 8 and 19; severe physical aggression at ages 19, 30, and 48; and aggressive personality at ages 19, 30, and 48. The "severe physical aggression" measure assessed how often the person punched, choked, beat up, or used a knife or a gun against another person in the preceding year. The "aggressive personality" measure was the sum of the F, 4, and 9 scales of the Minnesota Multiphasic Personality Inventory (MMPI; Hathaway & McKinley, 1940). For the G3 data, we used the same two indicators of adult aggression as with G2: aggressive personality and behaving severely physically aggressively. However, we analyzed these indicators separately because the sample sizes are quite different for the two variables, given that only those G3 offspring who were over 13 received the aggressive personality assessment.

In Table 7.1, the intergenerational correlations are shown from G2 to G3 for these variables. One can see substantial cross-generational correlations between the G2 parent's aggression at age 8, 19, 30, and 48 and the G3 offspring's aggressive personality and severe physical aggression at the time the G2 parent was 48. For a subsample of 125 of the G3 offspring we had data on the aggressiveness of the other parent as well. Their aggressiveness correlated about .20 ($p < .05$) with the G2 spouses' aggressiveness at both age 30 and 48 and with the G3 offsprings' aggressiveness. However, the total prediction of G3s' aggression was not enhanced by adding in this other parent's aggression to a prediction equation.

TABLE 7.1
Correlations Between Generation G2's (Parents') Aggression at Four Ages and Generation G3's Aggression When G2 Parent Was Age 48

	Child aggression when parent was age 48	
G2 parent's aggression at different ages	G3 child's aggressive personality ($N = 212$)	G3 child's severe physical aggression ($N = 348$)
Age 8		
G2's composite aggression	0.24***	0.09*
Age 19		
G2's composite aggression	0.26***	0.18***
Age 30		
G2's composite aggression	0.46***	0.17***
Age 48		
G2's composite aggression	0.19***	0.26***

*$p < .10$. ** $p < .05$. *** $p < .01$.

The correlations with G2s' age-8 aggression are consistent with genetic and biological predisposition models of intergenerational transfer, whereas the correlations between G2s' later aggression and the G3 offsprings' aggression are consistent with learning models that emphasize transmission of aggressive behavior during the child-rearing years. Although the differences are not large, an inspection of the correlations suggests that the strongest relations with the offspring's aggressive personality are from the parent's aggression years earlier when the parent was a child, adolescent, or young adult. However, the strongest correlations with the G3 offsprings' actual physically aggressive behavior are with the G2 parents' aggressiveness later in life at age 19, 30, and 48 (i.e., during the early child-rearing years). These results are consistent with the concept that characteristically aggressive personalities are influenced by predisposing genetic and biological factors modified by learning experiences during the early child-rearing years, whereas the emergence of adult aggressive behaviors is influenced more by the child-rearing environment in which the offspring develops. The highest correlations with G3s' aggressive personality around age 18 is with the parents' age 30 aggressiveness for both genders 18 years earlier. However, the highest correlations with G3s' physically aggressive behavior around age 18 is with the parents' concurrent age 48 aggressiveness.

These specific relations are illustrated in more detail in Figure 7.1, which displays the mean aggression scores for the offspring of G2 parents who scored low (i.e., < 25th percentile), medium, or high (i.e., > 75th percentile) on aggression concurrently at age 48 or 18 years earlier at age 30. The effects

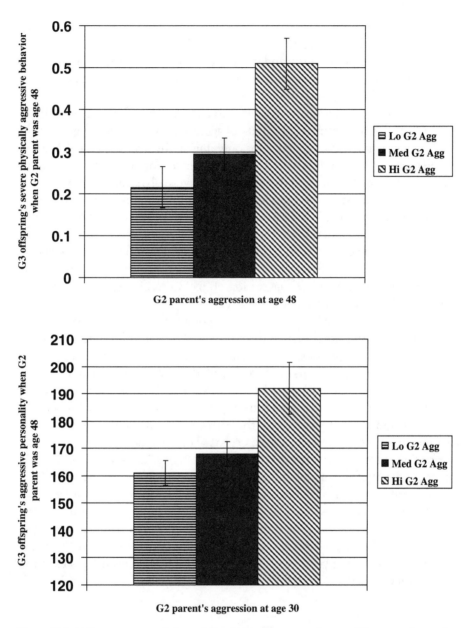

Figure 7.1. In the upper panel, the relation between a parent's age-48 aggression and their offspring's concurrent severe physical aggression when the offspring averaged 18 years of age, $F(2, 312) = 11.7$, $p < .001$. In the lower panel, the relation between a parent's age-30 aggression and their offspring's aggressive personality 18 years later (i.e., when the offspring averaged 18 years of age), $F(2, 113) = 6.24$, $p < .01$. G3 aggression is low if G2 is below the 25th percentile, medium if G2 is between the 25th to 75th percentile, and high if G2 is above the 75th percentile.

are significant and illustrate that it is the offspring of parents who were above the 75th percentile on aggression at age 30 who are most at risk of developing an aggressive personality, and it is the offspring of parents who are above the 75th percentile on aggression at age 48 who are most at risk of being seriously physically aggressive around age 18.

Given these relations, we decided to test a model of cross-generational transmission that combines continuity of aggression within the G2 generation with transmission across generations only during the age 30 to age 48 period when the G3 child is being reared. The model incorporated both the measure of aggressive personality and the measure of severe physical aggression. This two-generational structural model for continuity of aggression is shown in the left panel of Figure 7.2. The model assumes that the only path from generation G2 to generation G3 is the path from the aggression of the G2 parent at age 30 to the aggression of the child 18 years later. The model fits the data well with a nonsignificant chi-square statistic and other reasonable goodness-of-fit statistics. The path from G2 aggression at age 30 to G3 aggression 18 years later is a highly significant and large effect.

We next expanded the model to incorporate all three generations we had studied. The results are shown in the right panel of Figure 7.2. Unfortunately, our only good measure of G1's aggression is the individual's tendency to hit G2 when G2 was age 8. This measure is related to G2s' aggression, but it probably represents G2s' tendency to behave badly as well; thus, the path relating it to G2s' aggression at the same time is bidirectional. Still, the model fits the data well, and the best estimates of the path coefficients for the model suggest a total cross-generational effect from G1 to G3 of .15. Adding a path from G2s' aggression at age 48 directly to G3s' concurrent aggression did not significantly improve the fit of the model, indicating that the strong relation between G2s' age 48 aggression and G3s' concurrent severe physical aggression (see Table 7.1 and Figure 7.1) is a consequence of the stability of G2s' aggression through the child-rearing years. Thus, the estimated path coefficients are consistent with the concept that aggression is transmitted across generations primarily during the child-rearing years, with genetic and biological influences exerting long-term effects through within-generation continuity.

SUMMARY

In this chapter, we argued that cross-generational continuity in aggressiveness is undoubtedly the product of four factors: biological predispositions that are inherited by offspring, continuity in environment across generations, and conditioning and observational learning experienced by the child. We elaborated a model that takes into consideration all of these factors, and

Continuity of Aggression Over 40 Years Across 2 Generations

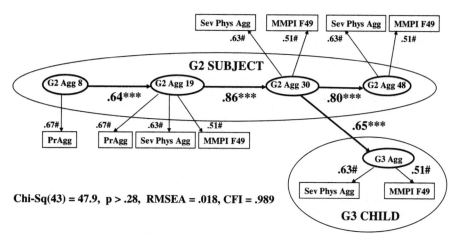

Chi-Sq(43) = 47.9, p > .28, RMSEA = .018, CFI = .989

Continuity of Aggression Over 40 Years Across 3 Generations

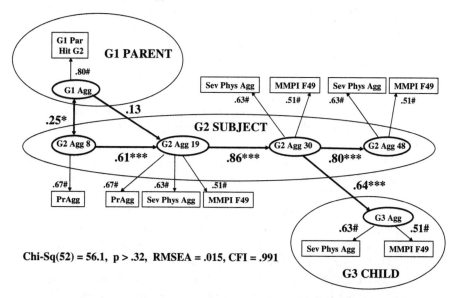

Chi-Sq(52) = 56.1, p > .32, RMSEA = .015, CFI = .991

Figure 7.2. In the upper panel, the continuity of aggression over 40 years across 2 generations (G2 and G3). X^2 (43) = 47.9, p > .28, RMSEA = .018, Cumulative Fit Index = .99. In the lower panel, the continuity of aggression over 40 years across 3 generations (G1, G2, and G3). X^2 (52) = 56.1, p > .32, RMSEA = .015, Goodness of Fit Index = .991. # indicates that the measurement parameter was fixed at the value estimated in the within-generation model. Correlated errors were specified for the same measures across ages. PrAgg = peer nominated aggression; Sev Phys Agg = severe physical aggression; MMPI F49 = the sum of scales F, 4, and 9 on the Minnesota Multiphasic Personality Inventory; G1 Par Hit G2 = the amount of hitting of G2 child at age 8 by the G1 parents; G2 Agg 'n' = G2's composite aggression score at age 'n'. *p<.05 **p<.01 ***p<.001.

we applied it to data from a three-generation longitudinal study. The data showed significant cross-generational continuity including significant relations between an offspring's aggressive behavior as an adult and their parents' aggressive behaviors in both childhood and during the time the child was being raised. A model fits the data well in which the cross-generational effects across two and three generations are mostly mediated by the parent's aggression during the child-rearing period.

REFERENCES

Anderson, C. A., & Huesmann, L. R. (2003). Human aggression: A social–cognitive view. In M. Hogg & J. Cooper (Eds.), *Handbook of social psychology* (pp. 296–323). London, England: Sage.

Bandura, A. (1977). *Social learning theory.* Englewood Cliffs, NJ: Prentice Hall.

Bergman, L. R., & Andershed, A. (2009). Predictors and outcomes of persistent or age-limited registered criminal behavior: A 30-year longitudinal study of a Swedish urban population. *Aggressive Behavior, 35,* 164–178. doi:10.1002/ab.20298

Broidy, L. M., Nagin, D. S., Tremblay, R. E., Bates, J. E., Brame, B., Dodge, K. A., . . . Vitaro, F. (2003). Developmental trajectories of childhood disruptive behaviors and adolescent delinquency: A six-site, cross-national study. *Developmental Psychology, 39,* 222–245. doi:10.1037/0012-1649.39.2.222

Cairns, R. B., Cairns, B. D., Xie, H., Leung, M. C., & Hearne, S. (1998). Paths across generations: Academic competence and aggressive behaviors in young mothers and their children. *Developmental Psychology, 34,* 1162–1174. doi:10.1037/0012-1649.34.6.1162

Capaldi, D. M., & Clark, S. (1998). Prospective family predictors of aggression toward female partners for at-risk young men. *Developmental Psychology, 34,* 1175–1188. doi:10.1037/0012-1649.34.6.1175

Capaldi, D. M., Pears, K. C., Patterson, G. R., & Owen, L. D. (2003). Continuity of parenting practices across generations in an at-risk sample: A prospective comparison of direct and mediated associations. *Journal of Abnormal Child Psychology, 31,* 127–142. doi:10.1023/A:1022518123387

Caspi, A., McClay, J., Moffitt, T. E., Mill, J., Martin, J., Craig, I. W., . . . Poulton, R. (2002, August). Role of genotype in the cycle of violence in maltreated children. *Science, 297,* 851–854. doi:10.1126/science.1072290

Caspi, A., Sugden, K., Moffitt, T. E., Taylor, A., Craig, I. W., Harrington, H., . . . Poulton, R. (2003, July). Influence of life stress on depression: Moderation by a polymorphism in the 5-HTT gene. *Science, 301,* 386–389. doi:10.1126/science.1083968

Cicchetti, D., Ackerman, B. P., & Izard, C. E. (1995). Emotions and emotion regulation in developmental psychopathology. *Development and Psychopathology, 7,* 1–10. doi:10.1017/S0954579400006301

Cloninger, C. R., & Gottesman, I. I. (1987). Genetic and environmental factors in antisocial behavior disorders. In S. A. Mednick, T. E. Moffitt, & S. A. Stack (Eds.), *The causes of crime: New biological approaches* (pp. 92–109). New York, NY: Cambridge University Press.

Conger, R. D., Neppl, T., Kim, K. J., & Scaramella, L. (2003). Angry and aggressive behavior across three generations: A prospective, longitudinal study of parents and children. *Journal of Abnormal Child Psychology, 31*, 143–160. doi:10.1023/A:1022570107457

Constantino, J. N. (1996). Intergenerational aspects of the development of aggression: A preliminary report. *Journal of Developmental and Behavioral Pediatrics, 17*, 176–182. doi:10.1097/00004703-199606000-00006

Deater-Deckard, K., & Plomin, R. (1999). An adoption study of the etiology of teacher and parent reports of externalizing behavior problems in middle childhood. *Child Development, 70*, 144–154. doi:10.1111/1467-8624.00011

Dodge, K. A. (1982). Social cognition and children's aggressive behavior. *Child Development, 53*, 620–635. doi:10.2307/1129373

Dubow, E. F., Huesmann, L. R., & Boxer, P. (2003). Theoretical and methodological considerations in cross-generational research on parenting and child aggressive behavior. *Journal of Abnormal Child Psychology, 31*, 185–192. doi:10.1023/A:1022526325204

Duncan, G. J. (2002). The PSID and me. In E. Phelps, F. F. Furstenberg, & A. Colby (Eds.), *Looking at lives: American longitudinal studies of the twentieth century* (pp. 133–166). New York, NY: Russell Sage Foundation.

Eisenberg, N., Cumberland, A., & Spinrad, T. L. (1998). Parental socialization of emotion. *Psychological Inquiry, 9*, 241–273. doi:10.1207/s15327965pli0904_1

Farrington, D. P. (2003). Key results from the first forty years of the Cambridge Study in delinquent development. In T. P. Thornberry & M. D. Krohn (Eds.), *Taking stock of delinquency: An overview of findings from contemporary longitudinal studies* (pp. 137–183). New York, NY: Kluwer/Plenum.

Farrington, D. P., Ttofi, M. M., & Coid, J. W. (2009). Development of adolescence-limited, late-onset, and persistent offenders from age 8 to age 48. *Aggressive Behavior, 35*, 150–163. doi:10.1002/ab.20296

Flouri, E., & Buchanan, A. (2002). What predicts good relationships with parents in adolescence and partners in adult life: Findings from the 1958 British birth cohort. *Journal of Family Psychology, 16*, 186–198. doi:10.1037/0893-3200.16.2.186

Frick, P. J., & Morris, A. (2004). Temperament and developmental pathways to conduct problems. *Journal of Clinical Child and Adolescent Psychology, 33*, 54–68. doi:10.1207/S15374424JCCP3301_6

Gallese, V., Fadiga, L., Fogassi, L., & Rizzolatti, G. (1996). Action recognition in the premotor cortex. *Brain, 119*, 593–609. doi:10.1093/brain/119.2.593

Hathaway, S. R., & McKinley, J. C. (1940). *The MMPI manual*. New York, NY: Psychological Corporation.

Helson, R., Jones, C., & Kwan, V. S. Y. (2002). Personality change over 40 years of adulthood: Hierarchical linear modeling analyses of two longitudinal samples. *Journal of Personality and Social Psychology, 83*, 752–766. doi:10.1037/0022-3514.83.3.752

Higgins, E. T., & Parsons, J. E. (1983). Social cognition and the social life of the child: Stages as subcultures. In E. T. Higgins, D. W. Ruble, & W. W. Hartup (Eds.), *Social cognition and social behavior: Developmental issues* (pp. 15–62). New York, NY: Cambridge University Press.

Hops, H., Davis, B., Leve, C., & Sheeber, L. (2003). Cross-generational transmission of aggressive parent behavior: A prospective, mediational examination. *Journal of Abnormal Child Psychology, 31*, 161–169. doi:10.1023/A:1022522224295

Huesmann, L. R. (1988). An information processing model for the development of aggression. *Aggressive Behavior, 14*, 13–24.

Huesmann, L. R. (1998). The role of social information processing and cognitive schema in the acquisition and maintenance of habitual aggressive behavior. In R. G. Geen & E. Donnerstein (Eds.), *Human aggression: Theories, research, and implications for social policy* (pp. 73–109). San Diego, CA: Academic Press.

Huesmann, L. R., Dubow, E. F., Eron, L. D., & Boxer, P. (2006). Middle childhood family-contextual and personal factors as predictors of adult outcomes. In A. C. Huston & M. N. Ripke (Eds.), *Developmental contexts in middle childhood: Bridges to adolescence and adulthood* (pp. 62–86). New York, NY: Cambridge University Press. doi:10.1017/CBO9780511499760.005

Huesmann, L. R., Dubow, E. F., & Boxer, P. (2009). Continuity of aggression from childhood to early adulthood as a predictor of life outcomes: Implications for the adolescent-limited and life-course-persistent models. *Aggressive Behavior, 35*, 136–149. doi:10.1002/ab.20300

Huesmann, L. R., Eron, L. D., & Dubow, E. F. (2002). Childhood predictors of adult criminality: Are all risk factors reflected in childhood aggressiveness? *Criminal Behaviour and Mental Health, 12*, 185–208. doi:10.1002/cbm.496

Huesmann, L. R., Eron, L. D., Lefkowitz, M. M., & Walder, L. O. (1984). The stability of aggression over time and generations. *Developmental Psychology, 20*, 1120–1134. doi:10.1037/0012-1649.20.6.1120

Huesmann, L. R., & Guerra, N. G. (1997). Children's normative beliefs about aggression and aggressive behavior. *Journal of Personality and Social Psychology, 72*, 408–419. doi:10.1037/0022-3514.72.2.408

Huesmann, L. R., & Kirwil, L. (2007). Why observing violence increases the risk of violent behavior in the observer. In D. J. Flannery, A. T. Vazsonyi, & I. D. Waldman (Eds.), *The Cambridge handbook of violent behavior and aggression* (pp. 545–570). Cambridge, England: Cambridge University Press.

Hurley, S., & Chater, N. (Eds.). (2005). *Perspectives on imitation: From neuroscience to social science*. Cambridge, MA: The MIT Press.

Knoblich, G., & King, R. (1992). Biological correlates of criminal behavior. In J. McCord (Ed.), *Advances in criminological theory* (Vol. 3, pp. 1–21). New Brunswick, NJ: Transaction.

Kokko, K., & Pulkkinen, L. (2000). Aggression in childhood and long-term unemployment in adulthood: A cycle of maladaptation and some protective factors. *Developmental Psychology, 36,* 463–472. doi:10.1037/0012-1649.36.4.463

Kokko, K., Pulkkinen, L., Huesmann, L. R., Dubow, E. F., & Boxer, P. (2009). Intensity of aggression in childhood as a predictor of different forms of adult aggression: A two-country (Finland and United States) analysis. *Journal of Research on Adolescence, 19,* 9–34. doi:10.1111/j.1532-7795.2009.00579.x

Loeber, R., & Dishion, T. (1983). Early predictors of male delinquency: A review. *Psychological Bulletin, 94,* 68–99. doi:10.1037/0033-2909.94.1.68

MacEwen, K. E. (1994). Refining the intergenerational transmission hypothesis. *Journal of Interpersonal Violence, 9,* 350–365. doi:10.1177/088626094009003005

Meltzoff, A. N. (2007). Like me: A foundation for social cognition. *Developmental Science, 10,* 226–134. doi:10.1111/j.1467-7687.2007.00574.x

Mednick, S. A., Gabrielli, W. F., Jr., & Hutchings, B. (1984, May). Genetic influences in criminal convictions: Evidence from an adoption cohort. *Science, 224,* 891–894. doi:10.1126/science.6719119

Meltzoff, A. N., & Moore, M. K. (1983). Newborn infants imitate adult facial gestures. *Child Development, 54,* 702–709. doi:10.2307/1130058

Miles, D. R., & Carey, G. (1997). Genetic and environmental architecture of human aggression. *Journal of Personality and Social Psychology, 72,* 207–217. doi:10.1037/0022-3514.72.1.207

Moffitt, T. E. (1993). Adolescence-limited and life-course-persistent antisocial behavior: A developmental taxonomy. *Psychological Review, 100,* 674–701. doi:10.1037/0033-295X.100.4.674

Munafò, M. R., Clark, T. G., Moore, L. R., Payne, E., Walton, R., & Flint, J. (2003). Genetic polymorphisms and personality in healthy adults: A systematic review and meta-analysis. *Molecular Psychiatry, 8,* 471–484. doi:10.1038/sj.mp.4001326

Olweus, D. (1979). The stability of aggressive reaction patterns in males: A review. *Psychological Bulletin, 86,* 852–875. doi:10.1037/0033-2909.86.4.852

Olweus, D., Mattsson, A., Schaling, D., & Loew, H. (1988). Circulating testosterone levels and aggression in adolescent males: A causal analysis. *Psychosomatic Medicine, 50,* 261–272.

Patterson, G. R. (1986). Performance models for antisocial boys. *American Psychologist, 41,* 432–444. doi:10.1037/0003-066X.41.4.432

Pulkkinen, L., Lyyra, A.-L., & Kokko, K. (2009). Life success of males on nonoffender, adolescence-limited, persistent, and adult-onset antisocial pathways: Follow-up from age 8 to 42. *Aggressive Behavior, 35,* 117–135. doi:10.1002/ab.20297

Pulkkinen, L., Nygren, H., & Kokko, K. (2002). Successful development: Childhood antecedents of adaptive psychosocial functioning in adulthood. *Journal of Adult Development, 9,* 251–265. doi:10.1023/A:1020234926608

Raine, A., Brennan, P., & Mednick, S. A. (1995). Birth complications combined with early maternal rejection at age 1 year predispose to violent crime at age

18 years. *Obstetrical & Gynecological Survey, 50*, 775–776. doi:10.1097/00006254-199511000-00010

Raine, A., & Jones, F. (1987). Attention, autonomic arousal, and personality in behaviorally disordered children. *Journal of Abnormal Child Psychology, 15*, 583–599. doi:10.1007/BF00917243

Rönkä, A., Oravala, S., & Pulkkinen, L. (2002). "I met this wife of mine and things got on a better track": Turning points in risk development. *Journal of Adolescence, 25*, 47–63. doi:10.1006/jado.2001.0448

Rutter, M. (1996). Transitions and turning points in developmental psychopathology: As applied to the age span between childhood and mid-adulthood. *International Journal of Behavioral Development, 19*, 603–626. doi:10.1080/016502596385712

Rutter, M. (1998). Some research considerations on intergenerational continuities and discontinuities: Comment on the special section. *Developmental Psychology, 34*, 1269–1273. doi:10.1037/0012-1649.34.6.1269

Sameroff, A. J. (1983). Developmental systems: Contexts and evolution. In W. Kessen (Ed.), *Handbook of child psychology: Vol. 1. History, theory, and methods* (pp. 237–294). New York, NY: Wiley.

Sameroff, A. J., Seifer, R., Baldwin, A., & Baldwin, C. (1993). Stability of intelligence from preschool to adolescence: The influence of social and family risk factors. *Child Development, 64*, 80–97. doi:10.2307/1131438

Serbin, L. A., Cooperman, J. M., Peters, P. L., Lehoux, P. M., Stack, D. M., & Schwartzman, A. E. (1998). Intergenerational transfer of psychosocial risk in women with childhood histories of aggression, withdrawal, or aggression and withdrawal. *Developmental Psychology, 34*, 1246–1262. doi:10.1037/0012-1649.34.6.1246

Shaw, D. S. (2003). Advancing our understanding of intergenerational continuity in antisocial behavior. *Journal of Abnormal Child Psychology, 31*, 193–199. doi:10.1023/A:1022578309274

Smith, C. A., & Farrington, D. P. (2004). Continuities in antisocial behavior and parenting across three generations. *Journal of Child Psychology and Psychiatry, 43*, 230–247.

Thornberry, T. P., Freeman-Gallant, A., Lizotte, A. J., Krohn, M., & Smith, C. A. (2003). Linked lives: The intergenerational transmission of antisocial behavior. *Journal of Abnormal Child Psychology, 31*, 171–184. doi:10.1023/A:1022574208366

Werner, E. E. (2002). Looking for trouble in paradise: Some lessons learned from the Kauai longitudinal study. In E. Phelps, F. F. Furstenberg, & A. Colby (Eds.), *Looking at lives: American longitudinal studies of the twentieth century* (pp. 297–314). New York, NY: Russell Sage Foundation.

8

GENETIC AND ENVIRONMENTAL INFLUENCES ON AGGRESSION

SOO HYUN RHEE AND IRWIN D. WALDMAN

Considerable research has been conducted on the etiology of aggression and antisocial behavior, and it has relied on many different theoretical and empirical approaches. Of these, behavior genetic methods have the advantages of testing competing alternative etiological models and of clearly distinguishing genetic from environmental influences and estimating their relative magnitudes. More than 100 twin and adoption studies of antisocial behavior have been published, which led us (Rhee & Waldman, 2002) to conduct a meta-analysis of twin and adoption studies of antisocial behavior in general and several specific operationalizations of antisocial behavior, including aggression.

The role of familial influences on antisocial behavior has been studied extensively. Dysfunctional familial influences, such as parental psychopathology (e.g., Robins, 1966), coercive parenting styles (e.g., Patterson, Reid, & Dishion, 1992), physical abuse (Dodge, Bates, & Pettit, 1990), and family

---

This work was supported in part by NIDA DA-13956 to Soo Hyun Rhee and NIMH MH-01818 to Irwin D. Waldman. Earlier versions of this chapter were presented at the meeting of the American Society of Criminology in 1996 and the meeting of the Behavior Genetics Association in 1997, and a more extensive version has been published in *Psychological Bulletin, 128*, pp. 490–529.

conflict (e.g., Norland, Shover, Thornton, & James, 1979), are significantly associated with antisocial behavior. Often, these variables are considered to be environmental influences, and the possibility that they may also reflect genetic influences is not considered. This is unfortunate because disentangling the influences of nature and nurture is the first step toward reaching the eventual goal of explaining the specific etiology of antisocial behavior (see Chapter 7, this volume). Also, estimating the relative magnitude of genetic and environmental influences on antisocial behavior is an important step in the search for specific candidate genes and environmental risk factors underlying antisocial behavior. Although it is not possible to disentangle genetic from environmental influences in family studies because genetic and environmental influences are confounded in nuclear families, twin and adoption studies have the unique ability to disentangle genetic and environmental influences and to estimate the magnitude of both simultaneously.

Twin studies can disentangle genetic and environmental influences on a trait by comparing the similarity between monozygotic (MZ) twin pairs, who are genetically identical, with the similarity between dizygotic (DZ) twin pairs, who share 50% of their genes, on average. Traits with genetic influences will show greater similarity between MZ twins than between DZ twins. Adoption studies demonstrate (a) genetic influences on a trait if there is a significant correlation between the trait in adoptees and their biological relatives and (b) environmental influences if there is a significant correlation between the trait in adoptees and their adoptive parents or siblings.

In this chapter, we address the specific question of the magnitude of genetic and environmental influences on aggression (see also Chapters 7 and 9) and explore how the pattern and magnitude of these influences compare with those on antisocial behavior in general. In the twin and adoption studies reviewed here, aggression is usually studied as a personality characteristic and assessed with such measures as the Adjective Checklist (Gough & Heilbrun, 1972) and the Multidimensional Personality Questionnaire (as cited in Tellegen et al., 1988). The operationalizations of aggression have been diverse, ranging from reports of negative affect (Partanen, Bruun, & Markkanen, 1966) to observations of the number of times a child hits a Bobo doll (Plomin, Foch, & Rowe, 1981). For the present review, the operationalization of aggression was restricted to behavior that meets the *Diagnostic and Statistical Manual of Mental Disorders* (4th ed.; American Psychiatric Association, 1994) criteria for conduct disorder (e.g., bullying, initiating physical fights, using a weapon that can cause serious physical harm). Toward the end of the chapter, we qualitatively review the emerging behavior genetic literature on specific forms of aggression in children, including reactive, proactive, and relational aggression. We also briefly describe the burgeoning molecular genetic literature examining the association of aggression with relevant candidate genes.

META-ANALYSIS OF BEHAVIOR GENETIC
STUDIES OF AGGRESSION

We began our search for twin and adoption studies of aggression by examining the PsycINFO and Medline databases. The search terms used in this process were *aggressive, aggression, crime, criminality, delinquent,* or *delinquency* in combination with the terms *twin(s), adoptee(s), adoptive, genetic, genetics, genes, environmental,* and *environment.* We examined the references cited in research articles and review articles found in the search process, to locate any additional studies that might have been missed or published before the databases were established.

Inclusion Criteria

After excluding unsuitable studies according to the criteria described later (i.e., construct validity, inability to calculate tetrachoric or intraclass correlations, and assessment of related disorders) and addressing the problem of nonindependence in these studies, 14 studies examining aggression remained. Table 8.1 lists the behavior genetic studies examining aggression included in the meta-analysis. Also listed are the method of assessment and method of zygosity determination (in twin studies) used in each study, the mean or median age of the sample, the sex of the participants, the number of pairs, the relationship of the pairs, and the effect sizes.

Construct Validity

Studies examining aggression were included if they examined behavioral aggression (e.g., physical fighting, cruelty to animals, bullying). Studies that examined other related variables, such as anger, hostility, or impulsivity, were not included because it was not clear whether they examined aggression or some related but distinct trait. An additional study (Partanen et al., 1966) was excluded because the aggression items used by the authors (e.g., "Are you readily insulted?" and "Do you easily become unhappy about even small things?") suggested that negative affect or anger, rather than aggression per se, was being assessed.

Inability to Calculate Tetrachoric or Intraclass Correlations

The effect sizes used in this meta-analysis were the Pearson product-moment or intraclass correlations that were reported in the studies, or the tetrachoric correlations that were estimated from the concordances or percentages reported in the studies. These effect sizes were analyzed using model-fitting programs that estimate the relative contribution of genetic and environmental influences and test the fit of alternative etiological models.

TABLE 8.1
Effect Sizes for Behavior Genetic Studies Examining Aggression

Study	Assessment	Zygosity	Age	Sex	N	Relationship	Effect size
Midwest twins (Cates, Houston, Vavak, Crawford, & Uttley, 1993)	Self-report	Blood grouping/ questionnaire	42.50	F–F	77	MZ	.07 (assault)
					21	DZ	.41 (assault)
					77	MZ	.41 (verbal)
					21	DZ	.06 (verbal)
					77	MZ	.40 (indirect)
					21	DZ	.01 (indirect)
California twins (Ghodsian-Carpey & Baker, 1987)	Parent report	Questionnaire	5.20	Both–both	21	MZ	.78
					17	DZ	.31
London twins (adults, 1970s; Wilson, Rust, & Kasriel, 1977)	Reaction to stimuli		30.50	Both–both	49	MZ	.59
					52	DZ	.34
London twins (adults, 1980s; Rushton, Fulker, Neale, Nias, & Eysenck, 1986)	Self-report	Blood grouping/ questionnaire	30.00	M–M	90	MZ	.33
					46	DZ	.16
				F–F	206	MZ	.43
					133	DZ	.00
				M–F	98	DZ	.12
Minnesota twins (reared together, 1970s; Tellegen et al., 1988)	Self-report	Blood grouping	21.65	Both–both	217	MZ	.43
					114	DZ	.14
Minnesota twins (1990s, adults; Finkel & McGue, 1997)	Self-report	Blood grouping/ questionnaire	37.76	M–M	220	MZ	.37
					165	DZ	.12
				F–F	406	MZ	.39
					352	DZ	.14
				M–F	114	DZ	.12

Study	Rater	Measure	Age	Sex	N	Zygosity	r
Boston twins (children; Scarr, 1966)	Parent report	Blood grouping	8.08	F–F	24	MZ	.35
					28	DZ	-.08
Philadelphia twins (Meininger, Hayman, Coates, & Gallagher, 1988)	Teacher report	Blood grouping	8.50	Both–both	61	MZ	.67
					34	DZ	.11
Missouri twins (Owen & Sines, 1970)	Reaction to stimuli	Blood grouping	10.00	M–M	10	MZ	.09
					11	DZ	-.24
				F–F	11	MZ	.58
					13	DZ	.22
Colorado twins (1980s; Plomin, Foch, & Rowe, 1981)	Objective test	Questionnaire	7.60	Both–both	53	MZ	.42
					32	DZ	.42
California twins (Rahe, Hervig, & Rosenman, 1978)	Self-report	Blood grouping	48.00	M–M	82	MZ	.31
					79	DZ	.21
British Columbia twins (Blanchard, Vernon, & Harris, 1995)	Self-report	Blood grouping	36.18	Both–both	96	MZ	.59
					48	DZ	.34
Dutch twins (van den Oord, Verhulst, & Boomsma, 1996)	Parent report	Blood grouping (questionnaire)	3.00	M–M	210	MZ	.81
					265	DZ	.49
				F–F	236	MZ	.83
					238	DZ	.49
				M–F	409	DZ	.45
Swedish Twins (adults; Gustavsson, Pedersen, Åsberg, & Schalling, 1996)	Self-report			Both–both	15	MZ ra	.22 (indirect)
					26	MZ	.41 (indirect)
					29	DZ	.27 (indirect)
					15	MZ ra	-.03 (verbal)
					26	MZ	.22 (verbal)
					29	DZ	.23 (verbal)

Note. M = male; F = female; Both = both male and female; MZ = monozygotic twin pairs; DZ = dyzygotic twin pairs; MZ ra = monzygotic twin pairs reared apart.

Nonindependent Samples

Another justification for exclusion from the meta-analysis was nonindependent sampling. Several effect sizes from studies in the original reference list were based on nonindependent samples because researchers examined more than one dependent measure of antisocial behavior in their sample or published follow-up data from the same sample in separate publications. Several suggestions for dealing with nonindependent samples have been offered in the meta-analytic literature (Mullen, 1989; Rosenthal, 1991). For example, Mullen (1989) gave four options for dealing with this problem: choosing the best dependent measure, averaging the effect sizes of the different dependent measures, conducting separate meta-analyses for each of the dependent measures, or using nonindependent samples as if they were independent samples (the least recommended approach). We did not follow the option of choosing the best dependent measure unless one of the dependent measures did not fulfill the inclusion criteria described previously, making the decision easy. Taking this option would have required making subjective choices because we were aware of the effect sizes associated with each of the dependent measures. The option of conducting separate meta-analyses for each of the dependent measures was not chosen simply because it was impractical: There were many effect sizes from nonindependent samples. The most practical and prudent option was to average the effect sizes from nonindependent samples.

Given that model-fitting analyses require specification of the sample size, we used the option of averaging multiple effect sizes in cases where the sample size was identical across the nonindependent samples. If the sample size was not identical across the nonindependent samples, we used the effect size from the largest sample. More specifically, in cases of nonindependence where the same dependent measure was used in the same sample multiple times (e.g., in follow-up analyses), we chose the effect size estimated from the largest sample. In cases of nonindependence in which different dependent measures were used in the same sample (e.g., when the author of one publication examined more than one dependent measure or authors of different publications examined different dependent measures in one sample), the effect sizes were averaged if the sample size was the same across the nonindependent samples, and the effect size from the largest sample was used if the sample size differed across the nonindependent samples.

Determination of Effect Sizes

Some adoption and twin studies used a continuous variable to measure antisocial behavior and reported either Pearson product-moment or intraclass correlations, which were the effect sizes used from these studies in the meta-analysis. In other studies, a dichotomous variable was used, and concordances, percentages, or a contingency table (including the number of twin pairs with both members affected, one member affected, and neither member affected) were reported. The information from the concordances or percentages was transformed into a contingency table, which was then used to estimate the tetrachoric correlation (i.e., the correlation between the latent continuous variables that are assumed to underlie the observed dichotomous variables), which was the effect size used in the meta-analysis. For some studies, we directly estimated the tetrachoric correlation from the raw data because it had to be estimated from contingency tables. For these studies, we were also able to estimate the weight matrix (i.e., the asymptotic covariance matrix of the correlation matrix). If the weight matrix can be estimated, it is possible to use weighted least squares estimation in the model-fitting analyses, which is more appropriate for nonnormally distributed variables (e.g., diagnoses) than maximum likelihood estimation.

Model-Fitting Analyses

The magnitude of additive and nonadditive genetic influences (a^2 and d^2) constitutes the proportion of variance in the liability for aggression that is due to genetic differences among individuals. If genetic influences are additive, the effects of alleles from different loci are independent and "add up" to influence the liability underlying a trait. If genetic influences are nonadditive, the alleles interact with each other to influence the liability for a trait, either at a single genetic locus (i.e., dominance) or at different loci (i.e., epistasis). Many studies report the magnitude of additive and nonadditive genetic influences combined, and this estimate of broad-sense heritability is symbolized by h^2. Shared environmental influences (c^2) represent the proportion of liability variance that is due to environmental influences that are experienced in common and make family members similar to one another, whereas nonshared environmental influences (e^2) represent the proportion of liability variance that is due to environmental influences that are experienced uniquely and make family members different from one another. It is important to note that estimates of nonshared environmental influences also include measurement error.

It is customary in contemporary behavior genetic analyses to compare alternative models containing different sets of causal influences for their fit to the observed data (i.e., twin or familial correlations or covariances). These models posit that aggression is caused by the types of influences described previously: additive genetic influences (A), nonadditive genetic influences (D), shared environmental influences (C), and nonshared environmental influences (E). In the present meta-analysis, we contrasted the fit of the ACE model, the AE model, the CE model, and the ADE model. We assessed the fit of each model, as well as of competing models, using both the chi-square statistic and the Akaike information criterion (AIC), a fit index that reflects both the fit of the model and its parsimony (Loehlin, 1992). The AIC has been used extensively in both the structural equation modeling and behavior genetic literatures. Among competing models, that with the lowest AIC and the lowest χ^2 relative to its degrees of freedom is considered to be the best-fitting model.

Unfortunately, it is not possible to estimate c^2 and d^2 simultaneously or test an ACDE model with data only from twin pairs reared together because the estimation of c^2 and d^2 both rely on the same information (i.e., the difference between the MZ and DZ twin correlations). If the DZ correlation is greater than half the MZ correlation, the ACE model is the correct model, and the estimate of d^2 in the ADE model is always zero. If the DZ correlation is less than half the MZ correlation, however, the ADE model is the correct model, and the estimate of c^2 in the ACE model is always zero.

Meta-Analytic Findings

The ACE model was the best-fitting model for aggression ($a^2 = .44$, $c^2 = .06$, $e^2 = .50$), although the fit of this model was close to that of the AE model, and the magnitude of shared environmental influences on aggression is modest. Models that included nonadditive genetic influences instead of shared environmental influences or that omitted additive genetic influences fit less well. By comparison, in our omnibus meta-analysis of behavior genetic studies of antisocial behavior there were moderate additive genetic ($a^2 = .32$), nonadditive genetic ($d^2 = .09$), shared environmental ($c^2 = .16$), and nonshared environmental ($e^2 = .43$) influences. These results suggest that the magnitude of genetic and nonshared environmental influences is slightly higher for aggression than for antisocial behavior in general and that evidence for the role of shared environmental influences on aggression is at best tentative pending future studies.

New Directions in Behavior Genetic Studies of Aggression

Unfortunately, we were unable to examine a meaningful distinction between overt and relational aggression (Crick, Casa, & Mosher, 1997; Crick & Grotpeter, 1995) because there are no published twin or adoption studies of relational aggression. Overt aggression harms others through physical damage or the threat thereof, whereas relational aggression harms others by damaging their peer relationships or reputation (e.g., spreading rumors, excluding them from a peer group). Although relational aggression does not physically harm the victims, it has serious consequences for both the aggressors (e.g., higher levels of loneliness, depression, and negative self-perceptions, as well as concurrent and future peer rejection; Crick & Grotpeter, 1995) and the victims (e.g., depression, anxiety; Crick & Grotpeter, 1996). The distinction between overt and relational aggression is especially important when examining sex differences in aggression and its causes, given that females are significantly more relationally aggressive and less overtly aggressive than males (Crick & Grotpeter, 1995; Crick et al., 1997). Given the evidence that overt and relational aggression are correlated but distinct (Crick et al., 1997), behavior genetic studies are necessary to determine the degree of genetic and environmental influences that are common to both overt and relational aggression rather than being specific to each.

Similarly, few behavior genetic studies have distinguished between reactive and proactive aggression (Dodge, Lochman, Harnish, Bates, & Pettit, 1997; Vitaro, Brendgen, & Tremblay, 2002; Waschbusch, Willoughby, & Pelham, 1998). *Reactive aggression* is characterized by impulsive "hot-blooded" anger, appears to be a response to frustration or perceived threat, and is associated with lack of self-control. In contrast, *proactive aggression* is premeditated and "cold-blooded," less emotional, and more likely to be driven by expected rewards (Dodge et al., 1997). Evidence suggests that reactively and proactively aggressive children differ in developmental histories, adjustment, and social information-processing patterns and that reactive and proactive aggression are distinct (Dodge et al., 1997; Vitaro et al., 2002; see also Chapter 9, this volume). Therefore, behavior genetic studies of antisocial behavior should distinguish between reactive and proactive aggression, and multivariate studies should examine the etiology of the overlap between different forms of antisocial behavior. Genetically informative studies of aggression have recently made important strides along these lines. In addition, several behavior genetic studies examining the development of aggression have been conducted.

The Overlap Between Different Forms of Aggression

Two genetically informative studies have examined the common and unique etiologies of proactive and reactive aggression, with differing results. Brendgen, Vitaro, Boivin, Dionne, and Pérusse (2006) examined the association between proactive and reactive aggression in a sample of 172 six-year-old twin pairs from Quebec. The magnitude of genetic influences was similar for proactive ($h^2 = .41$, $e^2 = .59$) and reactive aggression ($h^2 = .39$, $e^2 = .61$). The correlation between proactive and reactive aggression ranged from .51 to .60 in this sample, with the correlation between genetic influences on the two types of aggression being .87, and the correlation between nonshared environmental influences being .34. Brendgen et al. (2006) also found that most of the association between proactive and reactive aggression was due to common etiological factors influencing physical aggression.

The second study examining proactive and reactive aggression was Baker, Raine, Liu, and Jacobson's (2008) study of 1,219 nine- to 10-year-old twins from southern California. Results were presented separately for child, mother, and teacher report, because the correlation between these sources was low (.18 to .26). Baker et al. found a significant sex difference in the magnitude of genetic and environmental influences on aggression according to child reports, such that moderate genetic influences were present for boys but not girls, whereas moderate shared environmental influences were present for girls but not boys (boys: $h^2 = .38$ and $e^2 = .62$ for reactive aggression and $h^2 = .50$ and $e^2 = .50$ for proactive aggression; girls: $c^2 = .36$ and $e^2 = .64$ for reactive aggression and $c^2 = .14$ and $e^2 = .86$ for proactive aggression). In contrast, no differences were found for mother reports ($h^2 = .26$, $c^2 = .27$, and $e^2 = .46$ for reactive aggression and $h^2 = .32$, $c^2 = .21$, and $e^2 = .47$ for proactive aggression) or teacher reports ($h^2 = .20$, $c^2 = .43$, and $e^2 = .37$ for reactive aggression and $h^2 = .45$, $c^2 = .14$, and $e^2 = .41$ for proactive aggression). The phenotypic correlation between proactive and reactive aggression ranged from .46 to .80. The authors suggest that both common genetic and environmental influences are responsible for this correlation, but results varied across the three sources (child report: $r_g = .57$ and $r_e = .46$ for boys, $r_c = .53$ and $r_e = .53$ for girls; mother report: $r_g = .76$, $r_c = .76$, $r_e = .43$; teacher report: $r_g = 1.0$, $r_c = 1.0$, $r_e = .53$).

As stated previously, another meaningful distinction between forms of aggression is that between overt and relational aggression (Crick & Grotpeter, 1995; Crick et al., 1997). Two recent twin studies have examined the association between relational and overt aggression. Brendgen et al. (2005) examined the association between physical aggression (i.e., overt aggression) and social aggression (i.e., relational aggression) in 234 six-year-old twin pairs from Quebec. Teacher and peer reports of physical and social aggression were obtained, and the magnitude of genetic and environmental influences was similar for the two sources (teacher report: $h^2 = .63$, $e^2 = .37$ for physical aggression; $h^2 = .20$, $c^2 = .20$, $e^2 = .60$ for social aggression; peer report: $h^2 = .54$, $e^2 = .46$ for physical aggression; $h^2 = .23$, $c^2 = .23$, $e^2 = .54$ for social aggression). The phenotypic correlation between physical and social aggression was .43 for teacher ratings and .41 for peer ratings, and there was evidence of common genetic and nonshared environmental influences on the two types of aggression (teacher report: $r_g = .79$, $r_e = .31$; peer report: $r_g = 1.0$, $r_e = .12$). Ligthart et al. (2005) examined relational versus direct (i.e., overt) aggression in 7,449 seven-year-old Dutch twin pairs. They found evidence of genetic, shared environmental, and nonshared environmental influences on both relational and direct aggression and found evidence of significant sex differences in the magnitude of genetic and environmental influences for direct aggression, such that genetic influences were stronger for girls and shared environmental influences were stronger for boys (relational aggression, boys and girls combined: $h^2 = .66$, $c^2 = .16$, $e^2 = .18$; direct aggression: $h^2 = .53$, $c^2 = .23$, $e^2 = .24$ for boys; $h^2 = .60$, $c^2 = .13$, $e^2 = .27$ for girls). The phenotypic correlation between relational and direct aggression was .58 for boys and .47 for girls, and this correlation was due to both common genetic and shared environmental influences (55% genetic, 33% shared environmental, and 12% nonshared environmental influences in boys; 58% genetic, 30% shared environmental, and 12% nonshared environmental influences in girls).

The Overlap Between Aggression and Other Types of Antisocial Behavior

Several studies have examined differences in the etiology of aggressive and nonaggressive antisocial behavior. As shown in Table 8.2, although the results from these studies are not uniform, several general conclusions can be drawn from them. First, although most studies reported similar, moderate heritabilities for both types of antisocial behavior, some studies (e.g., Eley, Lichtenstein, & Stevenson, 1999) suggest that aggressive behavior is more heritable than nonaggressive antisocial behavior. This conclusion is borne out by findings from a recent meta-analysis of 19 studies of aggressive and 15 studies of nonaggressive antisocial behavior (Burt, 2009). In this meta-analysis, the etiology of aggression included additive genetic and non-shared environmental influences but no evidence for shared environmental influences ($h^2 = .65$, $c^2 = .00$, $e^2 = .35$), whereas the etiology of nonaggressive antisocial behavior also included shared environmental influences and showed a lower magnitude of genetic influences ($h^2 = .48$, $c^2 = .18$, $e^2 = .34$).

Second, the phenotypic correlation between aggressive and nonaggressive antisocial behavior was moderate in most studies (e.g., .32 in Gelhorn et al., 2006, and .48 to .76 in Bartels et al., 2003). Third, most studies suggest that there are significant common genetic influences on the covariance between aggressive behavior and nonaggressive antisocial behavior. Fourth, there was phenotypic continuity between aggressive and nonaggressive antisocial behavior from childhood to adolescence ($r = .28$ to .61 in Eley, Lichtenstein, & Moffitt, 2003), which also had genetic influences. However, it is possible that some of this phenotypic continuity is due to shared method variance, because the correlation between aggressive behavior in childhood assessed via parent report and nonaggressive antisocial behavior in adolescent assessed via self-report was lower ($r = .07$ to .15 in Tuvblad, Eley, & Lichtenstein, 2005).

TABLE 8.2
Results of Studies Examining Aggressive and Nonaggressive Antisocial Behavior

Study	Operationalization/ Assessment	Etiology of Aggressive Behavior	Etiology of Nonaggressive Behavior	Etiology of Phenotypic Covariance
Bartels (2003)	Parent report of aggressive/ rule breaking behavior	$h^2 = .69$, $c^2 = .00$, $e^2 = .31$ (males) $h^2 = .72$, $c^2 = .00$, $e^2 = .28$ (females)	$h^2 = .79$, $c^2 = .00$, $e^2 = .21$ (males) $h^2 = .56$, $c^2 = .23$, $e^2 = .21$ (females)	$h^2 = .80$, $c^2 = .02$-.06, $e^2 = .12$-.14
Button (2004)	Self-report of aggressive and nonaggressive antisocial behavior	$h^2 = .58$-68 $c^2 = .00$-09 $e^2 = .32$-33	$h^2 = .59$-74 $c^2 = .00$-14 $e^2 = .26$-27	$h^2 = .87$, $c^2 = .00$, $e^2 = .13$
Eley (1999)	Parent report of aggressive and nonaggressive behavior	$h^2 = .55$, $c^2 = .18$, $e^2 = .27$ (Swedish males) $h^2 = .42$, $c^2 = .25$, $e^2 = .33$ (British males) $h^2 = .76$, $c^2 = .06$, $e^2 = .19$ (Swedish females) $h^2 = .71$, $c^2 = .04$, $e^2 = .25$ (British females)	$h^2 = .30$, $c^2 = .44$, $e^2 = .26$ (Swedish males) $h^2 = .13$, $c^2 = .54$, $e^2 = .32$ (British males) $h^2 = .45$, $c^2 = .34$, $e^2 = .22$ (Swedish females) $h^2 = .42$, $c^2 = .30$, $e^2 = .28$ (British females)	$h^2 = .38$, $c^2 = .53$, $e^2 = .09$ (Swedish males) $h^2 = .25$, $c^2 = .56$, $e^2 = .19$ (British males) $h^2 = .72$, $c^2 = .18$, $e^2 = .10$ (Swedish females) $h^2 = .88$, $c^2 = .06$, $e^2 = .06$ (British females)

Study	Description			
Eley (2003)	Parent report of aggressive nonaggressive antisocial behavior at two time points (childhood and adolescence)	$h^2 = .60$, $c^2 = .15$, $e^2 = .24$ (time 1); $h^2 = .46$, $c^2 = .30$, $e^2 = .24$ (time 2)	$h^2 = .49$, $c^2 = .35$, $e^2 = .16$ (time 1); $h^2 = .44$, $c^2 = .42$, $e^2 = .14$ (time 2)	$h^2 = .70$, $c^2 = .28$, $e^2 = .02$ (aggressive at time 1 and non-aggressive at time 2); $h^2 = .69$, $c^2 = .27$, $e^2 = .04$ (non-aggressive at time 1 and aggressive at time 2)
Gelhorn (2006)	Self-report of aggressive and nonaggressive conduct disorder symptoms	$h^2 = .49$, $c^2 = .00$, $e^2 = .51$	$h^2 = .55$, $c^2 = .00$, $e^2 = .45$	$h^2 = .61$, $c^2 = .00$, $e^2 = .39$
Tuvblad (2005)	Parent report of aggressive behavior in childhood and self-report of non-aggressive behavior in adolescence	$h^2 = .59$, $c^2 = .18$, $e^2 = .23$ (girls); $h^2 = .67$, $c^2 = .04$, $e^2 = .29$ (boys)	$h^2 = .37$, $c^2 = .30$, $e^2 = .33$ (girls); $h^2 = .27$, $c^2 = .43$, $e^2 = .30$ (boys)	$h^2 = 1.00$ (girls); $h^2 = .39$, $c^2 = .47$, $e^2 = .14$ (boys)

Note. h^2 = heritability, or magnitude of genetic influences; c^2 = magnitude of shared environmental influences; e^2 = magnitude of nonshared environmental influences.

Behavior Genetic Studies of the Development of Aggression

Several researchers have examined the stability of aggressive behavior in behavior genetic studies. The overall conclusion is that aggressive behavior is moderately stable from childhood to adolescence (for a similar conclusion, see Chapter 7) and that genetic influences explain a larger percentage of the stability of aggressive behavior than do shared or nonshared environmental influences. Van der Valk, Verhulst, Neale, and Boomsma (1998) conducted a longitudinal study of aggressive behavior in 111 pairs of adopted biological siblings, 221 pairs of adopted nonbiological siblings, and 1,484 adopted singletons from the Netherlands. Aggressive behavior was assessed via parent questionnaires at age 10 to 15 years, then again 3 years later. The correlation between the two time points ranged from .51 to .70, and the covariance between the two time points was due 69% to genetic influences, 14% to shared environmental influences, and 17% to nonshared environmental influences. Van Beijsterveldt, Bartels, Hudziak, and Boomsma (2003) examined the stability of aggression at ages 3, 7, 10, and 12 in a large sample of Dutch twin pairs (ranging from 1,509 pairs at age 12 to 6,488 pairs at age 3). Aggressive behavior was assessed via parent questionnaires. The correlations for aggression assessed at different ages ranged from .41 to .77. Genetic influences explained approximately 65% of the total stability of aggression, whereas shared environmental influences accounted for approximately 25% of the total stability of aggression. A simplex model, wherein a dynamic developmental process consisting of transmission of existing influences interacting with new influences, fit best for genetic influences. In contrast, there was a stable set of the same shared environmental influences and age-specific nonshared environmental influences.

In a longitudinal twin study, Haberstick, Schmitz, Young, and Hewitt (2006) examined the development of aggressive behavior from childhood to early adolescence (through parent report at ages 7, 9, 10, 11, and 12 and teacher report at ages 7, 8, 9, 10, 11, and 12) and reached conclusions slightly different from those of van Beijsterveldt et al. (2003). The contribution of common genetic influences to the stability of aggression ranged from 66% to 87% for parent report and 59% to 95% for teacher report, and the rest was attributable to nonshared environmental influences that were common across age. There was no evidence of significant shared environmental influences that were common across age. The authors noted that there is consistent evidence of common genetic influences on aggression assessed at different ages despite the fact that different teachers rated the children at each age. Eley, Lichtenstein, and Moffitt (2003) examined over 1,000 twin pairs from the Swedish Twin Registry assessed at ages 8 to 9 and 13 to 14 years. Aggressive behavior was assessed via parent report at both time points. Continuity in aggression between childhood and adolescence ranged from .53 to .69 and was due 84% to genetic influences, 8% to shared environmental influences, and 8% to nonshared environmental influences.

Candidate Genes for Aggression and Antisocial Behavior

Based on the evidence that aggression is heritable, researchers have initiated attempts to find specific genes that contribute to its etiology using a candidate gene approach. In well-designed candidate gene studies, genes are selected based on the known or hypothesized involvement of their gene product in the etiology of a trait or disorder (i.e., its pathophysiological function and etiological relevance). Whereas genome scans may be thought of as exploratory searches for putative genes that underlie a disorder or trait, well-conducted candidate gene studies are targeted tests of the role of specific genes in the etiology of a disorder or trait, as the location, function, and etiological relevance of candidate genes are most often known a priori.

Genes underlying various aspects of the dopaminergic, noradrenergic, and serotonergic neurotransmitter pathways represent viable candidates given the role of these neurotransmitter systems in the etiology and pathophysiology of aggression. For example, there is considerable overlap between antisocial behavior and childhood attention-deficit hyperactivity disorder (ADHD; e.g., Lilienfeld & Waldman, 1990); thus, candidate genes for ADHD may also be relevant candidates for aggression and antisocial behavior. Several genes within the dopamine system appear to be risk factors for ADHD (Waldman & Gizer, 2006). Dopamine genes are plausible candidates for ADHD, given that the stimulant medications that are the most frequent and effective treatments for ADHD appear to act primarily by regulating dopamine levels in the brain (Seeman & Madras, 1998; Solanto, 1984), although they also affect noradrenergic and serotonergic function (Solanto, 1998). In addition, knock-out gene studies in mice, which examine the behavioral effects of the deactivation of specific genes, have further demonstrated the potential relevance of genes within these neurotransmitter systems. Results of such studies have markedly strengthened the consideration as candidate genes for ADHD of dopaminergic genes, such as the dopamine transporter gene (*DAT1*; Giros, Jaber, Jones, Wightman, & Caron, 1996) and the dopamine receptor D3 and D4 genes (*DRD3* and *DRD4*; Accili et al., 1996; Dulawa, Grandy, Low, Paulus, & Geyer, 1999; Rubinstein et al., 1997), as well as genes within the serotonergic system, such as the serotonin 1β receptor gene (*HTR1β*; Saudou et al., 1994). Serotonergic genes also are plausible candidates for aggression, given the demonstrated relations between serotonergic function and aggression (Berman, Kavoussi, & Coccaro, 1997).

Although a comprehensive review of molecular genetic studies of aggression and antisocial behavior is beyond the scope of this chapter, several lines of research suggest an association between serotonin and aggression. Several researchers have found lower cerebrospinal fluid levels of 5-hydroxyindoleacetic acid, a serotonin metabolite, in aggressive or violent individuals (e.g., Brown, Goodwin, Ballenger, Goyer, & Major,1979; Linnoila et al., 1983). Mice lacking the *HTR1β* gene show enhanced aggressive behavior (Saudou et al., 1994), and a serotonin transporter (*5HTT*) polymorphism is associated with aggression in nonhuman primates who experienced insecure early attachment relationships (Suomi, 2003).

Candidate genes for neurotransmitter systems may include (a) *precursor genes* that affect the rate at which neurotransmitters are produced from precursor amino acids (e.g., tyrosine hydroxylase for dopamine, tryptophan hydroxylase for serotonin), (b) *receptor genes* that are involved in receiving neurotransmitter signals (e.g., genes corresponding to the five dopamine receptors, *DRD1, D2, D3, D4,* and *D5,* and to the serotonin receptors, such as *HTR1β* and *HTR2A*), (c) *transporter genes* that are involved in the reuptake of neurotransmitters back into the presynaptic terminal (e.g., the dopamine and serotonin transporter genes, *DAT1* and *5HTT*), (d) *metabolite genes* that are involved in the metabolism or degradation of these neurotransmitters (e.g., the genes for catechol-o-methyl-transferase and for monoamine oxidase A and B), and (e) genes that are responsible for the conversion of one neurotransmitter into another (e.g., dopamine beta hydroxylase, or *DβH,* which converts dopamine into norepinephrine). We anticipate that there will be a steep increase in the number of studies of the involvement of such candidate genes in aggression and antisocial behavior over the next decade.

CONCLUSIONS

In conclusion, the results of a meta-analysis suggest that there are moderate additive genetic and nonshared environmental influences and modest shared environmental influences on aggression. Behavior genetic studies examining relational versus overt aggression and reactive versus proactive aggression have recently been undertaken. The first set of these studies demonstrates moderate heritabilities and nonshared environmental influences on these aggression dimensions, with genetic influences contributing substantially to their overlap. Shared environmental influences were also found to underlie some of these dimensions of aggression, particularly social or relational aggression. An association between dopamine and serotonin and aggression has been implicated in some early candidate gene studies, although human studies examining the association between the serotonin transporter gene and violence or aggression have yielded conflicting results. Future molecular genetic studies will illuminate the specific genetic underpinnings of aggression and antisocial behavior.

REFERENCES

Note: References marked with an asterisk indicate studies included in the meta-analysis.

Accili, D., Fishburn, C. S., Drago, J., Steiner, H., Lachowicz, J. E., Park, B. H., ... Fuchs, S. (1996). A targeted mutation of the D3 dopamine receptor gene is associated with hyperactivity in mice. *Proceedings of the National Academy of Sciences of the United States of America, 93,* 1945–1949. doi:10.1073/pnas.93.5.1945

American Psychiatric Association. (1994). *Diagnostic and statistical manual of mental disorders* (4th ed.). Washington, DC: Author.

Baker, L. A., Raine, A., Liu, J., & Jacobson, K. C. (2008). Differential genetic and environmental influences on reactive and proactive aggression in children. *Journal of Abnormal Child Psychology, 36,* 1265–1278. doi:10.1007/s10802-008-9249-1

Bartels, M., Hudziak, J. J., van den Oord, E. J., van Beijsterveldt, C. E., Rietveld, M. J., & Boomsma, D. I. (2003). Co-occurrence of aggressive behavior and rule-breaking behavior at age 12: Multi-rater analyses. *Behavior Genetics, 33,* 607–621. doi:10.1023/A:1025787019702

Berman, M. E., Kavoussi, R. J., & Coccaro, E. F. (1997). Neurotransmitter correlates of human aggression. In D. M. Stoff, J. Breiling, & J. D. Maser (Eds.), *Handbook of antisocial behavior* (pp. 305–313). New York, NY: Wiley.

*Blanchard, J. M., Vernon, P. A., & Harris, J. A. (1995). A behavior genetic investigation of multiple dimensions of aggression. *Behavior Genetics, 25,* 256.

Brendgen, M., Dionne, G., Girard, A., Boivin, M., Vitaro, F., & Pérusse, D. (2005). Examining genetic and environmental effects on social aggression: A study of 6-year-old twins. *Child Development, 76,* 930–946. doi:10.1111/j.1467-8624.2005.00887.x

Brendgen, M., Vitaro, F., Boivin, M., Dionne, G., & Pérusse, D. (2006). Examining genetic and environmental effects on reactive versus proactive aggression. *Developmental Psychology, 42,* 1299–1312. doi:10.1037/0012-1649.42.6.1299

Brown, G. L., Goodwin, F. K., Ballenger, J. C., Goyer, P. F., & Major, L. F. (1979). Aggression in humans correlates with cerebrospinal fluid amine metabolites. *Psychiatry Research, 1,* 131–139. doi:10.1016/0165-1781(79)90053-2

Burt, S. A. (2009). Are there meaningful etiological differences within antisocial behavior? Results of a meta-analysis. *Clinical Psychology Review, 29.* 163–178. doi:10.1016/j.cpr.2008.12.004

Button, T. M., Scourfield, J., Martin, N., & McGuffin, P. (2004). Do aggressive and nonaggressive antisocial behavior in adolescents result from the same genetic and environmental effects? *American Journal of Medical Genetics, 129B*, 59–63. doi:10.1002/ajmg.b.30045

*Cates, D. S., Houston, B. K., Vavak, C. R., Crawford, M. H., & Uttley, M. (1993). Heritability of hostility-related emotions, attitudes, and behaviors. *Journal of Behavioral Medicine, 16*, 237–256. doi:10.1007/BF00844758

Crick, N. R., Casa, J. F., & Mosher, M. (1997). Relational and overt aggression in preschool. *Developmental Psychology, 33*, 579–588. doi:10.1037/0012-1649.33.4.579

Crick, N. R., & Grotpeter, J. K. (1995). Relational aggression, gender, and social-psychological adjustment. *Child Development, 66*, 710–722. doi:10.2307/1131945

Crick, N. R., & Grotpeter, J. K. (1996). Children's treatment by peers: Victims of relational and overt aggression. *Development and Psychopathology, 8*, 367–380. doi:10.1017/S0954579400007148

Dodge, K. A., Bates, J., & Pettit, G. S. (1990, December). Mechanisms in the cycle of violence. *Science, 250*, 1678–1683. doi:10.1126/science.2270481

Dodge, K. A., Lochman, J. E., Harnish, J. D., Bates, J. E., & Pettit, G. S. (1997). Reactive and proactive aggression in school children and psychiatrically impaired chronically assaultive youth. *Journal of Abnormal Psychology, 106*, 37–51. doi:10.1037/0021-843X.106.1.37

Dulawa, S. C., Grandy, D. K., Low, M. J., Paulus, M. P., & Geyer, M. A. (1999). Dopamine D4 receptor-knock-out mice exhibit reduced exploration of novel stimuli. *The Journal of Neuroscience, 19*, 9550–9556.

Eley, T. C., Lichtenstein, P., & Moffitt, T. E. (2003). A longitudinal behavioral genetic analysis of the etiology of aggressive and nonaggressive antisocial behavior. *Development and Psychopathology, 15*, 383–402. doi:10.1017/S095457940300021X

Eley, T. C., Lichtenstein, P., & Stevenson, J. (1999). Sex differences in the etiology of aggressive and nonaggressive antisocial behavior: Results from two twin studies. *Child Development, 70*, 155–168. doi:10.1111/1467-8624.00012

*Finkel, D., & McGue, M. (1997). Sex differences and nonadditivity in heritability of the multidimensional personality questionnaire scales. *Journal of Personality and Social Psychology, 72*, 929–938. doi:10.1037/0022-3514.72.4.929

Gelhorn, H., Stallings, M., Young, S., Corley, R., Rhee, S. H., Christian, H., & Hewitt, J. (2006). Common and specific genetic influences on aggressive and nonaggressive conduct disorder domains. *Journal of the American Academy of Child and Adolescent Psychiatry, 45*, 570–577. doi:10.1097/01.chi.0000198596.76443.b0

*Ghodsian-Carpey, J., & Baker, L. A. (1987). Genetic and environmental influences on aggression in 4- to 7-year-old twins. *Aggressive Behavior, 13*, 173–186. doi:10.1002/1098-2337(1987)13:4<173::AID-AB2480130402>3.0.CO;2-Y

Giros, B., Jaber, M., Jones, S. R., Wightman, R. M., & Caron, M. G. (1996, February). Hyperlocomotion and indifference to cocaine and amphetamine in mice lacking the dopamine transporter. *Nature, 379*, 606–612. doi:10.1038/379606a0

Gough, H. G., & Heilbrun, A. B. (1972). *The Adjective Checklist manual*. Palo Alto, CA: Consulting Psychologists Press.

*Gustavsson, J. P., Pedersen, N. L., Åsberg, M., & Schalling, D. (1996). Exploration into the sources of individual differences in aggression-, hostility-, and anger-related (AHA) personality traits. *Personality and Individual Differences, 21,* 1067–1071. doi:10.1016/S0191-8869(96)00146-8

Haberstick, B. C., Schmitz, S., Young, S. E., & Hewitt, J. K. (2006). Genes and developmental stability of aggressive behavior problems at home and school in a community sample of twins aged 7–12. *Behavior Genetics, 36,* 809–819. doi:10.1007/s10519-006-9092-5

Ligthart, L., Bartels, M., Hoekstra, R. A., Hudziak, J. J., & Boomsma, D. I. (2005). Genetic contributions to subtypes of aggression. *Twin Research and Human Genetics, 8,* 483–491. doi:10.1375/twin.8.5.483

Lilienfeld, S. O., & Waldman, I. D. (1990). The relation between childhood attention-deficit hyperactivity disorder and adult antisocial behavior reexamined: The problem of heterogeneity. *Clinical Psychology Review, 10,* 699–725. doi:10.1016/0272-7358(90)90076-M

Linnoila, M., Virkkunen, M., Scheinin, M., Nuutila, A., Rimon, R., & Goodwin, F. K. (1983). Low cerebrospinal fluid 5-hydroxyindoleacetic acid concentration differentiates impulsive from nonimpulsive violence behavior. *Life Sciences, 33,* 2609–2614. doi:10.1016/0024-3205(83)90344-2

Loehlin, J. C. (1992). *Latent variable models: An introduction to factor, path, and structural analysis* (2nd ed.). Hillsdale, NJ: Erlbaum.

*Meininger, J. C., Hayman, L. L., Coates, P. M., & Gallagher, P. (1988). Genetics or environment? Type A behavior and cardiovascular risk factors in twin children. *Nursing Research, 37,* 341–346. doi:10.1097/00006199-198811000-00006

Mullen, B. (1989). *Advanced BASIC meta-analysis.* Hillsdale, NJ: Erlbaum.

Norland, S., Shover, N., Thornton, W., & James, J. (1979). Intrafamily conflict and delinquency. *Pacific Sociological Review, 22,* 233–237.

*Owen, D., & Sines, J. O. (1970). Heritability of personality in children. *Behavior Genetics, 1,* 235–248. doi:10.1007/BF01074655

Partanen, J., Bruun, K., & Markkanen, T. (1966). *Inheritance of drinking behavior: A study on intelligence, personality, and use of alcohol of adult twins.* Helsinki, Finland: The Finnish Foundation for Alcohol Studies.

Patterson, G. R., Reid, J. B., & Dishion, T. J. (1992). *Antisocial boys.* Eugene, OR: Castalia Publishing.

*Plomin, R., Foch, T. T., & Rowe, D. C. (1981). Bobo clown aggression in childhood: Environment, not genes. *Journal of Research in Personality, 15,* 331–342. doi:10.1016/0092-6566(81)90031-3

*Rahe, R. H., Hervig, L., & Rosenman, R. H. (1978). Heritability of type A behavior. *Psychosomatic Medicine, 40,* 478–486.

Rhee, S. H., & Waldman, I. D. (2002). Genetic and environmental influences on antisocial behavior: A meta-analysis of twin and adoption studies. *Psychological Bulletin, 128,* 490–529. doi:10.1037/0033-2909.128.3.490

Robins, L. N. (1966). *Deviant children grown up*. Baltimore, MD: Williams & Wilkins.

Rosenthal, R. (1991). *Meta-analytic procedures for social research*. Newbury Park, CA: Sage.

Rubinstein, M., Phillips, T. J., Bunzow, J. R., Falzone, T. L., Dziewczapolski, G., Zhang, G., . . . Chester, J. (1997). Mice lacking dopamine D4 receptors are supersensitive to ethanol, cocaine, and methamphetamine. *Cell, 90*, 991–1001. doi:10.1016/S0092-8674(00)80365-7

*Rushton, J. P., Fulker, D. W., Neale, M. C., Nias, D. K. B., & Eysenck, H. J. (1986). Altruism and aggression: The heritability of individual differences. *Journal of Personality and Social Psychology, 50*, 1192–1198. doi:10.1037/0022-3514.50.6.1192

Saudou, F., Amara, D. A., Dierich, A., LeMeur, M., Ramboz, S., Segu, L., . . . Hen, R. (1994, September). Enhanced aggressive behavior in mice lacking 5-HT1B receptor. *Science, 265*, 1875–1878. doi:10.1126/science.8091214

*Scarr, S. (1966). Genetic factors in activity motivation. *Child Development, 37*, 663–673. doi:10.2307/1126688

Seeman, P., & Madras, B. K. (1998). Anti-hyperactivity medication: Methylphenidate and amphetamine. *Molecular Psychiatry, 3*, 386–396. doi:10.1038/sj.mp.4000421

Solanto, M. V. (1984). Neuropharmacological basis of stimulant drug action in attention deficit disorder with hyperactivity: A review and synthesis. *Psychological Bulletin, 95*, 387–409. doi:10.1037/0033-2909.95.3.387

Solanto, M. V. (1998). Neuropsychopharmacological mechanisms of stimulant drug action in attention-deficit hyperactivity disorder: A review and integration. *Behavioural Brain Research, 94*, 127–152. doi:10.1016/S0166-4328(97)00175-7

Suomi, S. J. (2003). Gene-environment interactions and the neurobiology of social conflict. *Annals of the New York Academy of Sciences, 1008*, 132–139. doi:10.1196/annals.1301.014

*Tellegen, A., Lykken, D. T., Bouchard, T. J., Wilcox, K., Segal, N., & Rich, S. (1988). Personality similarity in twins reared apart and together. *Journal of Personality and Social Psychology, 54*, 1031–1039. doi:10.1037/0022-3514.54.6.1031

Tuvblad, C., Eley, T. C., & Lichtenstein, P. (2005). The development of antisocial behaviour from childhood to adolescence. A longitudinal twin study. *European Child & Adolescent Psychiatry, 14*, 216–225. doi:10.1007/s00787-005-0458-7

van Beijsterveldt, C. E., Bartels, M., Hudziak, J. J., & Boomsma, D. I. (2003). Causes of stability of aggression from early childhood to adolescence: A longitudinal genetic analysis in Dutch twins. *Behavior Genetics, 33*, 591–605. doi:10.1023/A:1025735002864

*van den Oord, E. J. C. G., Verhulst, F. C., & Boomsma, D. I. (1996). A genetic study of maternal and paternal ratings of problem behaviors in 3-year-old twins. *Journal of Abnormal Psychology, 105*, 349–357. doi:10.1037/0021-843X.105.3.349

van der Valk, J. C., Verhulst, F. C., Neale, M. C., & Boomsma, D. I. (1998). Longitudinal genetic analysis of problem behaviors in biologically related and unrelated adoptees. *Behavior Genetics, 28*, 365–380. doi:10.1023/A:1021621719059

Vitaro, F., Brendgen, M., & Tremblay, R. E. (2002). Reactively and proactively aggressive children: Antecedent and subsequent characteristics. *Journal of Child Psychology and Psychiatry, and Allied Disciplines, 43*, 495–505. doi:10.1111/1469-7610.00040

Waldman, I. D., & Gizer, I. (2006). The genetics of attention deficit hyperactivity disorder. *Clinical Psychology Review, 26*, 396–432. doi:10.1016/j.cpr.2006.01.007

Waschbusch, D. A., Willoughby, M. T., & Pelham, W. E. (1998). Criterion validity and utility of reactive and proactive aggression: Comparisons to attention deficit hyperactivity disorder, oppositional defiant disorder, conduct disorder, and other measures of functioning. *Journal of Clinical Child Psychology, 27*, 396–405. doi:10.1207/s15374424jccp2704_3

*Wilson, G. D., Rust, J., & Kasriel, J. (1977). Genetic and family origins of humor preferences: A twin study. *Psychological Reports, 41*, 659–660.

9

SOCIAL INFORMATION PROCESSING PATTERNS AS MEDIATORS OF THE INTERACTION BETWEEN GENETIC FACTORS AND LIFE EXPERIENCES IN THE DEVELOPMENT OF AGGRESSIVE BEHAVIOR

KENNETH A. DODGE

It is well established that social–cognitive processes correlate with aggressive behavioral acts (see Chapters 1, 2, and 7). For example, in response to an ambiguous provocation by another person, when a respondent infers that the act was committed with hostile intent (a *hostile attribution*), the probability that the respondent will react aggressively is high (about .76; Dodge, 1980), whereas when that same respondent infers that the act was committed benignly, the probability of an aggressive behavioral reaction is low (about .25). Likewise, if during another stage of processing information the respondent evaluates an aggressive response as being likely to lead to desired outcomes, the probability of engaging in aggression is high (Fontaine, Yang, Dodge, Bates, & Pettit, 2008). Although the evidence is less clear that these social–cognitive processes cause the aggressive behavioral response during the microseconds of interpersonal interaction, the correlation has been found over and over, suggesting that social–cognitive processes, and the developmental processes that support them, are closely intertwined with the matrix of causes of aggression.

It has also been found that individuals develop characteristic styles of processing social information within specific social situations. These styles act as acquired personality characteristics. They correlate significantly with and predict individual differences in aggressive behavior in particular situations. In this chapter, the empirical evidence on this topic will be reviewed briefly and integrated with recent discoveries regarding psychophysiology and neural processes. A general model will be advanced that proposes that (a) processing patterns provide the proximal mechanism through which aggressive behavior occurs; (b) these patterns correlate with neural and psychophysiological processes; (c) these patterns are acquired through genetic and environmental processes, especially in interaction; and (d) acquired processing patterns account for the effects of genetic and environmental factors in behavioral development and provide the mechanism through which these factors exert their impact. Findings will be presented from the Child Development Project (CDP), an ongoing longitudinal study of 585 boys and girls followed from age 4 through young adulthood.

SOCIAL INFORMATION PROCESSING MECHANISMS IN AGGRESSIVE BEHAVIORS

Models of the processing of information in response to social stimuli posit a sequence of steps that lead to behavioral responding including aggression toward others (Crick & Dodge, 1994; see also Chapter 7, this volume). These steps are logically ordered and assumed to flow temporally, although evidence for the sequential ordering is scant (see Chapter 1, this volume). Methods to assess an individual's self-report of her or his processing have been developed using hypothetical situational vignettes as stimuli. In each vignette, the person is asked to contemplate a hypothetical scenario in which a social event occurs and then to answer questions about attributions and possible responses (Dodge, 1980). The stimuli have been presented orally, in the form of cartoons, or by video.

The first several steps of processing describe the sensation and interpretation of cues, and the latter steps describe behavioral decision making. The first step is attention to and sensation of the stimulus. Because the stimulus array is so large, selective attention to some cues over others is inevitable. In a situation involving provocation by another—for example, being pushed to the ground—one child might attend to the provocation itself and the pain it causes, whereas a second child might attend to the teacher watching in the background, and a third child might attend to the peers who are laughing nearby. Attention to cues can obviously influence downstream processing and ultimate behavior, for example, when attention to the provocateur's look of surprise and regret might mitigate a retaliatory response. Numerous factors affect selective attention to hostile versus other cues, such as recent threat, fatigue, and stress. A pattern of habitual selective attention to hostile cues (e.g., the provocateur's angry voice, repeated negative behavior, lack of sensitivity to the child's pain) has been associated with chronic aggressive behavior (Dodge, Pettit, McClaskey, & Brown, 1986).

Closely following the sensation of cues is a mental representation of those cues, often involving an interpretation of the other person's intention. As noted earlier, when a hostile intent is inferred, aggressive behavior likely ensues, in contrast with an inference of a benign intention. The process of mental representation occurs in microseconds and may be updated across time during a social interaction. It is not usually a conscious process, although it can become so if prompted. The process undoubtedly involves neural activity that is conditioned by experience (for evidence regarding neural activity underlying mental representations of social intent, see Chapter 6). Inferences of hostile intent have also been found to correlate with heightened autonomic reactivity (Crozier et al., 2008). Numerous studies have shown a robust pattern in which hostile attributional biases are associated with aggressive behavior, especially reactive aggression (Dodge, 1980). A review by Orobio de Castro, Veerman, Koops, Bosch, and Monshouwer (2002) indicates that this pattern holds across ages, demographic and cultural groups, and contexts.

The third step is goal selection, in which the mentally represented stimulus is associated with an emotional reaction and the narrowing of a goal. Again, the respondent is not usually aware of this process but might reflect afterward on the cognitive processes involved. Children who experience anger and regularly select instrumental and self-defensive goals are likely to behave aggressively, whereas children who select social goals are likely to behave nonaggressively (Crick & Dodge, 1994).

Steps of response generation, response evaluation, and enactment constitute the response–decision phase of processing. Mental representation and goal selection trigger one or more possible behavioral responses such as aggression, withdrawal, and social deflection. The trigger from mental representation of hostile intent to aggressive response generation is a neural association that is probably both "ready" at birth (because of evolutionary adaptation) and conditioned from experience and observation (see Chapter 6). One of the most frequently replicated findings in this area is the empirical association between the generation of aggressive responses to hypothetical social stimuli and actual chronic aggressive behavior, beginning at about age 4 and continuing through adolescence (Dodge, Coie, & Lynam, 2006).

Generation of an aggressive response does not lead inevitably to aggressive behavior (see Chapters 3 and 6, this volume). Processes of response evaluation and decision (called *RED* by Fontaine & Dodge, 2006) follow. During RED, the respondent immediately decides (nonconsciously, in microseconds) to accept the generated response without any consideration of consequences or to consider multiple domains of evaluative judgment, including (a) *response efficacy*, the estimation of how likely the respondent is to be successful if the considered response were to be carried out; (b) *response valuation*, which is the assignment of value to the response in terms of its social and moral qualities; (c) *outcome expectancy*, which is the estimation of the likelihood of various consequences of a behavior; and (d) *outcome valuation*, in which the estimated outcome is given value. Fontaine and Dodge (2006) hypothesized that different possible responses are compared (*response comparison*) before the most appropriate response is selected (*response selection*). Measurement of response decision during hypothetical social stimuli has yielded robust correlations between all of these subprocesses and chronic aggressive behavior, especially proactive aggression (see the review by Fontaine & Dodge, 2006).

SOCIAL INFORMATION PROCESSING PATTERNS AS PREDICTORS OF INDIVIDUAL DIFFERENCES IN AGGRESSIVE BEHAVIOR

Although these processing patterns are empirically correlated with individual differences in aggressive behavior, the correlational findings often suffer from two problems. First, because the measurement of processing is typically based on individuals' self-report, the data depend on self-observation of cognitive processing and not processing itself, which occurs at the neural level and nonconsciously. Even self-reports that are collected "online" are immediate self-observations. Recent evidence suggests that individuals actually begin to respond with neural activity in microseconds prior to self-awareness of responding. The second problem is that the empirical correlation between patterns of processing and patterns of behavior might reflect an opposite causal direction than proposed in the model or might be attributable to an unmeasured third variable. Two kinds of evidence have been mounted to test the hypothesis that chronic patterns of processing improve the prediction of aggressive behavior.

Controlling for Prior Aggression

The first evidence comes from prospective studies in which early levels of problematic aggressive conduct are controlled statistically. In the CDP of a community sample of 585 boys and girls followed for 20 years, we assessed both aggressive behavior and processing patterns recurrently. We know that during the early elementary school years, children develop patterns of processing social information that become stable when measured annually for 4 years, as assessed by cross-time internal consistency coefficients of .70 to .79 (Dodge, Pettit, Bates, & Valente, 1995). These patterns function as acquired personality characteristics. During this period, the continuity in aggressive behavior also becomes strong. Aggressive behavior measured by teacher assessments at age 5 was found to predict patterns of social information processing in kindergarten through Grade 3, which in turn predicted aggressive behavior at age 10 and improved the prediction of aggressive behavior even when early levels of aggression were statistically controlled (Dodge et al., 2003). This pattern supports the hypothesis that social information processing plays a causal role in generating aggressive behavior.

We also found that we could predict adolescent conduct problems from kindergarten processing patterns. Here, we scored children as displaying problems in social information processing at the early steps (i.e., hypervigilance and hostile attributional biases) or later steps (i.e., response generation or evaluation) or at both steps or neither step. We found, while controlling for kindergarten externalizing problems as assessed by both mothers and teachers, that the four groups differed in mother- and teacher-rated externalizing behavior problems at the end of Grade 11 (Lansford et al., 2006). Furthermore, the effect was cumulative or synergistic, in that the group of children with kindergarten problems at both stages of processing was especially likely to show conduct problems in high school.

The prediction was even stronger for processing patterns in Grade 8. Controlling for conduct problems before and during Grade 8, the four groups of children as assessed by processing patterns during Grade 8 differed in mother- and teacher-rated conduct problems in Grade 11. Again, a cumulative or interactive effect was found, with the group displaying the highest levels of problematic conduct being the one with problems at both early and later stages of processing.

The relation between processing patterns and aggressive behavior is iterative and reciprocal (Fontaine & Dodge, 2006). That is, aggressive behavior at age 14 predicted processing patterns the next year, which in turn predicted growth in aggression the following year, even controlling for prior aggression. Likewise, processing patterns in one year predicted aggression in the following year, which altered processing patterns in the subsequent year. Across adolescence, this reciprocal effect continues.

Intervention as Experimental Evidence

The second kind of evidence comes from intervention experiments in which explicit attempts to alter processing patterns are manipulated by random assignment and the effect on aggressive behavior is assessed. Graham and Hudley (1993) developed a brief intervention to help young African American boys process information in more benevolent ways (i.e., with a lessened hostile attribution bias). They found that random assignment to this intervention led to lower scores on measures of hostile attribution bias, and this impact mediated a change in aggressive behavior. Guerra and Slaby (1990) also randomly assigned aggressive adolescents to intervention or control conditions. Their intervention involved multiple components of social information processing. They also found that random assignment to the intervention condition was associated with improvements in processing patterns and reduced aggressive behavior.

Situation and Relationship Specificity

A pivotal issue in constructing models of social information processing is situational specificity in the link between processing patterns and behavior. Processing patterns within a certain kind of situation, such as being provoked or attempting to enter a peer group or handling conflict in a romantic relationship or with a coworker, predict behavior within that type of situation more strongly than behavior in other situations. For example, Dodge et al. (1986) assessed processing patterns in provocative peer interactions and peer-group entry situations. We then placed children in a laboratory setting and exposed them to a provocation by a confederate peer and an entry situation in which they were asked to initiate entry into a strange peer group. We found that processing patterns predicted behavior, and the predictions were stronger within kinds of situations than across kinds of situations.

More recently, we found similar evidence for young adults. Two kinds of situations are important in young adulthood, defined by relationships. The establishment of successful romantic relationships is a key developmental task in that age period (Collins & van Dulmen, 2006). Unfortunately, violence is fairly common in these relationships, as indicated by surveys showing that 20% to 50% of intimate relationships during adulthood involve violence toward a partner (Silverman, Raj, Mucci, & Hathaway, 2001). Likewise, relationships with adult peers are essential to work and community success (Arnett, 2006). Although some individuals display violence across different kinds of relationships, many adults behave violently only in romantic relationships (Archer, 2000), and some research indicates that peer violence and partner violence have distinguishable antecedents (Brendgen, Vitaro, Tremblay, & Lavoie, 2001).

We were able to interview 85% of the original CDP sample at age 22 and follow them through age 24. We assessed processing patterns in situations involving conflict with a romantic partner (e.g., "You are at a gathering with a group of friends and your girl/boyfriend and learn that your girl/boyfriend and one of the people at the gathering used to be a couple; they spend most of the night talking with each other") and conflict with a coworker or peer (e.g., "You tell a friend something personal and ask your friend not to discuss it with anyone else. However, a couple of weeks later, you find out that a lot of people know about it").

We (Pettit, Lansford, Dodge, & Bates, 2009) were able to predict violent behavior in each of these types of relationships as well as evidence of relationship specificity. Processing patterns in a hypothetical romantic relationship predicted violent behavior in actual romantic relationships 2 years later, as reported by both the participant and his or her romantic partner. Also, processing patterns within the peer relationship predicted violent behavior toward peers 2 years later. Furthermore, the predictions were stronger within kinds of relationships than across kinds of relationships.

NEURAL AND PSYCHOPHYSIOLOGICAL PROCESSES AND SOCIAL INFORMATION PROCESSING

A misconception about information processing is that it occurs independently of biological processes in real time. Accumulating evidence indicates that psychophysiological and neural processes co-occur with information processing (see Chapter 6, this volume). Most likely, these processes occur in real time outside a person's awareness, and measures of information processing represent the individual's postbehavioral reflection on her or his thoughts and actions. This suggests that the measures of information processing may be imprecise and subject to self-presentation and other biases.

Psychophysiological Processes

Ortiz and Raine (2004) reviewed evidence indicating that resting heart rate is inversely related to individual differences in aggressive behavior (i.e., low resting heart rate predicts higher aggressive behavior), especially proactive and life-persistent aggression but not situational or adolescence-limited aggression (Moffit & Caspi, 2001). Raine, Venables, and Mednick (1997) found that low resting heart rate at age 3 predicted aggressive behavior 8 years later at age 11. Raine (2002) hypothesized that deficits in volume and function of prefrontal cortex may be responsible for low autonomic activity as well as aggressive behavior.

However, during the processing of social cues, the autonomic nervous system reacts with rapid changes in heart rate (Crozier et al., 2008). While the individual is attending to cues, heart rate decreases. When a provocation occurs, heart rate increases and then slowly returns to baseline when the threat subsides. Lorber (2004) summarized evidence from numerous studies showing that aggressive children display higher heart rate reactivity to provocative cues than do nonaggressive children. Furthermore, Crozier et al. (2008) found that high heart rate reactivity to provocation was correlated with several stages of social information processing. Furthermore, processing responses mediate the link between heart rate changes and aggressive behavior.

Thus, two separate psychophysiological processes may be related to aggressive behavior. Both low resting heart rate and high heart rate reactivity in response to threatening cues appear to predict aggressive behavior. These processes may have their antecedents in both life events and heritable biological processes, and their impact on aggressive behavior may be mediated by the manner in which the individual processes social information in response to threat.

Neural Processes

Neuroimaging studies suggest that regions of the prefrontal cortex (e.g., the dorsolateral prefrontal cortex and ventral prefrontal cortex) and the limbic system (e.g., amygdala) are activated during information processing in response to interpersonal provocations such as unfair allocation of resources by a peer (Meyer-Lindenberg et al., 2006; see also Chapter 6, this volume). Meyer-Lindenberg et al. (2006) found significant activation of the amygdala in response to experimental presentation of stimuli similar to those used to assess social information processing, such as angry and fearful faces and aversively valenced cues. Presentation of threatening faces (Pezawas et al., 2005), the perception of anger in others, and the experience of anger in oneself (Murphy, Nimmo-Smith, & Lawrence, 2003) all reliably activate the amygdala. The prefrontal cortex is activated during executive function tasks involved in processing information, such as planning, inhibitory control, and decision making (Raine, Buchsbaum, & LaCasse, 1997). Raine (2008) stated that "the prefrontal cortex acts as an 'emergency brake' on runaway emotions generated by limbic structures" (p. 324).

The activation of these brain regions, in turn, appears to be mediated by the release of neurotransmitters. Monoamine oxidase-A (MAO-A) appears to correlate with amygdala volume and probably with its activation (Meyer-Lindenberg et al., 2006). Release of 5-HT in the prefrontal cortex is thought to regulate an individual's impulsive desire to retaliate aggressively to perceived hostile treatment (Evers et al., 2006), although the evidence was only correlational until recently. Crockett, Clark, Tabibnia, Lieberman, and Robbins (2008) experimentally manipulated serotonin levels in each of 20 human subjects through an acute tryptophan depletion procedure that temporarily lowered 5-HT levels. In contrast with a placebo condition, when subjects had lower serotonin levels they responded to unfair treatment by a peer with greater retaliatory behavior (for more evidence concerning the role of serotonin in aggressive behavior, see Chapters 7 and 8, this volume).

Thus, in the same way that social information processing involves multiple, relatively independent steps, functional brain imaging studies have identified multiple brain regions that are implicated in different aspects of responding to social stimuli.

ANTECEDENTS OF SOCIAL INFORMATION PROCESSING PATTERNS AND NEURAL PROCESSES

I turn now to the antecedents of processing patterns and neural processes that mediate aggressive behavior. Given the empirical findings of both general prediction and situation-specific prediction, I hypothesize that some antecedent factors apply generally and some apply to specific domains, situations, or relationships.

Child Maltreatment

The experience of abuse by one's parent during the first 5 years of life is devastating and has been hypothesized to alter one's central working models of how human relationships work. Children develop basic trust through interaction with caring adults, and violation of that trust through extreme or ongoing maltreatment is hypothesized to lead to schemas, scripts, knowledge structures, and working models that others will act maliciously (see Chapters 4, 13, 14, and 19). Thus, the child develops hypervigilant and selective attentional patterns, becomes quick to attribute hostile motives to others, adopts self-defensive rather than social goals, develops a repertoire of self-defensive behavioral responses, and comes to evaluate self-protective behaviors as effective and desirable. Given the centrality of these working models, it is hypothesized that this experience will lead to long-term and pervasive patterns of processing information across a range of social situations and relationships.

Evidence supporting this hypothesis comes from several sources, including Pollack's work on attention patterns in maltreated children and findings from the CDP study. Dodge, Bates, and Pettit (1990) and Weiss, Dodge, Bates, and Pettit (1992) found that maltreatment in the first 5 years of life predicted processing patterns at school entry that included hypervigilance, hostile attributional biases, aggressive response generation, and favorable evaluation of aggressive behaviors. In turn, these patterns predicted aggressive behavior and mediated the impact of maltreatment on aggression. Dodge et al. (2003) extended the measurement of aggressive outcomes through adolescence and found a similar pattern of prediction and mediation. Edwards et al. (2009)

found that 30.4% of the maltreated children had an official court record of arrest by age 24, in contrast with 16.5% of the nonmaltreated children.

Lansford et al. (2007) found that the outcomes that accrue from early-life maltreatment are broad and include not only aggressive behavior but also early pregnancy, anxiety, depressive symptoms, school dropout, substance-use problems, and arrests for a variety of crimes (for a review of these long-term effects of child maltreatment, see Chapter 19, this volume). The processing patterns that were assessed in early elementary school mediated some but not all of these outcomes, perhaps because the stimuli that were used to assess processing patterns were restricted to only selected domains. It is plausible that maltreatment alters processing in multiple domains, which then mediate behavioral outcomes. More comprehensive assessments of processing patterns are necessary to test this hypothesis.

Peer Social Rejection

Other life experiences appear to have more circumscribed effects. In American elementary schools, chronic peer social rejection is a fairly common painful experience. We hypothesized, and found empirically, that this experience would exacerbate children's aggressive behavior problems beyond whatever aggressive behavior led to the peer response of rejection (Dodge et al., 2003). That is, rejection during kindergarten through Grade 2 predicted aggressive behavior in Grade 4, even controlling for early aggressive behavior. Furthermore, patterns of social information processing about peer events partially mediated the growth in aggressive behavior during this period.

More recently, Pettit et al. (2009) found that the impact of early peer rejection lasts through young adulthood. Recall the CDP findings presented earlier about the significant relation between processing patterns in peer relationships at age 22 and aggressive behavior toward peers at age 24. It turns out that the experience of peer rejection in kindergarten significantly predicts these processing patterns at age 22, which in turn mediate the impact of kindergarten peer rejection on aggressive behavior toward peers in young adulthood.

To describe these relations in person-centered terms, we dichotomized participants into those who had been rejected by peers in elementary school and those who had not, those who displayed problematic processing about peer relationships at age 22 and those who did not, and those who displayed violence toward adult peers versus those who did not. Among those who were not rejected by peers and who displayed nonproblematic processing about peers, the probability of becoming violent toward a peer was relatively low (.43), whereas among rejected children who displayed problematic processing, the probability was high (.70). In between were nonrejected children who displayed problematic processing (.47) and rejected children who did not display problematic processing (.51).

Exposure to Romantic Relationship Violence

The antecedents of romantic relationship violence may differ from those for peer-directed violence. Exposure to parents' domestic violence in early life predicts later violence in romantic relationships (Nay, Dodge, Lansford, Pettit, & Bates, 2009), but disentangling the effect of this particular exposure from other family violence may prove difficult. We explored the effect of victimization during adolescent romantic relationships on young adult violent behavior toward a romantic partner (for a review of consequences of aggression within romantic relationships, see Chapter 20, this volume).

We found that being victimized violently during an adolescent romantic relationship did indeed predict violent behavior toward a romantic partner in young adulthood. Also, this adolescent experience predicted problematic processing patterns in romantic relationships, which partially mediated the effect of victimization on later violent behavior toward a romantic partner. Among non-victims who display non-problematic processing, the probability of later becoming violent toward a romantic partner was low (.29), whereas among victims who displayed problematic processing, the probability was high (.62). In between were nonvictims who displayed problematic processing (.42) and nonvictims who did not display problematic processing (.43).

Because of the unique paths from problematic processing within a relationship type to violence in that kind of relationship, it follows that mediation by processing patterns was found only within relationship types and not across relationship types.

Genetic Factors

Individual differences in genetic variation in the serotonin transporter 5-HT gene have been associated with increased amygdala activation (Pezawas et al., 2005) and prefrontal cortex functions (Raine, 2008), as assessed through functional magnetic resonance imaging (fMRI). Also, a common variation in the X-linked MAO-A gene has been correlated with amygdala volume and activation in response to threatening stimuli (Meyer-Lindenberg et al., 2006). That is, individuals, especially males, with a polymorphism in the gene for MAO-A demonstrate greater amygdala activation when presented with threatening faces and aversive emotional situations. It follows, then, that variation in these genes would correlate with individual differences in processing patterns in response to threatening social situations.

Environmental and Genetic Factors

A comprehensive model of the development of chronic aggressive behavior must account for both genetic and life-experience factors (see Chapters 7 and 8). The major environmental factors in early life have been reviewed elsewhere (Dodge et al., 2006; Dodge & Pettit, 2003); they include the kinds of personally threatening experiences addressed earlier, such as early physical maltreatment, peer social rejection, and victimization, as well as exposure to stressful contexts such as poverty and disadvantage. The latter factors are likely to operate through their effects on life experiences such as parenting quality and success in life tasks such as getting an education (Dodge, Pettit, & Bates, 1994). Major environmental variables in mid-childhood and adolescence involve exposure to deviant peers who influence high-risk youth to engage in aggressive behavior and also involve parental failure to supervise and monitor youths' activities, thus increasing their exposure to violence and precipitators of violence (Dodge et al., 2006).

Environmental variables that have an enduring effect are likely to be ones that alter brain processes. Evidence has been growing that life stressors and early trauma have enduring effects on both prefrontal cortex and amygdala processes measured through fMRI. Liston, McEwan, and Casey (2009) reported that the natural experiment of a potent stressor (an upcoming academic examination) had observable effects on decreasing dorsolateral prefrontal cortex activity during laboratory tasks. Ganzel, Casey, Glover, Voss, and Temple (2007) found that individuals who had been exposed to major trauma during the September 11, 2001, attack on the World Trade Center displayed heightened amygdala activation when presented with emotionally aversive and fearful faces.

The heritability of criminal and aggressive behavior patterns has been evident for some time (see Chapter 8), although adoption studies have identified a heritability-by-environment interaction effect. Cloninger, Sigvardsson, Bohman, and von Knorring (1982) found that under conditions of low heritable risk (i.e., having a biological parent who was not a criminal), the impact of the environment (i.e., having an adoptive parent who was or was not a criminal) on later criminality was rather small (a rate of .03 for noncriminal adoptive parents vs. .07 for criminal adoptive parents). However, under conditions of high heritable risk, the effect of the environment was strong (.12 for noncriminal adoptive parents vs. .40 for criminal adoptive parents). Jaffee et al. (2005) studied monozygotic and dizygotic twins from the British E-Risk study and identified four rank-ordered groups of increasing heritable risk, with the lowest heritable-risk group being children whose monozygotic twin was not conduct disordered (CD), the next lowest group being children whose dizygotic twin was not CD, the next highest group being children whose dizygotic twin was CD, and the highest group being children whose monozygotic twin was CD. The experience of child physical maltreatment was determined by clinical interview with the mother, following procedures used by Dodge, Bates, and Pettit (1990). Among the group at lowest heritable risk, the experience of physical maltreatment had little effect on conduct disorder outcomes (for the nonmaltreated group, the rate was .02; for maltreated group it was .04). Among those at the next highest level of heritable risk, the effect of maltreatment was small (.06 vs. .13). Among the group at the next highest level, the effect of maltreatment grew larger (.19 vs. .37). Finally, among those at the highest level, the effect of maltreatment was largest (.46 vs. .70).

The search for specific genetic variables that predict aggressive behavior has been plagued by both political pressures and empirical failures to replicate published findings, perhaps because of atheoretical approaches to gene analyses that capitalize on chance (Kim-Cohen et al., 2006). Several theorists argue that genetic factors are likely to operate indirectly through their effects on neurally and biologically mediated dispositions to act impulsively without planning, without empathy, or without consideration of extenuating circumstances (Caspi et al., 2002). These dispositions have been called *executive functions* (Morgan & Lilienfeld, 2000), and they likely affect processing responses (or are measured as processing responses) during social interactions. For example, a deficit in considering another's feelings would lead to inaccurate interpretations of stimulus events, and impulsivity would lead to premature decision making that failed to consider long-term consequences.

In line with this hypothesis, the genetic polymorphisms that have been most frequently correlated with aggressive behavior are ones that relate to neurotransmitter functions, especially dopamine (Dick et al., 2006; Moffitt et al., 2008; see also Chapter 8, this volume). Three genes are discussed here. First, MAO-A is an enzyme that selectively metabolizes serotonin, norepinephrine, and dopamine (Shih, Chen, & Ridd, 1999), which are involved in brain actions associated with stress regulation (Charney, 2004) and biological sensitivity to adverse social contexts (Boyce & Ellis, 2005). A polymorphism in the X-chromosome-linked gene that encodes MAO-A has been identified in about one third of all human males, suggesting that it might have adaptive value across evolution but is still nonnormative. In rodents, this polymorphism has been correlated with both aggressive behavior and lower brain serotonin and norepinephrine levels (Cases et al., 1995). In humans, a modest main effect of a polymorphism in MAO-A on aggressive behavior has been found (Brunner, Nelen, Breakefield, Ropers, & van Oost, 1993), but other studies have found contradictory patterns (Kim-Cohen et al., 2006).

More likely in my estimation is a gene-by-environment interaction effect. Eisenberger, Way, Taylor, Welch, and Lieberman (2007) found that individuals with the low-expression allele form of MAO-A demonstrated heightened dorsal anterior cingulate cortex activity but only in response to an environmental stressor of peer social rejection and not to peer inclusion. They suggested that MAO-A may dispose individuals to become "hypersensitive" to interpersonal rejection.

If the MAO-A enzyme is involved in regulating stress, especially in reaction to trauma and threat, then it might play a role in moderating the effect of early physical maltreatment on the development of aggressive behavior. Caspi et al. (2002) found this interaction effect in their Dunedin longitudinal sample, and Kim-Cohen et al. (2006) replicated the pattern in the British E-Risk study. In the CDP, we recently replicated this interaction effect on externalizing behavior patterns (Edwards et al., 2009). Among children without the MAO-A polymorphism, those who had been maltreated did not differ from those who had not been maltreated in the proportion who had been arrested by age 22 (.28 vs. .25), but among children with the polymorphism, those who had been maltreated had a much higher probability of criminal arrest by age 22 than those who had not been maltreated (.71 vs. .26).

A second gene that has been implicated in a variety of externalizing and addiction disorders is the gamma-aminobutyric acid (GABA) A receptor, alpha 2, also known as GABRA2 (Dick et al., 2006). GABA is the major inhibitory neurotransmitter in the mammalian brain. A polymorphism in GABRA2 has been associated with conduct disorder, but the more powerful pattern again is a gene-by-environment interaction in which high parental supervision during early adolescence has been found to buffer children from the adverse effect of the GABRA2 polymorphism (Dick et al., 2006). Among children whose parents engaged in low rates of supervision, the likelihood of being in a persistently high trajectory of conduct problems across adolescence increases dramatically with the number of copies of the risk allele of GABRA2, from .07 to .19 to .28 for 0, 1, or 2 copies, respectively, whereas among children whose parents engaged in high rates of supervision, the likelihood of being in the persistently high trajectory of conduct problems increases modestly from .10 to .12 to .13 for 0, 1, or 2 copies, respectively.

A third gene that has been found to correlate with aggressive behavior is 5-HT. Recall that polymorphisms in 5-HT have been associated with impaired limbic structures and increased amygdala function. Waldman (2008; see also Chapter 8, this volume) recently took this work a step further by finding a significant relation between a polymorphism in 5-HT and individual differences in reactive but not proactive aggressive behavior. Even more striking was that, using the social information processing instruments described earlier, it was possible to find a significant association between

5-HT and hostile attributional biases. Finally, the effect of 5-HT on reactive aggression was mediated by hostile attributional biases. This work is the first known attempt to identify molecular genetic bases for social information processing patterns.

In sum, a comprehensive model of the development of chronic aggressive behavior must take into account environmental main effects, gene main effects, and gene-by-environment interaction effects. Furthermore, the environmental variables are likely to include both broad factors that influence aggression across many situations as well as factors that influence aggression within particular kinds of situations.

A PROPOSED MODEL OF SOCIAL INFORMATION PROCESSING MECHANISMS IN GENE-BY-ENVIRONMENT INTERACTION EFFECTS

Integration of the distal genetic and environmental factors with social information processing proximal mechanisms requires a final leap of theorizing. The model proposed here builds on models by van Goozen, Fairchild, and Harold (2008) and Raine (2008) but is unique in positing that within-situation processing patterns mediate the effects of genes, environments, and their interactions. The overall model is depicted in Figure 9.1, which posits that specific (albeit as yet unidentified) genes and an early environment characterized by threat, trauma, or adversity pose risks for the long-term development of chronically violent behavior. These distal factors operate as main effects and in interaction with each other. Throughout development, particular environments also lead to the development of situation-specific processing patterns that mediate aggressive behavior within those situations. When these situations present themselves, they pose proximal risk of violent behavior.

These distal and proximal risk factors are mediated by brain processes that operate in response to proximal situational stimuli. Three aspects of functioning are hypothesized to co-occur during responding: neural activity in synapses (most likely involving neurotransmitters such as dopamine), social information processing as described earlier, and psychophysiological activity in the autonomic nervous system. These brain processes, in turn, mediate aggressive behavioral responses within these situations.

A RESEARCH AGENDA

This model suggests numerous studies that have yet to be completed. To understand the intricate interactions among specific genes and specific environments, existing large-sample longitudinal studies need to be mined to test

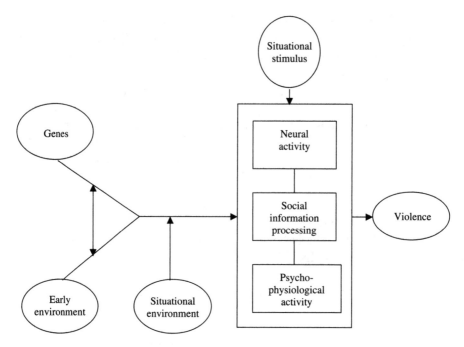

Figure 9.1. A proposed model of genetic, environmental, and processing mechanisms in the development of aggressive behavior.

gene–environment hypotheses. Subgroups of individuals who fit profiles of gene–environmental risk need to be exposed to situational stimuli that elicit processing responses while the individuals are being observed via fMRI and psychophysiological recording.

Such studies are likely to produce both support and disconfirmation of different components of the proposed model, hopefully with iterative refinement of the model over time. Although empirical studies have already yielded promising results, it is highly unlikely that any single gene or group of genes, even in interaction with environmental histories, will account for much of the variance in aggressive behavior.

The implications of these empirical findings and the model in Figure 9.1 for the design of preventive interventions suggest an additional research agenda. Environmental engineering in light of personalized genetic information has the exciting but unrealized potential to reduce or prevent the development of chronic violence. So, too, environments and training interventions that alter social information processing patterns offer the hope of secondary prevention among individuals at high risk in terms of gene–environment risk profiles. Thus, despite an enormous amount of progress so far, research on the determinants of aggressive behavior still has a long way to go.

REFERENCES

Archer, J. (2000). Sex differences in aggression between heterosexual partners: A meta-analytic review. *Psychological Bulletin, 126,* 651–680. doi:10.1037/0033-2909.126.5.651

Arnett, J. J. (2006). The psychology of emerging adulthood: What is known, and what remains to be known? In J. J. Arnett & J. L. Tanner (Eds.), *Emerging adults in America: Coming of age in the 21st century* (pp. 303–330). Washington, DC: American Psychological Association. doi:10.1037/11381-013

Brendgen, M., Vitaro, F., Tremblay, R. E., & Lavoie, F. (2001). Reactive and proactive aggression: Predictions to physical violence in different contexts and moderating effects of parental monitoring and caregiving behavior. *Journal of Abnormal Child Psychology, 29,* 293–304. doi:10.1023/A:1010305828208

Boyce, W. T., & Ellis, B. (2005). Biological sensitivity to context: I. An evolutionary–developmental theory of the origins and functions of stress reactivity. *Development and Psychopathology, 17,* 271–301. doi:10.1017/S0954579405050145

Brunner, H. G., Nelen, M., Breakefield, X., Ropers, H., & van Oost, B. (1993, October). Abnormal behavior associated with a point mutation in the structural gene for monoamine oxidase A. *Science, 262,* 578–580. doi:10.1126/science.8211186

Cases, O., Seif, I., Grimsby, J., Gaspar, P., Chen, K., Pournin, S., . . . De Maeyer, E. (1995, June). Aggressive behavior and altered amounts of brain serotonin and norepinephrine in mice lacking MAOA. *Science, 268,* 1763–1766. doi:10.1126/science.7792602

Caspi, A., McClay, J., Moffitt, T. E., Mill, J., Martin, J., Craig, I.,W., . . . Poulton, R. (2002, August). Role of genotype in the cycle of violence in maltreated children. *Science, 297,* 851–854. doi:10.1126/science.1072290

Charney, D. S. (2004). Psychobiological mechanisms of resilience and vulnerability: Implications for successful adaptation to extreme stress. *The American Journal of Psychiatry, 161,* 195–216. doi:10.1176/appi.ajp.161.2.195

Cloninger, C. R., Sigvardsson, S., Bohman, M., & von Knorring, A. (1982). Predisposition to petty criminality in Swedish adoptees. *Archives of General Psychiatry, 39,* 1242–1247.

Collins, W. A., & van Dulmen, M. (2006). "The course of true love(s) . . .": Origins and pathways in the development of romantic relationships. In A. C. Crouter & A. Booth (Eds.), *Romance and sex in adolescence and emerging adulthood: Risks and opportunities* (pp. 63–86). Mahwah, NJ: Erlbaum.

Crick, N. R., & Dodge, K. A. (1994). A review and reformulation of social information-processing mechanisms in children's social adjustment. *Psychological Bulletin, 115,* 74–101. doi:10.1037/0033-2909.115.1.74

Crockett, M. J., Clark, L., Tabibnia, G., Lieberman, M. D., & Robbins, T. W. (2008, June). Serotonin Modulates Behavioral Reactions to Unfairness. *Science, 320,* 1739. doi:10.1126/science.1155577

Crozier, J. C., Dodge, K. A., Fontaine, R. G., Lansford, J. E., Bates, J. E., Pettit, G. S., & Levenson, R. W. (2008). Social information processing and cardiac predictors of adolescent antisocial behavior. *Journal of Abnormal Psychology, 117,* 253–267. doi:10.1037/0021-843X.117.2.253

Dick, D. M., Bierut, L., Hinrichs, A., Fox, L., Bucholz, K. K., Kramer, J., . . . Foroud, T. (2006). The role of GABRA2 in risk for conduct disorder and alcohol and drug dependence across developmental stages. *Behavior Genetics, 36,* 577–590. doi:10.1007/s10519-005-9041-8

Dodge, K. A. (1980). Social cognition and children's aggressive behavior. *Child Development, 51,* 162–170. doi:10.2307/1129603

Dodge, K. A., Bates, J. E., & Pettit, G. S. (1990, December). Mechanisms in the cycle of violence. *Science, 250,* 1678–1683. doi:10.1126/science.2270481

Dodge, K. A., Coie, J. D., & Lynam, D. (2006). Aggression and antisocial behavior in youth. In N. Eisenberg, W. Damon, & R. M. Lerner (Eds.), *Handbook of child psychology: Vol. 3. Social, emotional, and personality development* (6th ed., pp. 719–788). New York, NY: Wiley.

Dodge, K. A., Lansford, J. E., Burks, V. S., Bates, J. E., Pettit, G. S., Fontaine, R., & Price, J. M. (2003). Peer rejection and social information-processing factors in the development of aggressive behavior problems in children. *Child Development, 74,* 374–393. doi:10.1111/1467-8624.7402004

Dodge, K. A., & Pettit, G. S. (2003). A biopsychosocial model of the development of chronic conduct problems in adolescence. *Developmental Psychology, 39,* 349–371. doi:10.1037/0012-1649.39.2.349

Dodge, K. A., Pettit, G. S., & Bates, J. E. (1994). Socialization mediators of the relation between socioeconomic status and child conduct problems. *Child Development, 65,* 649–665. doi:10.2307/1131407

Dodge, K. A., Pettit, G. S., Bates, J. E., & Valente, E. (1995). Social information-processing patterns partially mediate the effect of early physical abuse on later conduct problems. *Journal of Abnormal Psychology, 104,* 632–643. doi:10.1037/0021-843X.104.4.632

Dodge, K. A., Pettit, G. S., McClaskey, C. L., & Brown, M. (1986). Social competence in children. *Monographs of the Society for Research in Child Development, 51*(2), 1–85.

Edwards, A. C., Dodge, K. A., Latendresse, S. J., Lansford, J. E., Bates, J. E., Pettit, G. S., . . . Dick, D. M. (2009). MAOA-uVNTR and early physical discipline interact to influence delinquent behavior. *Journal of Child Psychology and Psychiatry.* doi:10.1111/j.1469-7610.2009.02196.x

Eisenberger, N. I., Way, B. M., Taylor, S. E., Welch, W. T., & Lieberman, M. D. (2007). Understanding genetic risk for aggression: Clues from the brain's response to social exclusion. *Biological Psychiatry, 61,* 1100–1108. doi:10.1016/j.biopsych.2006.08.007

Evers, E. A. T., Van der Veen, F. M., Van Deursen, J. A., Schmitt, J. A. J., Deutz, N. E. P., & Jolles, J. (2006). The effect of acute tryptophan depletion on the BOLD response during performance monitoring and response inhibition in healthy male volunteers. *Psychopharmacology, 187,* 200–208. doi:10.1007/s00213-006-0411-6

Fontaine, R. G., & Dodge, K. A. (2006). Real-time decision making and aggressive behavior in youth: A heuristic model of response evaluation and decision (RED). *Aggressive Behavior, 32,* 604–624. doi:10.1002/ab.20150

Fontaine, R. G., Yang, C., Dodge, K. A., Bates, J. E., & Pettit, G. S. (2008). Testing an individual systems model of Response Evaluation and Decision (RED) and anti-social behavior across adolescence. *Child Development, 79,* 462–475. doi:10.1111/j.1467-8624.2007.01136.x

Ganzel, B., Casey, B. J., Glover, G., Voss, H. U., & Temple, E. (2007). The after-math of 9/11: Effect of intensity and recency of trauma on outcome. *Emotion, 7,* 227–238. doi:10.1037/1528-3542.7.2.227

Graham, S., & Hudley, C. (1993). An attributional intervention to reduce peer-directed aggression among African-American boys. *Child Development, 64,* 124–138.

Guerra, N. G., & Slaby, R. G. (1989). Evaluative factors in social problem solving by aggressive boys. *Journal of Abnormal Child Psychology, 17,* 277–289.

Jaffee, S. R., Caspi, A., Moffitt, T. E., Dodge, K. A., Rutter, M., Taylor, A., & Tully, L. A. (2005). Nature × nurture: Genetic vulnerabilities interact with physical maltreatment to promote conduct problems. *Development and Psychopathology, 17,* 67–84. doi:10.1017/S0954579405050042

Kim-Cohen, J., Caspi, A., Taylor, A., Williams, B., Newcombe, R., Craig, I. W., & Moffit, T. E. (2006). MAOA, maltreatment, and gene–environment interaction predicting children's mental health: New evidence and a meta-analysis. *Molecular Psychiatry, 11,* 903–913. doi:10.1038/sj.mp.4001851

Lansford, J. E., Malone, P. S., Dodge, K. A., Crozier, J. C., Pettit, G. S., & Bates, J. E. (2006). A 12-year prospective study of patterns of social information processing problems and externalizing behaviors. *Journal of Abnormal Child Psychology, 34,* 709–718. doi:10.1007/s10802-006-9057-4

Lansford, J. E., Miller-Johnson, S., Berlin, L. J., Dodge, K. A., Bates, J. E., & Pettit, G. S. (2007). Early physical abuse and later violent delinquency: A prospective longitudinal study. *Child Maltreatment, 12,* 233–245. doi:10.1177/1077559507301841

Liston, C., McEwan, B. S., & Casey, B. J. (2009). Psychosocial stress reversibly disrupts prefrontal processing and attentional control. *Proceedings of the National Academy of Sciences of the United States of America, 106,* 912–917. doi:10.1073/pnas.0807041106

Lorber, M. F. (2004). Psychophysiology of aggression, psychopathy, and conduct problems: A meta-analysis. *Psychological Bulletin, 130,* 531–552.

Meyer-Lindenberg, A., Buckholtz, J. W., Kolachana, B., Hariri, A., Pezawas, L., Blasi, G., . . . Weinberger, D. R. (2006). Neural mechanisms of genetic risk for impulsivity and violence in humans. *Proceedings of the National Academy of Science Early Edition, 103,* 6269–6274. doi: 10.1073/pnas.0511311103

Moffitt, T. E., Arseneault, L., Jaffee, S. R., Kim-Cohen, J., Koenen, K. C., Odgers, C. L., . . . Viding, E. (2008). DSM-V conduct disorder: Research needs for an evidence base. *Journal of Child Psychology and Psychiatry, 49,* 3–33.

Moffitt, T. E., & Caspi, A. (2001). Childhood predictors differentiate life-course persistent and adolescence-limited antisocial pathways among males and females. *Development and Psychopathology, 13,* 355–375. doi:10.1017/S0954579401002097

Morgan, A. B., & Lilienfeld, S. O. (2000). A meta-analytic review of the relation between antisocial behavior and neuropsychological measures of executive function. *Clinical Psychology Review, 20,* 113–136. doi:10.1016/S0272-7358(98)00096-8

Murphy, F. C., Nimmo-Smith, I., & Lawrence, A. D. (2003). Functional neuroanatomy of emotions: A meta-analysis. *Cognitive, Affective, & Behavioral Neuroscience, 3,* 207–233. doi:10.3758/CABN.3.3.207

Nay, S., Dodge, K. A., Lansford, J., Pettit, G. S., & Bates, J. E. (2009). *Rejection sensitivity as a mediator of the effect of romantic relationship history on violent behavior in romantic relationships.* Unpublished manuscript.

Orobio de Castro, B., Veerman, J. W., Koops, W., Bosch, J. D., & Monshouwer, H. J. (2002). Hostile attribution of intent and aggressive behavior: A meta-analysis. *Child Development, 73,* 916–934. doi:10.1111/1467-8624.00447

Ortiz, J., & Raine, A. (2004). Heart rate level and antisocial behavior in children and adolescents: A meta-analysis. *Journal of the American Academy of Child and Adolescent Psychiatry, 43,* 154–162. doi:10.1097/00004583-200402000-00010

Pettit, G. S., Lansford, J. E., Dodge, K. A., & Bates, J. E. (2009). *Domain specificity in social information processing and violent behavior in early adulthood.* Manuscript submitted for publication.

Pezawas, L., Meyer-Lindenberg, A., Drabani, E. M., Verchinski, B. A., Munoz, K. E., Kolachana, B. S., . . . Weinberger, D. R. (2005). 5-HTTLPR polymorphism impacts human cingulate-amygdala interactions: a genetic susceptibility mechanism for depression. *Nature Neuroscience, 8,* 828–834. doi:10.1038/nn1463

Raine, A. (2002). Annotation: The role of prefrontal deficits, low autonomic arousal and early health factors in the development of antisocial and aggressive behavior in children. *Journal of Child Psychology and Psychiatry, and Allied Disciplines, 43,* 417–434. doi:10.1111/1469-7610.00034

Raine, A. (2008). From genes to brain to antisocial behavior. *Current Directions in Psychological Science, 17,* 323–328. doi:10.1111/j.1467-8721.2008.00599.x

Raine, A., Buchsbaum, M., & LaCasse, L. (1997). Brain abnormalities in murderers indicated by positron emission tomography. *Biological Psychiatry, 42,* 495–508. doi:10.1016/S0006-3223(96)00362-9

Raine, A., Venables, P. H., & Mednick, S. A. (1997). Low resting heart rate at age 3 years predisposes to aggression at age 11 years: Evidence from the Mauritius Child Health Project. *Journal of the American Academy of Child and Adolescent Psychiatry, 36,* 1457–1464.

Shih, J. C., Chen, K., & Ridd, M. (1999). Monoamine oxidase: From genes to behavior. *Annual Review of Neuroscience, 22*, 197–217. doi:10.1146/annurev.neuro.22.1.197

Silverman, J. G., Raj, A., Mucci, L. A., & Hathaway, J. E. (2001). Dating violence against adolescent girls and associated substance use, unhealthy weight control, sexual risk behavior, pregnancy, and suicidality. *JAMA, 286*, 572–579. doi:10.1001/jama.286.5.572

van Goozen, S. H. M., Fairchild, G., & Harold, G. T. (2008). The role of neurobiological deficits in childhood antisocial behavior. *Current Directions in Psychological Science, 17*, 224–228. doi:10.1111/j.1467-8721.2008.00579.x

Waldman, I. D. (2008, June). *The etiology of hostile perceptual biases and their relation with children's aggression.* Paper presented at the annual meeting of the Behavior Genetics Association, Louisville, KY.

Weiss, B., Dodge, K. A., Bates, J. E., & Pettit, G. S. (1992). Some consequences of early harsh discipline: Child aggression and a maladaptive social information processing style. *Child Development, 63*, 1321–1335. doi:10.2307/1131558

10

VIOLENCE AND CHARACTER: A CuPS (CULTURE × PERSON × SITUATION) PERSPECTIVE

DOV COHEN AND ANGELA K.-Y. LEUNG

Individual-differences and cultural approaches to the study of violence have both contributed greatly to our understanding, but both approaches face some inherent difficulties. A cultural approach that ignores individual differences can explain differences between cultures in rates of violence, but it has difficulty predicting who will be violent and what this means for the violent individuals' behavior in other contexts. Two problems with an individual-difference approach that ignores culture are that (a) the approach may fail to explain differences in rates of violence between societies and (b), perhaps more problematically, it may discover "truths" about violence that hold in only one cultural context but do not hold, or even reverse, in others.

In this chapter, we argue for the value of combining an individual-differences approach with a cultural-differences approach in a way that treats both individual differences and cultural differences seriously. Specifically, we argue for taking culture seriously by examining differences between cultural logics. Such logics structure behaviors, situations, scripts, and values in ways that make sense to people within a culture, even if they do not make sense to people outside that culture. We also argue for taking individual differences seriously by treating people as more than cultural robots who mechanically follow cultural dictates. In the combined approach advocated here, the key notion is that individuals are always in a culture, though they are not always of it. We outline this combined approach, the CuPS approach (culture × person × situation) and demonstrate its value by describing experiments conducted with three different cultural groups.

Before doing so, it is important to say what the CuPS approach is not. CuPS is not a mediational approach. It does not assume that there is some underlying individual difference that plays itself out similarly across cultures, and it does not assume that cultural differences would simply derive from such an underlying difference. As such, it does not follow the common procedures for studying cultural and individual differences, namely, (a) showing that there are cultural differences between some dependent variables; (b) measuring an individual-difference variable that also predicts the dependent variable and differs in mean levels across cultures; and (c) showing that the cultural difference is entirely a product of this individual difference, disappearing when the individual difference is controlled for.

We have no doubt that this mediational approach is important and that it is extremely useful for understanding various phenomena. However, our approach differs in that it treats culture seriously by considering the way cultural logics structure and give psychological meaning to behaviors and situations, and it allows for different cultures to have different cultural logics. Triandis's (1994) notion of a cultural syndrome and Mischel and colleagues' (Mendoza-Denton & Mischel, 2007) conception of personality as defined by a *behavioral signature* are both essential for the CuPS approach.

SYNDROMES AND SIGNATURES

A *cultural syndrome* is a central organizing theme of a culture (e.g., "honor," "dignity") structured by a cultural logic that clusters behaviors, situations, scripts, and values in a coherent, meaningful way. This coherence is internal in that it is coherent according to a distinct cultural logic for a given culture or subculture, and it may be completely incoherent for outsiders whose own cultures are structured by a different cultural logic. Thus, clusters of behavior that make perfect sense in one culture may seem puzzling to people outside that culture: "How come he would risk his life to help me out of a jam, but if I insult his mother, he'd kill me?" "How can this person be so trustworthy when he has no backbone and won't stand up for himself?" "How can this person be so arrogant that he ignores other people's opinions, and yet he is also so kind and dependable?"

Individual differences arise because people are not automata following the dictates of their culture. People can follow the ideals of their culture, or they can reject them. However, their behavior should not be considered random, because it is in fact patterned. People choose their behavior, but these choices are often influenced by ready-made cultural templates that structure certain sorts of behaviors as belonging together. Thus, within an honor culture, an individual who endorses retributive violence may be embracing the honor ideal and thus may be more honest and trustworthy, these virtues also being elements of the honor ideal. Conversely, within an honor culture, an individual who rejects retributive violence may be rejecting the honor ideals, including those related to being an honest and trustworthy person. Outside of an honor culture, the pattern is likely quite different. In a nonhonor culture, a person who endorses retributive violence may be rejecting his culture's ideals, including ideals of honesty and trustworthiness as well as nonviolence. The particular cultural logics have to be understood in greater detail, but the point is that the person × situation behavioral signatures in one culture may be very different from the person × situation behavioral signatures in another culture.

ORDER AND VALUE IN HONOR, DIGNITY, AND FACE CULTURES

Cultures are defined by how they solve certain problems. Two of the most salient of these are the problem of order and the problem of value. The first relates to how cooperation and order emerge in a society, with a central question being: Who has legitimate authority to use violence and when can they use it? The second relates to how worth is provisioned: Is personal worth something that is inherent in the individual and inalienable, or is worth something that must be socially conferred?

Our research has been mostly concerned with cultural syndromes of honor, dignity, and face, and we provide brief sketches of these as "ideal types," centering on the two issues mentioned previously. In a culture of *dignity*, a defining idea is that "each individual at birth possess[es] an intrinsic value at least theoretically equal to that of every other person" (Ayers, 1984, p. 19). Dignity is inalienable in that others cannot take it away. Thus, a person of dignity is relatively impervious to insults or affronts by others. A person with a sense of dignity has an integrity that comes from a sturdy moral core, centered on a belief in the inherent worth of individual human beings. This sturdy moral core—rather than the threat of being shamed by others— is presumed to keep the individual behaving correctly, regardless of the whims of the situation, the temptations of expediency, or the desire to curry favor with others. When individual conscience fails, however, an effective system of law enforcement is there to back it up. Dignity cultures tend to be found in societies such as market economies, where individuals act as relatively autonomous agents who work within a system of law that protects property rights and punishes predation. Violations of the rules are offenses against the state, and it is the state that punishes, rather than vigilantes.

In a culture of honor, honor is both internal and external; it must be claimed from and paid by others. *Honor* is defined by Pitt-Rivers (1966) as follows:

> The value of a person in his own eyes, but also in the eyes of his society. It is his estimation of his own worth, his claim to pride, but it is also the acknowledgement of that claim . . . his right to pride. (p. 21)

An individual must assertively strive for honor, but if that honor is not ultimately conferred by other people, it is a big problem. Thus, honor requires fortitude but is itself fragile and precarious. In Ayers's (1984) metaphor, it is unlike dignity, which resembles

> an internal skeleton, . . . a hard structure at the center of the self; honor, on the other hand, resembles a . . . suit of armor that, once pierced, leaves the self . . . no alternative except to strike back in desperation. (p. 20)

The fragility of honor derives from the context in which cultures of honor typically develop. They arise in contexts where the state is weak, where there is no effective law enforcement, no mechanism to guarantee contracts, no police to prevent predation, and no justice system to punish the guilty (Pitt-Rivers, 1966). In such an environment, "every man should be sheriff on his own hearth" (as an old North Carolina proverb put it; Fischer, 1988, p. 765). A reputation for reciprocity is key here because one must be known as someone who will pay back, who can be relied on to pay back a good turn, who will deliver on promises (and threats), and who will avenge wrongs done to him (see Chapter 12, this volume). Insults and trivial conflicts take on great importance in such cultures because they are probes or tests of who can do what to whom. A man who will not let himself be trifled with on small matters surely will not let himself be trifled with on big matters either. In this context, it pays to have a reputation as a man of honor who will show positive reciprocity and, if wronged, a thirst for vengeance (see Chapters 3 and 12, this volume).

Cultures of face exist within strong hierarchical structures. *Face*, as defined by Ho (1976) and by Heine, Lehman, Markus, and Kitayama (1999), is "the respectability and/or deference which a person can claim . . . by virtue of [his or her] relative position" in a hierarchy and is the proper fulfillment of his or her role. A person's performance in his or her role is not for him or her to judge but rather must be judged by others; thus, face has primarily an external quality (Kim & Cohen, 2010). Face can be gained, but the focus is mostly on not losing it—for oneself and for others one interacts with. Indeed, unlike honor cultures, where one person can often increase his honor by taking someone else's, in face cultures people often work together to save each other's face, avoiding the direct conflicts that become such important contests for status in competitive honor cultures.

Bad behavior in a face culture is not supposed to be punished by the victim. Doing so would only further upset the harmony that is supposed to prevail in the stable hierarchy of a face culture. Instead, the group or someone further up the hierarchy will do the punishing. Generally, the three Hs that characterize face cultures are harmony, hierarchy, and humility. The latter, humility, is quite functional, because in a system where face must be socially conferred, it is not good to claim too much for oneself; otherwise, one may receive a painful and humiliating lesson about where one really falls in the status hierarchy.

These sketches of three kinds of cultures are ideal types (Weber, 1920/1997), and ideal types do not actually exist in the world. However, the sketches are useful because they lead us to predict different behavioral signatures among people from honor, dignity, and face cultures. It is not the case that individuals all follow the ideals of their culture. However, when individuals depart from the ideals, their departures tend to be systematic. Individuals who depart from the ideals are not simply people who are oblivious to cultural norms, and they are not random noise. Rather, their behavior—even when they reject their culture's dominant ideals—tends to fit preexisting cultural templates, patterned by the culture's logic even as its ideals are rejected. Again, individuals are always in a culture, even if they are not always of it.

TWO EXPERIMENTS

We attempted to demonstrate how this works with two laboratory experiments showing the different person × situation behavioral signatures that occur in different cultures. In our first study we examined positive reciprocity, and in our second we examined the virtue of trustworthiness, as shown by whether participants cheated on a memory test to earn money. In both studies, University of Illinois students were participants. Our dignity culture group comprised northern Anglo American students, our honor culture group comprised Latino and southern Anglo American students, and our face culture group comprised Asian Americans whose ancestors were from East Asia (for supporting evidence, see Ayers, 1984; Cohen, Hoshino-Browne, & Leung, 2007; Hamamura & Heine, 2008; Heine et al., 1999; Ho, 1976; Kim, Cohen, & Au, in press; Triandis, 1994; Vandello & Cohen, 2003; Vandello, Cohen, Grandon, & Franiuk, 2009). Obviously, all of the participants were American, so we speak of our groups not as coming from different societies but as people whose relative familiarity with dignity, face, and honor differs as a function of the dominant theme within their subculture.

In both experiments, we obtained individual-difference measures of the participant's (a) endorsement of honor-related violence and (b) belief that a person's worth is either inalienable or must be socially conferred. The measure of (a) was obtained by showing video clips in which someone responded violently to an insult, affront, or threat, and the participants had to indicate how justified the violence was, how much the insulter deserved to be beaten, how reasonable the violent person's actions were, and so on. The measure of (b) was obtained with simple Likert scale items: "How others treat me is irrelevant to my worth as a person," "How much I respect myself is far, far more important than how much others respect me," "No one (except me) can make me feel diminished," and "No one can take a person's self-respect away from him or her." Participants' endorsements of (a) or (b) were person-level variables in the design.

In Experiment 1, participants were given a cover story, according to which we were examining people's attitudes toward violence in the media. This was the putative reason for showing film clips and asking about violence. The cover story was followed by a questionnaire that asked about demographics and also contained the questions described earlier concerning inalienable versus socially conferred worth. As far as the participant knew, that was the entire experiment. However, there was, of course, more to it than this. The participant came into the study with two fellow confederates. On learning that the experiment involved watching movies, one of the confederates pulled out a small bag of candies and offered some to the participant and the other confederate. In half the cases, the candy offerer turned out to be the "disk confederate" and in the other half, the offerer turned out to be the "distraction confederate" (the reason for the names will become obvious in a moment).

After filling out their questionnaires, participants and confederates received a false debriefing and were then dismissed. After they left the lab room, the distraction confederate buttonholed the participant and started talking to him as the disk confederate rummaged through his own backpack at a table 15 feet down the hall. The disk confederate pulled a crumpled piece of paper out of his backpack and asked the participant and confederate, "Do either of you know where room 25 is? I've got to meet a study group there in 5 minutes." Either the participant or the distraction confederate would reply that room 25 was in the basement, and after learning this, the disk confederate packed his bag up and left. In doing so, however, he "inadvertently" left behind and forgot his bright, neon-colored computer disk that now lay on the desk.

After allowing the disk confederate to make his getaway, the distraction confederate ended his conversation with the participant. Both of them then walked down the hall, having to walk past the "lost" disk. If the participant did not notice the disk, the confederate drew attention to it and gave the participant a few subtle opportunities to volunteer to find the disk confederate. If the participant did not take up the offer, the study ended. If the participant did take up the offer, he needed to find the disk confederate, not an easy task given that (a) the directional signs in the University of Illinois psychology building are confusing, contradictory, and occasionally completely misleading (pointing to the wrong floor) and (b) room 25 is actually a locked broom closet, tucked behind a set of doors at the bottom of a ramp.

Though a few participants could not or did not find room 25, the majority of those who attempted to do so succeeded. (Participant progress was monitored by confederates hidden throughout the building and by the exits, communicating via walkie-talkies.) If a participant reached room 25, however, his journey might continue, because room 25 had a sign on the door, "Meeting moved to room 841 (8th floor)." The participant then had to decide either to walk up the nine floors, take the elevator (if he had the time—the elevators were slow), or abandon the search altogether (the building's exit was located tantalizingly nearby). For those who chose to go on to the eighth floor and found room 841 (a broom closet again), there was another sign on the door, "Went to get TV and VCR. Will be back soon." A confederate hidden in the hallway watched to see whether the participant waited for at least 1 minute for someone to return. The participant's degree of helping could thus be measured, with higher scores indicating that the participant had gone further in trying to find the disk confederate. Because we manipulated whether it was the disk confederate or the distraction confederate who offered the participant candy, this situational manipulation dictated whether finding the disk confederate was or was not an act of reciprocity for his offer of the candy.

The key prediction involved a three-way interaction: culture (honor vs. nonhonor culture) × person (high vs. low endorsement of honor-related violence) × situation (helping is reciprocity vs. not reciprocity). The interaction was significant in a regression analysis. In analyzing the interaction, we found two very different patterns for our honor and nonhonor respondents. Among the honor group in the reciprocity condition, there were people who paid back and people who did not. That is, those who paid back insults and affronts ("negative gifts," as Miller, 1993, called them) were those who also went the furthest to pay back a favor, traipsing all over the psychology building to help out the person who offered them a piece of candy. Thus, the people who paid back the negative were also the people who paid back the positive. However, in the nonhonor groups, the pattern was the opposite: Those who rejected retributive violence were most likely to return the favor to the disk confederate who had offered them candy. "Good" people eschewed violence and good people repaid the confederate.

The moral obligation to repay the confederate was binding for both honor culture participants who embraced the ideal of honor and for face and dignity participants who embraced the ideals of face and dignity, respectively. (With regard to this latter distinction, we further found that the dignity culture participants who were most likely to pay back a favor were also the ones who endorsed the notion that personal worth is inalienable; conversely, among nondignity participants, this relationship between paying back favors and endorsing the principle of inalienable worth did not hold.) Finding the disk confederate was a matter of fulfilling a duty to reciprocate rather than a simple act of altruism. The effects described earlier held for the situation where the disk confederate had offered the participant candy; they did not hold when the disk confederate had not offered candy.

The experiment illustrates in static form the argument that (a) cultural syndromes differ in the way they cluster behaviors together and (b) individuals position themselves toward or against the dominant syndromes of their culture or subculture. The experiment we describe next demonstrates this dynamically, illustrating the way this process works in microcosm. That is, our bicultural honor culture participants (i.e., Latinos and southern Anglos at the University of Illinois) may live in two worlds and may structure their behavior according to different cultural logics, depending on which one happens to be salient for them in a given situation.

The University of Illinois at Urbana–Champaign is an overwhelmingly White campus in a northern part of the state. Most psychology experiments there take place in a laboratory room in the Department of Psychology. The default ideal in such a context is dignity. In the experiment we just described, honor was "primed" in that all participants watched the film clips before having to find the confederate. In the next experiment, half the participants were unprimed, whereas the other half were primed with honor, watching the film clips before engaging in the crucial behavior (again, as in the experiment already described).

In this study, we also examined a different behavior, one related to trustworthiness and integrity (an ideal embraced under the mantle of honor in honor cultures, the mantle of dignity in dignity cultures, and the mantle of face in face cultures). The trustworthiness ideal is a universal good, but depending on the cultural syndrome from which it derives, it can be clustered with different sorts of behaviors.

For this study, we adapted a procedure from Houston and Ziff (1976), giving participants an opportunity to win money by cheating on a memory test. Briefly, the participant was instructed to remember words from two lists; the experimenter "accidentally" left one of these two lists exposed, and the dependent variable was (roughly) the likelihood that the participant cheated (as opposed to remembering words from the exposed list due to chance alone). Our person-level variable for the endorsement of retributive violence was measured in the same way as in the previous experiment; however, for half the participants, the honor–violence film clips were shown before the memory test was given and for the other half, the film clips came after.

Again, the key prediction concerned a three-way interaction: culture (honor vs. nonhonor culture) × person-level endorsement of violence (high vs. low) × situation (honor is primed vs. honor is not primed). The prediction can be illustrated by imagining two hypothetical people. Imagine person A from an honor culture who endorses the notion that insults and affronts need to be paid back with violence if necessary. Imagine person B from an honor culture, a person who lives by the mantra "Sticks and stones may break my bones but names will never hurt me" and thus rejects honor-related violence. In the unprimed condition, in the context of a psychology laboratory on a northern, predominately White campus, the cultural ideal that is salient and that one reacts toward or against is dignity. In this case, person A, who embraces the idea of paying back insults, is a rejecter of the ideal of dignity, and as a rejecter of dignity's ideal, should be less likely to act in an upright and trustworthy fashion. However, person B is an endorser of the dignity ideal, and as such, should be more likely to act with integrity.

Now, change the salient cultural syndrome to which A and B are reacting by administering the honor prime. When honor is the salient ideal, person A is an endorser of honor and, as such, should follow honor's strictures against cheating and be more honest. In contrast, person B goes from being an endorser of dignity to a rejecter of honor and, as a rejecter of honor, should be more likely to cheat. This is what happened in our experiment. The honor prime made endorsers of retributive violence less likely to cheat whereas making rejecters of retributive violence more likely to cheat.

It interesting that the priming effect was most pronounced among those most steeped in the culture of honor tradition. In the unprimed condition, for both the honor and the nonhonor groups, more endorsement of violence was correlated with more cheating. In the primed condition, among those who grew up entirely in the South, the correlation flipped dramatically: For those who grew up entirely in the South, the correlation between honor–violence endorsement and cheating was $r = -.87$. For these Southerners, endorsing honor violence meant embracing all that honor entails, including honesty. This did not occur for people from nonhonor groups or for people who spent much less of their life in the South. For these groups, one cannot prime—or perhaps more correctly, cannot easily prime—honor as the salient syndrome to which one reacts.

A few caveats are needed, and they derive from a more general point about priming. The effectiveness of a prime depends on both (a) the "strength" of the prime and (b) the participant's susceptibility to being primed by a given stimulus. Regarding susceptibility, the strong results with the lifelong Southerners are suggestive but must be regarded with caution due to the small n (we had only 16 lifelong Southerners in our sample). Although, regarding the strength of the prime, we could not effectively activate honor as an ideal for our nonhonor groups, this is not to say that the ideal can never be activated. Our participants watched five film clips. Perhaps stronger primes could induce honor as a salient ideal, but in the current studies we have no evidence for this (see also Cohen, 2007).

Cultural Rejectionism

As illustrated previously, being an endorser of honor (when honor is the salient ideal) is not the same thing as being a rejecter of dignity (when dignity is the salient ideal). And conversely, being a rejecter of honor is not the same thing as being an endorser of dignity. The same inclination toward or against retributive violence positions one as either a rejecter or endorser of a cultural system (of honor, dignity, or face), and positioning oneself with respect to this cultural system has implications for a wide variety of behaviors, including positive reciprocity, honesty, and (as illustrated in our other work not discussed here) financial as well as political actions (see Leung & Cohen, 2008).

A point that these studies reiterate is that cultural rejecters are not simply oblivious folks who just don't "get it." They are not simply undersocialized. Sometimes they understand the cultural ideals perfectly well and just choose to reject them. In our studies, cultural rejectionists behaved badly in ways that were striking. In the disk study, Southerners and Latinos who rejected honor-related violence actually helped someone less after that person offered them candy than they did when the person did not offer them candy. The same was true of northern Anglo and Asian Americans who endorsed honor-related violence. And the same was true of northern Anglo Americans who rejected the ideal of inalienable worth. These participants all helped the confederate less after the confederate had done something nice for them. They behaved most badly when social obligations pressed most heavily on them.

It would be worthwhile to study further this seeming desire to violate norms—to act badly when one is most obligated not to—perhaps because of a motivation to assert one's own autonomy, perhaps because of some other motive, or perhaps simply for the sake of spite. There is a Yiddish word— *aftselakhis*—translated "very literally, 'in order to provoke anger,' the impulse to do things only because someone else doesn't want you to" (Wex, 2005, p. 2). In the case of the experiments described here, the word may not apply because the participants in our studies were not angering the confederate by not returning his disk. However, the word perhaps captures some of the spirit of how our cultural rejectionists behaved (or misbehaved) when they faced social obligations. Again, the deeper underlying motives for their behavior, the feelings they experience when they violate social norms (e.g., glee?

shame? dejection? mastery? freedom?), and the circumstances that provoke such reactions seem worth studying if we want to avoid what Dennis Wrong (1961) famously called "the oversocialized conception of man" (p. 183). There may be individual differences in the desire to act spitefully, but the results from the second experiment showing that participants from honor cultures can go from endorsers of dignity to rejecters of honor (or from rejecters of dignity to endorsers of honor) by changing the salience of a cultural syndrome suggests that we should consider not just person-level effects but also the interaction of person-level variables with situational and cultural variables as well. (For more on these effects, see Cohen, 2009; Kim & Cohen, 2010.)

Rejecting the Logic

We have argued that individuals are always in a cultural context, although they are not always of it. That is, people react toward or against the salient ideals of their culture—embracing them or rejecting them. Individuals are "free" to go against the ideals of their culture. Our most important caveat is that there is another level of freedom beyond this. That is, individuals are free to reject not just the ideals of their culture but also the cultural logic itself that binds together and organizes sets of behaviors, values, and scripts. Thus, it is one thing to reject the ideals of honor as a package, to reject retributive violence, reject prosocial reciprocity, and reject honest behavior. However, it is another thing altogether to reject the logic that weaves together honor by, for example, embracing the notion that one is obligated to pay back good things but not obligated to pay back bad ones or by embracing the notion that one can show integrity without having to stand up for him- or herself if challenged. There are obviously people who do this (though in the first experiment there were not many). It seems worthwhile to study how, when, and why people challenge not just the ideals but also the underlying logic of their culture. Again, our second study provides a clue: At least for our bicultural respondents, one might be able to replace one cultural logic (e.g., honor) with that of another (e.g., dignity), or vice versa (see Leung & Cohen, 2009). Particularly in a rather loose social system such as that of the United States, people can operate in not just one culture but also in subcultures and sub-subcultures. Research exploring how people pick the niches they occupy in a culture or subculture may be particularly useful (Morris, 2009).

Our caveat does not modify the claim that individuals are always in a cultural context even if they are not always aware of it. However, it does make the claim more complex by noting that sometimes people can choose the salient cultural or subcultural system they are responding to. "Choice" does not apply to our experiments because participants were randomly assigned to a condition that made honor salient or not. But the point about choice applies to the larger sense in which people have some freedom to decide which subcultural systems they will be part of (see also Oishi, 2004; Zou, Morris, & Benet-Martinez, 2008).

CONCLUSION

In sum, all societies must solve the problem of order. How they solve it and how they conceive of individual worth help to define whether a society resembles the prototype of an honor, dignity, face, or some other sort of culture. Different cultural logics operate in different cultures, meaning that different sorts of behaviors, scripts, and values get bundled together in different ways. These bundles are coherent to people in the culture even if they do not always seem coherent to those outside the culture.

Individuals react toward or against the salient ideals of their culture, and even when they choose to reject the culture's ideals, they are still often guided by its logic and fit their behavior to preexisting cultural templates. The CuPS approach helps to explain the distinct patterns of within-culture, as well as between-culture, variation, and it takes both cultural logics and individual differences seriously. The acceptance or rejection of salient cultural ideals of honor, dignity, and face entail consequences for patterning a range of behaviors beyond violence, including whether one is an honest, trustworthy person who can be counted on to pay back favors. Individuals are always in a cultural context even if they are not always of it. Further research into the way people position themselves with respect to cultural ideals, their motives for doing so, and the forces and choices that influence the cultural syndrome to which they are responding seems likely to be very productive.

REFERENCES

Ayers, E. (1984). *Vengeance and justice*. New York, NY: Oxford University Press.

Cohen, D. (2007). Methods of cultural psychology. In S. Kitayama & D. Cohen (Eds.), *Handbook of cultural psychology* (pp. 196–236). New York, NY: Guilford Press.

Cohen, D. (2009). How do personal experience and cultural traditions interact to give rise to intracultural/regional variations within a national culture? In R. Wyer, C. Y. Chiu, & Y. Y. Hong (Eds.), *Understanding culture* (pp. 487–489). New York, NY: Taylor & Francis.

Cohen, D., Hoshino-Browne, E., & Leung, A. K.-y. (2007). Culture and the structure of personal experience: Insider and outsider phenomenologies of the self and social world. In M. Zanna (Ed.), *Advances in experimental social psychology* (Vol. 39, pp. 1–67). San Diego, CA: Academic Press.

Fischer, D. H. (1988). *Albion's seed.* New York, NY: Oxford University Press.

Hamamura, T., & Heine, S. (2008). The role of self-criticism in self-improvement and face maintenance among Japanese. In E. C. Chang (Ed.), *Self-criticism and self-enhancement* (pp. 105–122). Washington, DC: American Psychological Association. doi:10.1037/11624-007

Heine, S. J., Lehman, D., Markus, H., & Kitayama, S. (1999). Is there a universal need for positive self-regard? *Psychological Review, 106,* 766–794. doi:10.1037/0033-295X.106.4.766

Ho, D. (1976). On the concept of face. *American Journal of Sociology, 81,* 867–884. doi:10.1086/226145

Houston, J. P., & Ziff, T. (1976). Effects of success and failure on cheating behavior. *Journal of Educational Psychology, 68,* 371–376. doi:10.1037/0022-0663.68.3.371

Kim, Y. H., & Cohen, D. (2010). Information, perspective, and the self in face and dignity cultures. *Personality and Social Psychology Bulletin, 36,* 537–550. doi:10.1177/0146167210362398

Kim, Y. H., Cohen, D., & Au, W. T. (in press). The jury and abjury of my peers. *Journal of Personality and Social Psychology.*

Leung, A. K.-y., & Cohen, D. (2008). *Within- and between-culture variation: Individual differences and the cultural logics of honor, face, and dignity cultures.* Unpublished manuscript, Singapore Management University.

Leung, A. K.-y., & Cohen, D. (2009). *The embodiment of moral systems.* Unpublished manuscript, Singapore Management University.

Mendoza-Denton, R., & Mischel, W. (2007). Integrating system approaches to culture and personality. In S. Kitayama & D. Cohen (Eds.), *Handbook of cultural psychology* (pp. 175–195). New York, NY: Guilford Press.

Miller, W. (1993). *Humiliation.* Ithaca, NY: Cornell University Press.

Morris, M. (2009). How do personal experience and cultural traditions interact to give rise to intracultural/regional variations within a national culture? In R. Wyer, C. Y. Chiu, & Y. Y. Hong (Eds.), *Understanding culture* (pp. 484–487). New York, NY: Taylor & Francis.

Oishi, S. (2004). Personality in culture. *Journal of Research in Personality, 38,* 68–74. doi:10.1016/j.jrp.2003.09.012

Pitt-Rivers, J. (1966). Honour and social status. In J. Peristiany (Ed.), *Honour and shame* (pp. 19–78). London, England: Weidenfeld & Nicholson.

Triandis, H. C. (1994). *Culture and social behavior.* New York, NY: McGraw-Hill.

Vandello, J. A., & Cohen, D. (2003). Male honor and female fidelity: Implicit cultural scripts that perpetuate violence. *Journal of Personality and Social Psychology, 84,* 997–1010. doi:10.1037/0022-3514.84.5.997

Vandello, J., Cohen, D., Grandon, R., & Franiuk, R. (2009). Stand by your man. *Journal of Cross-Cultural Psychology, 40*, 81–104. doi:10.1177/0022022108326194

Weber, M. (1997). *The theory of social and economic organization*. New York, NY: Free Press. (original work in German published 1920)

Wex, M. (2005). *Born to kvetch*. New York, NY: St. Martin's Press.

Wrong, D. (1961). The oversocialized conception of man in modern sociology. *American Sociological Review, 26*, 183–193. doi:10.2307/2089854

Zou, X., Morris, M., & Benet-Martinez, V. (2008). Identity motives and cultural priming. *Journal of Experimental Social Psychology, 44*, 1151–1159. doi:10.1016/j.jesp.2008.02.001

III

PSYCHOLOGICAL AND RELATIONAL PROCESSES

11

MIRROR, MIRROR, ON THE WALL, WHO'S THE MOST AGGRESSIVE OF THEM ALL? NARCISSISM, SELF-ESTEEM, AND AGGRESSION

SANDER THOMAES AND BRAD J. BUSHMAN

What we have to fight for is the necessary security for the existence and increase of our race and people, the subsistence of its children and the maintenance of our racial stock unmixed, the freedom and independence of the Fatherland; so that our people may be enabled to fulfill the mission assigned to it by the Creator.

—Adolf Hitler

Do aggressive people typically think poorly of themselves? Are they full of self-doubt and feelings of inadequacy? Do they feel inferior to others? Or, instead, are aggressive people typically absorbed with themselves, thinking they are better than others? Do they overestimate rather than underestimate their qualities? Although controversies still exist, research has provided several important insights into the link between self-views and aggression. This chapter provides an overview of historical perspectives and more recent research findings; it addresses several existing controversies (and suggests ways to solve them), discusses possible interventions for reducing aggression, and recommends directions for future research.

HISTORICAL PERSPECTIVES

One long-standing view in psychology has held that low self-esteem causes aggression. Although the origins of this view are difficult to establish (there is no landmark work that made the original observation or theoretical statement that aggressive people suffer from low self-esteem), a few reasons may explain why this notion sneaked into conventional wisdom. Most important, we believe, is that it is intuitively compelling to believe that low self-esteem is a cause of aggression. Having low self-esteem feels bad, whereas having high self-esteem feels good. It may therefore seem logical to infer that having low self-esteem is associated with bad things (e.g., behaving aggressively) and having high self-esteem is associated with good things (e.g., behaving prosocially). Moreover, it is well established that unpleasant events, which make people feel bad, increase aggression (e.g., Berkowitz, 1983). As Nathaniel Branden (1984), one of the most fervent advocates of the idea that self-esteem is the key determinant of good adjustment, said: "I cannot think of a single psychological problem—from anxiety and depression, to fear of intimacy or of success, to spouse battery or child molestation—that is not traceable to the problem of low self-esteem" (p.12).

A few scholars have gone beyond correlations and tried to explain why low self-esteem should cause aggression. According to one explanation, people generally want to experience high self-esteem, so individuals with low self-esteem should suffer from distress and frustration and may behave aggressively in an attempt to feel better about themselves. Aggression is viewed as a strategy to regulate the pain and distress associated with one's negative self-feelings (Horney, 1950; Toch, 1969/1993). According to a second explanation, individuals with low self-esteem often reject societal norms, which include norms restricting aggressive behavior (Rosenberg, 1965). In the absence of firm empirical data, it was understandable for early psychologists to believe that low self-esteem is a cause of aggression. More recently, however, several well-designed, rigorous studies have examined the relationship between self-views and aggression. Is it still valid to believe that low self-esteem is a cause of aggression?

Does Low Self-Esteem Influence Aggressive Behavior?

In 1996, Roy Baumeister and his colleagues reviewed the literature and found little support for the view that low self-esteem increases aggression (Baumeister, Smart, & Boden, 1996). In fact, they concluded that inflated self-views increase aggression, especially when people suffer a blow to their ego. It is possible, however, that more recent findings have yielded a different picture, especially because the review sparked reevaluations and much new research (i.e., it has been cited hundreds of times). Here we provide an overview of research conducted since 1996.

Research on the Low Self-Esteem Hypothesis as it Applies to Adults

Research involving adult participants (mostly undergraduate college students) has typically found a negative association between self-esteem and self-reported aggression (e.g., Bradshaw & Hazan, 2006; Donnellan, Trzesniewski, Robins, Moffitt, & Caspi, 2005, Study 3; D'zurilla, Chang, & Sanna, 2003). Negative correlations in the range of −.20 to −.50 have typically been found between self-esteem and self-reported hostility and anger. More pertinent to the present purposes, weak but significant negative correlations have also been found between self-esteem and self-reported physical aggression. For example, one study found a correlation of −.11 in a sample of more than 3,000 undergraduate college students (Donnellan et al., 2005, Study 3). The main exception to this pattern of findings is the absence of a correlation between low self-esteem and self-reported verbal aggression. Thus, although low self-esteem individuals do not claim to be more verbally aggressive, they do claim to be more prone to anger, more likely to harbor hostile feelings toward others, and more likely to be physically aggressive than their high self-esteem counterparts.

Do these findings justify the claim that low self-esteem is an important cause of aggression? We believe not. Self-report measures are often problematic (e.g., Nisbett & Wilson, 1977), especially when examining aggression. Self-report studies typically find that high self-esteem individuals overstate their good qualities and understate their negative traits (Baumeister, Campbell, Krueger, & Vohs, 2003). Aggression is generally considered to be socially unacceptable, so people with high self-esteem should report low aggression. Thus, studies that relate self-esteem to self-reports of aggression are relevant only to the extent that their findings generalize to more objective measures of aggression. We know of one study that found a negative link between self-esteem and a behavioral measure of provoked aggression (i.e., preparing samples of hot sauce for a provocative confederate to consume; Webster & Kirkpatrick, 2006). However, this effect became significant only after a range of closely related self-regard variables (i.e., superiority, mate value, social inclusion) were statistically controlled. Moreover, another study in the same lab found no link between self-esteem and the same behavioral measure of aggression (Kirkpatrick, Waugh, Valencia, & Webster, 2002). It is this latter finding that is consistent with the majority of findings based on objective aggression measures. Whether these measures involved blasting opponents with painful noise (e.g., Bushman & Baumeister, 1998; Twenge & Campbell, 2003), giving a confederate less money (Bushman, Bonacci, van Dijk, & Baumeister, 2003), or third-party observations of real-world aggression (Goldberg et al., 2007), the bulk of studies found no correlations, or even small positive correlations between self-esteem and objectively observed aggression. In summary, the research conducted after Baumeister and colleagues published their 1996 review has provided no compelling reason to challenge their conclusion that low self-esteem does not cause aggression and violence.

Research on the Low Self-Esteem Hypothesis as It Applies to Children

It is possible that low self-esteem does not cause aggression in adulthood but does cause aggression in children. Indeed, aggression is much more common in late childhood and adolescence than it is in adulthood, perhaps increasing the likelihood of establishing a link with low self-esteem. In addition, late childhood and adolescence are developmental periods marked by profound concern with maintaining desired self-images (Harter, 2006). If it is true that aggression is a regulatory strategy people use to protect their feelings of self-worth (Morf & Rhodewalt, 2001), then children and adolescents who are low in self-esteem may be more likely than their adult counterparts to behave aggressively.

A pair of studies that used the same longitudinal sample (i.e., a complete birth cohort of over 1,000 participants from Dunedin, New Zealand) provided evidence that appears to be consistent with this reasoning (Donnellan et al., 2005, Study 2; Trzesniewski et al., 2006). One study found a small but significant negative relationship between self-esteem at age 11 and teacher- and parent-reported externalizing problems (including some items assessing aggression) at age 13 (Donnellan et al., 2005). The other study found a negative relationship between young adolescents' self-esteem and court convictions for violent offenses in adulthood (Trzesniewski et al., 2006). It is important that these findings were based on observational measures of aggression and externalizing problems, so they cannot be explained by self-report biases.

Unfortunately, however, these studies were limited in one important respect. They did not rule out the possibility that the link between low self-esteem and aggression was actually due to social or contextual factors related to both self-esteem and (later) violent and aggressive behavior. This is important because third variables often inflate the relationship between self-esteem and its supposed correlates (Baumeister et al., 2003). A different group of researchers tried to replicate the findings from these two studies using a similar New Zealand birth cohort of over 1,000 participants (Boden, Fergusson, & Horwood, 2007). These researchers also found that low self-esteem at ages 10 and 15 predicted aggressive and violent behavior at ages 18, 21, and 25. However, the relationship became nonsignificant when the researchers controlled for Maori ethnicity, parent education, and other family background factors that were potentially confounded with self-esteem. They concluded the following:

> While it may be possible to observe bivariate relationships between self-esteem and later violent and aggressive behavior, these associations are in fact very modest in nature, and can be explained by the effects of family background and contextual factors that are confounded with self-esteem, rather than the direct effects of self-esteem per se. (Boden et al., 2007, p. 888)

Taken together, many studies have appeared since Baumeister and colleagues (1996) challenged the notion that low self-esteem causes aggression. A few studies have sought to revive the low self-esteem hypothesis. However, these studies were methodologically flawed in important respects and consistently failed to replicate when more rigorous research designs were used. Regardless of whether one studies children, adolescents, or adults, low self-esteem generally fails to predict objective measures of aggressive behavior. Then we might ask another question: What kind of self-views, if any, predispose people to behave aggressively?

DOES NARCISSISM INFLUENCE AGGRESSIVE BEHAVIOR?

Baumeister and his colleagues (1996) proposed that aggression most commonly stems from *threatened egotism*. In other words, people with big egos become aggressive when others threaten their inflated egos. Thus, "grandiose" and "inflated" self-views, rather than simply "positive" self-views, were predicted to lead to aggressive and violent behavior. Such forms of exaggerated self-love are characteristic of narcissism. In its extreme form, *narcissism* is a personality disorder defined by grandiose self-views and an inflated sense of entitlement and personal superiority (American Psychiatric Association, 1994). Most current psychological research focuses on *normal narcissism*, operationalized as a trait on which people in the general population vary (Morf & Rhodewalt, 2001). Normal narcissism is typically measured using self-report questionnaires such as the Narcissistic Personality Inventory (NPI). Recent research has confirmed the view that NPI-measured narcissism is distributed dimensionally in the general population (Foster & Campbell, 2007).

The threatened egotism hypothesis has gained abundant empirical support. Bushman and Baumeister (1998) conducted two laboratory experiments in which participants were given the opportunity to aggress against individuals who insulted or praised them or against an innocent third person. The results showed that people with low self-esteem were not more aggressive than others. Narcissists who aggressed directly against the person who insulted them showed the highest aggression levels. The finding that narcissism is positively related to aggressive behavior in adults has been replicated by other researchers using self-report aggression questionnaires (Donnellan et al., 2005, Study 3; Lawrence, 2006), laboratory aggression measures (e.g., Bushman et al., 2003; Konrath, Bushman, & Campbell, 2006; Reidy, Zeichner, Foster, & Martinez, 2008; Stucke & Sporer, 2002; Twenge & Campbell, 2003), and real-world aggression measures (Bushman & Baumeister, 2002; Goldberg et al., 2007).

It is possible that self-esteem could have an indirect effect on aggression, so we recently examined the joint and interactive effects of self-esteem and narcissism on aggression (Bushman et al., 2009). Interactions between self-esteem and narcissism are relevant because clinical theories and empirical research have suggested that there are various kinds of narcissists who differ in their level of self-esteem (Dickinson & Pincus, 2003; Kernberg, 1975; Kohut, 1977). *Covert narcissists* have relatively low self-esteem and are described as socially avoidant individuals who are self-absorbed yet shy and introverted. In contrast, *overt narcissists* have much higher self-esteem and are described as self-assured extraverts who have a dominant interpersonal orientation. We reanalyzed data from a previous experiment (Bushman & Baumeister, 1998) and conducted a new experiment, finding that aggression was highest in threatened narcissists who also had high levels of self-esteem (i.e., in overt narcissists). To the extent that threatened narcissists harbored somewhat lower levels of self-esteem (characteristic of covert narcissists), they were much less aggressive.

Some scholars, however, have argued that laboratory findings may not generalize to the real world because the setting and measures are artificial (e.g., Donnellan et al., 2005). We therefore conducted a follow-up study as a naturalistic extension of our laboratory work (Bushman et al., 2009, Study 3). We used a nonlaboratory, naturally occurring situation in which students from a class were able to evaluate each other's work and influence each other's grade. Ego threat was not manipulated or artificially induced. Instead, it was measured in the form of naturally occurring feelings of humiliation experienced after receiving negative feedback from a fellow student. Similarly, the target of aggression was not an unseen confederate but a fellow student with whom participants actually interacted in the classroom. These features of the study made the events seem real and consequential: People were genuinely affected and sometimes humiliated by the criticisms they received of their actual class work, and they believed they could lower the grades of their evaluator by giving the evaluator negative feedback.

The results of this field study were the same as those from the laboratory experiments. The most aggressive people were those who experienced feelings of humiliation and had high levels of both narcissism and self-esteem. Humiliated narcissists who held lower levels of self-esteem were the least aggressive. Taken together, this set of studies provides new evidence against the view that low self-esteem causes aggression. There were indirect (rather than direct) effects of low self-esteem on aggression, but they were in the direction opposite of the low self-esteem hypothesis. Low self-esteem reduced or eliminated the independent effect of narcissism on aggression.

Although early work on narcissism focused on adults, narcissism can also be reliably identified and distinguished from related personality constructs in children and adolescents (Thomaes, Stegge, Bushman, Olthof, & Denissen, 2008). In a recent study, we examined whether narcissism and self-esteem also jointly predict aggression in children who undergo shameful experiences (Thomaes, Bushman, Stegge, & Olthof, 2008). Shameful experiences are fairly common in late childhood and adolescence, due in part to developmental increases in self-consciousness (Ryan & Kuczkowski, 1994). In our experiment, participants lost to an ostensible opponent in a competitive task. In the shame condition, they were told their opponent was really bad on the task and that they should easily win. After losing, they saw their own name at the bottom of a ranking list on a bogus web page, below their opponent's name. In the control condition, they were told nothing about their opponent and did not see any rankings. Next, participants could blast their opponent with loud noise through headphones (a measure of aggression). Consistent with previous studies of adults, narcissists were more aggressive than others but only when they were shamed. No support was found for the traditional view that low self-esteem underlies aggression. In fact, that view was contradicted by the finding that high self-esteem increased narcissistic shame-induced aggression. Once again, low self-esteem eliminated the aggressive behavior characteristic of shamed narcissists.

Taken together, these studies indicate that narcissistic self-views predispose people to behave aggressively. The link between narcissism and aggression generalizes across research settings and methodologies and seems to be independent of such factors as age, gender, and type of aggression measure. Narcissists are especially aggressive when their grandiose self-images are challenged. Self-esteem affects narcissists' aggressive inclinations by heightening aggression when self-esteem is high and reducing or inhibiting aggression when self-esteem is low.

Controversies

Although we have tried to explain and reconcile many of the conflicting findings that mark the literature on self-views and aggression, a number of unanswered questions and controversies remain. The first controversy concerns the shape of the relation between self-views and aggression. One might wonder whether the relationship is U-shaped, such that people holding negative, deflated self-views and people holding positive, inflated self-views are aggression prone. Such a U-shaped relationship would be supported by theories that argue that extremes of self-esteem (both low and high) are maladaptive because they typically reflect distorted perceptions (Jahoda, 1958; Kernis, 2003). Prior research has mainly tested linear relationships between self-views and aggression. We know of only two studies that examined the possibility of a curvilinear relationship (Perez, Vohs, & Joiner, 2005; Webster, 2007). The results from both studies provided little support for a U-shaped relationship, but both studies used self-report measures of aggression, which as we noted earlier are problematic. Thus, the issue remains open and awaits further scientific scrutiny.

Another controversy—one that we already touched on briefly—concerns the best way to measure aggressive behavior (see Chapters 1, 8, and 9). Some scholars have faulted laboratory aggression studies because they are artificial. Indeed, participants in laboratory studies are likely aware that researchers will not let them seriously injure or abuse anyone. However, research consistently finds that the same factors that increase aggression in the real world also increase aggression in the laboratory and that the same individual differences in aggression that exist in the real world also exist in the laboratory (Anderson & Bushman, 1997; Anderson, Lindsay, & Bushman, 1999). Clearly, one advantage of field studies of aggression is that they do not suffer from lack of ecological validity. However, field studies typically use informant-based measures of aggression (e.g., teacher, parent, or peer report measures) that also have limitations (see Chapter 7, this volume). Most important, informants may not validly report on targets' aggression in response to specific situational contexts, which makes it difficult to use informant-based measures to test situation-dependent theories of aggression (e.g., threatened egotism theory).

A third controversy concerns what we think of as the "doughnut theory" of narcissistic aggression. This theory recognizes that aggressive people typically hold inflated, narcissistic self-views, but it argues that hidden behind this veneer of grandiosity are deeper feelings of insecurity and insufficiency (much like a doughnut with an empty hole in the middle). Is there any evidence to support this notion? No and yes.

When self-esteem is defined in the usual way—as one's conscious appreciation of one's worth as a person—there is no support for the doughnut theory. In fact, the theory is directly contradicted by the finding that low self-esteem decreases (rather than increases) narcissistic aggression. Moreover, if low self-esteem does not cause aggression, how could hidden low self-esteem cause aggression? However, recent developments indicate that the distinction between explicit (i.e., conscious, controlled) and implicit (i.e., unconscious, uncontrolled) self-esteem may be important. Some people hold "balanced" explicit and implicit self-esteem (i.e., they hold similar levels of relatively high or low explicit and implicit self-esteem), but other people hold "discrepant" explicit and implicit self-esteem. The doughnut theory argues that people holding a combination of high explicit self-esteem and low implicit self-esteem are exceptionally aggressive. Perhaps these people are aggressive in an attempt to ward off threatening information that would otherwise prime their implicit feelings of insecurity. Initial research findings provide some support for this notion. One study involving middle school students found an interaction between explicit and implicit self-esteem in predicting teacher-reported aggression, such that the most aggressive children tended to have high explicit and low implicit self-esteem (with implicit self-esteem measured using a categorization task that assesses the ease with which participants associate positive and negative words with themselves; Sandstrom & Jordan, 2008). We know of no research designed to replicate this finding with adults. However, there is evidence that narcissistic adults can have high explicit and low implicit self-esteem (Jordan, Spencer, Zanna, Hoshino-Browne, & Correll, 2003). Future research is needed to determine whether these kinds of adults are especially prone to aggression.

A final controversy concerns how aggression is conceptualized. *Aggression* is generally defined as any behavior intended to harm another person who does not want to be harmed (Bushman & Thomaes, 2008). Some researchers have focused on more broadly defined categories of behavior that include not only aggression but also other antisocial behaviors such as lying, stealing, vandalism, and being disruptive in class (e.g., Donnellan et al., 2005; Trzesniewski et al., 2006). It is entirely plausible that the relationship between self-views and aggression is different from the relationship between self-views and other antisocial behaviors (for a review of different genetic markers for aggression and other antisocial behaviors, see Chapter 8, this volume). Low self-esteem may foster a tendency to break society's rules because people with low self-esteem regard themselves as unsuccessful or marginalized members of society. Thus, low self-esteem may make people willing to violate social norms, such as by lying, cheating, or stealing. Indeed, most research suggests that low self-esteem increases the chance that individuals will engage in antisocial or delinquent behavior (Baumeister et al., 2003; Donnellan et al., 2005; Trzesniewski et al., 2006). There is abundant evidence, however, that low self-esteem does not make people more likely to behave aggressively. We believe the field will benefit from studies that focus on well-defined, homogeneous categories of behavior (i.e., either aggressive behavior or other antisocial, delinquent, norm-violating behavior). Research is also needed on the different motivational processes that may underlie various categories of antisocial behavior.

Clinical Implications

What do the research findings reviewed in this chapter imply for prevention and intervention strategies designed to reduce aggression? Aggression and violence are complex phenomena that have multiple causes (e.g., Chapters 1, 2, and 7). Individual differences in aggression are stable over time and typically emerge by early childhood (see Chapter 7). This means that effective prevention and intervention strategies should be (a) broadly targeted at a constellation of determinants of aggressive behavior and (b) initiated early in children's development (e.g., Dodge, Coie, & Lynam, 2006; see also Chapter 9, this volume).

Among the many factors that influence aggression, perpetrators' self-regard is important. Until now, many prevention and intervention strategies designed to reduce aggression in children and adolescents have been aimed at boosting their self-esteem (e.g., Kusché & Greenberg, 1994). For example, boosting self-esteem is a central goal of the Promoting Alternative Thinking Strategies program, one of the most popular classroom-based aggression prevention programs worldwide. According to the author of the program, "high self-esteem makes it more likely that children will develop internal motivation to eschew antisocial behavior and violence," whereas "low self-esteem is emotionally painful and frequently results in . . . angry outbursts including violent and delinquent behavior" (Kusché, 2002, pp. 294–295). The empirical evidence we have reviewed in this chapter contradicts these claims. In fact, if well-intended efforts to boost self-esteem cultivate the inflated self-views characteristic of narcissism, they may inadvertently increase (rather than decrease) the aggressive behavior of at-risk youth.

The existing evidence suggests that prevention and intervention strategies should target inflated (rather than deflated) self-views to reduce aggression. The important work by Michael Kernis (2003) on the nature of "optimal" self-esteem promises to be useful as a framework for developing such strategies. From Kernis's perspective, it is important to assist aggressive narcissists in (a) being aware of their strengths and weaknesses, (b) being able to present themselves in an open and truthful way to others rather than rigidly seeking to promote their self-image, and (c) being able to process self-relevant information in an objective and accepting way rather than in a defensive and biased way. Because self-views may be most amenable to intervention in childhood and the foundation for lifelong aggressive behavior styles is laid in childhood, these interventions are likely to be most effective when implemented in childhood.

One other perhaps complementary way of reducing narcissistic aggression is based on the rationale that narcissists are aggressive only when their egos are threatened and that intervention techniques that reduce the psychological impact of ego-threatening experiences may thus lessen narcissistic aggression. One such technique is to allow individuals to reaffirm their sense of self (Sherman & Cohen, 2006; Steele, 1988). Self-affirmation theory holds that individuals' overall sense of self is based on multiple domains of functioning, and a threat to one domain of functioning can be compensated for by reflecting on the personal importance of a different domain (e.g., a self-defining skill or interest). Previous research has shown that self-affirmations reduce the psychological impact of threatening feedback and social-evaluative stress (e.g., Cohen, Garcia, Apfel, & Master, 2006; Sherman & Cohen, 2006).

We recently conducted a field experiment to examine whether self-affirmation can reduce narcissistic aggression (Thomaes, Bushman, Orobio de Castro, Cohen, & Denissen, 2009). Participants were 405 middle-school students who completed either a self-affirmation or a control writing exercise in their classes. In the affirmation condition, participants wrote about their most important values and why these are important to them. In the control condition, participants wrote about their least important values and why these may be important to others (Cohen et al., 2006). The intervention was administered on a Monday morning so that we could examine its possible effect on aggressive incidents in class during the following week. These aggressive incidents were measured on Friday afternoon using peer reports. We also obtained a measure of ego threats that had been experienced during the past week. In the control condition, the now familiar pattern of results emerged, with narcissists being more aggressive than others but only when they experienced relatively high levels of ego threat. In the intervention condition, however, that standard pattern of results was eliminated by the self-affirmation writing exercise. Thus, as predicted, the self-affirmation intervention reduced narcissistic aggression for a period of 1 week, presumably by attenuating the ego protective motives that normally drive narcissists' aggression. We hope this result will encourage the development of theory and evidence-based aggression interventions aimed at buttressing people's self-views against ego threats.

FUTURE RESEARCH

Three main issues need to be addressed to improve our understanding of how self-views relate to aggression. First, we need to know more about developmental processes (see Chapter 7). From what point in development do children's narcissistic traits predispose them to behave aggressively? Young children typically hold unrealistically positive and grandiose self-views, but these self-views typically become increasingly realistic later in childhood (Harter, 2006). It may be that from late childhood, individual differences in narcissism come to influence children's aggressive behavior. Research is needed to test this hypothesis and to help clinicians identify critical age periods in which to influence the self-views underlying children's aggressive behavior. It is also important to know more about the developmental origins of narcissism. Why do some people grow up to be narcissists, whereas others do not? Two theories attribute the development of narcissism to dysfunctional parenting. From a social learning perspective, it is parental overvaluation (i.e., excessive praise, the tendency to rigidly link children's efforts and achievements to their worth as a person) that leads to narcissism (Damon, 1995; Millon, 1981; Twenge, 2006). From a psychodynamic perspective, it is parental coldness and rejection that leads to narcissism (Kernberg, 1975; Kohut, 1977). According to this perspective, children may learn to seek continuous attention and admiration to compensate for a lack of parental warmth. The few empirical studies available provide some evidence for both theories (Horton, Bleau, & Drwecki, 2006; Otway & Vignoles, 2006). These data, however, were based on retrospective adult reports of childhood experiences. Longitudinal research that includes early assessments of parenting behavior and children's experience with parents is needed. This research should also examine possible interactions with children's genetically based temperamental traits.

Second, virtually all research on self-views and aggression has been conducted in individualistic countries (e.g., United States, Canada, Great Britain, Germany, the Netherlands, Finland, Australia, New Zealand). Research suggests that self-views may play a different motivational role in the lives of people from collectivistic cultures. Whereas people from individualistic cultures are typically motivated to enhance their self-views, people from collectivistic cultures tend to be less concerned about sustaining favorable self-views, at least as a goal in itself (Heine, Lehman, Markus, & Kitayama, 1999). People from collectivistic cultures tend to view themselves in terms of the social roles they play and the relationships they have with others (see Chapter 10, this volume). In fact, it has been argued that the concept of self-esteem is itself a Western phenomenon and that positive self-views in collectivistic cultures result from a sense of satisfaction with the social role one plays rather than from standing out as an exceptionally admirable individual (Markus & Kitayama, 1991). It is possible that these different self-construals have different effects on aggressive behavior. Moreover, the types of experiences that are perceived as ego threatening are likely to be different in different cultures. Researchers typically focus on threats to people's personal worth as situational triggers of narcissistic aggression, but such experiences may not be experienced as threatening in collectivistic cultures. A key aim for future research is to explore cultural differences and similarities in the links between self-views and aggression.

Third, whereas research thus far has focused on self-views that increase people's aggressive inclinations, little is known about self-views that may decrease aggressive inclinations. If narcissism predisposes people to behave aggressively, what self-views influence people not to behave aggressively? Recent research has characterized *self-compassion* as a healthy cousin of self-esteem (Leary, Tate, Adams, Allen, & Hancock, 2007). Whereas self-esteem essentially involves a judgment of oneself, self-compassion involves an orientation to be kind, caring, and supportive of oneself when things go badly

(Neff, 2003a, 2003b). Self-compassion may be a key self-trait that disengages people's inclinations to aggress. People often aggress when they encounter adversity and experience high levels of emotional distress or frustration. Self-compassion mitigates the emotional impact of adverse events (Leary et al., 2007), and so it may also mitigate the aggressive behaviors that often follow from such events.

We recommend that researchers broaden their scope and begin to study self-compassion or related adaptive self-traits that may reduce aggressive behavior. It would be particularly informative if researchers could show that self-compassion plays a causal role in determining people's inclinations to aggress. Research has shown that it is possible to induce feelings of self-compassion, allowing for such a causal test (Leary et al., 2006). This would not only increase our knowledge of how the self is involved in aggressive behavior, but it might also suggest further ways to use self-views as a remedy for violence and aggression.

REFERENCES

American Psychiatric Association. (1994). *Diagnostic and statistical manual of mental disorders* (4th ed.). Washington, DC: Author.

Anderson, C. A., & Bushman, B. J. (1997). External validity of "trivial" experiments: The case of laboratory aggression. *Review of General Psychology, 1,* 19–41. doi:10.1037/1089-2680.1.1.19

Anderson, C. A., Lindsay, J. J., & Bushman, B. J. (1999). Research in the psychological laboratory: Truth or triviality? *Current Directions in Psychological Science, 8,* 3–9. doi:10.1111/1467-8721.00002

Baumeister, R. F., Campbell, J. D., Krueger, J. I., & Vohs, K. D. (2003). Does high self-esteem cause better performance, interpersonal success, happiness, or healthier lifestyles? *Psychological Science in the Public Interest, 4,* 1–44. doi:10.1111/1529-1006.01431

Baumeister, R. F., Smart, L., & Boden, J. M. (1996). Relation of threatened egotism to violence and aggression: The dark side of high self-esteem. *Psychological Review, 103,* 5–33. doi:10.1037/0033-295X.103.1.5

Berkowitz, L. (1983). Aversively stimulated aggression: Some parallels and differences in research with animals and humans. *American Psychologist, 38,* 1135–1144. doi:10.1037/0003-066X.38.11.1135

Boden, J. M., Fergusson, D. M., & Horwood, L. (2007). Self-esteem and violence: Testing links between adolescent self-esteem and later hostility and violent behavior. *Social Psychiatry and Psychiatric Epidemiology, 42,* 881–891. doi:10.1007/s00127-007-0251-7

Bradshaw, C. P., & Hazan, C. (2006). Examining views of self in relation to views of others: Implications for research on aggression and self-esteem. *Journal of Research in Personality, 40,* 1209–1218. doi:10.1016/j.jrp.2005.11.004

Branden, N. (1984, August–September). In defense of self. *Association for Humanistic Psychology,* pp. 12–13.

Bushman, B. J., & Baumeister, R. F. (1998). Threatened egotism, narcissism, self-esteem, and direct and displaced aggression: Does self-love or self-hate lead to violence? *Journal of Personality and Social Psychology, 75,* 219–229. doi:10.1037/0022-3514.75.1.219

Bushman, B. J., & Baumeister, R. F. (2002). Does self-love or self-hate lead to violence. *Journal of Research in Personality, 36,* 543–545. doi:10.1016/S0092-6566(02)00502-0

Bushman, B. J., Baumeister, R. F., Thomaes, S., Ryu, E., Begeer, S., & West, S. G. (2009). Looking again, and harder, for a link between low self-esteem and aggression. *Journal of Personality, 77,* 427–446. doi:10.1111/j.1467-6494.2008.00553.x

Bushman, B. J., Bonacci, A. M., van Dijk, M., & Baumeister, R. F. (2003). Narcissism, sexual refusal, and aggression: Testing a narcissistic reactance model of sexual coercion. *Journal of Personality and Social Psychology, 84,* 1027–1040. doi:10.1037/0022-3514.84.5.1027

Bushman, B. J., & Thomaes, S. (2008). Aggression. In R. F. Baumeister & K. D. Vohs (Eds.), *Encyclopedia of social psychology* (Vol. 1, pp. 20–25). Thousand Oaks, CA: Sage.

Cohen, G. L., Garcia, J., Apfel, N., & Master, A. (2006, September). Reducing the racial achievement gap: A social–psychological intervention. *Science, 313,* 1307–1310. doi:10.1126/science.1128317

Damon, W. (1995). *Greater expectations: Overcoming the culture of indulgence in our homes and schools.* New York, NY: Free Press.

Dickinson, K. A., & Pincus, A. L. (2003). Interpersonal analysis of grandiose and vulnerable narcissism. *Journal of Personality Disorders, 17,* 188–207. doi:10.1521/pedi.17.3.188.22146

Dodge, K. A., Coie, J. D., & Lynam, D. (2006). Aggression and antisocial behavior in youth. In W. Damon, R. Lerner, & N. Eisenberg (Eds.), *Handbook of child psychology: Vol. 3. Social, emotional, and personality development* (pp. 719–788). New York, NY: Wiley.

Donnellan, M. B., Trzesniewski, K. H., Robins, R. W., Moffitt, T. E., & Caspi, A. (2005). Low self-esteem is related to aggression, antisocial behavior, and delinquency. *Psychological Science, 16,* 328–335. doi:10.1111/j.0956-7976.2005.01535.x

D'zurilla, T. J., Chang, E. C., & Sanna, L. J. (2003). Self-esteem and social problem solving as predictors of aggression in college students. *Journal of Social and Clinical Psychology, 22,* 424–440. doi:10.1521/jscp.22.4.424.22897

Foster, J. D., & Campbell, W. K. (2007). Are there such things as "narcissists" in social psychology? A taxometric analysis of the Narcissistic Personality Inventory. *Personality and Individual Differences, 43,* 1321–1332. doi:10.1016/j.paid. 2007.04.003

Goldberg, B. R., Serper, M. R., Sheets, M. M. A., Beech, D., Dill, C., & Duffy, K. G. (2007). Predictors of aggression on the psychiatric inpatient service: Self-esteem, narcissism, and theory of mind deficits. *Journal of Nervous and Mental Disease, 195,* 436–442.

Harter, S. (2006). The self. In W. Damon, R. M. Lerner, & N. Eisenberg (Eds.), *Handbook of child psychology: Vol. 3. Social, emotional, and personality development* (pp. 505–570). New York, NY: Wiley.

Heine, S. J., Lehman, D. R., Markus, H. R., & Kitayama, S. (1999). Is there a universal need for positive self-regard? *Psychological Review, 106,* 766–794. doi:10.1037/ 0033-295X.106.4.766

Horney, K. (1950). *Neurosis and human growth.* New York, NY: Norton.

Horton, R. S., Bleau, G., & Drwecki, B. (2006). Parenting narcissus: Does parenting contribute to the development of narcissism? *Journal of Personality, 74,* 345–376. doi:10.1111/j.1467-6494.2005.00378.x

Jahoda, M. (1958). *Current concepts of positive mental health.* New York, NY: Basic Books. doi:10.1037/11258-000

Jordan, C. H., Spencer, S. J., Zanna, M. P., Hoshino-Browne, E., & Correll, J. (2003). Secure and defensive high self-esteem. *Journal of Personality and Social Psychology, 85,* 969–978. doi:10.1037/0022-3514.85.5.969

Kernberg, O. (1975). *Borderline conditions and pathological narcissism.* New York, NY: Jason Aronson.

Kernis, M. H. (2003). Toward a conceptualization of optimal self-esteem. *Psychological Inquiry, 14,* 1–26. doi:10.1207/S15327965PLI1401_01

Kirkpatrick, L. A., Waugh, C. E., Valencia, A., & Webster, G. D. (2002). The functional domain specificity of self-esteem and the differential prediction of aggression. *Journal of Personality and Social Psychology, 82,* 756–767. doi:10.1037/ 0022-3514.82.5.756

Kohut, H. (1977). *The restoration of the self.* Madison, WI: International Universities Press.

Konrath, S., Bushman, B. J., & Campbell, W. K. (2006). Attenuating the link between threatened egotism and aggression. *Psychological Science, 17,* 995–1001. doi:10.1111/j.1467-9280.2006.01818.x

Kusché, C. (2002). Psychoanalysis as prevention. Using PATHS to enhance ego-development, object relations, and cortical integration in children. *Journal of Applied Psychoanalytic Studies, 4,* 283–301. doi:10.1023/A:1015773327131

Kusché, C., & Greenberg, M. (1994). *PATHS: Promoting alternative thinking strategies.* South Deerfield, MA: Developmental Research Programs.

Lawrence, C. (2006). Measuring individual responses to aggression-triggering events: Development of the Situational Triggers of Aggressive Responses (STAR) scale. *Aggressive Behavior, 32,* 241–252. doi:10.1002/ab.20122

Leary, M. R., Tate, E. B., Adams, C. E., Allen, A. B., & Hancock, J. (2007). Self-compassion and reactions to unpleasant self-relevant events: The implications of treating oneself kindly. *Journal of Personality and Social Psychology, 92,* 887–904. doi:10.1037/0022-3514.92.5.887

Markus, H. R., & Kitayama, S. (1991). Culture and the self: Implications for cognition, emotion, and motivation. *Psychological Review, 98,* 224–253.

Millon, T. (1981). *Disorders of personality. DSM-III: Axis II.* New York, NY: Wiley.

Morf, C. C., & Rhodewalt, F. (2001). Unraveling the paradoxes of narcissism: A dynamic self-regulatory processing model. *Psychological Inquiry, 12,* 177–196. doi:10.1207/S15327965PLI1204_1

Neff, K. D. (2003a). The development and validation of a scale to measure self-compassion. *Self and Identity, 2,* 223–250. doi:10.1080/15298860309027

Neff, K. D. (2003b). Self-compassion: An alternative conceptualization of a healthy attitude toward oneself. *Self and Identity, 2,* 85–101. doi:10.1080/15298860309032

Nisbett, R. E., & Wilson, T. D. (1977). Telling more than we can know: Verbal reports on mental processes. *Psychological Review, 84,* 231–259. doi:10.1037/0033-295X.84.3.231

Otway, L. J., & Vignoles, V. L. (2006). Narcissism and childhood recollections: A quantitative test of psychoanalytic predictions. *Personality and Social Psychology Bulletin, 32,* 104–116. doi:10.1177/0146167205279907

Perez, M., Vohs, K. D., & Joiner, T. E., Jr. (2005). Discrepancies between self- and other-esteem as correlates of aggression. *Journal of Social and Clinical Psychology, 24,* 607–620. doi:10.1521/jscp.2005.24.5.607

Reidy, D. E., Zeichner, A., Foster, J. D., & Martinez, M. A. (2008). Effects of narcissistic entitlement and exploitativeness on human physical aggression. *Personality and Individual Differences, 44,* 865–875. doi:10.1016/j.paid.2007.10.015

Rosenberg, M. (1965). *Society and the adolescent self-image.* Princeton, NJ: Princeton University Press.

Ryan, R. M., & Kuczkowski, R. (1994). The imaginary audience, self-consciousness, and public individuation in adolescence. *Journal of Personality, 62,* 219–238. doi:10.1111/j.1467-6494.1994.tb00292.x

Sandstrom, M. J., & Jordan, R. (2008). Defensive self-esteem and aggression in childhood. *Journal of Research in Personality, 42,* 506–514. doi:10.1016/j.jrp.2007.07.008

Sherman, D. K., & Cohen, G. L. (2006). The psychology of self-defense: Self-affirmation theory. In M. P. Zanna (Ed.), *Advances in experimental social psychology* (Vol. 38, pp. 183–242). San Diego, CA: Academic Press.doi:10.1016/S0065-2601(06)38004-5

Steele, C. M. (1988). The psychology of self-affirmation: Sustaining the integrity of the self. In L. Berkowitz (Ed.), *Advances in experimental social psychology* (Vol. 21, pp. 261–302). New York, NY: Academic Press.

Stucke, T. S., & Sporer, S. L. (2002). When a grandiose self-image is threatened: Narcissism and self-concept clarity as predictors of negative emotions and aggression following ego-threat. *Journal of Personality, 70*, 509–532. doi:10.1111/1467-6494.05015

Thomaes, S., Bushman, B., Orobio de Castro, B., Cohen, G., Denissen, J. J. A. (2009). Reducing narcissistic aggression by buttressing self-esteem: An experimental field study. *Psychological Science, 20*, 1536–1542.

Thomaes, S., Bushman, B. J., Stegge, H., & Olthof, T. (2008). Trumping shame by blasts of noise: Narcissism, self-esteem, shame, and aggression in young adolescents. *Child Development, 79*, 1792–1801. doi:10.1111/j.1467-8624.2008.01226.x

Thomaes, S., Stegge, H., Bushman, B. J., Olthof, T., & Denissen, J. (2008). Development and validation of the Childhood Narcissism Scale. *Journal of Personality Assessment, 90*, 382–391. doi:10.1080/00223890802108162

Toch, H. (1993). *Violent men: An inquiry into the psychology of violence*. Washington, DC: American Psychological Association. (Original work published 1969)

Trzesniewski, K. H., Donnellan, M. B., Moffitt, T. E., Robins, R. W., Poulton, R., & Caspi, A. (2006). Low self-esteem during adolescence predicts poor health, criminal behavior, and limited economic prospects during adulthood. *Developmental Psychology, 42*, 381–390. doi:10.1037/0012-1649.42.2.381

Twenge, J. M. (2006). *Generation me: Why today's young Americans are more confident, assertive, entitled—and more miserable than ever before*. New York, NY: Free Press.

Twenge, J. M., & Campbell, W. K. (2003). "Isn't it fun to get the respect that we're going to deserve?" Narcissism, social rejection, and aggression. *Personality and Social Psychology Bulletin, 29*, 261–272. doi:10.1177/0146167202239051

Webster, G. D. (2007). Is the relationships between self-esteem and aggression necessarily U-shaped? *Journal of Research in Personality, 41*, 977–982. doi:10.1016/j.jrp.2007.01.001

Webster, G. D., & Kirkpatrick, L. A. (2006). Behavioral and self-reported aggression as a function of domain-specific self-esteem. *Aggressive Behavior, 32*, 17–27. doi:10.1002/ab.20102

12

EVOLVED MECHANISMS FOR REVENGE AND FORGIVENESS

MICHAEL E. McCULLOUGH, ROBERT KURZBAN,
AND BENJAMIN A. TABAK

In this chapter, we describe our efforts to understand the functions of the cognitive systems that underlie humans' capacities for revenge and forgiveness. A better understanding of these concepts is not only scientifically interesting but socially important as well. In developed nations, the desire for revenge is cited as a causal factor in as many as 20% of homicides (Kubrin & Weitzer, 2003). Roughly 20% of the perpetrators of violent assault and criminal property damage in the United Kingdom cite the desire for revenge as a motive (Home Office, 2003), and 61% of U.S. school shootings between 1974 and June 2000 were vengeance-motivated (Vossekuil, Fein, Reddy, Borum, & Modzeleski, 2002). The desire for revenge also motivates people to enlist in terrorist organizations (Speckhard & Ahkmedova, 2006).

Perhaps because revenge is so closely linked to aggression and violence, it has been fashionable in Western thought since the Stoic (and, later, Christian) philosophers to view revenge as immoral, irrational, or both (Murphy, 2003). As if seeking to restate this dim view of revenge in modern, therapeutic terms,

We gratefully acknowledge the support of the National Institute of Mental Health Grant 5R01MH071258, a grant from the Fetzer Institute, and support from the Center for the Study of Law and Religion at Emory University to the first author.

social scientists in the past century have also promulgated the idea that the desire for revenge is indicative of psychological dysfunction (Murphy, 2003).

The "revenge as disease" conceit had a predictable effect on how forgiveness came to be studied empirically as well: If the desire for revenge is a disease, then perhaps forgiveness is the cure. Indeed, many of the earliest empirical studies on forgiveness were related to the use of interventions for promoting forgiveness in therapeutic settings (DiBlasio & Benda, 1991; Hebl & Enright, 1993). These treatments do promote forgiveness—and reduce psychological symptoms of anxiety and depression and boost self-esteem (Lundahl, Taylor, Stevenson, & Roberts, 2008)—but such facts do not even come close to proving that forgiveness is a "cure" for revenge.

Evolutionary research and scholarship cast considerable doubt on "disease" and "cure" conceits for conceptualizing the human capacities for revenge and forgiveness. In this chapter, we propose that revenge and forgiveness are the results of distinct psychological adaptations that evolved to solve specific adaptive problems. We posit that one or more revenge mechanisms evolved because of their efficacy in deterring interpersonal harms and that one or more forgiveness mechanisms evolved because of their efficacy in preserving valuable relationships despite those harms. Here, we attempt to define revenge and forgiveness in functional terms that will make them more amenable to evolutionary analysis (Williams, 1966), to describe the selection pressures that gave rise to them, and to outline what we think are the proximate causes and the computations involved when people make choices to forgive or to avenge a wrong.

EVOLUTION OF REVENGE

In the section that follows, we attempt to outline a functional approach to understanding revenge. In particular, we attempt to define revenge functionally rather than behaviorally and demonstrate the value of such a definitional approach. Second, we attempt to outline the evolutionary selection pressures that might have given rise to psychological mechanisms that produce revenge as a functional output.

Revenge: A Functional Definition

A great deal of research and writing has been devoted to revenge, and people have powerful intuitions about it. Still, we believe it is worthwhile to take a step back and reflect on the evolved function of putative revenge systems. At its heart, revenge solves a problem that is faced to varying degrees by many species: how to change other organisms' incentives to induce them to emit benefits and refrain from imposing costs on oneself (see Chapter 3). To the extent that other organisms can learn that a target organism will retaliate (or conditionally benefit) as a function of their behavior, it is beneficial for the target organism to signal that it will do so. One (albeit imperfect) way to signal that one will retaliate if harmed (or benefit if helped) is to actually do so. If neural tissue is assembled that reliably motivates these sorts of contingent punishments and contingent rewards, it may boost lifetime reproductive fitness of its bearer and therefore evolve precisely because of these functions. Our analysis begins with this simple, but crucial, idea.

This notion contrasts with the way some philosophers have defined revenge, but we think some of the previous definitions create as many problems as they solve. For example, Govier (2002) wrote, "When we seek revenge, we seek satisfaction by attempting to harm the other (or associated persons) as a retaliatory measure" (p. 2). Elster (1990) likewise defined revenge as "the attempt, at some cost or risk to oneself, to impose suffering upon those who have made one suffer, because they have made one suffer" (p. 862). Uniacke (2000) also claimed that "revenge is personal and noninstrumental: With revenge we seek to make people suffer because they have made us suffer, not because their actions or values require us to bring them down" (p. 62).

These definitions, because they are proximate and do not commit to any function, make no obvious predictions about the design features of the psychology of revenge. "Enjoyment" and other proximate explanations (see Govier's, 2002, definition) leave a promissory note for an ultimate explanation that must be paid. Why should revenge produce pleasure? For no organism except humans would we accept that an explanation for a behavior is that it brings enjoyment.

In short, functional thinking about cognition and behavior reminds us that there is no free lunch. Why would a species such as *Homo sapiens* engage in costly behavior such as revenge unless the mechanism that creates revenge was designed to produce benefits in the currency of fitness or is a by-product of a structure that does yield fitness payoffs (Andrews, Gangestad, & Matthews, 2002)? What could maintain revenge in humans' behavioral repertoire?

The definitions cited earlier also introduce problems related to intentionality. What does it mean that revenge involves an attempt to impose retaliatory harm on an aggressor? Does the word *attempt* imply a conscious and deliberate effort to make another individual suffer? Is consciousness necessary? Is deliberation necessary? Or can this striving to harm one's provoker be automatic and/or unconscious? And is this distinction critical in any case?

We think a functional definition of revenge can clarify some of these points. Biologists regularly define behavior functionally, as when Maynard Smith and Harper (2003) defined a *signal* as "any act or structure which alters the behaviour of other organisms, which evolved because of that effect, and which is effective because the receiver's response has also evolved" (p. 3). By designating a function, it becomes possible to search for evidence of the features—behavioral or physiological—that contribute to accomplishing the putative function.

In similar fashion, we define *revenge* functionally as behavior resulting from a mechanism designed to deter the imposition of costs on (or the withholding of benefits from) oneself or one's allies by the imposition of costs following a target's imposition of costs (or withholding of benefits), where costs and benefits are defined in terms of their effects on lifetime reproductive fitness. That is, revenge is a deterrence system designed to change others' incentives regarding the self and one's kin or allies (see Chapter 4 for a similar functional analysis of what the chapter authors call the *power behavioral system*). By imposing costs after harm (or withheld benefits), revenge signals that subsequent acts will be subject to the same contingent response, thereby altering others' incentives. We hypothesize that humans possess psychological adaptations designed specifically to produce revenge.

This functional definition has several important features. First, it replaces considerations of intentionality (e.g., whether the organism is deliberately or consciously attempting to do something) with considerations of design (e.g., what the system that motivates revenge was designed to do). Moreover, the concept of design makes powerful empirical commitments; adaptation is a strong claim (Williams, 1966), and to the extent that the psychological mechanisms do not show features that support a deterrence function, the hypothesis that humans possess an innate psychology of revenge is undermined.

Our definition of revenge incorporates as instances of revenge all retaliatory impositions of costs that are caused by a mechanism designed for this purpose, even acts that are not based on deliberation or awareness and even those that do not actually manage to deter anything (as when people behave aggressively toward a driver whom they perceive to have mistreated them on the road). Such a definition also permits a distinction between costs to the provoker that arise from design for that function versus costs that arise as a by-product. Harming a provoker is only revenge when the system that motivated the harmful behavior was crafted for that purpose. Avoiding a provoker to avert a second harm is not revenge, but avoiding a provoker to limit his or her access to benefits might be. Likewise, the phenomenon of *displaced aggression*, in which a victim of aggression proceeds later to harm a third party (Miller, Pedersen, Earleywine, & Pollock, 2003; see also Chapter 6, this volume), may not be revenge, even if the third party is a genetic relative or ally of the original aggressor. If displaced aggression of this nature is not produced by a system designed for deterrence but rather is produced by the psychological processes that Miller et al. (2003) implicated (e.g., residual arousal and postaggression rumination that lead to what are, essentially, cognitive errors)—that is to say, if displaced aggression is a mere by-product of other psychological processes—then it is not revenge. As a side note, to us it is an open question whether some instances of triggered displaced aggression might actually reflect the operation of a revenge system. What we wish to point out here is that this "triggered displaced aggression as revenge" hypothesis—though it might be wrong—would likely never have been generated solely by relying on the standard, nonfunctional framework that researchers commonly use to understand displaced aggression.

Selection Pressures That Gave Rise to Mechanisms for Revenge

In an influential review article, Clutton-Brock and Parker (1995) noted that retaliation (which they called *punishment*) is common among nonhuman animals (for a more recent example, see Jensen, Call, & Tomasello, 2007). They speculated that retaliation yields fitness gains by reducing the probability that the targets of retaliation will repeat their injurious actions against the retaliator in the future. Consistent with Clutton-Brock and Parker's analysis, we hypothesize that natural selection gave rise to one or more comparable deterrence systems in humans. In this sense, the adaptive consequences of revenge come not from what revenge causes per se but from what it prevents. For illustrative purposes here, we distinguish among three types of deterrence. The first two, direct and indirect deterrence of aggression, involve deterring the imposition of costs. The third involves deterring the withholding of benefits.

Direct Deterrence

By *direct deterrence*, we mean that revenge discourages aggressors from harming the avenger a second time. The logic of direct deterrence is straightforward: If a potential aggressor must make a decision in which he or she can take an action that imposes costs on a potential victim to acquire some benefit, then the potential victim is better off if he or she can change the potential aggressor's incentives so that the expected value of the cost-imposing action on the potential victim is negative. Revenge can accomplish this transformation of expected value by conveying to an aggressor that the retaliatory infliction of fitness costs will exceed the potential benefits to be gained by aggressing against the potential victim a second time (see Chapter 3). Nevertheless, direct deterrence gives rise to strategic complications. For example, although revenge at Time 1 might predict revenge at Time 2, there is nothing that forces this to be true. An organism could be, for example, intermittently vengeful. This leads to well-known problems of signaling that one's vengeful dispositions are stable over time (Frank, 1988).

Experimental evidence in support of revenge's effectiveness as a direct deterrent comes from experiments involving economic games such as the sequential and iterated prisoner's dilemma (Axelrod, 1984). In the *sequential* prisoner's dilemma game, there is one round of play, but the second mover chooses only after seeing the first player's choice. In such games, the second player is much more likely to cooperate after a cooperative move than after a defecting move. More relevant to our present point, defection is almost always met with retaliatory defection (Clark & Sefton, 2001, Table 6), an observation that holds not only in the United States (Hayashi, Ostrom, Walker, & Yamagishi, 1999). However, because noncooperation and punishment are the same in the prisoner's dilemma, such findings must be interpreted with care.

In the *iterated* prisoner's dilemma, subjects play multiple rounds of the game with either the same partner or different ones. For the present purpose, key issues are whether people respond to defection with defection—moves plausibly interpretable as revenge—and whether such moves elicit subsequent cooperation from one's partner. Experiments using large numbers of trials in prisoner's dilemma games suggest that people do respond to defection with defection (Bixenstine & Wilson, 1963), though the details vary across studies (Rapoport & Chammah, 1965). Reciprocal strategies such as "tit for tat" or variants of it tend to elicit cooperation from experimental subjects (e.g., Wilson, 1971), hinting at their effectiveness in deterring defection.

Moreover, in an analysis of data from five different laboratory studies of dyadic negotiation in which partners played 250 consecutive trials during which they could either punish, reward, or withhold reward (and punishment) from each other, Molm (1997) found that the frequency with which retaliatory punishment was used (i.e., the infliction of punishment after one's negotiation partner had previously punished the actor) was positively associated with the frequency with which partners rewarded each other. Likewise, the use of punishment following nonreward (i.e., the withholding of benefits) was associated with higher rates of rewarding. These findings suggest that retaliatory infliction of punishments in response to punishments and the withholding of rewards creates a relational climate in which the exchange of reward is more frequent. In contrast, Molm reported that the frequency with which dyads punished *noncontingently* (i.e., independently of whether the punishment was a retaliatory response to punishment or the withholding of benefits) was associated with lower rates of rewarding: It is only when punishment is contingent on previous punishment or nonreward that it promotes cooperation.

In some situations, one can benefit from revenge's efficacy as a deterrent simply by possessing the ability to retaliate against one's interaction partners; it is not always necessary to retaliate directly. Work in behavioral economics also illustrates this basic point. Consider the difference in play in the dictator game (DG) as opposed to the ultimatum game (UG). In both games, some amount of money, say $10, is to be divided between two people. In the DG, one person unilaterally decides how to split the money. In the UG, one person, the "proposer," proposes a split, and the other person, the "responder," can either accept that split or reject it, in which case both players receive nothing. Rejection in the UG is revenge; the cost imposed is the amount that the proposer allocated to him- or herself. It is not surprising that typical proposals in the UG (roughly 40% of the stake), in which revenge is possible, are larger than in the DG (roughly 20% of the stake), in which revenge is not possible (Forsythe, Horowitz, Savin, & Sefton, 1994).

Social psychology experiments also show how the prospect of suffering revenge can deter aggressors from harming the prospective avenger. In one study (Diamond, 1977), undergraduate men wrote an essay, which a confederate then derogated. Participants were then brought back to the laboratory 24 hours later and were given the opportunity to give 10 (bogus) shocks of varying intensities to the person who wrote the insulting reviews. Half were led to believe that after they administered shocks, they would then switch roles and receive the shocks themselves. People who believed that they could harm their insulting evaluators without the threat of retaliation gave stronger shocks to the evaluators.

The lessons of empirical studies on the direct deterrent effects of punishment are not always straightforward, however. For example, Fehr and List (2004) used the trust game, a two-step dyadic game in which an "investor" first entrusts a sum of money to a second person called the "trustee"; the money is then multiplied by some constant (often tripled) by the researchers. In the second step, the trustee is given the opportunity to return some amount of money to the investor. Fehr and List permitted investors to indicate a minimum amount of money they required from their trustees in return. If trustees failed to return that minimum amount, that amount was automatically deducted from the trustees' payoffs. Return transfers were highest when this punishment option was available but left unused by investors. Nonetheless, the majority of investors used the punishment option. Houser et al. (2008), using a similar design, found that the threat of punishment reduced the fraction of money trustees returned to investors even if the threat of punishment was applied as a result of a random process rather than as a decision on the part of the investor. Likewise, revenge in some experimental settings increases, rather than deters, noncooperation. Dreber, Rand, Fudenberg, and Nowak (2008) found that using punishment against noncooperators reduced players' gains in an iterated prisoner's dilemma, possibly because punishment in this experiment imposed large costs: The cost of punishment and the size of the damage it inflicts clearly influence revenge's deterrent effects.

Deterring Third Parties

Mechanisms for revenge may also have been naturally selected for their efficacy in deterring would-be aggressors by virtue of revenge's ability to signal the avenger's aggressive potential. Reputation is important for understanding how third-party deterrence might work. Ancestral humans lived in small, close-knit groups (Boehm, 2008) without the benefit of institutions for protecting individual rights, so a readiness to retaliate against interpersonal harms might have been an important component of people's social reputations. Researchers have documented the importance of defense of honor (i.e., more or less, the perceived ability to defend one's interests with violent force when necessary) and the revenge that it stimulates as a major cause of violence among individuals from many societies (for a review, see McCullough, 2008; see also Chapter 10, this volume).

Consistent with the idea that revenge is enacted partly out of reputational concerns, laboratory studies show that the psychological mechanisms that cause revenge are sensitive to the presence of third parties. Victims retaliate more strongly against their provokers when an audience has witnessed the provocation, especially if the audience communicates to the victim that he or she looks weak because of the harm suffered or if the victim knows that the audience is aware that he or she has suffered particularly unjust treatment (Brown, 1968; Kim, Smith, & Brigham, 1998). Also, when two men get into an argument, the mere presence of a third person doubles the likelihood that the argument will escalate to a violent encounter (Felson, 1982).

Deterring the Withholding of Benefits

Finally, we think mechanisms for revenge might have been naturally selected because of their efficacy in changing others' behavior to increase the delivery of benefits (as opposed to only reducing harm). Public goods games are useful for illustrating how revenge can deter the withholding of benefits. In these games, a few (often four to six) participants receive an initial endowment of money and are instructed to choose how to split that endowment between two different pools. One pool is private, and participants simply keep any money they place in it. The other pool is shared; money placed into this pool is multiplied by some amount greater than one, and the resultant total is subsequently divided evenly among all the players in the group. Money maximizers keep everything in their private pools; aggregate group wealth is maximized when everyone contributes to the public pool. These games are social dilemmas because they create a tension between individual and group outcomes. (The fact that they involve groups rather than dyads is incidental.)

Yamagishi (1986) had subjects play public goods games in groups of four, repeated over 12 trials. He varied whether participants could punish other members of the group and varied the price of punishment, that is, the cost one had to spend to reduce another player's payoff by one unit. Players used the sanctioning system when it was provided, and, in its presence, players contributed greater amounts to the public good. However, these results do not distinguish the proximate motive, that is, whether sanctioning is instrumental (i.e., the result of a motive to increase one's benefits through the use of incentives) or vengeful (i.e., the result of a motive to impose costs on individuals who had an opportunity to deliver benefits but chose not to do so).

Fehr and Gächter's (2002) results help to clarify the proximate motive for punishment in this context. Fehr and Gächter ran a similar game with a few modifications, the most important of which was that players changed groups from round to round, so punishment could not be used to induce group members who were uncooperative in round r to benefit the subject in round $r + 1$. Nevertheless, their results were similar to Yamagishi's (1986): Participants sanctioned uncooperative group members, and group members cooperated more when the punishment option was available (see also Anderson & Putterman, 2006). These results imply the operation of the revenge system, given that instrumental motives were ruled out. Fehr and Gächter would not agree. They coined a new term, *altruistic punishment,* to describe their findings.

Carpenter and Matthews (in press) conducted an experiment that contained an important control condition that helps to identify the limits of any altruism that might be present in so-called altruistic punishment. They ran noniterated public goods games and varied whether participants could punish members of their own groups or members of other people's groups. In the key treatment, the "one-way TPP" (third-party punishment) condition, almost no one punished. The fact that one-way third-party punishment was so minimal when directed toward noncooperators in groups to which the subjects themselves did not belong strongly suggests that without the possibility of revenge, people tend not to punish.

EVOLUTION OF FORGIVENESS

In the section to follow, we attempt to outline the basics of a functional approach to understanding forgiveness. As we did in outlining the basics of a functional approach to revenge, we offer a functional definition of forgiveness and illustrate its advantages over previous definitional approaches. We also outline the evolutionary selection pressures that might have given rise to psychological mechanisms that produce forgiveness as a functional output.

Forgiveness: A Functional Definition

Natural selection gave rise to one or more psychological systems that produce revenge, we posit, by virtue of the fitness payoffs associated with direct deterrence, third-party deterrence, and, possibly, deterrence of benefit-withholding. However, avengers trade off the potential benefits lost by virtue of any damage that revenge does to relations with the harm doer, and they incur the (probabilistic) costs associated with any counterrevenge that might ensue as the result of their revenge. We therefore presume that the revenge system is designed to adjust its operation in response to the potential costs and benefits associated with revenge in any particular instance. When the costs of revenge are too high relative to its expected deterrence benefits, an organism might pursue an alternative course of behavior—forgiveness being one of the more likely ones.

Over the past decade, the first author's research group has defined *forgiveness* as a set of motivational changes whereby an organism becomes (a) decreasingly motivated to retaliate against an offending relationship partner; (b) decreasingly motivated to avoid the offender; and (c) increasingly motivated by good will for, and a desire to reconcile with, the offender, despite the offender's harmful actions (McCullough, 2008; McCullough, Worthington, & Rachal, 1997). Here, we refine this definition by adding a functional addendum: that one or more "forgiveness systems" produce these motivational changes because of their efficacy during evolution in promoting the restoration of beneficial relationships in the aftermath of interpersonal harms.

This newly "functionalized" definition of forgiveness permits all of the important conceptual distinctions that other theorists (e.g., Enright & Coyle, 1998; Worthington, 2005) consider important (e.g., that forgiveness is different from forgetting an offense, denying its reality, condoning it, or attempting to minimize its significance), and it enables a tighter conceptual link between forgiveness and reconciliation than has previously been recognized. Many theorists have been careful to distinguish forgiveness from *reconciliation*, with the latter concept indicating a restoration of the relationship between offender and victim (Worthington, 2005). In light of the functional definition of forgiveness that we propose, it might be possible to forgive a harm doer (i.e., to experience motivational changes by which one becomes less vengeful, less avoidant, and more benevolently disposed toward him or her) without reconciling (i.e., restoring the relationship). Nevertheless, we reason that modern humans are capable of forgiving because ancestral humans who deployed this strategy enjoyed the fitness benefits that came from restoring potentially valuable relationships.

Nevertheless, forgiveness, like revenge, involves costs. Forgiveness prepares a victim to reenter constructive relations with a harm doer based on the prospect of capturing benefits from that relationship, but forgiveness entails foregoing revenge and its deterrent effects. Forgiveness, therefore, involves a loss of gains from changing the harm doer's incentives, potentially inviting recidivism (e.g., see Gordon, Burton, & Porter, 2004) and attacks from those who see the opportunity to exploit the forgiver. In short, forgiveness undermines the function of the revenge system by undermining deterrence. Thus, a forgiveness system, like a revenge system, should be sensitive to costs and benefits, and these costs and benefits should have shaped the suite of proximate social–psychological factors that turn the system on and off.

Forgiveness: Selection Pressures

As noted earlier, we hypothesize that putative forgiveness systems evolved in response to selection pressures for restoring relationships that, on average, would have boosted lifetime reproductive fitness, a quality that researchers have called *relationship value* (de Waal, 2000). The role of relationship value in determining animals' propensity to forgive and/or reconcile after conflict has been demonstrated in many simulations of the evolution of cooperation among dyads and networks of individuals (e.g., Axelrod, 1984; Hruschka & Henrich, 2006). Similar findings (Koski, Koops, & Sterck, 2007; Watts, 2006) have emerged from behavioral studies of many mammalian species' postconflict conciliatory behaviors. It is in relationships in which substantial potential fitness gains are possible (e.g., kin, mates, allies, exchange partners) that forgiveness and/or reconciliation appear to be most common in nonhuman animals.

The benefits to lifetime reproductive fitness differ by relationship type. They might entail, of course, inclusive fitness benefits (Hamilton, 1964). After all, imposing costs on one's close genetic relatives directly impairs one's own inclusive fitness. Also, kin are most likely, all else being equal, to be the source of direct and reciprocal benefits for reasons associated with kin altruism. Therefore, one might expect forgiveness to be more likely in the context of kin relationships, with closer relatives being more easily forgiven than more distant ones.

Social organisms will also undergo selection pressure for forgiveness in the context of cooperation between nonrelatives when repeated encounters are likely (Axelrod, 1984; Trivers, 1971). Individuals who could forgive in such contexts would acquire two fitness benefits. First, forgiving isolated transgressions would have inhibited the *echo effect* (Axelrod, 1984), whereby individuals who are cooperatively disposed nevertheless become locked in costly cycles of retaliation when initial unintended defections occur due to noise. Second, individuals who can forgive their reciprocal altruism partners following defections would have been able to preserve their access to benefits that their partners would have been able to provide them and would have spared themselves the costs associated with establishing new relationships with new individuals whose social dispositions would be unknown (Hruschka & Henrich, 2006). On average, it may simply be less costly to forgive some number of defections from a well-established relationship partner than to retaliate, or to withdraw from the relationship, following an isolated defection.

Indeed, in computer simulations of the evolution of reciprocal altruism—especially when the possibility of noise is assumed—evolutionarily stable strategies tend to be more forgiving than tit for tat, which responds to defection with defection and to cooperation with cooperation (Frean, 1994; Hauert & Schuster, 1998; Wu & Axelrod, 1995). This is especially true when one models reciprocal altruism as occurring largely among small networks of individuals (e.g., friendship groups, individuals within small living groups) who focus their cooperative efforts on other individuals within the network and limit their cooperation with individuals outside of the network (Levine & Kurzban, 2006). Under such circumstances, agents are expected to forgive up to 80% of other network members' defections (Hruschka & Henrich, 2006).

Other types of relationships generate still other types of benefits that redound to lifetime reproductive fitness. The benefits that might accrue from forgiving a mate are different from the benefits that might accrue by forgiving a friend, which in turn are different from the benefits that a forgiver might receive by forgiving an ally. Because the fitness-enhancing properties come in different currencies, the psychological systems that produce forgiveness are likely set up to identify the types of benefits that a particular type of relationship is likely to confer (and to weight them appropriately with respect to the probability of capturing those benefits, the time horizon at which they will be realized, etc.) and then weigh those benefits against the deterrent value of revenge, which the organism would trade off if it chose to forgive instead of seeking revenge (McCullough, Luna, Berry, Tabak, & Bono, in press).

CHOOSING FORGIVENESS OVER VENGEANCE: PROXIMATE CAUSATION

If, as we hypothesize, forgiveness systems are sensitive to tradeoffs associated with sacrificing the deterrence benefits of revenge for the relationship-restoration benefits of forgiveness, then such systems should be acutely sensitive to variables that influence the value of each option. These variables include, but are not necessarily limited to, characteristics of the offender, the transgression itself, and cues that predict the probabilities of future attacks and/or the potential future value of the restored relationship. In other words, we predict that forgiveness is generated by systems designed to compute and compare the cost of forgone revenge and the benefits that are expected to accrue from a restored relationship.

Value of Deterrence

The value of revenge diminishes to the extent that it does not change behavior that would otherwise occur. In the limiting case, suppose that after an offense, the transgressor could persuasively signal that he or she would never—or could never—again inflict costs. In such a case, revenge would yield no benefit (except through third-party deterrence).

Information relevant to inferring intent can come from various sources. For instance, a transgressor's apology, expression of sympathy for a victim's suffering, and declaration of his or her intention to behave better in the future could indicate a low likelihood of trying to harm the victim in the future (McCullough et al., 1997). Verbal declarations such as these are susceptible to strategic manipulation, of course. Nonverbal displays such as blushing, which facilitate forgiveness after some transgressions (de Jong, Peters, & de Cremer, 2003), also contain information about changed intent and a transgressor's eagerness to distance himself or herself from a transgression, and their reliability may come from their unfakeability (Frank, 1988).

Other situational features might reduce the perceived deterrent value of revenge by convincing a victim that the transgressor's harmful actions were unintentional in the first place. People more readily forgive transgressors whose behavior was unintentional, unavoidable, or committed without awareness of the potential negative consequences (McCullough et al., in press). Also, it is unnecessary to engage in deterrence when additional transgressions are impossible. When the aggressor's capacity for violence is removed, for instance, vengeance yields little additional deterrent value. In some ethnographic accounts, reconciliation rituals involve the surrender of weapons (e.g., Boehm, 1987), which seems well suited to conveying an unwillingness to commit future aggressive acts. Trust may be a key psychological process by which the aforementioned factors that cue benevolent intentions lower the likelihood of revenge and raise the likelihood of forgiveness (Kurzban, 2003). People more readily forgive people whom they trust (Hewstone, Cairns, Voci, Hamberger, & Niens, 2006) and people who are reputed to be trustworthy (Vasalou, Hopfensitz, & Pitt, 2008) despite their recent bad behavior.

Expected Value of the Relationship

Against the costs of forgone revenge is the expected value of future benefits in a relationship in which intentions are positive rather than negative. The expected future value of a relationship is computed, we hypothesize, in much the same way that it would be in contexts other than the aftermath of a transgression. Because of the well-known principles of kin selection, close relatives are likely to be a source of benefits, and thus, we expect that cues of kinship will facilitate forgiveness, just as they evidently facilitate the restraint of vengeance (Lieberman & Linke, 2007).

In similar fashion, those with whom one has a close history of association, shared interests, and many opportunities for mutually beneficial transactions are good candidates for forgiveness because of the possibility of continued gains. Indeed, priming people with the names of close others (e.g., via subliminal presentation) leads to increased judgments of forgiveness, increased accessibility of the concept of forgiveness, and reduced deliberation about whether forgiveness is an appropriate course of action (Karremans & Aarts, 2007). Karremans and Aarts's (2007) results complement those from several previous studies showing that people are more inclined to forgive individuals with whom they feel close and committed (Finkel, Rusbult, Kumashiro, & Hannon, 2002; McCullough et al., 1998; see also Chapter 2, this volume). We would argue that the reason for these associations of closeness and/or commitment with forgiveness is that relationship closeness and commitment act as cues of relationship value in many types of relationships. We think the importance of relationship value can also explain why people tend to want some form of compensation prior to forgiving (Boehm, 1987; Bottom, Gibson, Daniels, & Murnighan, 2002): Compensation may serve as a cue of (among other things) a transgressor's ability or willingness to be a valuable relationship partner in the future.

In computations of expected value, empathy may play a special role. Empathy for transgressors, which is a sympathy- or pity-like response to the plight of another person, appears to be a reliable facilitator of forgiveness (McCullough et al., 1997), perhaps as a result of empathy's long phylogenetic history as a motivator of care for valuable relationship partners (Preston & de Waal, 2002). Whether the empathy–forgiveness link is part of the design of the forgiveness system or merely an incidental effect that empathy can exert within the existing forgiveness system, however, is currently difficult to know.

SUMMARY

The desire for revenge and the ability to forgive seem to be universal psychological endowments of humans (Boehm, 2008; Daly & Wilson, 1988; McCullough, 2008). Species-typical traits call out for explanations in terms of the mind's evolved mental structures, either as direct products or as by-products of what those structures were designed to do (Andrews et al., 2002). Here, we have taken an adaptationist stance and posited that revenge and forgiveness result from computational mechanisms designed to produce them. Once one has moved into a functional framework, we think it becomes easier to see what should qualify as revenge and forgiveness—and what should not—and what the important questions are if one wants to understand what revenge and forgiveness are really all about. By outlining the selection pressures that likely gave rise to humans' penchants for revenge and forgiveness, we have also tried here to identify the types of information that the structures that produce revenge and forgiveness should be designed to process. We hope that introducing this sort of thinking can help investigators prioritize their research efforts in the future.

REFERENCES

Anderson, C., & Putterman, L. (2006). Do non-strategic sanctions obey the law of demand? The demand for punishment in the voluntary contribution mechanism. *Games and Economic Behavior, 54,* 1–24. doi:10.1016/j.geb.2004.08.007

Andrews, P. W., Gangestad, S. W., & Matthews, D. (2002). Adaptationism—How to carry out an exaptationist program. *Behavioral and Brain Sciences, 25,* 489–504. doi:10.1017/S0140525X02000092

Axelrod, R. (1984). *The evolution of cooperation.* New York, NY: Basic Books.

Bixenstine, V. E., & Wilson, K. V. (1963). Effects of level of cooperative choice by the other player on choices in a prisoner's dilemma game. Part II. *Journal of Abnormal and Social Psychology, 67,* 139–147. doi:10.1037/h0044242

Boehm, C. (1987). *Blood revenge: The enactment and management of conflict in Montenegro and other tribal societies* (2nd ed.). Philadelphia: University of Pennsylvania Press.

Boehm, C. (2008). Purposive social selection and the evolution of human altruism. *Cross-Cultural Research, 42,* 319–352. doi:10.1177/1069397108320422

Bottom, W. P., Gibson, K., Daniels, S. E., & Murnighan, J. K. (2002). When talk is not cheap: Substantive penance and expressions of intent in rebuilding cooperation. *Organization Science, 13,* 497–513. doi:10.1287/orsc.13.5.497.7816

Brown, B. R. (1968). The effects of need to maintain face on interpersonal bargaining. *Journal of Experimental Social Psychology, 4,* 107–122. doi:10.1016/0022-1031 (68)90053-X

Carpenter, J. P., & Matthews, P. H. (in press). Norm enforcement: Anger, indignation, or reciprocity? *Journal of the European Economic Association.*

Clark, K., & Sefton, M. (2001). The sequential prisoner's dilemma: Evidence on reciprocation. *The Economic Journal, 111,* 51–68. doi:10.1111/1468-0297.00588

Clutton-Brock, T. H., & Parker, G. A. (1995). Punishment in animal societies. *Nature, 373,* 209–216. doi:10.1038/373209a0

Daly, M., & Wilson, M. (1988). *Homicide.* New York, NY: Aldine de Gruyter.

de Jong, P. J., Peters, M. L., & de Cremer, D. (2003). Blushing may signify guilt: Revealing effects of blushing in ambiguous social situations. *Motivation and Emotion, 27*, 225–249. doi:10.1023/A:1025059631708

de Waal, F. B. M. (2000, July). Primates: A natural heritage of conflict resolution. *Science, 289*, 586–590. doi:10.1126/science.289.5479.586

Diamond, S. R. (1977). The effect of fear on the aggressive responses of anger aroused and revenge motivated subjects. *Journal of Psychology, 95*, 185–188.

DiBlasio, F., & Benda, B. B. (1991). Practitioners, religion and the use of forgiveness in the clinical setting. *Journal of Psychology and Christianity, 10*, 166–172.

Dreber, A., Rand, D. G., Fudenberg, D., & Nowak, M. A. (2008, March 20). Winners don't punish. *Nature, 452*, 348–351. doi:10.1038/nature06723

Elster, J. (1990). Norms of revenge. *Ethics, 100*, 862–885. doi:10.1086/293238

Enright, R. D., & Coyle, C. T. (1998). Researching the process model of forgiveness within psychological interventions. In E. L. Worthington (Ed.), *Dimensions of forgiveness: Psychological research and theological perspectives* (pp. 139–161). Philadelphia, PA: Templeton Foundation Press.

Fehr, E., & Gächter, S. (2002). Altruistic punishment in humans. *Nature, 415*, 137–140. doi:10.1038/415137a

Fehr, E., & List, J. A. (2004). The hidden costs and returns of incentives: Trust and trustworthiness among CEOs. *Journal of the European Economic Association, 2*, 743–771. doi:10.2139/ssrn.364480

Felson, R. B. (1982). Impression management and the escalation of aggression and violence. *Social Psychology Quarterly, 45*, 245–254. doi:10.2307/3033920

Finkel, E. J., Rusbult, C. E., Kumashiro, M., & Hannon, P. A. (2002). Dealing with a betrayal in close relationships: Does commitment promote forgiveness? *Journal of Personality and Social Psychology, 82*, 956–974. doi:10.1037/0022-3514.82.6.956

Forsythe, R., Horowitz, J. L., Savin, N. E., & Sefton, M. (1994). Fairness in simple bargaining experiments. *Games and Economic Behavior, 6*, 347–369. doi:10.1006/game.1994.1021

Frank, R. H. (1988). *Passions within reason: The strategic role of the emotions.* New York, NY: Norton.

Frean, M. R. (1994). The prisoner's dilemma without synchrony. *Proceedings of the Royal Society of London B, 257*, 75–79. doi:10.1098/rspb.1994.0096

Gordon, K. C., Burton, S., & Porter, L. (2004). Predicting the intentions of women in domestic violence shelters to return to partners: Does forgiveness play a role? *Journal of Family Psychology, 18*, 331–338. doi:10.1037/0893-3200.18.2.331

Govier, T. (2002). *Forgiveness and revenge.* New York, NY: Routledge.

Hamilton, W. D. (1964). The genetical evolution of social behaviour. Parts I & II. *Journal of Theoretical Biology, 7*, 1–52.

Hauert, C., & Schuster, H. G. (1998). Extending the iterated prisoner's dilemma without synchrony. *Journal of Theoretical Biology, 192*, 155–166. doi:10.1006/jtbi.1997.0590

Hayashi, N., Ostrom, E., Walker, J., & Yamagishi, T. (1999). Reciprocity, trust, and the sense of control: A cross-societal study. *Rationality and Society, 11*, 27–46. doi:10.1177/104346399011001002

Hebl, J., & Enright, R. D. (1993). Forgiveness as a psychotherapeutic goal with elderly females. *Psychotherapy, 30*, 658–667. doi:10.1037/0033-3204.30.4.658

Hewstone, M., Cairns, E., Voci, A., Hamberger, J., & Niens, U. (2006). Intergroup contact, forgiveness, and experience of "The Troubles" in Northern Ireland. *Journal of Social Issues, 62*, 99–120. doi:10.1111/j.1540-4560.2006.00441.x

Home Office. Research, Development and Statistics Directorate. Offending Surveys and Research, National Centre for Social Research and BMRB. (2003). *Social Research, Offending, Crime and Justice Survey, 2003* [computer file] (Report No. SN: 5248, 3rd ed.). Retrieved from http://www.data-archive.ac.uk/doc/5248%5Cmrdoc%5CUKDA%5CUKDA_Study_5248_Information.htm

Houser, D., Xiao, E., McCabe, K., & Smith, V. (2008). When punishment fails: Research on sanctions, intentions and noncooperation. *Games and Economic Behavior, 62*, 509–532.

Hruschka, D. J., & Henrich, J. (2006). Friendship, cliquishness, and the emergence of cooperation. *Journal of Theoretical Biology, 239*, 1–15. doi:10.1016/j.jtbi.2005.07.006

Jensen, K., Call, J., & Tomasello, M. (2007). Chimpanzees are vengeful but not spiteful. *Proceedings of the National Academy of Sciences of the United States of America, 104*, 13046–13050. doi:10.1073/pnas.0705555104

Karremans, J. C., & Aarts, H. (2007). The role of automaticity in determining the inclination to forgive close others. *Journal of Experimental Social Psychology, 43*, 902–917. doi:10.1016/j.jesp.2006.10.012

Kim, S. H., Smith, R. H., & Brigham, N. L. (1998). Effects of power imbalance and the presence of third parties on reactions to harm: Upward and downward revenge. *Personality and Social Psychology Bulletin, 24*, 353–361. doi:10.1177/0146167298244002

Koski, S. E., Koops, K., & Sterck, E. H. M. (2007). Reconciliation, relationship quality, and postconflict anxiety: Testing the integrated hypothesis in captive chimpanzees. *American Journal of Primatology, 69*, 158–172. doi:10.1002/ajp.20338

Kubrin, C. E., & Weitzer, R. (2003). Retaliatory homicide: Concentrated disadvantage and neighborhood culture. *Social Problems, 50*, 157–180. doi:10.1525/sp.2003.50.2.157

Kurzban, R. (2003). Trust, reciprocity, and gains from association: Interdisciplinary lessons from experimental research. In E. Ostrom & J. Walker (Eds.), *Biological foundations of reciprocity* (pp. 105–127). New York, NY: Sage.

Levine, S. S., & Kurzban, R. (2006). Explaining clustering in social networks: Towards an evolutionary theory of cascading benefits. *Managerial and Decision Economics, 27*, 173–187. doi:10.1002/mde.1291

Lieberman, D., & Linke, L. (2007). The effect of social category on third party punishment. *Evolutionary Psychology, 5*, 289–305.

Lundahl, B. W., Taylor, M. J., Stevenson, R., & Roberts, K. D. (2008). Process-based forgiveness interventions: A meta-analytic review. *Research on Social Work Practice, 18*, 465–478. doi:10.1177/1049731507313979

Maynard Smith, J., & Harper, D. (2003). *Animal signals*. Oxford, England: Oxford.

McCullough, M. E. (2008). *Beyond revenge: The evolution of the forgiveness instinct*. San Francisco, CA: Jossey-Bass.

McCullough, M. E., Luna, L. R., Berry, J. W., Tabak, B. A., & Bono, G. (in press). On the form of forgiving: Modeling the time-forgiveness relationship and testing the valuable relationships hypothesis. *Emotion*.

McCullough, M. E., Rachal, K. C., Sandage, S. J., Worthington, E. L., Brown, S. W., & Hight, T. L. (1998). Interpersonal forgiving in close relationships. II: Theoretical elaboration and measurement. *Journal of Personality and Social Psychology, 75*, 1586–1603. doi:10.1037/0022-3514.75.6.1586

McCullough, M. E., Worthington, E. L., & Rachal, K. C. (1997). Interpersonal forgiving in close relationships. *Journal of Personality and Social Psychology, 73*, 321–336. doi:10.1037/0022-3514.73.2.321

Miller, N., Pedersen, W. C., Earleywine, M., & Pollock, V. E. (2003). A theoretical model of triggered displaced aggression. *Personality and Social Psychology Review, 7*, 75–97. doi:10.1207/S15327957PSPR0701_5

Molm, L. D. (1997). *Coercive power in social exchange*. New York, NY: Cambridge University Press.

Murphy, J. G. (2003). *Getting even: Forgiveness and its limits*. New York, NY: Oxford.

Preston, S. D., & de Waal, F. B. M. (2002). Empathy: Its ultimate and proximate bases. *Behavioral and Brain Sciences, 25*, 1–72.

Rapoport, A., & Chammah, A. M. (1965). *The prisoner's dilemma*. Ann Arbor: University of Michigan Press.

Speckhard, A., & Ahkmedova, K. (2006). The making of a martyr: Chechen suicide terrorism. *Studies in Conflict and Terrorism, 29*, 429–492. doi:10.1080/10576100 600698550

Trivers, R. L. (1971). The evolution of reciprocal altruism. *The Quarterly Review of Biology, 46*, 35–57. doi:10.1086/406755

Uniacke, S. (2000). Why is revenge wrong? *The Journal of Value Inquiry, 34*, 61–69. doi:10.1023/A:1004778229751

Vasalou, A., Hopfensitz, A., & Pitt, J. V. (2008). In praise of forgiveness: Ways for repairing trust breakdowns in one-off online interactions. *International Journal of Human-Computer Studies, 66*, 466–480. doi:10.1016/j.ijhcs.2008.02.001

Vossekuil, B., Fein, R. A., Reddy, M., Borum, R., & Modzeleski, W. (2002). *The final report and findings of the Safe School Initiative: Implications for the prevention of school attacks in the United States*. Washington, DC: U.S. Department of Education, Office of Elementary and Secondary Education, Safe and Drug-Free Schools Program and U.S. Secret Service, National Threat Assessment Center.

Watts, D. (2006). Conflict resolution in chimpanzees and the valuable-relationships hypothesis. *International Journal of Primatology*, *27*, 1337–1364. doi:10.1007/s10764-006-9081-9

Williams, G. C. (1966). *Adaptation and natural selection. A critique of some current evolutionary thought.* Princeton, NJ: Princeton University Press.

Wilson, W. (1971). Reciprocation and other techniques for inducing cooperation. *The Journal of Conflict Resolution*, *15*, 167–195. doi:10.1177/002200277101500205

Worthington, E. L. (2005). More questions about forgiveness: Research agenda for 2005–2015. In E. L. Worthington (Ed.), *Handbook of forgiveness* (pp. 557–573). New York, NY: Routledge.

Wu, J., & Axelrod, R. (1995). How to cope with noise in the iterated prisoner's dilemma. *The Journal of Conflict Resolution*, *39*, 183–189. doi:10.1177/0022002795039001008

Yamagishi, T. (1986). The provision of a sanctioning system as a public good. *Journal of Personality and Social Psychology*, *51*, 110–116. doi:10.1037/0022-3514.51.1.110

13

ATTACHMENT, ANGER, AND AGGRESSION

MARIO MIKULINCER AND PHILLIP R. SHAVER

In recent years, attachment theory (Bowlby, 1973, 1980, 1982), designed originally to characterize infant–parent emotional bonding, has been applied first to the study of adolescent and adult romantic relationships (e.g., Hazan & Shaver, 1987) and then more broadly to the study of emotion regulation, social motives, and diverse forms of social behavior (Mikulincer & Shaver, 2003; see also Chapter 4, this volume). In this chapter, we explore the theory's relevance to understanding both normative and individual-difference aspects of human power and aggression. We begin with a brief summary of attachment theory and an account of the two major dimensions of attachment insecurity in adulthood. We then present a model of attachment-related processes in adulthood, based on an extensive review of the attachment research literature (Mikulincer & Shaver, 2007a). Next, we focus on the experience of anger and on destructive forms of aggression (see Chapter 14, this volume). We review research on ways in which attachment processes included in our model affect (a) functional and dysfunctional forms of anger, (b) domestic violence, (c) antisocial criminal behavior, and (d) intergroup hostility and aggression. Finally, we consider the main adaptive goal of human aggression: to maintain power and dominance (see Chapter 4, this volume). We consider how attachment orientations and the experience and exercise of power are related. We also present some new exploratory research concerning the influence of attachment-related processes on cognition and action when a person's sense of power is experimentally enhanced.

ATTACHMENT THEORY AND ATTACHMENT STYLE

According to Bowlby (1982), human beings are born with an innate psychobiological system (the *attachment behavioral system*) that motivates them to seek proximity to supportive others (*attachment figures*) in times of need. This system accomplishes basic regulatory functions (protection from threats and alleviation of distress) in humans of all ages, but it is most directly observable during infancy and early childhood (Bowlby, 1988). Bowlby (1973) described important individual differences in the functioning of the attachment system. Interactions with attachment figures who are available and responsive in times of need facilitate optimal attachment-system functioning and promote a sense of attachment security, a sense that the world is safe, that attachment figures are helpful when called on, and that it is possible to explore the environment curiously and engage effectively and enjoyably with other people. This sense of security is rooted in positive mental representations of self and others, which Bowlby called *internal working models*. When attachment figures are not reliably available and supportive, however, a sense of security is not attained, negative internal working models are formed, and strategies of affect regulation other than appropriate proximity seeking (*secondary attachment strategies*, conceptualized in terms of two major dimensions, avoidance and anxiety) are adopted.

In studies of adolescents and adults, tests of these theoretical ideas have generally focused on a person's *attachment style*, that is, the pattern of relational expectations, emotions, and behavior that results from a particular history of attachment experiences (Fraley & Shaver, 2000). Initially, research on individual differences in attachment was based on Ainsworth, Blehar, Waters, and Wall's (1978) three-category typology of attachment patterns in infancy (i.e., secure, anxious, and avoidant) and on Hazan and Shaver's (1987) conceptualization of similar adult styles in the romantic relationship domain. Subsequent studies (e.g., Brennan, Clark, & Shaver, 1998) revealed, however, that attachment styles are more appropriately conceptualized as regions in a two-dimensional space. The first dimension, attachment *anxiety*, reflects the degree to which a person worries that an attachment figure (including adult relationship partners) will not be available in times of need. The second dimension, attachment-related *avoidance*, reflects the extent to which a person distrusts relationship partners' goodwill and strives to maintain behavioral independence and emotional distance from partners. People who score low on both dimensions are said to be secure or to have a secure attachment style. The two dimensions can be measured with reliable and valid self-report scales and are associated in theoretically predictable ways with various aspects of personal adjustment and relationship quality (for a review, see Mikulincer & Shaver, 2007a).

Attachment styles are initially formed in interactions with primary caregivers during early childhood, as a large body of research has shown (Cassidy & Shaver, 2008), but Bowlby (1988) claimed that memorable interactions with others throughout life can alter a person's working models and move the person from one region of the two-dimensional space to another. Moreover, although attachment style is often conceptualized as a single global orientation toward close relationships, it is actually rooted in a complex network of cognitive and affective processes and mental representations, which includes many episodic, context-related, and relationship-specific as well as general attachment representations (Mikulincer & Shaver, 2003). In fact, many studies indicate that a person's attachment style can change depending on context and recent experiences (Mikulincer & Shaver, 2007b). This makes it possible to study the effects of security and insecurity experimentally.

ATTACHMENT-SYSTEM FUNCTIONING IN ADULTHOOD

On the basis of an extensive review of adult attachment studies, Mikulincer and Shaver (2003) proposed that when the attachment system is activated, an affirmative answer to the implicit or explicit question "Is an attachment figure available and likely to be responsive to my needs?" heightens the sense of attachment security and facilitates the use of constructive emotion-regulation strategies. These strategies are aimed at alleviating distress, maintaining supportive intimate relationships, and bolstering a person's sense of love-worthiness and self-efficacy. Moreover, they sustain what Shaver and Mikulincer (2002), following Fredrickson (2001), called a *broaden-and-build* cycle of attachment security, which expands a person's resources for maintaining coping flexibility and emotional stability in times of stress, broadens the person's perspectives and capacities, and facilitates the incorporation of mental representations of security-enhancing attachment figures into the self. This broaden-and-build process allows relatively secure individuals to maintain an authentic sense of personal efficacy, resilience, and optimism even when social support is temporarily unavailable (Mikulincer & Shaver, 2007a).

Perceived unavailability of an attachment figure results in attachment insecurity, which compounds the distress aroused by the appraisal of a situation as threatening. This state of insecurity forces a decision about the viability of further (more active) proximity seeking as a protective strategy. The appraisal of proximity as feasible or essential—because of attachment history, temperamental factors, or contextual cues—results in energetic, insistent attempts to attain proximity, support, and love. These attempts are called *hyperactivating strategies* (Cassidy & Kobak, 1988) because they involve up-regulation of the attachment system, including constant vigilance and intense concern until an attachment figure is perceived to be available and supportive. Hyperactivating strategies include attempts to elicit a partner's involvement, care, and support through clinging and controlling responses (Shaver & Mikulincer, 2002); overdependence on relationship partners as a source of protection (Shaver & Hazan, 1993); and perception of oneself as relatively helpless with respect to emotion regulation (Mikulincer & Shaver, 2003). These strategies help to explain the psychological correlates and consequences of attachment anxiety.

If a person has learned instead that relying on attachment figures is not a safe or effective way to cope with threats, he or she is likely to downplay such threats, inhibit worries and negative emotions, and defensively engage in what Bowlby (1982) called *compulsive self-reliance*. These coping strategies are called *deactivating* (Cassidy & Kobak, 1988) because their goal is to keep the attachment system down-regulated rather than experience the frustration and pain of rejection, punishment for expressing feelings, or abandonment. These strategies help to explain the psychological correlates and consequences of avoidant attachment.

In short, each attachment strategy has a major regulatory goal (i.e., insisting on proximity to an attachment figure or on self-reliance), which goes along with particular cognitive and affective processes that facilitate goal attainment. These strategies affect the experience, regulation, and expression of emotions (Mikulincer & Shaver, 2007a), including anger, which is of special concern in the present chapter. Moreover, the strategies affect the functioning of other behavioral systems, such as exploration and caregiving, as we and others have shown in numerous studies (reviewed by Mikulincer & Shaver, 2007a). As explained by Shaver et al. in Chapter 4 of the present volume, power and dominance can be viewed as the goals of a separate behavioral system. We expect the functioning of that system to be affected by differences in attachment style (i.e., attachment anxiety and avoidance) just as the other behavioral systems are.

ATTACHMENT AND ANGER

In Bowlby's (1973) analysis of infants' emotional reactions to separation from an attachment figure, he viewed anger as a functional reaction to separation because it sometimes motivates an attachment figure to pay more attention in the future and thereby provide better, more reliable care. In general, especially for adults, anger is functional to the extent that it communicates an intense but justifiable reaction to inconsiderate or undeserved ill treatment, rather than simply being a way to injure or destroy a relationship partner through acts of revenge (see Chapters 3 and 12, this volume). Bowlby (1973) called this constructive form of anger the "anger of hope" because it is intended to bring about a better future state of a relationship. He also mentioned, however, that anger can become so intense that it alienates or injures a partner, in which case it becomes destructive to a relationship and can even lead to violence or death. He called this the "anger of despair."

Functional anger is typical of people who feel secure in attachment relationships. Mikulincer (1998) found, for example, that when secure adults were hurt or frustrated by relationship partners' behavior, they were optimistic about the partners' willingness to apologize and "reform." Moreover, secure people's memories of their reactions to anger-provoking events were characterized by the constructive goal of repairing the relationship, engaging in adaptive problem-solving, and restoring a positive mood following a conflict. Another study explored the functional nature of secure adolescents' anger (Zimmermann, Maier, Winter, & Grossmann, 2001). Adolescent research participants performed a difficult, frustrating problem-solving task with the help of a friend, and their disappointment and anger during the task and their negative behavior toward the friend (e.g., rejecting the friend's suggestions without discussion) were coded. Disappointment and anger were associated with more aggressive behavior only in the case of insecure adolescents.

Avoidant individuals' deactivating strategies favor suppression of anger because anger implies emotional investment in a relationship, which is incongruent with avoidant people's emotional distance and extreme self-reliance (Cassidy & Kobak, 1988). Avoidant people's anger tends to be expressed only in indirect ways and to take the form of nonspecific hostility or generally hateful attitudes. Mikulincer (1998) found, for example, that avoidant adults did not report intense anger in response to provocative experiences, but they were aroused physiologically and attributed hostile intent to a hurtful other, even when the other's behavior was unintentional. In a laboratory study of support seeking in dating couples, Rholes, Simpson, and Orina (1999) found in a sample of women that avoidant attachment was associated with hostility toward their partner (coded from video recordings) when they worried about an upcoming painful task. Thus, although avoidant individuals are rarely comfortable describing themselves as needy or angry, they nevertheless react with hostility and hatred.

Attachment-anxious individuals, because of their tendency to intensify distress and ruminate about distressing experiences, are vulnerable to intense and prolonged bouts of anger. However, their fear of separation, desperate desire for love, and high dependency may keep them from expressing anger while causing them to direct it toward themselves. They may react to provocations and insults with a tangled mixture of resentment, hostility, anger, self-criticism, fear, sadness, and depression. Indeed, Mikulincer (1998) found that anxious people's memories of prior anger-provoking events included a flood of angry feelings, intense rumination, and a variety of negative emotions.

In a study of couple interactions, Simpson, Rholes, and Phillips (1996) found that attachment anxiety was associated with displaying and reporting more anger, hostility, and distress while discussing with a dating partner an unresolved problem in their relationship. In a study of support seeking, Rholes et al. (1999) found that, although anxious attachment was unrelated to anger toward a dating partner while waiting to undergo an anxiety-arousing experience, after participants were told they would not have to undergo the stressful task, attachment anxiety was associated with more intense expressions of anger toward one's partner. This pattern was particularly strong if participants had been more worried about the upcoming experience and had sought more support from their partner. Thus, it seems that anxious individuals' need for reassurance and support caused them to hold back feelings of frustration and anger while seeking a partner's support. But once the support was no longer needed (in that particular laboratory setting), the angry feelings surfaced and were expressed.

In a study using psychophysiological measures, Diamond and Hicks (2005) presented men with anger-provoking tasks (e.g., performing serial subtraction while being criticized by an experimenter), measured anger during and after the tasks, and recorded the men's *vagal tone*, a physiological indicator of down-regulation of negative emotions. They found that attachment anxiety was associated with both greater self-reported anger and lower vagal tone during and after the tasks, suggesting intense anger that was difficult to subdue.

ATTACHMENT AND AGGRESSION

So far, we have shown that attachment insecurities make it difficult for people to confine themselves to the constructive form of anger that Bowlby called the anger of hope. These insecurities make it more likely that people will experience anger of despair, which may provoke destructively aggressive behavior. In this section, we review studies of attachment insecurities and destructive aggression at three levels of analysis: domestic violence in couples; antisocial behavior that affects communities, such as delinquency and criminality; and intergroup (e.g., inter-ethnic or international) violence (for a more detailed review of the attachment-aggression link at the intergroup level, see Chapter 14).

Domestic Violence

From an attachment perspective, domestic violence is an exaggerated form of protesting a partner's hurtful behavior (see Chapters 2, 14, and 20). It is meant to discourage or prevent a partner from violating or breaking off the relationship (e.g., Bartholomew & Allison, 2006). We expect this kind of behavior to be more common among insecurely attached individuals, especially the anxious ones, who are especially vulnerable to hurt feelings and threats of abandonment (Mikulincer & Shaver, 2007a). Avoidant individuals, in contrast, might be expected to withdraw from conflict rather than escalate it, because they try to dismiss hurt feelings and avoid expressing vulnerability or need. Nevertheless, Bartholomew and Allison (2006) found that avoidant people sometimes became violent in the midst of escalating domestic conflicts, especially if their partner was anxiously attached and demanded their involvement.

Anxious attachment has been associated with domestic violence in two kinds of studies (reviewed by Mikulincer & Shaver, 2007a). First, anxious attachment has been found to correlate with measures of domestic violence across different samples of couples, whether married or cohabiting, and the correlation cannot be explained by other relational or personality factors. Second, abusive men who score relatively high on attachment anxiety report more severe and more frequent acts of coercion and abuse during couple conflicts.

Research also indicates that victims of domestic violence suffer from attachment insecurities, with most studies finding elevations in attachment anxiety and some finding elevations in avoidance as well (Mikulincer & Shaver, 2007a). Because of the cross-sectional nature of these studies, however, the findings may indicate either that attachment insecurity puts people at risk of being abused or that abuse increases attachment insecurity, or both. Also, because violence in relationships is often reciprocal, many victims are also perpetrators (Bartholomew & Allison, 2006), which creates a strong correlation between perpetration and victimization (for a more detailed discussion, see Chapter 20, this volume).

Antisocial Behavior

Adult attachment researchers have found links between attachment insecurities and antisocial behavior, such as delinquency and criminality (reviewed by Mikulincer & Shaver, 2007a). Although both anxious and avoidant individuals are more likely than their secure counterparts to engage in antisocial behavior, they do so for different reasons. Anxiously attached people sometimes engage in delinquent or criminal behavior as a way of crying out for attention and care or of expressing anger and resentment (Allen, Moore, Kuperminc, & Bell, 1998). Avoidant individuals engage in antisocial behavior to distance themselves from others (e.g., parents) or to demonstrate, by violating rules and laws, their lack of concern for others (Allen et al., 1998).

Levinson and Fonagy (2004) compared the attachment patterns of 22 imprisoned delinquents, 22 patients with personality disorder without a criminal history, and 22 healthy controls. They noted a higher prevalence of avoidant attachment in the delinquent group than in the other groups. Moreover, delinquents who had committed violent offenses (e.g., murder, malicious wounding) exhibited the same inability or unwillingness to talk coherently about their emotional experiences that has been noted in other studies of insecure attachment. In a related study, van IJzendoorn et al. (1997) interviewed 40 male criminals and found that 95% of them had insecure attachment patterns.

If antisocial behavior is associated with attachment insecurity, then interventions aimed at strengthening a person's sense of attachment security might help with rehabilitation. In fact, there is evidence from studies of residential treatment programs for troubled and delinquent adolescents that forming and maintaining a secure attachment relationship with a staff member can reduce antisocial behavior (e.g., Born, Chevalier, & Humblet, 1997). In a yearlong study of adolescents residing in an Israeli treatment center, Gur (2006) found that those who formed secure attachment bonds with staff members had lower rates of anger, depression, and behavioral problems and more positive emotional experiences during the year. Adolescents who formed more secure attachment bonds with staff members changed in the direction of security on measures of attachment orientation and exhibited less aggressive behavior toward peers and authorities.

Intergroup Aggression

The link between attachment insecurity and aggression is also evident in the field of intergroup relations. In a series of five studies, Mikulincer and Shaver (2001) found that higher levels of self-reported attachment anxiety were associated with more hostile responses to a variety of out-groups (as defined by secular Israeli Jewish students): Israeli Arabs, Ultra-Orthodox Jews, Russian immigrants, and homosexuals. In addition, we found that experimental heightening of the sense of attachment security (by subliminally presenting security-related words or asking study participants to visualize the faces of security-providing attachment figures) eliminated negative responses to out-groups. These effects were found even when participants' sense of personal value was threatened or their ingroup had been insulted by an outgroup member. That is, experimentally augmented attachment security reduced the sense of threat created by encounters with outgroup members and seemed to eliminate defensive and hostile responses toward outgroup members.

Building on these studies, Mikulincer and Shaver (2007b) found that increasing people's sense of attachment security reduced actual aggression between contending or warring social groups. Specifically, Israeli Jewish under-graduates participated in a study together with another Israeli Jew or an Israeli Arab (in each case, the same confederate of the experimenter) and were sub-liminally and repeatedly exposed (for 20 ms on each trial) to the name of their own security-enhancing attachment figure, the name of a familiar person who was not viewed as an attachment figure, or the name of an acquaintance. Fol-lowing the priming procedure, participants were informed that they would evaluate a food sample and that they had been randomly selected to give the confederate hot sauce to evaluate. They also learned indirectly that the con-federate strongly disliked spicy foods. (This procedure has been used in other studies of interpersonal aggression, e.g., McGregor et al., 1998.) The dependent variable was the amount of hot sauce allocated to the confederate.

When participants had been subliminally primed with the name of someone who was not an attachment figure, they delivered a larger amount of hot sauce to the Arab confederate than to the Jewish confederate, a sign of intergroup aggression. But security priming eliminated this difference: Participants whose sense of security had been enhanced delivered equal (relatively low) amounts of hot sauce to both the Arab and the Jewish con-federate. In addition, participants scoring higher on attachment anxiety gave more hot sauce to the outgroup member (Israeli Arab) than to the ingroup member (Israeli Jew). Thus, it seems that people who are either dispositionally secure or induced to feel more secure in a particular setting are better able than their insecure counterparts to tolerate intergroup differences and to refrain from intergroup aggression.

ATTACHMENT AND POWER

So far, we have considered the association between attachment insecu-rities and destructive forms of anger and aggression: domestic violence, anti-social behavior, and intergroup violence. As explained in Chapter 4 of this volume, however, aggression is not exclusively maladaptive or destructive; it is presumably an adaptive strategy that arose and was maintained in evolution because it contributed to attaining the set goal of a hypothesized power/

dominance behavioral system (for similar analyses, see Chapters 3 and 12). Following Sroufe and Waters's (1977) analysis of "felt security" as the proximal psychological goal of the attachment system, we propose that something we call "felt power" is the goal of the power/dominance system. This "felt sense" is associated with feeling that one can control resources without undue social interference. Only when this goal is blocked by social interference do aggressive behaviors become pervasive, extreme, destructive, or dysfunctional (see Chapter 4, this volume). In this section, we focus on times when feelings of power and dominance are elevated and aggression serves its adaptive function. In particular, we explore whether and how attachment insecurities affect the experience and exercise of power.

According to the *approach/inhibition theory of power* (e.g., Galinsky, Gruenfeld, & Magee, 2003; Keltner, Gruenfeld, & Anderson, 2003), experiencing a sense of power facilitates what Carver and White (1994) called an *approach orientation* and Higgins (1998) called a *promotion orientation*, that is, a motivated state involving reward-related thoughts, heightened attention to rewards, and positive emotions related to rewards. The sense of power also seems to counteract what Carver and White (1994) called an *inhibition orientation* and Higgins (1998) called a *prevention orientation*, a state aimed at avoiding threats, heightened attention to threats, activation of threat-related thoughts, and negative emotions. Galinsky et al. (2003) reasoned that a sense of power strengthens an approach orientation because powerful people expect to have greater access to rewards and less interference from others when pursuing rewards. For the same reasons, powerlessness favors an inhibition orientation because powerless people expect to be subject to more social and material threats and are aware of the constraints that these threats impose on one's actions.

The approach/inhibition theory of power has received strong empirical support. For example, Keltner et al. (2003) reviewed evidence that elevated power increases the experience and expression of positive emotions, sensitivity and responsiveness to potential rewards, the automaticity of social cognitions, and the likelihood of approach, disinhibition, and extraverted behavior. In subsequent studies, experimental augmentation of the sense of power (e.g., asking people to recall an episode in which they had power over others) elevated risk-taking in negotiations; engagement in risky, unprotected sex; and competitive behavior (e.g., Anderson & Galinsky, 2006; Magee, Galinsky, & Gruenfeld, 2007).

An increased sense of power also protects people from others' influence and social pressure (Galinsky, Magee, Gruenfeld, Whitson, & Liljenquist, 2008). At the same time, because powerful people feel they have control over others and do not feel constrained by them, increasing people's sense of power may increase their psychological distance from others (Smith & Trope, 2006) and their tendency to objectify others and perceive them as means for attaining personal goals (Gruenfeld, Inesi, Magee, & Galinsky, 2008). Galinsky, Magee, Inesi, and Gruenfeld (2006) found that increasing people's sense of power reduced their inclination to adopt others' perspectives and to empathize with others.

We suspect that these consequences of elevated power are moderated by people's attachment orientations because they are likely to depend on how one relates to others and on the goals, wishes, and fears that underlie one's social behavior. For example, people who hold negative views of others and dislike closeness and intimacy (i.e., people with an avoidant attachment style) are likely to construe power as a way to gain distance from others and freedom from their influence. In contrast, people who hold positive views of others and are able to balance dependence and autonomy (i.e., relatively secure people) are probably able to use power and influence to improve their interpersonal relations, respond to others' needs, and resolve interpersonal conflicts without deferring too much to a partner's needs. Moreover, people who fear rejection and abandonment (i.e., anxiously attached people) may feel uneasy when granted power and be reluctant to act freely, take risks, and step outside the boundaries of conformity. In subsequent sections, we report findings from two studies that examine these ideas.

Attachment Anxiety Weakens the Link Between Power and an Approach Orientation

Our first hypothesis is that increasing a person's sense of power will strengthen his or her tendency to adopt an approach orientation (e.g., be optimistic and take risks) as long as the person scores low on attachment anxiety but not if he or she scores high. People with an anxious attachment style are likely to be ambivalent about power and dominance. On the one hand, they want to have control over relationship partners (Shaver & Hazan, 1993); on the other hand, they may be reluctant to assert themselves (e.g., Bartholomew & Horowitz, 1991), because this could provoke a partner's resentment, create conflict, and threaten relationship stability.

To test this hypothesis, in Study 1 we examined the effects of priming a sense of power (using Galinsky et al.'s, 2003, technique) on optimism and risk, taking into account individual differences in attachment anxiety and avoidance. Eighty Israeli undergraduate students (60 women and 20 men) completed in a class the Experiences in Close Relationships (ECR) measure of attachment anxiety and avoidance (Brennan et al., 1998), which had alpha reliability coefficients of .90 and .83 in this sample. Weeks later they came to a laboratory individually and were randomly assigned to a power priming or a control condition. In the power priming condition ($n = 40$), participants were asked to recall a particular incident in which they had power over one or more other people and to write about what happened, how they felt, and what they did during and after the episode (for instructions, see Galinsky et al., 2003). In the control condition ($n = 40$), participants were asked to recall a particular TV program they had watched the previous week and to write about it.

All of the participants then completed Weinstein's (1980) 15-item optimism scale (with an alpha of .85) and Tversky and Kahneman's (1981) measure of risk preference. They were told the following:

> Imagine that you work for a large hi-tech company that is experiencing serious economic troubles and needs to lay off 6000 employees. Plan A will save 2,000 jobs, whereas plan B has a one third probability of saving all 6,000 jobs but a two thirds probability of saving no jobs.

Participants were asked to indicate the extent to which they would favor one option over the other using a scale ranging from 1 (*very much prefer program* A) to 7 (*very much prefer program* B). Higher scores reflected greater preference for the riskier program (program B).

Hierarchical regression analyses examining the unique and interactive effects on optimism and risk preference of being primed with memories of power (a dummy variable contrasting the power condition with the control condition), avoidant attachment, and attachment anxiety revealed significant main effects of power priming and attachment anxiety. Replicating Galinsky et al.'s (2006) findings, participants in the power condition were more optimistic, $\beta = .27, p < .05$, and more likely to prefer the riskier plan than participants in the control condition, $\beta = .29, p < .01$. In addition, more anxiously attached participants were less optimistic and less likely to prefer the riskier plan, βs of $-.33$ and $-.30$, $ps < .01$. These main effects were qualified by significant interactions between power priming and anxious attachment ($\beta = -.41, p < .01$, for optimism; $\beta = -.29, p < .01$, for risk preference). Simple slope tests revealed that power priming led to greater optimism and risk preference than the control condition mainly when participants scored relatively low on attachment anxiety, βs of .68 and .58, $ps < .01$. These effects of power priming were negative or nil and not significant when attachment anxiety was relatively high, βs of $-.14$ and .00. In sum, as expected, attachment anxiety disrupted the previously documented association between power and an approach orientation.

Power Increases Objectification of Others in the Context of Avoidant Attachment

Our second hypothesis is that increasing a person's sense of power will increase the objectification of others among people scoring high on avoidant attachment but not among less avoidant people. Avoidant people hold generally negative, uncompassionate views of others and try to remain emotionally distant and detached from them (see the review by Mikulincer & Shaver, 2007a). It seems likely that they will use power as an opportunity to act on their preferences for autonomy and distance, their critical view of others, and their perception of others as objects to be used instrumentally for personal need satisfaction. In contrast, more secure people, who hold positive, empathic views of others and are guided by a desire to form mutually satisfying and harmonious relationships, should be less likely to see others as objects even when they are granted a degree of power over them.

To test these ideas we conducted a second study (Study 2) with a new group of 60 Israeli undergraduate students (41 women and 19 men) who completed the ECR scale during a class period (with resulting alphas of .86 for anxiety and .88 for avoidance). Weeks later they came to a laboratory individually and were randomly assigned to a power priming or a control condition as in Study 1. All of them were then asked to think about their relationships with three other students in their classes. For each of these students, participants completed Gruenfeld et al.'s (2008) 10-item objectification scale (e.g., "I tend to contact this person only when I need something from him/her," "I try to get him/her to do things that will help me succeed"). Item ratings were made on a 7-point scale ranging from 1 (*not at all*) to 7 (*very much*). For each participant and each target student, we computed an objectification score by averaging the 10 item scores (with alphas ranging from .88 to .91). Because the correlations between the three different student scores were high ($rs > .64$), we computed a total objectification score by averaging them.

Hierarchical regression analyses examining the unique and interactive effects of power priming, avoidant attachment, and attachment anxiety on objectification revealed a significant main effect of avoidant attachment, $\beta = .34$, $p < .01$. This effect was qualified, as expected, by a significant interaction between power priming and avoidant attachment, $\beta = .29$, $p < .05$. Simple slope tests revealed that power priming led to greater objectification of others mainly when participants scored relatively high on avoidance, $\beta = .43$, $p < .01$. The effect was in the opposite direction but not significant when avoidance was low, $\beta = -.15$. Thus, as hypothesized, when people were primed with a sense of power, avoidant participants tended to objectify others more than less avoidant participants, suggesting that secure people might be able to maintain a sense of power without treating others as objects.

CONCLUDING REMARKS

As explained in Chapter 4 of this volume, Bowlby (1982) did not say much about anger, aggression, or power/dominance, partly because he wanted to part company with Freud's emphasis on sexual and aggressive "instincts" or "drives" and partly because he was concerned primarily with infant–parent relationships. He viewed anger in the context of infants' reactions to separation or abandonment. Some of his ideas about anger (i.e., anger of hope or anger of despair) can be extended to the realm of adult close relationships, and we have summarized some of the literature on that topic here. But infants are not prepared to occupy powerful or dominant roles in society, so Bowlby said virtually nothing about power and dominance in his books.

Nevertheless, attachment theory has been fruitfully expanded in several directions, including the conceptualization of leadership and group functioning in terms of attachment dynamics (Mikulincer & Shaver, 2007a). And Bowlby's behavioral-system construct has proven useful in the study of sexuality, empathy, and altruism from an attachment perspective (Mikulincer & Shaver, 2007a), partly because Bowlby explicitly referred to the existence of sexual and caregiving behavioral systems. Because we now want to extend the theory into the untouched domain of power and dominance, we have begun to conceptualize the existence of a power/dominance system. If such a system exists, we expect its operations to be colored by attachment security and the major forms of attachment insecurity. In this chapter, we have unveiled our first efforts to explore links between attachment and power. We think the results are interesting and well worth pursuing further.

REFERENCES

Ainsworth, M. D. S., Blehar, M. C., Waters, E., & Wall, S. (1978). *Patterns of attachment: Assessed in the strange situation and at home.* Hillsdale, NJ: Erlbaum.

Allen, J. P., Moore, C., Kuperminc, G. P., & Bell, K. (1998). Attachment and adolescent psychosocial functioning. *Child Development, 69,* 1406–1419. doi:10.2307/1132274

Anderson, C., & Galinsky, A. D. (2006). Power, optimism, and risk-taking. *European Journal of Social Psychology, 36,* 511–536. doi:10.1002/ejsp.324

Bartholomew, K., & Allison, C. J. (2006). An attachment perspective on abusive dynamics in intimate relationships. In M. Mikulincer & G. S. Goodman (Eds.), *Dynamics of romantic love* (pp. 102–127). New York, NY: Guilford Press.

Bartholomew, K., & Horowitz, L. M. (1991). Attachment styles among young adults: A test of a four-category model. *Journal of Personality and Social Psychology, 61,* 226–244. doi:10.1037/0022-3514.61.2.226

Born, M., Chevalier, V., & Humblet, I. (1997). Resilience, desistance, and delinquent career of adolescent offenders. *Journal of Adolescence, 20,* 679–694. doi:10.1006/jado.1997.0119

Bowlby, J. (1973). *Attachment and loss: Vol. 2. Separation: Anxiety and anger.* New York, NY: Basic Books.

Bowlby, J. (1980). *Attachment and loss: Vol. 3. Sadness and depression*. New York, NY: Basic Books.

Bowlby, J. (1982). *Attachment and loss: Vol. 1. Attachment* (2nd ed.). New York, NY: Basic Books.

Bowlby, J. (1988). *A secure base: Clinical applications of attachment theory*. London, England: Routledge.

Brennan, K. A., Clark, C. L., & Shaver, P. R. (1998). Self-report measurement of adult romantic attachment: An integrative overview. In J. A. Simpson & W. S. Rholes (Eds.), *Attachment theory and close relationships* (pp. 46–76). New York, NY: Guilford Press.

Carver, C. S., & White, T. L. (1994). Behavioral inhibition, behavioral activation, and affective responses to impending reward and punishment: The BIS/BAS scales. *Journal of Personality and Social Psychology, 67*, 319–333. doi:10.1037/0022-3514.67.2.319

Cassidy, J., & Kobak, R. R. (1988). Avoidance and its relationship with other defensive processes. In J. Belsky & T. Nezworski (Eds.), *Clinical implications of attachment* (pp. 300–323). Hillsdale, NJ: Erlbaum.

Cassidy, J., & Shaver, P. R. (Eds.). (2008). *Handbook of attachment: Theory, research, and clinical applications* (2nd ed.). New York, NY: Guilford Press.

Diamond, L. M., & Hicks, A. M. (2005). Attachment style, current relationship security, and negative emotions: The mediating role of physiological regulation. *Journal of Social and Personal Relationships, 22*, 499–518. doi:10.1177/0265407505054520

Fraley, R. C., & Shaver, P. R. (2000). Adult romantic attachment: Theoretical developments, emerging controversies, and unanswered questions. *Review of General Psychology, 4*, 132–154. doi:10.1037/1089-2680.4.2.132

Fredrickson, B. L. (2001). The role of positive emotions in positive psychology: The broaden-and-build theory of positive emotions. *American Psychologist, 56*, 218–226. doi:10.1037/0003-066X.56.3.218

Galinsky, A. D., Gruenfeld, D. H., & Magee, J. C. (2003). From power to action. *Journal of Personality and Social Psychology, 85*, 453–466. doi:10.1037/0022-3514.85.3.453

Galinsky, A. D., Magee, J. C., Gruenfeld, D. H., Whitson, J. A., & Liljenquist, K. A. (2008). Power reduces the press of the situation: Implications for creativity, conformity, and dissonance. *Journal of Personality and Social Psychology, 95*, 1450–1466. doi:10.1037/a0012633

Galinsky, A. D., Magee, J. C., Inesi, M. E., & Gruenfeld, D. H. (2006). Power and perspective not taken. *Psychological Science, 17*, 1068–1074. doi:10.1111/j.1467-9280.2006.01824.x

Gruenfeld, D. H., Inesi, M. E., Magee, J. C., & Galinsky, A. D. (2008). Power and the objectification of social targets. *Journal of Personality and Social Psychology, 95*, 111–127. doi:10.1037/0022-3514.95.1.111

Gur, O. (2006). *Changes in adjustment and attachment-related representations among high-risk adolescents during residential treatment: The transformational impact of the functioning of caregiving figures as a secure base* (Unpublished doctoral dissertation). Bar-Ilan University, Ramat Gan, Israel.

Hazan, C., & Shaver, P. R. (1987). Romantic love conceptualized as an attachment process. *Journal of Personality and Social Psychology, 52,* 511–524. doi:10.1037/0022-3514.52.3.511

Higgins, E. T. (1998). Promotion and prevention: Regulatory focus as a motivational principle. In M. P. Zanna (Ed.), *Advances in experimental social psychology* (Vol. 30, pp. 1–46). New York, NY: Academic Press.

Keltner, D., Gruenfeld, D. H., & Anderson, C. (2003). Power, approach, and inhibition. *Psychological Review, 110,* 265–284. doi:10.1037/0033-295X.110.2.265

Levinson, A., & Fonagy, P. (2004). Offending and attachment: The relationship between interpersonal awareness and offending in a prison population with psychiatric disorder. *Canadian Journal of Psychoanalysis, 12,* 225–251.

Magee, J. C., Galinsky, A. D., & Gruenfeld, D. H. (2007). Power, propensity to negotiate, and moving first in competitive interactions. *Personality and Social Psychology Bulletin, 33,* 200–212. doi:10.1177/0146167206294413

McGregor, H., Lieberman, J., Greenberg, J., Solomon, S., Arndt, J., Simon, L., & Pyszczynski, T. (1998). Terror management and aggression: Evidence that mortality salience promotes aggression against worldview-threatening individuals. *Journal of Personality and Social Psychology, 74,* 590–605. doi:10.1037/0022-3514.74.3.590

Mikulincer, M. (1998). Adult attachment style and individual differences in functional versus dysfunctional experiences of anger. *Journal of Personality and Social Psychology, 74,* 513–524. doi:10.1037/0022-3514.74.2.513

Mikulincer, M., & Shaver, P. R. (2001). Attachment theory and intergroup bias: Evidence that priming the secure base schema attenuates negative reactions to out-groups. *Journal of Personality and Social Psychology, 81,* 97–115. doi:10.1037/0022-3514.81.1.97

Mikulincer, M., & Shaver, P. R. (2003). The attachment behavioral system in adulthood: Activation, psychodynamics, and interpersonal processes. In M. P. Zanna (Ed.), *Advances in experimental social psychology* (Vol. 35, pp. 53–152). New York, NY: Academic Press.

Mikulincer, M., & Shaver, P. R. (2007a). *Attachment patterns in adulthood: Structure, dynamics, and change.* New York, NY: Guilford Press.

Mikulincer, M., & Shaver, P. R. (2007b). Boosting attachment security to promote mental health, prosocial values, and intergroup tolerance. *Psychological Inquiry, 18,* 139–156.

Rholes, W. S., Simpson, J. A., & Orina, M. (1999). Attachment and anger in an anxiety-provoking situation. *Journal of Personality and Social Psychology, 76,* 940–957. doi:10.1037/0022-3514.76.6.940

Shaver, P. R., & Hazan, C. (1993). Adult romantic attachment: Theory and evidence. In D. Perlman & W. Jones (Eds.), *Advances in personal relationships* (Vol. 4, pp. 29–70). London, England: Jessica Kingsley.

Shaver, P. R., & Mikulincer, M. (2002). Attachment-related psychodynamics. *Attachment & Human Development, 4*, 133–161. doi:10.1080/14616730210154171

Simpson, J. A., Rholes, W. S., & Phillips, D. (1996). Conflict in close relationships: An attachment perspective. *Journal of Personality and Social Psychology, 71*, 899–914. doi:10.1037/0022-3514.71.5.899

Smith, P. K., & Trope, Y. (2006). You focus on the forest when you're in charge of the trees: Power priming and abstract information processing. *Journal of Personality and Social Psychology, 90*, 578–596. doi:10.1037/0022-3514.90.4.578

Sroufe, L. A., & Waters, E. (1977). Attachment as an organizational construct. *Child Development, 48*, 1184–1199.

Tversky, A., & Kahneman, D. (1981, January). The framing of decisions and the psychology of choice. *Science, 211*, 453–458. doi:10.1126/science.7455683

van IJzendoorn, M. H., Feldbrugge, J., Derks, F. C. H., de Ruiter, C., Verhagen M. F., Philipse, M. W., . . . Riksen-Walraven, J. M. (1997). Attachment representations of personality-disordered criminal offenders. *American Journal of Orthopsychiatry, 67*, 449–459. doi:10.1037/h0080246

Weinstein, N. D. (1980). Unrealistic optimism about future life events. *Journal of Personality and Social Psychology, 39*, 806–820. doi:10.1037/0022-3514.39.5.806

Zimmermann, P., Maier, M. A., Winter, M., & Grossmann, K. E. (2001). Attachment and adolescents' emotion regulation during a joint problem-solving task with a friend. *International Journal of Behavioral Development, 25*, 331–343.

14

ATTACHMENT AND VIOLENCE:
AN ANGER BORN OF FEAR

DONALD G. DUTTON

Angry coercive behavior, acting in the service of an affectional bond, is not uncommon. It is seen when a mother, whose child has foolishly run across the road, berates and punishes him with an anger born of fear.

— Bowlby, 1973, p. 287

In this chapter I review the literature on attachment and violence. I begin by noting that early disruptions of attachment activate the attachment behavioral system, a systemic alarm reaction assuaged only by contact with an attachment figure (Ainsworth, Blehar, Waters, & Wall, 1978; Bowlby, 1982). Later in life, failures to reduce attachment-related alarm or to find a "safe haven" in times of external threat can produce a spiraling arousal reaction that lowers impulse control and increases the likelihood of violence. I review studies connecting certain types of personality organization to intimate partner violence, violence toward the self, and violence in military contexts. These forms of personality organization can be viewed as extreme forms of attachment insecurity persisting into adulthood and making an individual susceptible to high aversive arousal and hence to arousal-based violence. Finally, I discuss symbolic attachment as a major incentive for violence when a culture promises secure attachment in perpetuity if one martyrs oneself for a "holy" cause.

Bowlby (1982) viewed interpersonal anger as arising from frustrated attachment needs and serving as a form of protest behavior directed at regaining or maintaining contact with an attachment figure. In adulthood, such protest is often directed at a romantic partner and can take the form of verbal abuse, coercive control of a partner's behavior, and even violence (see Chapters 13 and 20, this volume). Such abusive behavior is most likely to be precipitated by real or imagined threats of rejection, separation, or abandonment by the partner. Hence, as Bowlby (1988) stated, "violence . . . can be understood as the distorted and exaggerated version of behavior that is potentially functional" (p. 12).

This perspective is consistent with a large body of literature indicating that abusive men tend to be insecure and overly dependent on their partners and that jealousy and fears of separation are common triggers of abusive episodes (Dutton, 2006). In adults, tests of the association between attachment insecurities and violence have indicated that attachment patterns that include considerable anxiety (often labeled preoccupied and fearful; e.g., Bartholomew & Horowitz, 1991) incline a person to become highly emotionally aroused in response to possible separation or rejection (Bartholomew & Allison, 2006; Bartholomew, Henderson, & Dutton, 2001). It follows that individuals with these kinds of insecure attachment may exhibit higher levels of violence toward their close relationship partners, either as a way of controlling the threat of separation from a partner or as an impulsive "acting out" of inner tensions resulting from anticipating and dreading separation.

"PRIMITIVE" ATTACHMENT THREAT: STRESS REACTIONS

According to Bowlby (1973, 1982), fear-based activation of the attachment system is similar to an alarm reaction in animals. It produces hormonal and neurobiological hyperactivity, including the release of cortisol and endogenous opioids (similar to low-dose morphine). Frequent experiences of this kind can affect neural development (Perry, 1997; Schore, 1994, 2003a, 2003b; D. J. Siegel, 2001a). There is clear evidence from several independent researchers that early infancy (a period called "primitive" by psychoanalytic researchers because it is "preoedipal" in Freud's psychoanalytic theory) is a critical or sensitive period for neural development (Perry, 1997; Pynoos & Eth, 1985; Schore, 1994; D. J. Siegel, 2001b). Neural structures such as the hypothalamus and the prefrontal and orbitofrontal cortex, which regulate emotion, develop rapidly at this time (Schore, 1994, 2003a). As D. J. Siegel (2001b) states: "When certain suboptimal attachment experiences occur, the mind of the child may not come to function as a well-integrated system" (p. 82).

Klein and Mahler's (e.g., Klein & Riviere, 1937; Mahler, 1971; Mahler, Pine, & Bergman, 1975) psychoanalytic emphasis on the phase of infant development in which the child first physically separates from the mother and initiates a separate sense of identity is supported by current research on neurological development (Dutton, 2006). Thus, rage is exhibited first in the context of an intimate relationship, usually with mother (Klein & Riviere, 1937), in a phase of life prior to language development and before autobiographical memory (Schore, 2003a). Such rage is more common in insecure relationships, and the neural and psychological effects of repeatedly experiencing it in early childhood, incoherently and unmediated by language, may make it more likely to erupt later in life, where it seems especially irrational when it leads to violence against an intimate adult attachment figure.

THE NEUROBIOLOGY OF ATTACHMENT

In an extremely detailed analysis, Schore (1994, 2003a, 2003b) showed how the capacity for attachment matures into a homeostatic self-regulatory system near the end of the first year of life. This occurs because dyadic communication with a parental figure generates intense positive affective states in the infant and high levels of dopamine and endogenous opiates. These neurotransmitters, in turn, promote growth in the prefrontal cortex, especially the orbitofrontal cortex, which is critically involved in the attachment process. Attachment therefore has a neuropsychological aspect that is itself based on dyadic interaction with caregivers during the first year of life (before extensive development of the left hemispheric structures involved in language). Thus, the problems that abusive individuals have with attachment and emotion regulation are often grounded in early relationships that are not recalled later in words. This suggests that the most important and long-lasting effects of early family dysfunction may be due not simply to imitation of specific abusive acts but rather to the inability to regulate painful and destructive emotions, such as panic and rage.

D. J. Siegel (2001a) explains that one form of insecure attachment, labeled *disorganized/disoriented* (Lyons-Ruth & Jacobwitz, 2008; Main & Solomon, 1986, 1990), has been associated with marked impairments in the emotional, social, and cognitive domains, and predisposes a person to a clinical condition known as *dissociation* in which the capacity to function in an organized, coherent manner is impaired (Carlson, 1998). Disorganized attachment in infancy includes a diverse array of fearful, odd, disorganized, or conflicted behaviors exhibited in the Strange Situation assessment procedure (Ainsworth et al., 1978). Main (1995) argued that this kind of behavior stems from parents with unresolved losses and traumas who are themselves susceptible to dissociative states. These parents generate in their young children "fright without solution."

Recent studies have shown that youths with a history of disorganized attachment are at great risk of expressing hostility with peers and have the potential for extreme interpersonal violence (Lyons-Ruth, Bronfman, & Atwood, 1999; Lyons-Ruth & Jacobwitz, 2008). This implies that lack of resolution of trauma in a parent, leading to what Lyons-Ruth and her colleagues call hostile or helpless behavior, can cause parents to create frightening, paradoxical, and unsolvable problematic situations for their children. The adult attachment figure, who, according to Bowlby (1982) is equipped with a caregiving behavioral system that evolved because it provided a safe haven and secure base for children who were then more likely to live and reproduce, paradoxically becomes also a source of alarm, leaving a dependent child with no clear strategy for getting attachment needs met.

EMPIRICAL STUDIES OF ATTACHMENT STYLE, ANGER, AND INTIMATE PARTNER VIOLENCE

Adult attachment patterns or styles can be conceptualized in terms of two continuous dimensions, attachment anxiety and avoidance, as explained elsewhere in this volume (Chapter 13). Mikulincer (1998) examined a college sample and found that experiences and expressions of anger were related to attachment insecurities. Participants who scored relatively high on avoidance attempted to deny their anger but nevertheless revealed it in the form of smoldering hostility and physiological arousal, of which the avoidant individuals seemed to be unaware. The more anxious participants, in contrast, exhibited intense anger and a lack of anger control.

Mikulincer's findings motivated me to reexamine anger data that my associates and I had collected from abusive men using the subscales of the Siegel Multidimensional Anger Inventory (MAI; J. M. Siegel, 1986): anger-in, anger-out, and frequency, duration, and magnitude of anger and hostility. In our study, *fearful attachment* (a combination of attachment anxiety and avoidance, conceptually similar to infant disorganized attachment) correlated consistently higher than other adult attachment patterns with every subscale on the MAI. In my work (e.g., Dutton, 2006), I have described what I call "the abusive personality in males," which includes several characteristics that are significantly correlated with partners' reports of abusiveness. This personality pattern includes what I call a "fearful–angry" attachment style, and I hypothesized that some aspect of male socialization helped shape the fear to anger. Intimate abuse, I argue, is literally "an anger born of fear" (Bowlby 1973, p. 287).

The relationship of attachment to anger and violence has been studied in a sample selected for problems in intimate relationships, a court mandated group of men convicted of wife assault ($N = 160$). In this group, my colleagues and I (Dutton, Starzomski, Saunders, & Bartholomew, 1994) examined associations between attachment style (measured with the Relationship Styles Questionnaire [RSQ]; Griffin & Bartholomew, 1994) and emotional, cognitive, and behavioral reactions to intimacy. Specifically, the men completed a battery of questionnaires including the RSQ and measures of borderline personality traits (Oldham et al., 1985), trauma symptoms (Briere & Runtz, 1989), trait anger (J. M. Siegel, 1986), recalled parental treatment (Perris, Jacobsson, Lindstrom, von Knorring, & Perris, 1980), verbal and physical abusiveness (Straus, 1992; Tolman, 1989), and jealousy (Mathes & Severa, 1981). The men's spouses also completed the latter two scales to describe their husbands. We found that the more anxious attachment styles, fearful and preoccupied, were significantly correlated with most features of intimate abusiveness and with spouses' reports of abusiveness. The secure attachment style, even in this self-selected, court-mandated population, was negatively correlated with these features of abusiveness.

A recent study of dating violence in a college sample examined associations between attachment insecurities and these same features of abusiveness in women (Clift, 2008). A comparison of their findings with those obtained by Dutton et al. (1994) indicated that there is remarkable similarity across genders in the associations between forms of attachment insecurity and certain features of abusiveness.

Henderson and her colleagues (Henderson, Bartholomew, Trinke, & Kwong, 2005) also found attachment anxiety (in this case, preoccupied attachment) to be associated with women's violence toward their male partners. In fact, preoccupied attachment was associated with both perpetration and receipt of violence, regardless of gender. Bartholomew, Oram, and Landolt (2008) also found attachment anxiety to be associated with intimate partner violence in gay male relationships. In addition, Follingstad, Bradley, Helff, and Laughlin (2002) found that attachment anxiety and angry temperament were related to controlling behavior and physical violence in both partners in heterosexual dating relationships.

Mauricio, Tein, and Lopez (2007) examined 192 men who had been court mandated to participate in a batterer intervention program. They completed measures of anxious and avoidant attachment (the Experiences in Close Relationships questionnaire; Brennan, Clark, & Shaver, 1998), borderline and antisocial personality disorders, psychological and physical violence, and social desirability. The authors used structural equation modeling to test hypotheses that associations between anxious attachment and physical and psychological violence were mediated by borderline personality disorder and that associations between avoidant attachment and physical and psychological violence were mediated by antisocial personality disorder. Social desirability was included in the models as a covariate. The results indicated that personality disorders fully mediated the associations between avoidant attachment and physical and psychological abuse, and personality disorders fully mediated the association between anxious attachment and psychological abuse but only partially mediated the link between anxious attachment and psychological abuse.

These studies suggest that attachment insecurity, especially anxious attachment, may be a risk factor for violence, but for it to result in actual violence it has to "crystallize" into something more: a chronically angry temperament or a disturbance of the self that includes angry acting out.

THE ABUSIVE PERSONALITY: ATTACHMENT AND BORDERLINE PERSONALITY

My early work on the "abusive personality" was completed before the studies reviewed in the previous section were conducted, but it foreshadowed the importance of both attachment insecurities and personality dysfunctions (see also Westen & Shedler, 1999). At the time, I focused on borderline personality symptoms because of clinical descriptions of borderlines as exhibiting intermittent rage in intimate relationships (Gunderson, 1984). One of the main correlates of borderline functioning is attachment anxiety. The *Diagnostic and Statistical Manual of Mental Disorders* (4th ed., American Psychiatric Association, 1994) describes "frantic efforts to avoid real or imagined abandonment" (p. 710). However, at the time of our early research no one had connected borderline features or attachment insecurities with each other or with abusiveness.

Using a research strategy already mentioned (i.e., studying male perpetrators in court mandated groups and gathering data from them and their female partners), we (Dutton et al., 1994) found that fearful attachment (a combination of anxiety, anger, and discomfort with reliance on one's partner) was correlated significantly with wives' reports of abusiveness and perpetrators' self-reports of jealousy, anger, and trauma symptoms. Men who were abusive in intimate relationships exhibited both attachment insecurities and features of borderline personality. Subsequently, samples from several populations (i.e., court-mandated men in treatment programs, colleges students, working-class control men, clinical outpatients, gay men from urban communities) have also turned up strong and significant correlations (in the .45 to .65 range) between fearful attachment and borderline personality organization (as measured with the Borderline Personality Organization Scale; Oldham et al., 1985).

A central clinical feature of borderline individuals is their impulsivity. In examining an impulsive group of spouse abusers (compared with those who used violence instrumentally), we found that scores on fearful attachment were significantly higher in the impulsive group (Tweed & Dutton, 1998), a finding replicated by Edwards, Scott, Yarvis, Paizis, and Panizzon (2003) using an impulsive aggression questionnaire that assessed frequency of losing control, being suicidal, and displaying an extreme temper. Subsequent research with large samples of men (e.g., Henderson, Bartholomew, & Dutton, 1997; Mauricio et al., 2007) has largely confirmed the associations between attachment insecurity (especially of anxious varieties) and borderline traits, impulsivity, and abusiveness. The same pattern appears in abusive women as well (e.g., Clift 2008; Henning, Jones, & Holford, 2003).

We consider severely insecure early attachment to be a likely key to this personality constellation. The "modal family" for our court-mandated samples was notable for its abusiveness and lack of a safe haven and secure base for the children. Future research should explore the development of abusiveness in more detail, and further integrative theorizing should be attempted to bring into a single picture what we have learned and are still learning about early attachment experiences, neural development, impulsivity and poor emotion regulation, and clinically significant features of borderline personality and other personality disorders. Some of the pieces of this important story can be gleaned from other chapters in this volume (e.g., Chapters 1, 2, 7, and 9) and from chapters in the most recent edition of the *Handbook of Attachment* (Cassidy & Shaver, 2008), which includes many new findings regarding the neural underpinnings of attachment phenomena, the relation between genes and experiences in attachment relationships, and connections between attachment patterns and clinical disorders.

DYADIC PROCESSES CONNECTING ATTACHMENT AND VIOLENCE

Work by Bartholomew and her colleagues suggests that a dyadic or relationship perspective is important for understanding attachment dynamics. When pursuing this research strategy, it is important to assess attachment styles of both partners in a relationship. For example, Allison, Bartholomew, Mayseless, and Dutton (2008) used thematic interviews to assess attachment dynamics in heterosexual couples identified as involving male partner violence. The interviews revealed two attachment-related strategies, pursuit and distancing, which sometimes led to abuse. As a pursuit strategy, violence forced one partner to focus on the other. As a distancing strategy, violence served to push a partner away. Bartholomew et al. (2008) suggested that optimal social distance rather than physical proximity and contact (the goals of the attachment system highlighted by Ainsworth et al., 1978) might be considered the state in adult relationships that lowers or terminates attachment-system activation.

Referring to the frequent reciprocity of negative affect in relationships, Bartholomew and Allison (2006) analyzed the dyadic nature of interpersonal violence. Surveys in the United States indicate that bilateral violence is the most common form in intimate relationships (e.g., Stets & Straus, 1989; Whitaker, Haileyesus, Swahn, & Saltzman, 2007), and in laboratory studies of marital interactions, reciprocal negative affect is a consistent predictor of relationship dysfunction and deterioration (e.g., Cordova, Jacobson, Gottman, Rushe, & Cox, 1993; Leonard & Roberts, 1998; Margolin, John, & Gleberman, 1988). Future research should therefore consider both partners' attachment insecurities and their connections with both personality disorder symptoms and destructive reciprocal hostility and impulsive violence.

OTHER MANIFESTATIONS OF ATTACHMENT THREAT

Beyond the issues raised by relationship dynamics, several matters having to do with attachment insecurity and violence deserve attention. These include suicide, destructive behavior in military contexts, religion-based aggressive behavior, and violence against an outgroup as a means of defending oneself from death awareness.

Attachment Disruption and Aggression Toward the Self

One rarely reported aspect of attachment-related violence is suicide, which is especially common among men who have recently divorced. Using data from the U.S. National Morbidity Study, Kposowa (2000) found that divorced or separated persons were over twice as likely as married persons to commit suicide. Men were four times more likely than women to commit suicide under these conditions, and White males had the highest rate of all. If suicide is considered to be a form of aggression directed toward the self, we should consider why men are more prone than women to enact this form of aggression following relationship dissolution.

Attachment and Military Violence

The attachment behavioral system can be triggered by exposure to any kind of danger. Anecdotal reports from battlefields indicate that wounded and dying soldiers often call out for their mothers (Ferguson, 2006), recalling the well-documented reactions of young children. Under these extremely frightening conditions, soldiers sometimes engage in what Mawson (1987) called "transient criminality." He reviewed evidence that under conditions of extreme stress, such as found in natural disasters and combat, there are notable psychological changes of the following kind: partial identity diffusion, a sense of depersonalization, impaired sense of self-worth, impairments in memory and perceptual functioning, a partial loss of abstract standards including moral and legal rules, and a general decline in intellectual functioning (e.g., loss of concentration, decline in problem-solving ability).

According to Mawson (1987), combat stress produces chronic increases in sympathetic nervous system arousal, which in turn produces "seeking behavior" of the kind Bowlby (1973, 1982) attributed to the attachment behavioral system. In combat, because no security or familiar source of security is to be found, further increases in sympathetic arousal are generated. Under these conditions, a person's cognitive map begins to disintegrate; more patterned, abstract, differentiated mental processes situating the person in a complex of familiar people and places and normative obligations dissolve. According to Baumeister (1990), the situated identity or individuated self also breaks down and consciousness is altered so that it is completely focused on the present action, with autonomic arousal remaining very high. Instead of seeking the familiar (to reduce distress), the soldier is likely to engage in impulsive, enormously destructive behavior.

This is one way to think about the infamous My Lai massacre, perpetrated by a U.S. Army platoon during the Vietnam War. It followed weeks of losing comrades to booby-trapped mines while being unable to find the "enemy" on a search and destroy mission (Hersh, 1970). The testimony given at the war crimes trial of the perpetrators revealed a thought process that resembled paranoid schizophrenia (Dutton, 2007). The defendants described "booby-trapped babies" lobbed at them by mothers and referred to "the Battle of My Lai" although none of the villagers were armed or fired a weapon. This kind of mental breakdown in a situation in which violence is natural is often viewed by social psychologists as something that could happen to anyone under extreme stress. An attachment analysis suggests, however, that there may be important individual differences in behavior even under these conditions, as in fact was the case at My Lai (Hersh, 1970).

Attachment in Perpetuity and Holy War

Religious ideology has one great advantage over political ideology in generating violence. It can offer everlasting salvation, as Pope Urban II did to launch the First Crusade. The same strategy was used with Japanese kamikaze pilots in World War II, and it is used now to inspire Islamic suicide bombers (Dutton, 2007). The belief that is central to this kind of activity may be the most powerful motivating belief for human beings: that they will live with their loved ones (including an all-powerful symbolic parental figure) in everlasting bliss (i.e., they will enjoy attachment security in perpetuity). Cheung-Blunden and Blunden (2008), for example, found that Christian students exposed to images of the World Trade Center towers in flames on 9/11 were more likely than atheists to define the enemy in religious terms and to condone bombing and killing as a form of reprisal. Both Christianity and Islam have done this repeatedly throughout their histories, despite both the Bible and the Koran advocating peace and forgiveness.

A further motivating image resides in religious ideology: the notion of Armageddon. Asbridge (2004) describes how the recapturing of Jerusalem was consistent with the Christian belief that the "last days" before the Second Coming of Christ, foretold in the Bible, could come to pass only after Jerusalem was again in Christian hands. Phillips' 2006 volume, *American Theocracy*, points to the same belief among a sizeable number of fundamentalist Americans (called "end timers") today. He sees this belief as supportive of the 2003 invasion of Iraq, which end timers viewed as a way to reduce a threat to Israel and Jerusalem.

Although weaponry has improved immensely in the millennium since the crusades, the ideological belief structure and psychological need to belong to a like-minded "tribe" with a shared "worldview" (often articulated in religious terms) still persists. This raises a question of whether religion constitutes a symbolic form of attachment (Granqvist & Kirkpatrick, 2008; Kirkpatrick, 2005). Asbridge (2004) describes crusaders, still covered in blood and carrying booty, kneeling at the Holy Sepulchre to pray. This was not, he assures the reader, seen as contradictory in medieval times. Although the extreme violence displayed in response to a perceived threat to a central belief is sometimes described as primitive or "inhuman," it has been demonstrated across human history and diverse cultures with alarming consistency (Dutton, 2007).

Attachment and Terror Management Studies:
Violence Against a Worldview-Threatening Outgroup

Is secure attachment the antidote for death anxiety? Although Bowlby (1973) described an anger born of fear and Becker (1973) described evil as the "disguise of panic," for some strange reason attachment research and terror management theory research (TMT; Greenberg, Solomon, & Pyszcynski, 1997) rarely overlapped until recently. If death terror is a primary human motive, as TMT suggests, and secure attachment is a relief from terror, then attachment and TMT appear to be two sides of the same coin. Developmentally, attachment has to precede death terror, because attachment, as we described earlier, is a primitive process predating oedipal issues and coinciding with separation–

individuation around age 1.5 to 2 years (Schore, 1994, 2003a, 2003b), and children in the preschool years have little understanding of the universality, irreversibility, and inevitability of death (Nagy, 1948). However, studies showing that some of a person's defenses against death awareness are unrelated to death in any logical or semantic way (Pyszczynski, Greenberg, & Solomon, 1999) raise the question of whether unconscious awareness of death is prewired or precedes conscious development of notions of death.

Following this reasoning, Mikulincer and Florian (2000) performed five studies examining the contribution of attachment style to the psychological effects of experimentally enhanced mortality salience. Although defending one's worldview by punishing criminals or dissenters has been portrayed as the normative or natural defense against mortality salience (Greenberg et al., 1997), Mikulincer and Florian (2000) showed that this reaction is more characteristic of people who score high on measures of attachment insecurity than of those who score low. Specifically, experimentally induced death reminders produced more severe judgments and punishments of moral transgressors only among insecurely attached participants, whether they were primarily anxious or avoidant. Secure participants reacted to mortality salience with an increased sense of *symbolic immortality*—a transformational, constructive strategy that leads a person to invest in his or her children's care and to engage in creative activities whose products will live on after one's death—and a more intense desire for intimacy in close relationships (Mikulincer & Florian, 2000). Taubman–Ben-Ari, Findler, and Mikulincer (2002) also found that less insecure individuals reacted to mortality salience with greater willingness to initiate social interactions and more positive appraisals of their interpersonal competence.

The essential study, however—one examining attachment security as a moderator of aggression and violence motivated by fear of death—seems not to have been conducted. The theoretical question of whether insecure individuals would be more prone to outgroup violence during times of heightened stress and attachment-system activation remains to be conducted. However, the manipulation of attachment bonds has historically been used to shape child killers. In Rwanda, for example, child soldiers were forced to kill a resident of their own village to break attachment to the tribe and foster attachment to the killer group (Dutton, 2007; Human Rights Watch, 1999).

CONCLUSIONS

What, then, is the connection between attachment and violence? I have argued here that secure attachment diminishes both fear and anger born of fear and the converse, that insecure attachment increases both. When panic-driven anger is aroused, violence becomes much more likely. This process is most salient when anger arises in intimate relationships, especially ones perceived by the perpetrator to be the main or only potential source of security. It manifests as rage reactions to separation or threats of separation. If we take one more theoretical step and focus on symbolic attachment in the form of a tribe or family, then the evolutionary roots of Bowlby's (1982) formulation of attachment become salient. Threats to the tribe or, by extension, to the tribe's ideology or future ability to thrive can generate extreme violence that may have roots in attachment. Attachment and its ability to make us feel safe from death is perhaps the strongest human motive. The lure of secure attachment in perpetuity, unfortunately and tragically, can motivate people to kill themselves and strangers in a "holy war."

REFERENCES

Ainsworth, M. D. S., Blehar, M. C., Waters, E., & Wall, S. (1978). *Patterns of attachment: Assessed in the Strange Situation and at home*. Hillsdale, NJ: Erlbaum.

Allison, C. J., Bartholomew, K., Mayseless, O., & Dutton, D. G. (2008). Love as a battlefield: Attachment and relationship dynamics in couples identified for male partner violence. *Journal of Family Issues, 29*, 125–150. doi:10.1177/0192513X07306980

American Psychiatric Association. (1994). *Diagnostic and statistical manual of mental disorders* (4th ed.). Washington, DC: Author.

Asbridge, T. (2004). *The first crusade: A new history*. Oxford, England: Oxford University Press.

Bartholomew, K., & Allison, C. J. (2006). An attachment perspective on abusive dynamics in intimate relationships. In M. Mikulincer & G. S. Goodman (Eds.), *Dynamics of romantic love: Attachment, caregiving, and sex* (pp. 102–127). New York, NY: Guilford Press.

Bartholomew, K., Henderson, A. J. Z., & Dutton, D. G. (2001). Insecure attachment and abuse in intimate relationships. In C. Clulow (Ed.), *Adult attachment and couple psychotherapy: The "secure base" concept in practice and research* (pp. 43–61). London, England: Routledge.

Bartholomew, K., & Horowitz, L. W. (1991). Attachment styles among young adults: A test of a four-category model. *Journal of Personality and Social Psychology, 61*, 226–244. doi:10.1037/0022-3514.61.2.226

Bartholomew, K., Oram, D., & Landolt, M. A. (2008). Correlates of partner abuse in male same sex relationships. *Violence and Victims, 23*, 348–364.

Baumeister, R. F. (1990). Suicide as an escape from self. *Psychological Review, 97*, 90–113. doi:10.1037/0033-295X.97.1.90

Becker, E. (1973). *The denial of death*. New York, NY: Free Press.

Bowlby, J. (1973). *Attachment and loss: Vol. 2. Separation: Anxiety and anger.* New York, NY: Basic Books.

Bowlby, J. (1982). *Attachment and loss: Vol. 1. Attachment* (2nd ed.). New York, NY: Basic Books.

Bowlby, J. (1988). *A secure base: Clinical applications of attachment theory.* London, England: Routledge.

Brennan, K. A., Clark, C. L., & Shaver, P. R. (1998). Self-report measurement of adult romantic attachment: An integrative overview. In J. A. Simpson & W. S. Rholes (Eds.), *Attachment theory and close relationships* (pp. 46–76). New York, NY: Guilford Press.

Briere, J., & Runtz, M. (1989). The Trauma Symptom Checklist (TSC-33): Early data on a new scale. *Journal of Interpersonal Violence, 4,* 151–163. doi:10.1177/088626089004002002

Carlson, E. A. (1998). A prospective longitudinal study of attachment disorganization/disorientation. *Child Development, 69,* 1107–1128.

Cassidy, J., & Shaver, P. R. (Eds.). (2008). *Handbook of attachment: Theory, research, and clinical applications* (2nd ed.). New York, NY: Guilford Press.

Cheung-Blunden, V., & Blunden, B. (2008). Paving the road to war with group membership, appraisal antecedents, and anger. *Aggressive Behavior, 34,* 175–189. doi:10.1002/ab.20234

Clift, R. J. (2008). *The abusive personality in women in dating relationships.* (Unpublished doctoral dissertation). University of British Columbia, Vancouver, Canada.

Cordova, J. V., Jacobson, N. S., Gottman, J. M., Rushe, R., & Cox, G. (1993). Negative reciprocity and communication in couples with a violent husband. *Journal of Abnormal Psychology, 102,* 559–564. doi:10.1037/0021-843X.102.4.559

Dutton, D. G. (2006). *The abusive personality* (2nd ed.). New York, NY: Guilford Press.

Dutton, D. G. (2007). *The psychology of genocide, massacres, and extreme violence.* New York, NY: Praeger.

Dutton, D. G., Starzomski, A., Saunders, K., & Bartholomew, K. (1994). Intimacy-anger and insecure attachment as precursors of abuse in intimate relationships. *Journal of Applied Social Psychology, 24,* 1367–1386. doi:10.1111/j.1559-1816.1994.tb01554.x

Edwards, D. W., Scott, C. L., Yarvis, R. M., Paizis, C. L., & Panizzon, M. S. (2003). Impulsiveness, impulsive aggression, personality disorder and spousal violence. *Violence and Victims, 18,* 3–14. doi:10.1891/vivi.2003.18.1.3

Ferguson, N. (2006). *The war of the world.* New York, NY: Penguin.

Follingstad, D. R., Bradley, R. G., Helff, C. M., & Laughlin, J. E. (2002). A model for predicting dating violence: Anxious attachment, angry temperament and need for relationship control. *Violence and Victims, 17,* 35–47. doi:10.1891/vivi.17.1.35.33639

Granqvist, P., & Kirkpatrick, L. A. (2008). Attachment and religious representations and behavior. In J. Cassidy & P. R. Shaver (Eds.), *Handbook of attachment: Theory, research, and clinical applications* (2nd ed., pp. 906–933). New York, NY: Guilford Press.

Greenberg, J., Solomon, S., & Pyszcynski, T. (1997). Terror management theory of self-esteem and cultural worldviews: Empirical assessments and conceptual refinements. In M. P. Zanna (Ed.), *Advances in experimental social psychology* (Vol. 29, pp. 61–141). San Diego, CA: Academic Press.

Griffin, D. W., & Bartholomew, K. (1994). The metaphysics of measurement: The case of adult attachment. In K. Bartholomew & D. Perlman (Eds.), *Advances in personal relationships: Attachment processes in adulthood* (Vol. 5, pp. 17–52). London, England: Jessica Kinsley.

Gunderson, J. G. (1984). *Borderline personality disorder*. Washington, DC: American Psychiatric Press.

Henderson, A. J. Z., Bartholomew, K., & Dutton, D. G. (1997). He loves me, he loves me not: Attachment and separation resolution of abused women. *Journal of Family Violence, 12*, 169–192. doi:10.1023/A:1022836711637

Henderson, A. J. Z., Bartholomew, K., Trinke, S., & Kwong, M. J. (2005). When loving means hurting: An exploration of attachment and intimate abuse in a community sample. *Journal of Family Violence, 20*, 219–230. doi:10.1007/s10896-005-5985-y

Henning, K., Jones, A., & Holford, R. (2003). Treatment needs of women arrested for domestic violence: A comparison with male offenders. *Journal of Interpersonal Violence, 18*, 839–856. doi:10.1177/0886260503253876

Hersh, S. (1970). *My Lai: A report on the massacre and its aftermath*. New York, NY: Vintage Books.

Human Rights Watch. (1999). *Leave none to tell the tale: Genocide in Rwanda*. New York, NY: Author.

Kirkpatrick, L. A. (2005). *Attachment, evolution, and the psychology of religion*. New York, NY: Guilford Press.

Klein, M., & Riviere, J. (1937). *Love, hate, and reparation*. New York, NY: Norton.

Kposowa, A. J. (2000). Marital status and suicide in the National Longitudinal Mortality Study. *Journal of Epidemiology and Community Health, 54*, 254–261. doi:10.1136/jech.54.4.254

Leonard, K. E., & Roberts, L. J. (1998). The effects of alcohol on the marital interactions of aggressive and nonaggressive husbands and their wives. *Journal of Abnormal Psychology, 107*, 602–615. doi:10.1037/0021-843X.107.4.602

Lyons-Ruth, K., Bronfman, E., & Atwood, G. (1999). A relational diathesis model of hostile-helpless states of mind: Expressions in mother–infant interaction. In J. Solomon & C. George (Eds.), *Attachment disorganization* (pp. 33–70). New York, NY: Guilford Press.

Lyons-Ruth, K., & Jacobwitz, D. (2008). Attachment disorganization: Genetic factors, parenting contexts, and developmental transformation from infancy to adulthood. In J. Cassidy & P. R. Shaver (Eds.), *Handbook of attachment: Theory, research, and clinical applications* (2nd ed., pp. 666–697). New York, NY: Guilford Press.

Mahler, M. (1971). A study of the separation–individuation process and its possible application to borderline phenomena in the psychoanalytic situation. *The Psychoanalytic Study of the Child, 26,* 403–424.

Mahler, M., Pine, F., & Bergman, A. (1975). *The psychological birth of the human infant.* New York, NY: Basic Books.

Main, M. (1995). Attachment: Overview with implications for clinical work. In S. Goldberg, R. Muir, & J. Kerr (Eds.), *Attachment theory: Social, developmental, and clinical perspectives* (pp. 407–474). Hillsdale, NJ: Erlbaum.

Main, M., & Solomon, J. (1986). Discovery of a new, insecure disorganized/disoriented attachment pattern: Procedures, findings and implications for the classification of behavior. In T. B. Brazelton & M. W. Yogman (Eds.), *Affective development in infancy* (pp. 95–124). Norwood, NJ: Ablex.

Main, M., & Solomon, J. (1990). Procedures for identifying infants as disorganized/disoriented during the Ainsworth strange situation. In M. T. Greenberg, D. Cicchetti, & M. Cummings (Eds.), *Attachment in the preschool years: Theory, research, and intervention* (pp. 121–160). Chicago, IL: University of Chicago Press.

Margolin, G., John, R. S., & Gleberman, L. (1988). Affective responses to conflictual discussions in violent and nonviolent couples. *Journal of Consulting and Clinical Psychology, 56,* 24–33. doi:10.1037/0022-006X.56.1.24

Mathes, E. W., & Severa, N. (1981). Jealousy, romantic love, and liking: Theoretical considerations and preliminary scale development. *Psychological Reports, 49,* 23–31.

Mauricio, A. M., Tein, J. Y., & Lopez, F. G. (2007). Borderline and antisocial personality scores as mediators between attachment and intimate partner violence. *Violence and Victims, 22,* 139–157. doi:10.1891/088667007780477339

Mawson, A. W. (1987). *Transient criminality: A model of stress induced crime.* New York, NY: Praeger.

Mikulincer, M. (1998). Adult attachment style and individual differences in functional versus dysfunctional experiences of anger. *Journal of Personality and Social Psychology, 74,* 513–524. doi:10.1037/0022-3514.74.2.513

Mikulincer, M., & Florian, V. (2000). Exploring individual differences in reactions to mortality salience: Does attachment style regulate terror management mechanisms? *Journal of Personality and Social Psychology, 79,* 260–273. doi:10.1037/0022-3514.79.2.260

Nagy, M. (1948). The child's theories concerning death. *The Journal of Genetic Psychology, 73,* 3–27.

Oldham, J., Clarkin, J., Appelbaum, A., Carr, A., Kernberg, P., Lotterman, A., & Haas, G. (1985). A self-report instrument for Borderline Personality Organization. In T. H. McGlashan (Ed.), *The borderline: Current empirical research* (pp. 1–18). Washington, DC: American Psychiatric Press.

Perris, C., Jacobsson, L., Lindstrom, H., von Knorring, L., & Perris, H. (1980). Development of a new inventory for assessing memories of parental rearing behaviour. *Acta Psychiatrica Scandinavica, 61*, 265–274. doi:10.1111/j.1600-0447.1980.tb00581.x

Perry, B. (1997). Incubated in terror: Neurodevelopmental factors in the cycle of violence. In J. D. Osofsky (Ed.), *Children, youth and violence: Searching for solutions* (pp. 124–149). New York, NY: Guilford Press.

Phillips, K. (2006). *American theocracy*. New York, NY: Viking.

Pynoos, R. S., & Eth, S. (1985). Children traumatized by witnessing acts of personal violence: Homicide, rape, or suicide behavior. In S. Eth & R. S. Pynoos (Eds.), *Posttraumatic stress disorder in children* (pp. 17–44). Washington, DC: American Psychiatric Press.

Pyszczynski, T., Greenberg, J., & Solomon, S. (1999). A dual-process model of defense against conscious and unconscious death-related thoughts: An extension of terror management theory. *Psychological Review, 106*, 835–845. doi:10.1037/0033-295X.106.4.835

Schore, A. N. (1994). *Affect regulation and the origin of the self: The neurobiology of emotional development*. Hillsdale, NJ: Erlbaum.

Schore, A. N. (2003a). *Affect dysregulation and the disorders of the self*. New York, NY: Norton.

Schore, A. N. (2003b). *Affect regulation and the repair of the self*. New York, NY: Norton.

Siegel, D. J. (2001a). *The developing mind: How relationships and the brain interact to shape who we are*. New York, NY: Guilford Press.

Siegel, D. J. (2001b). Toward an interpersonal neurobiology of the developing mind: Attachment relationships, "mindsight," and neural integration. *Infant Mental Health Journal, 22*, 67–94. doi:10.1002/1097-0355(200101/04)22:1<67::AID-IMHJ3>3.0.CO;2-G

Siegel, J. M. (1986). The Multidimensional Anger Inventory. *Journal of Personality and Social Psychology, 51*, 191–200. doi:10.1037/0022-3514.51.1.191

Stets, J., & Straus, M. A. (1989). The marriage license as a hitting license: A comparison of dating, cohabiting and married couples. *Journal of Family Violence, 4*, 161–180. doi:10.1007/BF01006627

Straus, M. A. (1992). Measuring intrafamily conflict and violence: The Conflict Tactics Scale. In M. A. Straus & R. J. Gelles (Eds.), *Physical violence in American families* (pp. 29–46). New Brunswick, NJ: Transaction Publishers.

Taubman-Ben-Ari, O., Findler, L., & Mikulincer, M. (2002). The effects of mortality salience on relationship strivings and beliefs: The moderating role of attachment style. *The British Journal of Social Psychology, 41*, 419–441. doi:10.1348/014466602760344296

Tolman, R. M. (1989). The development of a measure of physiological maltreatment of women by their male partners. *Violence and Victims, 4*, 159–177.

Tweed, R. G., & Dutton, D. G. (1998). A comparison of instrumental and impulsive subgroups of batterers. *Violence and Victims, 13*, 217–230.

Westen, D., & Shedler, J. (1999). Revising and assessing Axis II, Part 1: Developing a clinically and empirically valid assessment instrument. *The American Journal of Psychiatry, 156*, 258–272.

Whitaker, D. J., Haileyesus, T., Swahn, M., & Saltzman, L. (2007). Differences in frequency of violence and reported injury between relationships with reciprocal and non-reciprocal intimate partner violence. *American Journal of Public Health, 97*, 941–947. doi:10.2105/AJPH.2005.079020

15

RESPECTING OTHERS AND BEING RESPECTED CAN REDUCE AGGRESSION IN PARENT–CHILD RELATIONS AND IN SCHOOLS

OFRA MAYSELESS AND MIRI SCHARF

This chapter examines the role that respect plays in mitigating aggression in two developmental contexts: parent–child relations and schools. The role of respect in reducing aggression and violence has been discussed and examined primarily by social psychologists who study adult relationships. In marriages, legal proceedings, politics, and intergroup conflicts, respect has been recognized as an important form of positive regard that helps to diffuse aggressive impulses (e.g., de Cremer & Tyler, 2005; Gottman, 1994; Janoff-Bulman & Werther, 2008). It is interesting that the term *respect* has rarely been used within the literature of developmental psychology, which examines the contexts in which children grow and develop. Hence we know little about the expression, experience, and effects of respect in developmental contexts; the possible inverse association between respect and aggression; and the ways in which respect can be encouraged and developed.

Building on conceptualizations in the literatures of philosophy and social psychology, we propose a conceptual framework for the study of respect in developmental contexts. In the following sections, we discuss two kinds of respect, unconditional and contingent, and distinguish between four related but distinct ways in which respect and disrespect are involved in preventing or fostering aggression: (a) respecting others, (b) being respected, (c) being disrespected or humiliated, and (d) respecting oneself. We then examine the role of respect in parent–child relationships and at school. Although respect per se, under that particular name, has rarely been examined in these contexts, several core characteristics of respect have been considered and discussed, and their association with aggression and the misuse of power has been investigated. In a final section we advocate an increased emphasis on respect in parent–child relationships, schools, and other contexts, because of its potential for reducing aggression and violence.

UNCONDITIONAL AND CONTINGENT FORMS OF RESPECT

The concept of respect is complex and multifaceted. It refers to several distinct yet interconnected processes and seems to have somewhat different implications in different contexts and relationships. Following previous writings (e.g., Frei & Shaver, 2002), we suggest that respect is an attitude rather than an emotion and includes cognitive evaluations, feelings, and behaviors with possible disparities among these different components. People may, for example, behave respectfully toward others but internally despise them and view them as immoral and unworthy. Conversely, a person may feel respect toward someone but not show it behaviorally. This may be the case, for instance, when adolescents internally respect their parents but at times behave in a defiant and disrespectful manner toward them.

Various researchers and thinkers have discussed different types or components of respect (Darwall, 1977; Frei & Shaver, 2002; Hendrick & Hendrick, 2006; Janoff-Bulman & Werther, 2008; Langdon, 2007; Lawrence-Lightfoot, 2000; Roland & Foxx, 2003). Here, we will refer mainly to two broad types of respect that have been discussed by most researchers, although under different names.

Unconditional Respect

The most general meaning of respect refers to a broad humanistic tendency to value each person as a worthy human being. We term this kind of respect *unconditional*. It is based on a moral contention that every human being has basic rights to freedom, dignity, and autonomy (e.g., Rawls, 1971; see also Chapter 10, this volume, for a related conceptualization of respect in what the authors call "cultures of dignity"). Some researchers rely on the writings of philosophers such as Kant (1959, p. 46), who viewed humans as rational beings and "ends in themselves" who deserve unconditional respect. Others (Lightfoot, 2000) rely on Piaget (1932), who considered the ability to recognize others as equals, and to appreciate them as having different and valuable points of view to be based on a major developmental accomplishment that he labeled *decentration*. The developmental emergence of this ability marks a move from cognitive egocentrism to a capacity for understanding and considering other points of view.

At a deeper level, such a stance often reflects a spiritual sense or belief that all humans have a common divine origin and share a divine quality. This belief implies a moral imperative to value, appreciate, and respect others, just as one respects the divine. This moral imperative is shared by many religions and religious movements, old and new, Eastern and Western, monotheistic or not (Smith, 1991).

Contingent Respect

The second broad meaning of respect, which, following Janoff-Bulman and Werther (2008), we label *contingent respect*, refers to an attitude toward an individual who possesses or embodies certain qualities or attributes or who has attained a certain admirable status. This general category of respect includes several types. For example, respect for social power (Langdon, 2007) includes respect for people with authority, such as parents or teachers, whose power is bestowed by their role or status regardless of their own specific qualities (e.g., warmth, competence, moral behavior; see Chapter 10, this volume, for a similar analysis of respect in what the author calls "face cultures"). A different kind of respect can be accorded individuals based on their moral character and integrity, for example, being hard working, trustworthy, sincere, altruistic, or honest (Darwall, 1977). A third kind of respect is a response to a person's special competence or a particular attribute that is valued by society (Chapter 10, this volume, offers a related analysis of respect in cultures of honor). Janoff-Bulman and Werther (2008) say that such respect is accorded to individuals or groups perceived as having the greatest potential to contribute to one's own group or organization. Whereas unconditional respect is not earned by any specific deed or accomplishment, the recipients of the other kinds of respect—the conditional forms—must earn their respect-worthiness by actions, efforts, or attainment of a certain social role or status.

Respect for Others and Its Relation to Aggression

Unconditional respect is closely related to foregoing aggression and violence. If a person respects others unconditionally, he or she values them in their own right and acknowledges that they are entitled to autonomy, privacy, and dignity and should not be injured, insulted, or humiliated. Such a person is polite and allows others to have a voice; above all, because such a person assumes others' divine or humanistic core, he or she refrains from any act that might damage or hurt the other person physically or psychologically.

Contingent respect for others is also likely to reduce aggression. First, people are naturally inclined to nurture and protect an entity (whether a person, a group, or "nature") that is valued and not to hurt, damage, or destroy it. Second, there is a moral aspect to contingent respect. A respected individual or a respected group is considered to be morally worthy and deserving of kind treatment (McCullough, 2008; see also Chapters 10 and 12, this volume). Hence, there is a moral prohibition against aggression toward a respected individual or group. Furthermore, in line with previous conceptual analyses (Frei & Shaver, 2002; Langdon, 2007), we contend that respecting others typically involves not just a general moral valuing of them but also a commitment to nurture, cherish, and support them. Thus, respect calls for a prosocial, caring orientation rather than an antagonistic or antisocial orientation. Finally, respecting others, particularly close relationship partners, encourages reciprocation of respect (Kumashiro, Finkel, & Rusbult, 2002). In relationships where one feels respected, there are fewer reasons to be frustrated, angry, or aggressive.

Being Respected and Its Relation to Aggression

Not just respecting others but being respected by others is likely to reduce aggression. First, when an individual is unconditionally respected, he or she feels valued, protected, and secure. In this situation there is little reason to behave aggressively (see Chapters 13 and 14). Further, as discussed more fully in the next section, being contingently respected fulfills people's basic needs, in close relationships and groups, for honor, dignity, and voice. Feeling respected therefore eliminates a common source of anger and aggression and contributes to an atmosphere of mutual understanding and appreciation (Miller, 2001; see also Chapter 10, this volume). Second, being and feeling respected by others often implies an expectation on the part of others that one will act morally. Such expectations tend to be fulfilled (e.g., Jussim, 1986), and they can attenuate, or even prevent, aggression, even in situations where frustration and anger might otherwise lead to aggressive acts. Finally, being respected often provides a person with greater social influence, so there is less need to resort to aggression to achieve desired ends.

Feeling Disrespected and Aggression

On the flip side of respecting others and receiving their respect is the possibility of losing respect or being disrespected. Not being especially singled out for respect is not necessarily negative; it may not lead to any particular feeling. But being disrespected is an extremely negative experience; it often amounts to being devalued, demeaned, or insulted, and it may include having one's rights to autonomy and dignity violated. Researchers have addressed this kind of disrespect in the context of expectations regarding fair and just treatment and reactions to perceived injustice (e.g., Heuer, Blumenthal, Douglas, & Weinblatt, 1999; Miller, 2001). According to Miller (2001), people generally believe they are entitled to fairness in the allocation of resources (*distributive justice*) and fairness in procedures used to determine the allocation of these resources (*procedural justice*). When such fairness—especially with regard to procedural justice—is enacted, individuals tend to feel respected even if their requests have not been granted. When individuals feel that their right to polite, fair, and respectful treatment has been violated, or that their honor has been violated, they are likely to feel hurt, frustrated, and disrespected, and therefore to react aggressively to restore self-esteem, save face, or educate the offender (see Chapters 1 and 2, this volume). In line with these contentions, disrespectful treatment, which denies people what they believe is rightfully theirs, is likely to cause both anger and aggression (Bettencourt & Miller, 1996; see also Chapter 10, this volume). Moreover, being subjected to disrespectful treatment is considered to justify aggression. People are less critical of aggressive acts when they are viewed as retaliation for disrespectful treatment (Harvey & Enzle, 1978; see also Chapter 12, this volume).

One interesting point in these discussions is the importance of behavioral signs of respect that serve as social signals of appreciation and recognition of a person's status (Janoff-Bulman & Werther, 2008; see also Chapter 12, this volume). For example, when discussing the negative effects of disrespect, it is often observed that public disrespect in front of an audience is more threatening, and hence has higher chances of evoking aggression, than a private display (Bies & Moag, 1986; Pitt-Rivers, 1965).

Self-Respect and Aggression

Self-respect, a sense of having personal moral standards and a sense of autonomy, freedom, and dignity (Roland & Foxx, 2003), is less discussed in the social psychological literature than respect for other people. Some of the negative effects of being disrespected or humiliated, and much of the resulting urge to retaliate, are said to derive from the damage incurred to one's self-respect (e.g., Roland & Foxx, 2003). Maintaining self-respect requires living and behaving in ways that accord with one's moral standards and expectations. Respecting oneself makes it more likely that one will not tolerate and accept disrespectful treatment by others (Roland & Foxx, 2003, p. 250). The relevance of self-respect to aggression and violence is thus clear. A self-respecting individual is likely to be committed to behaving morally and respectfully toward others and be motivated to do good. Hence he or she should not normally be aggressive or violent. Furthermore, self-respect is normally associated with a capacity for rationality and self-control. These qualities, in turn, are associated with lower levels of aggression and violence (see Chapters 1 and 2, this volume). Finally, individuals are likely to be less aggressive toward others who exhibit self-respect and dignity (Dillon, 2007).

How and where do people learn self-respect and respect of others? Two developmental contexts in which socialization of these dispositions occurs are (a) parent–child relationships and (b) schools. Both are contexts in which socialization agents are imbued with a moral and legal duty to educate and raise children to become competent adults and good citizens. How then does respect, with its different forms and facets, develop and function in these contexts?

RESPECT IN PARENT–CHILD RELATIONS AND ITS RELATION TO AGGRESSION

Respect, particularly of children toward their parents, has often been discussed. The fifth of the Bible's Ten Commandments is to "Honor your father and your mother, so that your days may be long in the land that the Lord your God is giving you." A similar moral and religious mandate is embedded in another ancient tradition, Chinese Confucian thought, which makes *filial piety*, love and respect for one's parents and ancestors, one of the most important virtues. This is respect of the contingent type, which is common in unilateral power relationships.

Children's respect for their parents involves demonstrations of honor and esteem toward parents and polite compliance with their instructions and requests (Langdon, 2007; Lightfoot, 2000). A child who disobeys his or her parents or shows defiance is considered disrespectful, whereas such behavior in a more egalitarian peer relationship might not be considered disrespectful. The underlying assumption seems to be that parents have a moral right to be obeyed, esteemed, and honored by their children because of their parental role, almost without consideration of the parents' actual expertise, competence, knowledge, or virtue. This is quite different from the conceptualization of respect within an egalitarian relationship, such as a romantic relationship, in which respect implies appreciation based on actual merit (Hendrick & Hendrick, 2006).

Parents, too, are expected to respect their children. In his book on 10 principles of good parenting, Steinberg (2004), a prominent developmental researcher, includes respecting your child as one of the principles. What is meant by respect in that case? As authority figures, parents are expected to consider their children's point of view and honor their autonomous decision processes and autonomous pursuits, while still providing rules and regulations and monitoring their implementation. Parents' respect for their children can be seen in the fair and just procedures they implement and in their acknowledgement of their children's right to have a "voice." This respect seems to be of the unconditional type, because it relates to the children's value as human beings and not to their specific moral character or accomplishments. Consequently, although respect in these relationships is expected to be mutual and is often described as such, the ways in which it is expected to be expressed differ somewhat in their qualities.

Both types of respect are related to aggression. When children respect, obey, and honor their parents, and comply with their parents' requests, they evince capacities for self-control and delay of gratification as well as appreciation of authority, rules, and regulations. Each of these qualities can reduce anger and aggression that children display toward their parents and that parents display toward their child (see Chapters 1, 2, and 9). Furthermore, children's respect for their parents usually puts the parents in the position of authority figures whom their children wish to emulate, thereby minimizing disagreements. Such a clear and predictable context enhances the child's sense of confidence and security. Securely attached children, who have a sense of direction and meaning, are usually less prone to aggression as either an instrumental means to attain a desired outcome or an uncontrolled reaction to an offence or frustration (see Chapters 13 & 14). Furthermore, parents' modeling of respect for their children tends to be emulated and internalized; hence, respected children tend to respect themselves and the people with whom they interact (see Chapter 7 for evidence of these intergenerational transmission processes). In addition, children who have been treated with respect tend to develop senses of security, autonomy, and competence, which render them happier, more self-controlled, and less often frustrated (see Chapter 7). Each of these qualities should reduce the prevalence of angry, aggressive behavior.

In a study of Singapore adolescents (Sim, 2000), regard for parents was associated with lower levels of antisocial behavior. Regard for parents further moderated the association between parental support and children's self-esteem, and mediated the association between parental monitoring and children's susceptibility to antisocial peer pressure. Similarly, in a large representative sample of Israeli youth (Scharf & Mayseless, 2005), respect for parents (e.g., "I respect them") predicted lower levels of aggression at school, over and above the contribution of perceived parental support and acceptance. In this study, we distinguished between respect as compliance (e.g., "It's important for me to do what my parent would like me to do") and respect as a positive valuation of parents (e.g., "They are wise and have had rich life experiences").

It is interesting that both forms of respect uniquely predicted less aggression at school, thus underscoring the importance of two different types of contingent respect, one based on the parental role as an authority figure and the other based on merit because of specific positive attributes (e.g., wisdom).

The effects of parental respect for children have been extensively studied by researchers examining the topic of disrespect for children's rights to autonomy and individuation. Parenting attitudes and practices that result in rejection of the child or invalidation of the child's autonomy—practices such as guilt induction and aversive psychological control—have clear negative consequences for the child's affect regulation and externalizing behavior problems (Barber, 2002; see also Chapter 7, this volume). Psychological control involves intrusive parenting practices such as instilling anxiety, inducing guilt, and withdrawing love in order to deny or suppress a child's thoughts, feelings, or desired actions (Barber, 2002; Mayseless & Scharf, 2009). In many studies, psychological control has been strongly associated with adverse outcomes, including delinquency and antisocial behavior (Barber, 2002).

Parents too, when they feel disrespected by their children, tend to be aggressive and abusive. Though not explicitly using the term respect, developmental researchers have examined the ramifications of parents' sense of humiliation and lack of power because of disrespect and defiance on the part of their children. In particular, Bugental and colleagues (Bugental & Lewis, 1999; Martorell & Bugental, 2006) have proposed a model of the misuse of power by people who perceive themselves as powerless yet are placed in a position of authority. Bugental and colleagues proposed and demonstrated that parents who feel powerless are more stressed by their children's misbehavior and tend more frequently to resort to coercive and abusive practices than parents who perceive themselves to have greater power in the parent–child relationship. Furthermore, the tendency to use abusive practices (e.g., spanking) is heightened when children are more challenging (Bugental & Happaney, 2004). We suspect, given these researchers' descriptions of what they observed, that parents' sense of low power in the parent–child relationship was related to being disobeyed and feeling disrespected by their children.

Researchers have also noted variability among cultures and ethnic groups with regard to the importance of respect in parent–child relationships (Rubin & Chung, 2006). For example, respect as a demonstration of filial piety is highly emphasized in some Asian cultures, especially Chinese culture (Ikels, 2004). In Western cultures, too, there are variations with regard to the importance of respect for parents. For example, Dixon, Graber, and Brooks-Gunn (2008) found higher respect for parental authority among African American and Latina girls compared with European American girls. Furthermore, low levels of respect were associated with more intense arguments in ethnic groups that placed higher value on respect (e.g., African American mother–daughter dyads and Latina mother–daughter dyads) than in other groups (e.g., European American).

In a binational study that included samples of middle-class families with late adolescent girls in the United States and Israel, we found another interesting example of cultural differences. The study included a videotaped interaction in which parents and their adolescent child were asked to discuss a conflictual issue. Based on the 10-minute interaction with each parent, several aspects of respect were coded. *Autonomy-inhibiting* behaviors included overpersonalizing the disagreement and pressuring the other person to agree, which were ways of expressing disrespect for the other's space, boundaries, and views; whereas *relatedness-inhibiting* behaviors included expressing hostility and rudely interrupting the other, showing disrespect for the other's right to be heard. Israeli girls were more autonomy-inhibiting toward both parents than U.S. girls. In addition, Israeli girls were more relatedness-inhibiting toward their mothers compared with the U.S. girls. These observations accord well with claims for low levels of respect toward authority in general, and for parents in particular, in Israeli society (Scharf & Mayseless, 2005; Golden & Mayseless, 2008).

RESPECT IN SCHOOLS AND ITS RELATION TO AGGRESSION

School is another developmental context in which respect is important. Respect in schools has been studied in terms of various constructs and in various kinds of relationships, for example, the general school climate, teacher–student relations, and peer relations. Many researchers have discussed the importance of respect in the school context, suggesting that respecting each student and his or her potential for growth and development should be a core aspect of education and a central component of school climate (Noddings, 1996). This contention has been emphasized in discussions of minority students, students with special needs, and students from high-risk backgrounds or environments (e.g., Battistich, Solomon, Watson, & Schaps, 1997).

This concern is part of a humanistic perspective on education and a moral perspective that advocates caring for students as valued human beings and ensuring that they flourish and actualize their potential (Noddings, 2005). Respecting individual differences in this context often means that authority figures are expected to create a school climate in which each student feels valued and competent and is helped to realize his or her potential. Such a climate is expected to prevent aggression and violence and to promote cooperation and benevolence (e.g., Mulcahy & Casella, 2005). Although past research has not assessed respect directly, it has demonstrated associations between a caring school climate and lower levels of violence, and between interventions aimed at creating such a climate and decreases in violence and aggression (e.g., Benbenishty & Astor, 2005; Kasen, Berenson, Cohen, & Johnson, 2004) In one of the few studies that directly focused on the expression of respect, LaRusso, Romer, and Selman (2008) found, in a representative sample of U.S. high schools, that greater perceived teacher support and regard for students' perspectives was associated with students' perception of their schools as having respectful climates and with positive outcomes, such as lower levels of drug use.

Students are generally expected to have and show respect for peers and teachers. Showing respect for peers often means not being aggressive toward them either physically or relationally, being polite to them, and refraining from damaging their belongings and blemishing their reputations (DioGuardi & Theodore, 2006) Within such an egalitarian context, mutual respect proved to be important in promoting friendships (Zongkui, Chumei, & Hsueh, 2006). On the flip side, disrespect for peers who have low social power has been considered one of the most serious causes of aggression at school: peer victimization and bullying. *Peer victimization* has been defined as repeated exposure to physical and verbal aggressive actions by peers (Olweus, 1997). Several studies have identified peer bullying as one of the major problems in U.S. schools (Espelage & Swearer, 2004). It is interesting that when discussing the factors in a school that affect peer bullying, Batsche and Knoff (1994) suggested that lack of respect for peers and the presence of teachers who seem to overlook the problem and not intervene are important. It is not surprising that some of the best-known intervention programs mention respect in their titles, although the focus on respect in the actual interventions is not strong (e.g., the Expect Respect Program described by Meraviglia, Becker, Rosenbluth, Sanchez, & Robertson, 2003; the Respect Program described by Ertesvåg & Vaaland, 2007).

Students are clearly expected to respect their teachers, and this type of respect closely resembles that expected from children in parent–child relationships. Respect for teachers is based on the teacher's role as an authority figure who is responsible for the children's acquisition of culturally valued knowledge and competencies, proper behavior, and a sense of value and well-being. In this context the student, especially in elementary school, is expected to obey the teachers and show respect by abiding by the teachers' rules and meeting their expectations (e.g., Hsueh, Zhou, Cohen, Hundley, & Deptula, 2005). Thus, in teacher–student relations, students are expected to show respect that is contingent on each teacher's role as an authority figure in charge of their education, whereas teachers are expected to show unconditional respect for their students as valuable human beings.

In line with the similarity between parents' and teachers' roles, several researchers have likened the teacher to a parent (e.g., Wentzel, 2002). For example, teachers' respect for students' autonomy, as in parent–child relationships, was associated with fewer behavioral problems (Wentzel, 2002).

Bugental and her colleagues (Bugental, Lyon, Lin, McGrath, & Bimbela, 1999) have similarly likened teachers and parents in their authority roles and found that a teacher's low perception of power is associated with intrusive and coercive educational practices.

As children grow older, respect is expected to be more reciprocal; that is, both teachers and students are expected to show respect of the unconditional type although, in addition, students have contingent respect for their teachers based on meritorious qualities, such as expertise, knowledge, or moral integrity (e.g., Chunmei, Zongkui, & Hse, 2005). In this context, students often respect their teachers in response to the respect they receive from them (Noddings, 1996). All types of respect—of teachers for students and of students for teachers and peers—are expected to be negatively associated with aggression. For example, victims of violence (i.e., both pure victims and bullies who are also victims) report feeling less respected at school than other students feel (Morrison, 2006). Langdon and Preble (2008) examined both adult respect (e.g., "Most of my teachers treat students with fairness and respect") and peer respect (e.g., "Students treat each other with fairness and respect at this school") in school using a large sample of 5th- through 12th-grade students. Each type of respect uniquely predicted lower levels of bullying at the school after controlling for background variables such as gender and ethnic origin.

In general, we would predict that respect from various sources—parents, peers, and teachers—are all relevant to lowering levels of aggression and violence. In our own study of a large representative sample of Israeli youth ($N = \sim 3500$), we examined the association between adolescents' respect for parents and respect for teachers on the one hand and various outcomes on the other. We found that respect for teachers was negatively associated with aggression after statistically controlling respect for parents and perceived acceptance by parents, which were also associated with lower aggression (Scharf & Mayseless, 2005).

Another indication of the role of various sources of respect in attenuating aggression comes from a study by Knafo, Daniel, and Khoury-Kassabri (2008). They examined the importance of students' hierarchy of values in predicting violence and aggression at school. Though they did not specifically use the term respect, they assessed values that are closely related to facets of respect. For example, the value called *universalism*, defined as "understanding, appreciation, tolerance, and protection of the welfare of all people and of nature" (p. 654), reflects the unconditional type of respect, whereas the value called *conformity*, defined as "limiting actions and urges that might violate social expectations and norms" (p. 654), reflects the contingent type of respect for authority. Using a large sample of Jewish and Arab students in Israel, Knafo et al. found that youth in both ethnic groups who endorsed these values were less inclined to be aggressive and violent at school. Furthermore, in schools in which violent behavior was more frequent, these values, and in particular universalism, were strongly negatively associated with self-reported violence and provided a stronger protective effect against violence than in schools where violent behavior was less frequent. It thus appears that values that reflect respect, either unconditional or contingent, are associated with lower levels of aggression and violence, and such values seem to be able to counteract contextual factors that favor aggression. In sum, although there are currently only a handful of studies examining respect in schools directly, there are promising empirical indications that respect of various kinds—teachers for students, students for teachers, and peers for peers—in addition to internalized values that foster respect are associated with lower levels of aggression and violence at school.

WHY IS RESPECT SO IMPORTANT AND HOW IS IT DIFFERENT FROM OTHER ATTITUDES OR EMOTIONS?

Respect is often conceptually and empirically associated with other attitudes and emotions. For example, examining respect in close relationships, Frei and Shaver (2002) found that when participants were asked to identify central features of respect in romantic relationships, loving and caring seemed to be central, in addition to more predictable qualities such as honesty, trustworthiness, reliability, and being considerate. Similarly, Hendrick and Hendrick (2006) devised a scale to assess respect for a romantic partner, and it focused on approval, communication, interest, and care. In addition, high status and power within a group was discussed as contributing to respect.

These characteristics might play an important role in mitigating aggression, but they are not equivalent to respect. Respect should not be confused with love and caring or with general power and value within a group. First, unlike empathy or caring, which are "warm" emotions that incline a person to take responsibility for the well-being of a needy other, *respect* is a moral attitude of appreciation of the other and a moral imperative to refrain from harming the other. It is a relatively "cooler" disposition. In general, love and caring are strong buffers against aggression, but they do not always have this beneficial effect. In fact, a large number of clinical case studies of marital violence and child abuse demonstrate that love and caring can sometimes lead to violence and aggression when they are not associated with respect for the other's autonomy and his or her value as a separate and unique human being (see Chapters 19 and 20). Similarly, viewing another person as having high status or great power is not synonymous with respect and may not be associated with lower levels of aggression toward the person. In fact, history is full of incidents in which people were aggressive toward others precisely because they valued them and wanted to possess them or tried to destroy them because of their unjustifiably high status or undeserved power (see Chapter 4). Respect for others is quite different from this love and status envy. Respect includes a moral imperative not to harm the other. The value accorded to the other entails consideration and acceptance of the other's right to dignity and autonomy.

HOW CAN RESPECT BE FOSTERED?

In every context in which children are reared and educated, a general attitude of respect can be demonstrated and taught. One of the most influential ways in which respect can be taught and transmitted is by modeling it in daily life. Respect breeds respect, and values and attitudes in particular are internalized by emulating authority figures (Grusec & Kuczynski, 1997). To foster and teach respect, parents, teachers, and other authority figures should behave respectfully toward others. Behaving respectfully means honoring and enabling the other's autonomy, showing interest and care, allowing the other to have a voice even when not approving its message, and appreciating the other's natural goodness. Contingent respect is learned when the unique qualities of each individual are acknowledged, valued, and appreciated. In the school context, this requires becoming better acquainted with each student's uniqueness and allowing each student to be successful in his or her own way and in his or her own preferred domains.

Another behavior that is important to model is not allowing disrespectful behavior toward oneself or others; that is, to foster respect, authority figures need to intervene when they observe disrespectful behavior. Such an intervention should in itself be done respectfully, but it should be clear and decisive. Children and adults learn respect or disrespect partly from the general climate in their environment. Observing disrespect on the part of parents toward each other, or disrespect shown by a school principal toward teachers, might be almost as harmful to a child's development of respect as being personally disrespected. In particular, to foster respect, authority figures should not allow disrespectful behavior toward themselves or among peers.

Another way to foster respect is to promote children's self-respect. Self-respect is linked to a sense of autonomy and self-control that includes personal and moral standards (Roland & Foxx, 2003). Authority figures can promote these aspects of self-respect by targeting them as socialization goals and promoting moral values, self-control, and autonomy. Thus, besides modeling respect and intervening when disrespect is shown, authority figures should teach children about respect more directly and verbally. This includes clear discussions of values and the importance of good character and moral conduct.

Articulating clear expectations for behaviors that are consistent with respect, as discussed in this chapter, provides children with concrete and much needed direction. Following through with helpful scaffolding (e.g., reminders, observations, examples) helps them internalize these standards and make them their own. This can be done by helping children articulate and discuss their feelings, hesitations, and decision processes with regard to their values. Contemporary parents and teachers sometimes shy away from a directive approach because they see themselves as living in a child-centered world. But good directions, as can be seen in athletic coaching situations, can be beneficial to novices.

CONCLUSION

In sum, the explicit study of respect within contexts in which children are raised, socialized, and educated is still fairly rare, and its results are not conceptually well integrated. Although constructs related to respect have been examined (e.g., psychological control by parents, acknowledgement of ethnic diversity in schools), research efforts to conceptualize and measure different types of respect in home and school contexts, their associations with various outcomes, and their unique contributions to these outcomes are scarce. We hope that the conceptual framework elucidated in this chapter will open new possibilities to study respect and its vicissitudes, including reductions in aggression and violence, in developmental contexts.

REFERENCES

Barber, B. K. (Ed.). (2002). *Intrusive parenting: How psychological control affects children and adolescents*. Washington, DC: American Psychological Association.

Batsche, G. M., & Knoff, H. M. (1994). Bullies and their victims: Understanding a pervasive problem in the schools. *School Psychology Review, 23*, 165–174.

Battistich, V., Solomon, D., Watson, M., & Schaps, E. (1997). Caring school communities. *Educational Psychologist, 32*, 137–151. doi:10.1207/s15326985ep3203_1

Benbenishty, R., & Astor, R. A. (2005). *School violence in context: Culture, neighborhood, family, school, and gender*. New York, NY: Oxford University Press.

Bettencourt, B. A., & Miller, N. (1996). Sex differences in aggression as a function of provocation: A meta-analysis. *Psychological Bulletin, 119*, 422–447. doi:10.1037/0033-2909.119.3.422

Bies, R. J., & Moag, J. S. (1986). Interactional justice: Communication criteria for fairness. In B. Sheppard (Ed.), *Research on negotiation in organizations* (pp. 43–55). Greenwich, CT: JAI Press.

Bugental, D. B., & Happaney, K. (2004). Predicting infant maltreatment in low-income families: The interactive effects of maternal attributions and child status at birth. *Developmental Psychology, 40*, 234–243. doi:10.1037/0012-1649.40.2.234

Bugental, D. B., & Lewis, J. C. (1999). The paradoxical misuse of power by those who see themselves as powerless: How does it happen? *Journal of Social Issues, 55*, 51–64. doi:10.1111/0022-4537.00104/

Bugental, D. B., Lyon, J. E., Lin, E. K., McGrath, E. P., & Bimbela, A. (1999). Children "tune out" in response to the ambiguous communication style of powerless adults. *Child Development, 70*, 214–230. doi:10.1111/1467-8624.00016

Chunmei, Z., Zongkui, Z., & Hse, Y. (2005). The conception of respect and its development in childhood. *Psychological Science (China), 28*, 337–341.

Darwall, S. L. (1977). Two kinds of respect. *Ethics, 88*, 36–48. doi:10.1086/292054

de Cremer, D., & Tyler, T. R. (2005). Am I respected or not? Inclusion and reputation as issues in group membership. *Social Justice Research, 18*, 121–153. doi:10.1007/s11211-005-7366-3

Dillon, R. S. (2007). Arrogance, self respect, and personhood. *Journal of Consciousness Studies, 14*, 101–126.

DioGuardi, R. J., & Theodore, L. A. (2006). Understanding and addressing peer victimization among students. In S. R. Jimerson & M. Furlong (Eds.), *Handbook of school violence and school safety: From research to practice* (pp. 339–352). Mahwah, NJ: Erlbaum.

Dixon, S. V., Graber, J., & Brooks-Gunn, J. (2008). The roles of respect for parental authority and parenting practices in parent–child conflict among African American, Latino, and European American families. *Journal of Family Psychology, 22*, 1–10. doi:10.1037/0893-3200.22.1.1

Ertesvåg, S. K., & Vaaland, G. S. (2007). Prevention and reduction of behavioral problems in school: An evaluation of the Respect program. *Educational Psychology, 27*, 713–736. doi:10.1080/01443410701309258

Espelage, D. L., & Swearer, S. M. (2004). *Bullying in American schools: A social–ecological perspective on prevention and intervention.* Hillsdale, NJ: Erlbaum.

Frei, J., & Shaver, P. R. (2002). Respect in close relationships: Prototype definition, self-report assessment, and initial correlates. *Personal Relationships, 9*, 121–139. doi:10.1111/1475-6811.00008

Golden, D., & Mayseless, O. (2008). On the alert in an unpredictable environment. *Culture and Psychology, 14*, 155–179. doi:10.1177/1354067X08088553

Gottman, J. M. (1994). *What predicts divorce? The relationship between marital processes and marital outcomes.* Hillsdale, NJ: Erlbaum.

Grusec, J. E., & Kuczynski, L. (1997). *Parenting and children's internalization of values: A handbook of contemporary theory.* Hoboken, NJ: Wiley.

Harvey, M. D., & Enzle, M. E. (1978). Effects of retaliation latency and provocation level on judged blameworthiness for retaliatory aggression. *Personality and Social Psychology Bulletin, 4*, 579–582. doi:10.1177/014616727800400417

Hendrick, S. S., & Hendrick, C. (2006). Measuring respect in close relationships. *Journal of Social and Personal Relationships, 23*, 881–899. doi:10.1177/0265407 506070471

Heuer, L., Blumenthal, E., Douglas, A., & Weinblatt, T. (1999). A deservingness approach to respect as a relationally based fairness judgment. *Personality and Social Psychology Bulletin, 25*, 1279–1292. doi:10.1177/0146167299258009

Hsueh, Y., Zhou, Z., Cohen, R., Hundley, R. J., & Deptula, D. P. (2005). Knowing and showing respect: Chinese and U.S. children's understanding of respect and its association to their friendships. *Journal of Psychology in Chinese Societies, 6*, 229–260.

Ikels, C. (Ed.). (2004). *Filial piety: Practice and discourse in contemporary East Asia.* Stanford, CA: Stanford University Press.

Janoff-Bulman, R., & Werther, A. (2008). The social psychology of respect: Implications for delegitimization and reconciliation. In A. Nadler, T. Malloy, & J. D. Fisher (Eds.), *The social psychology of inter-group reconciliation* (pp. 145–170). New York, NY: Oxford University Press. doi:10.1093/acprof:oso/9780195300314.003.0008

Jussim, L. (1986). Self-fulfilling prophecies: A theoretical and integrative review. *Psychological Review, 93*, 429–445. doi:10.1037/0033-295X.93.4.429

Kant, I. (1959). *Foundations of metaphysics of morals* (L. W. Beck, Trans.). Indianapolis, IN: Bobbs-Merrill.

Kasen, S., Berenson, K., Cohen, P., & Johnson, J. G. (2004). The effects of school climate on changes in aggressive and other behaviors related to bullying. In R. L. Espelage & S. M. Swearer (Eds.), *Bullying in American schools: A social–ecological perspective on prevention and intervention* (pp. 187–210). Hillsdale, NJ: Erlbaum.

Knafo, A., Daniel, E., & Khoury-Kassabri, M. (2008). Values as protective factors against violent behavior in Jewish and Arab high schools in Israel. *Child Development, 79*, 652–667. doi:10.1111/j.1467-8624.2008.01149.x

Kumashiro, M., Finkel, E. J., & Rusbult, C. E. (2002). Self-respect and prorelationship behavior in marital relationships. *Journal of Personality, 70*, 1009–1049.

Langdon, S. W. (2007). Conceptualizations of respect: Qualitative and quantitative evidence of four (five) themes. *Journal of Psychology, 141*, 469–484. doi:10.3200/JRLP.141.5.469-484

Langdon, S. W., & Preble, W. (2008). The relationship between levels of perceived respect and bullying in 5th through 12th graders. *Adolescence, 43*, 485–503.

LaRusso, M. D., Romer, D., & Selman, R. L. (2008). Teachers as builders of respectful school climates: Implications for adolescent drug use norms and depressive symptoms in high school. *Journal of Youth and Adolescence, 37*, 386–398. doi:10.1007/s10964-007-9212-4

Lawrence-Lightfoot, S. (2000). *Respect: An exploration*. New York, NY: Perseus.

Lightfoot, C. (2000). On respect. *New Ideas in Psychology, 18*, 177–185. doi:10.1016/S0732-118X(00)00007-6

Martorell, G. A., & Bugental, D. (2006). Maternal variations in stress reactivity: Implications for harsh parenting practices with very young children. *Journal of Family Psychology, 20*, 641–647. doi:10.1037/0893-3200.20.4.641

Mayseless, O., & Scharf, M. (2009). Too close for comfort: Inadequate boundaries with parents and individuation in late adolescent girls. *American Journal of Orthopsychiatry, 79*, 191–202. doi:10.1037/a0015623

McCullough, M. (2008). *Beyond revenge: The evolution of the forgiveness instinct*. San Francisco, CA: Jossey-Bass.

Meraviglia, M. G., Becker, H., Rosenbluth, B., Sanchez, E., & Robertson, T. (2003). The Expect Respect Project: Creating a positive elementary school climate. *Journal of Interpersonal Violence, 18*, 1347–1360. doi:10.1177/0886260503257457

Miller, D. T. (2001). Disrespect and the experience of injustice. *Annual Review of Psychology, 52*, 527–553. doi:10.1146/annurev.psych.52.1.527

Morrison, B. (2006). School bullying and restorative justice: Toward a theoretical understanding of the role of respect, pride, and shame. *Journal of Social Issues, 62*, 371–392. doi:10.1111/j.1540-4560.2006.00455.x

Mulcahy, D. G., & Casella, R. (2005). Violence and caring in school and society: Educational studies. *Educational Studies, 37*, 244–255. doi:10.1207/s15326993es3703_3

Noddings, N. (1996). Learning to care and to be cared for. In A. M. Hoffman (Ed.), *Schools, violence, and society* (pp. 185–198). Westport, CT: Praeger.

Noddings, N. (2005). What does it mean to educate the whole child? *Educational Leadership, 63*, 8–13.

Olweus, D. (1997). Bully/victim problems in school: Facts and intervention. *European Journal of Psychology of Education, 12*, 495–510. doi:10.1007/BF03172807

Piaget, J. (1932). *The moral judgment of the child*. Oxford, England: Harcourt, Brace.

Pitt-Rivers, J. (1965). Honour and social status. In J. G. Peristiany (Ed.), *The nature of human society: Honor and shame* (pp. 19–78). London, England: Weidenfeld & Nicholson.

Rawls, J. (1971). *A theory of justice*. Cambridge, MA: Harvard University Press.

Roland, C. E., & Foxx, R. M. (2003). Self-respect: A neglected concept. *Philosophical Psychology, 16*, 247–288. doi:10.1080/09515080307764

Rubin, K. H., & Chung, O. B. (2006). *Parenting beliefs, behaviors, and parent–child relations: A cross-cultural perspective*. New York, NY: Psychology Press.

Scharf, M., & Mayseless, O. (2005). *Parental authority and its associations with social and emotional functioning in school: Final research report*. Unpublished report submitted to the Ministry of Education, Israel (in Hebrew). Faculty of Education, University of Haifa, Haifa, Israel.

Sim, T. N. (2000). Adolescent psychosocial competence: The importance and role of regard for parents. *Journal of Research on Adolescence, 10,* 49–64. doi:10.1207/SJRA1001_3

Smith, H. (1991). *The world's religions: Our great wisdom traditions.* New York, NY: HarperCollins.

Steinberg, L. (2004). *The 10 basic principles of good parenting.* New York, NY: Simon & Schuster.

Wentzel, K. R. (2002). Are effective teachers like good parents? Teaching styles and student adjustment in early adolescence. *Child Development, 73,* 287–301. doi:10.1111/1467-8624.00406

Zongkui, Z., Chumei, Z., & Hsueh, Y. (2006). Relations between conception of respect and peer relationships in childhood. *Acta Psychologica Sinica, 38,* 232–239.

IV

AGGRESSION AT
THE SOCIETAL LEVEL

16

AN EXISTENTIAL PERSPECTIVE ON VIOLENT SOLUTIONS TO ETHNO–POLITICAL CONFLICT

GILAD HIRSCHBERGER AND TOM PYSZCZYNSKI

War would end if the dead could return.
—Stanley Baldwin, British Prime Minister

The outbreak of violence between Israel and Hamas on the eve of the year 2009 surprised hardly anyone. The fragile ceasefire had come to an end, and the renewed missile attacks on towns and villages in the south of Israel were the appetizer preceding the inevitable main course of massive violent retribution. But, although the ebbing and flowing of violence in this region has become habitual, for many it is accompanied by an increased sense of frustration caused by the inability to move beyond violence to find a rational solution that will bring peace to both Israelis and Palestinians.

And what would be the rational solution to this bitter and seemingly intractable conflict? The dictum that "war itself is the enemy," attributed to the Prussian philosopher von Clausewitz, has never resonated more strongly. The violent clashes between Israel and the Palestinians have resulted in significant losses to both sides with little gain, if any, to justify the price. Every round of violence ends with a new shaky agreement that differs ever so slightly from the shaky agreement that preceded the most recent violent outbreak. Thus, time and again when the dust settles from the futile attempt to subdue the other, Israelis and Palestinians find themselves with no viable option but to find a way to live peacefully with one another. But no one seems capable of finding a way to achieve this peace (see Chapter 17).

Even more perplexing is the fact that since the 1993 peace accord between Israel and the Palestine Liberation Organization (PLO), relations between the groups have significantly deteriorated and violence has reached an unprecedented level. The Israeli disengagement from Gaza in the summer of 2005 was intended to reduce friction between Israelis and Palestinians, but it failed to live up to its promise of breaking the cycle of violence and may have inadvertently contributed to the recent escalation of violent conflict. How can we explain that despite mounting evidence of the futility of violence, and the obvious need for reconciliation among the various factions, there seems to be no end in sight to perpetual warfare? And why has every step taken toward peace paradoxically resulted in a spiral of bitter violence?

One possible answer that many Israelis and Palestinians seem to adhere to is that the other side has proven to be duplicitous, inhumane, and ruthless, using peace as a cover for malevolent intentions (see Chapter 17). In the present chapter we provide an alternative answer to these questions and argue that powerful psychological forces underlying ethno–political conflict hamper the ability to achieve peace, even when peace seems to be a rational solution that would benefit all. We base our analysis on terror management theory (e.g., Greenberg, Pyszczynski, & Solomon, 1997) and demonstrate, with a body of research conducted recently in Iran, Israel, Europe, and the United States, how existential concerns underlie the proclivity to choose violent solutions to ethno–political conflicts. We also show that the link between mortality concerns and ethno–political violence is not inevitable, and that at times mortality concerns can even reduce violent inclinations. We suggest that a better understanding of the role played by mortality concerns in political reasoning provides insight into ways to move beyond violence and to promote peace.

TERROR MANAGEMENT THEORY

Terror management theory (TMT; e.g., Greenberg et al., 1997) contends that the instinctive animal desire for continued life juxtaposed with the uniquely human awareness of the inevitability of death creates a potential for paralyzing terror; effective regulation of ongoing human behavior requires that this potential for terror be effectively managed. According to TMT, existential terror is managed and security is provided by (a) a cultural worldview that provides an explanation for existence, standards through which one can attain a sense of personal value, and the promise of literal or symbolic immortality to those who live up to these standards; (b) self-esteem, which is acquired by believing in the cultural worldview and living up to its standards; and (c) close interpersonal relationships.

Terror management defenses are fragile social constructions that require ongoing validation from others if they are to promote effective functioning. Faith in one's worldview, the sense of personal value derived from living up to social and cultural standards, and the anxiety-buffering effectiveness of these structures is bolstered by others sharing one's beliefs and diminished when others adhere to a different system of values and beliefs. According to TMT, because these terror-management processes protect people from deeply rooted existential fears, much social thought and behavior is oriented toward maintaining them and defending them against threats.

Because of the fragile nature of culturally derived forms of defense, threats to these symbolic constructions undermine the emotional security that they provide and motivate people to protect their death-denying mechanisms to ward off the threats. When others hold beliefs that conflict with one's own basic conceptions and proclaim their culture's superiority or moral righteousness, they imply that one's worldview is incorrect and one's culture is inferior, which undermines one's sense of value and meaning. Such threats to worldviews and self-esteem strip away an individual's symbolic defensive shield and then people may express anger and derogate the source of the threats or choose to demonstrate their group's superiority by subduing, defeating, or even annihilating groups that challenge their worldview.

Terror management studies have tested these theoretical propositions by priming thoughts of death (i.e., heightening mortality salience [MS]) and examining cultural worldview defenses. The results of over 400 empirical studies conducted in 21 countries have provided support for the theoretical propositions of TMT. For example, studies have found that MS increases the motivation to invest in one's worldview and also leads to avoidance, derogation, and aggression against worldview-threatening others (e.g., Greenberg et al., 1990; Hirschberger & Ein-Dor, 2006; McGregor et al., 1998; Pyszczynski et al., 2006). These effects appear to be unique to thoughts about death. Other anxiety-producing activities, such as thinking about giving a speech, imagining physical pain, or worrying about life after college do not produce the same reactions as MS (e.g., Greenberg, Pyszczynski, Solomon, Simon, & Breus, 1994; Greenberg Simon, Porteus, Pyszczynski, & Solomon, 1995). Moreover, TMT effects are not accompanied by an increase in negative feelings or mediated by such feelings (Pyszczynski, Greenberg, & Solomon, 1999).

TERROR MANAGEMENT AND INTERGROUP CONFLICT

Much of the focus of terror management research has been on intergroup relations, showing that the need to defend symbolic death-denying mental structures often results in extreme reactions toward people who uphold different cultural, religious, or national worldviews (for a review, see Pyszczynski, Solomon, & Greenberg, 2003). For example, studies have shown that MS leads Christian participants to derogate a Jewish person (Greenberg et al., 1990), American college students to behave more aggressively toward those with different political orientations than their own (McGregor et al., 1998), White Americans to express sympathy for a White racist (Greenberg, Schimel, Martens, Pyszczynski, & Solomon, 2001), Italians to view their own nation as superior to other European countries (Castano, 2004), and even Israeli children as young as 11 to react more negatively to an immigrant child from Russia and more positively toward a child from Israel (Florian & Mikulincer, 1998).

These studies have consistently shown that brief, unobtrusive reminders of mortality lead people to view their group in a more positive light and view other groups in a more negative light to the extent of derogating and even aggressing against other groups. Thus, it may seem that reminders of mortality instantly turn people into ethnocentric, prejudiced, and potentially violent automatons. Fortunately, TMT views the effects of MS on intergroup attitudes as more complex and maintains that different people may react to MS in different ways, depending on individual differences and the situational context. For example, research has shown that whereas people with a conservative political orientation respond to MS with greater intolerance, people with a liberal political orientation respond to MS with greater tolerance (Greenberg, Simon, Pyszczynski, Solomon, & Chatel, 1992). Other research has shown that MS leads to heightened ingroup affiliation only when the ingroup is portrayed as strong and successful but leads to disaffiliation from elements of the worldview that reflect weakness or inferiority (Arndt, Greenberg, Schimel, Pyszczynski, & Solomon, 2002; Dechesne, Greenberg, Arndt, & Schimel, 2000).

In the realm of political conflict, additional variables may enter into the equation and further complicate the effect of existential concerns on violent inclinations so that mortality reminders may lead to support of violent solutions to conflict in some cases but to a rejection of violent means in others. In this chapter we demonstrate, first, that MS increases support for violent solutions to conflict but that this link between death concerns and violent outcomes depends on three major conditions: (a) social and national consensus on the use of violence, (b) a sense that violence is justified and necessary, and (c) a sense that violence is imminent and unavoidable. In the next step, we outline conditions that may disrupt the link between death concerns and support for violent solutions to conflict, and we demonstrate that thinking rationally about violence and considering the consequences of violence may moderate and even reverse the effects of MS on violent inclinations. In the final section of our analysis we focus on moving beyond violence and demonstrate that emphasizing basic human values and human similarities promotes more peaceful motives even when death is salient.

EXISTENTIAL CONCERNS PROMOTE POLITICAL VIOLENCE

> It is in the sphere of terrorism and counterterrorism that fear's most harmful manifestations flourish.
> —Irene Kahn, Amnesty International

The hypothesis that death awareness motivates violent solutions to political conflict is the most straightforward application of TMT to the realm of political psychology. War and terrorism simplify conflict and dichotomize groups into "us" and "them," "good" and "evil." Violence also offers hope for a clear-cut and long-lasting resolution of the conflict, the potential (or illusion) of pronouncing winners and losers, and a better future following victory. These attributes of political violence make it particularly attractive when death is salient, because under these conditions people are motivated to promote the triumph of their group and the thorough defeat of the opposition.

Indeed, research has revealed that among conservative Americans MS leads to greater support of extreme violence against countries or organizations that pose a threat to the United States (Pyszczynski et al., 2006, Study 2). It has led to Israeli settlers in the Gaza Strip, and their supporters who refused to accept the 2005 disengagement plan, to support more violent resistance (Hirschberger & Ein-Dor, 2006). Research has also shown that MS led participants in Iran (Pyszczynski et al., 2006, Study 1) and in Britain (Routledge & Arndt, 2008) to express greater willingness to sacrifice their life for their country. However, despite the seemingly clear link between mortality concerns and support for intergroup violence, we contend that this link is neither automatic nor inevitable. Instead, it depends on three major conditions: perceived consensus, justice, and inevitability of conflict.

Consensus

Organized forms of violence, such as war and terrorism, depend to a large extent on the broad support of the populations for whom these actions are purportedly undertaken. When leaders receive the support of their people, they feel less restrained in sending young men and women to the battlefield, and they are under less pressure from their publics to end the war. However, consensus is fragile, and often the price of war and the inability to achieve the expected outcomes instill doubt as to the legitimacy or efficacy of violent policies, concerns about the costs of such policies (in terms of loss of life, resources, and international respect), and the legitimacy and wisdom of the leader and his or her decisions. In such cases, public support at the beginning of a conflict can transform into disillusionment, frustration, and anger. Such was the case in the American war in Vietnam and more recently in the war in Iraq, where initial consensus and hope dissipated when the war failed to deliver its promise. In Israel, the Lebanon War of 1982 and, to some extent, the Lebanon War of 2006 were launched following missile attacks on Northern Israel and enjoyed public support until the death toll rose, and it became evident that the declared goals of the war were not attainable by violent means.

From a terror management perspective, consensus is a necessary ingredient for the functioning of the cultural worldview as an effective anxiety buffer. Because worldviews are symbolic social constructions that are fragile and susceptible to disconfirming information, they require constant consensual validation. For consensus to be established and maintained it is necessary to believe that the threat is of such magnitude that massive use of force is the only effective response.

Consensus is clearly a requirement for military action in democratic societies, where leaders receive their legitimacy from the support of their constituents. There is good reason to believe that consensus is important for violent behavior in nondemocratic societies as well. For example, in the Palestinian territories, suicide bombers are exalted as martyrs. Their pictures are posted on walls and buildings, and they are admired by children who view them as role models. Such idolization of people who are ready to kill themselves and others for what is considered a holy cause is necessary for the propagation of suicidal terrorism because in return for a shortened life, terrorists gain fame, adoration, respect, and honor (not to mention several afterlife virgins). According to TMT, long-lasting fame and admiration may be more appealing than a longer life because they provide a sense of symbolic immortality, the feeling that certain aspects of the self will survive physical death.

Empirical evidence supports the contention that MS elicits more consensus regarding violent responses to conflict as well as the contention that consensus is a necessary precondition for MS to elicit support for ethno–political violence. In a series of studies, Landau and his colleagues (Landau, Johns, et al., 2004) demonstrated that shortly after the beginning of the Iraq War, reminders of death increased support for American president George W. Bush and his counterterrorist policies. Other studies show that without a sense of consensus, MS may not lead to support of violence against other groups.

In a unique study conducted in Iran (Pyszczynski et al., 2006), participants were assigned to either an MS or control condition and then read a description of a student portrayed as holding commonly expressed views on political issues. Half of the participants read a description in which the student expressed support for martyrdom attacks against Western targets, and the other half read a description in which the student expressed disapproval of suicidal terrorism. The results indicated that MS led to greater support of martyrdom attacks only when the student expressed pro-martyrdom attitudes. However, when the student voiced opposition to suicidal terrorism, MS did not have a significant effect on support of violence. A more recent study demonstrated that MS increased support for terrorist violence among Iranians but that this effect was eliminated when participants were led to believe that the majority of their countrymen disapproved of such tactics (Abdollahi, Henthorn, & Pyszczynski, 2009). These results indicate that for MS to elicit support for suicidal terrorism, participants had to feel that there was consensus among their peers supporting such violence.

Justice

Consensus for violent solutions to conflict may be established when people feel that they are fighting for a just and noble cause. However, just because a cause is noble does not mean it will be achieved using violent means or that violence is the most effective route to attain the desired goal. Early scholars of war and conflict viewed the use of violence as a rational option that could advance a country's interests, as Clausewitz (1832/1976) contended, "War is not a mere act of policy but a true political instrument, a continuation of political activity by other means," implying that the decision to engage in war is the product of a rational cost–benefit analysis. From this perspective, war is waged when leaders conclude that war is a more efficient way to achieve political goals than other available means.

Expected utility theory (e.g., Bueno de Mesquita, 1988) formalizes this assumption and posits that by delineating the costs and benefits of conflict, political scientists may better understand the motives for going to war. However, over the years scholars of conflict resolution have concluded that rational factors alone do little to explain the outburst of violent conflict and that emotional and motivational factors such as anger, resentment, and revenge play a pivotal role in the decision to engage in war (e.g., Baumeister & Butz, 2005).

The decision to use violence in interethnic conflict may be driven so powerfully by emotional factors such as anger, revenge, and the need to restore a sense of justice, that utilitarian considerations, such as whether war is a good instrumental means of achieving a desired outcome, are ignored (see Chapter 17). In an analysis of five major international conflicts (including the two world wars), Welch (1993) concluded that the motivation to achieve justice or restore justice has been a major factor in most global conflicts. Welch further contended that the sense of injustice involves powerful emotions that often hinder a rational analysis of costs and benefits, and may lead to decisions that in retrospect seem hasty and impulsive.

TMT provides an opportunity to move beyond a rational analysis of violent conflict to better understand the underlying motives that instigate violence, even when violence makes little rational sense. In this section we argue that when death is salient, justice motives gain prominence and may override utilitarian considerations to the extent that violence may be exercised even when it is clearly counter to rational self-interest. Previous terror management research has already demonstrated that MS increases the propensity to strive for a just world (Hirschberger, 2006; Landau, Solomon, et al., 2004), and Pyszczynski et al. (2003) argued that part of the appeal of President Bush and his counter-terrorist polices immediately following 9/11 was that existential fear increased the desire to vanquish evil and restore justice.

In a series of four studies conducted in 2008 (Hirschberger, Pyszczynski, & Ein-Dor, 2009b), we examined whether MS would increase justice motives for violence and whether the motivation to achieve or restore justice would be greater than rational utilitarian considerations. In Study 1, Israeli participants were randomly assigned to MS and control conditions and then read a description of a missile attack from the Gaza Strip on an Israeli town. Some participants were told that security experts believed that a military incursion into Gaza was likely to significantly diminish Hamas's ability to fire more missiles (utility condition). Other participants were told that security experts believed that an incursion into Gaza would not reduce Hamas's ability to fire more missiles, nor would it effectively deter Hamas, but it would restore a sense of justice to the Israeli public (justice condition). All participants were asked to indicate their support for a military incursion into Gaza. The results revealed that in both the justice and utility conditions, MS led to greater support of a military strike. These findings suggest that reminders of death increase support of violence not only when violence has a clear purpose and is executed to obtain a concrete result but also when violence is considered to be ineffective but will contribute to feelings of greater justice. These findings seem to imply that people still desire violence even when they understand that it will not have the desired effect.

These findings indicated that MS leads to greater support of violence for both justice and utility reasons, but they did not indicate whether justice motives are more prominent than utility motives when death is salient. In the next study we developed a scale to measure justice and utility motives for violence, which would enable us to measure these motives within each subject rather than manipulate them between subjects as in Study 1. In Study 2, we developed the Justice, Utility, and Peace Inventory (JUPI), which consists of questions favoring violence to restore justice (justice factor; e.g., "A military strike on Gaza will make the Palestinians pay for their crimes"), favoring violence for utilitarian reasons (utility factor; e.g., "A military strike on Gaza will reduce missile attacks against Sderot"), or opposing violence altogether (peace factor; e.g., "A military strike on Gaza hurts the chances for peace"). A factor analysis confirmed the factorial structure of the JUPI, and correlations between the JUPI and other relevant instruments, such as the Right-Wing Authoritarianism Scale (Altemeyer, 1981) and the Need for Cognitive Closure

Scale (Webster & Kruglanski, 1994), established the construct, convergent, and discriminant validity of the JUPI.

Based on this second study, we examined the impact of MS on JUPI factors. Following the MS procedure, participants were instructed to read a description of a missile attack from Gaza on an Israeli town, as in the first study. However, half of the participants read that the attack resulted only in some minor damage and no casualties (mild outcome condition), and the other half read the description used in the first study wherein several people were killed or wounded during the attack (severe outcome condition). Then all participants completed the JUPI. Results revealed that in the mild outcome condition MS had no significant impact on the JUPI. However, in the severe outcome condition MS led to greater endorsement of the justice factor compared with the control condition. There was no significant effect of MS on the utility and peace items.

The results of this study indicate that when participants are given the opportunity to endorse both justice and utility items, MS has a significant effect only on the justice items and not on the utility items. Furthermore, the impact of MS on justice motives for violence was evident only when the outcome of the attack was severe and not when it was mild. Perhaps for MS to increase justice motives one needs to be in an enraged state of mind that overrides rational considerations.

To test this possibility, participants in a fourth study first read an essay that either recommended making decisions based on rational considerations or an essay that argued that decisions are best made on an emotional, intuitive basis. Then, participants completed the MS procedure and read a description of a panel of experts unanimously concluding that the appropriate response to a recent terrorist attack in Tel Aviv would be a limited attack targeting only the person responsible for the terrorist attack, rather than engaging in a full-scale attack against Gaza. Following this description, participants were asked to indicate whether, given the choice, they would favor a limited attack, as recommended, or a full scale attack, and they were asked to indicate to what extent they felt confident about their choice. Thus, MS, cognitive mode, and decision regarding the type of attack served as the independent variables. The level of confidence they expressed in the decision they made served as the dependent variable. Results revealed that participants who favored a limited attack were not significantly affected by experimental conditions. However, among those favoring a full-scale attack, MS led to greater support of an attack when participants were induced to make decisions based on emotions and intuitions. The results of this study suggest that confidence in the decision to endorse a full-scale attack that is considered by experts to be counterproductive is greater under MS conditions but only after participants are induced to think with their gut rather than their mind.

The prominence of justice and revenge motives in times of war is demonstrated in the following story. In the Gaza War of 2009 the three daughters of a Palestinian physician, Dr. Az-a-Din Abu El-Aish, who works at a large Israeli hospital, were killed while in their home. In his anguish and grief Dr. Abu El-Aish pleaded in a press conference that the violence be stopped and that Israelis and Palestinians find a way to live in peace. He also insisted that there was no reason to target his house, as there were no terrorists shooting from it. A mother of an Israeli soldier angrily interrupted his speech and accused him of harboring weapons or terrorists; otherwise why would anyone bomb his house?

At first sight, this rude and insensitive interruption could be seen as the epitome of coldheartedness. However, from a terror management perspective this behavior is different only in style, but not in essence, from other desperate attempts to defend the cultural worldview at all costs. From this point of view, Dr. Abu-Aish represented for two major reasons a severe threat to the predominant Israeli worldview that supported the war. First, he insisted that there were no hostile activities taking place in his house, undermining the position that all the casualties of the war were justified. For the accusing woman (a mother of a soldier), the possibility that some of the killing in Gaza could not be explained or justified posed an unbearable threat to her belief system. Second, in spite of his devastating loss, the doctor remained steadfast in his belief in peace and coexistence, threatening the need to believe that the other side of the conflict consists only of inhumane, cruel, and savage terrorists. In her almost instinctive attack on the doctor (which she later regretted), the Israeli woman defended her worldview from the possibility that the war was anything but a just, moral, and necessary clash between the forces of good and evil. This small episode in a larger war demonstrates the resistance of a population at war to any information that might undermine consensus that the war is righteous and justified. It is also a powerful demonstration of the workings of the justice motive and the mental acrobatics people will perform to convince themselves that wrongdoings committed on their behalf are justified.

The Inevitability of Violence

Rallying public support for a war not only requires that people perceive the cause as just and view their group as representing forces of good fighting against evil, but people also need to believe that there is no alternative and that war is imminent and unavoidable (see Chapter 17). For example, the American public perceived the September 11th attacks as the beginning of a violent and inevitable clash with radical Islam, and following the terrorist attacks support for President Bush and his war on terrorism was high. In contrast, the 2004 terrorist attacks on Madrid had the opposite effect: Support for the ruling Partido

Popular party diminished, probably in part because the Spanish population viewed the Madrid bombings as a reaction to Spanish support of the American war in Iraq and not as a direct conflict between Spain and radical Islam. In their view, the terrorist attacks were not inevitable and could be stopped if Spain changed its foreign policy and withdrew its support from the war in Iraq.

The difference between an imminent and inevitable war from an American perspective, and an undesirable and unnecessary war from a Spanish perspective, led to diametrically opposed reactions to the attacks in the two countries. For Americans, the seemingly inevitable route to violent conflict left the impression of no alternative options and perhaps elevated terror management mechanisms in the form of a symbolic war against evil. For the Spanish, who perceived the terrorist attacks as the price they were paying for the ill-considered policy of their government, the elevated death awareness following the attacks made their own vulnerability to harm salient, and they reacted by replacing their leadership with a more peaceful one. The fact that the Madrid attacks occurred several days before the election probably contributed to the Spanish sentiment that power was in their hands to avoid an unnecessary violent confrontation.

Recent research lends support to this analysis and indicates that when violence seems inevitable, MS leads to greater support for violent solutions to conflict. In one study (Hirschberger et al., 2009c, Study 1), MS led to greater support of a preemptive strike against Iran after participants read a speech that was purportedly delivered by an Iranian leader calling for the destruction of the State of Israel and for the continued development of Iran's nuclear program. In a similar study (Hirschberger et al., 2009c, Study 3), Israelis who lived in a region attacked by missiles during the 2006 Lebanon War expressed greater support of a preemptive strike against Hezbollah following MS, but only if they first read a passage describing Hezbollah as preparing for an imminent war with Israel.

SELF-PROTECTION MODERATES POLITICAL VIOLENCE

Previous terror management research has focused primarily on an abstract and nonimminent threat of death and on symbolic defenses used to quell existential anxieties. However, research conducted on current geopolitical conflicts and on the populations immersed in these conflicts must consider the fact that real-life conflict has not only symbolic but also real implications. That is, as much as people engaged in conflict are concerned about protecting their symbolic death-denying structures, so too are they concerned about their own physical safety. Reminders of personal mortality have been shown to engage motivation to defend the worldview, but it is also likely that they bring to mind the possibility of dying in a war. What determines people's choice of war or peace when mortality is salient? So far, we have demonstrated that MS leads to greater support for political violence when social consensus is high, when the cause is perceived as just, and when conflict seems inevitable. In this section we argue that MS will lead to less violent intentions when (a) perceived personal vulnerability to conflict-related injury or death is high, (b) adversary rhetoric raises the possibility of a nonviolent solution, (c) experts advise that violence is counterproductive, and (d) people are induced to think rationally.

To examine the role of perceived vulnerability and adversary intent in moderating the link between MS and political violence, we (Hirschberger et al., 2009c) conducted a series of studies to examine the dynamic interplay between symbolic terror management defenses, concrete self-protection from physical danger, and their effects on support of violent solutions to political conflict. In Study 1, we focused on the growing tensions between Israel and Iran over the development of Iran's nuclear program. Participants completed the typical MS procedure and were then randomly assigned to read either a conflict-escalating speech by an Iranian leader against Israel and the West or a conflict-de-escalating speech that implies that violence is not inevitable. Participants then rated their support of extremely violent reactions against Iran, including a preemptive nuclear strike. Results revealed that in the escalating rhetoric scenario condition, MS increased support of extreme violence against Iran, but in the de-escalating scenario the opposite pattern was observed, and MS decreased support of extreme preemptive violence relative to the control condition.

Our interpretation of the results of this study is that when violence seemed imminent and unavoidable, as in the escalation scenario, MS increased violent motives. However, because MS makes salient not only the need for a symbolic worldview but also the fact of personal vulnerability to harm and to death, when there were reasons to believe that violence might be averted, the need for personal safety overrode the defense of the symbolic worldview, and the motivation for violence was reduced.

To further test this explanation, we manipulated personal vulnerability in Study 2. Following the MS procedure and a description of the current state of tensions with Iran, participants were randomly assigned to two groups. The first group was asked to reflect on the possibility that they or their loved ones might be hurt in a future conflict between Iran and Israel. The second group was asked to reflect on the content of the passage. All participants then completed the same measure as in Study 1. Results revealed that participants who reflected only on the content of the passage responded to MS with increased support for preemptive violence. However, participants who reflected on their personal vulnerability to conflict-related harm responded to MS with decreased support for preemptive violence.

Based on the results of Studies 1 and 2, we attempted to better understand the impact on support of violence of the interaction between perceived adversary intent and perceived personal vulnerability. In Study 3, rather than manipulating personal vulnerability as in Study 2, we chose to focus on two groups of participants that differed in their level of exposure to war-related violence (matched on other potentially confounding variables). The first group consisted of participants who lived in Northern Israel during the Second Lebanon War against Hezbollah (summer, 2006) and had directly experienced missile attacks. The second group consisted of participants who lived in other parts of Israel and had never been directly exposed to conflict-related violence. All participants completed the MS procedure and then read either a conflict-escalating speech or a conflict-de-escalating speech by a leader of Hezbollah, and answered questions on support of a preemptive attack against Hezbollah.

Results revealed that for participants in the no-war-exposure group, MS led to greater support of violence regardless of Hezbollah rhetoric. However, among participants in the war-exposure group, MS led to greater support of violence in the escalation scenario but led to a reduced support of violence among participants in the de-escalation scenario. These findings suggest that among persons who feel less vulnerable to conflict-related violence, MS leads to increased support of violence regardless of whether the adversary's rhetoric is peaceful or belligerent. Ideological threat trumps practical concerns for one's safety. However, among participants who had experienced the war firsthand, the influence of MS on support of violence was contingent on adversary rhetoric: When it seemed that war was imminent, it increased support of violence, but when war seemed avoidable it had the opposite effect and reduced support of violence. When one's own life and that of one's family is on the line, people are more likely to consider nonviolent options when they perceive that violence can be averted.

Similar findings were obtained in the aforementioned research on justice and utility motives for violence (Hirschberger et al., 2009b). In Study 1, which measured whether utilitarian and justice motivations for violence would increase support of violence under MS conditions, a third group of participants were told that security experts believed that an incursion into Gaza would be counterproductive and was likely only to increase attacks against Israel (futility of violence condition). Counter to the other conditions, in this group MS significantly reduced support for political violence. In Study 3 of this research, which examined whether inducing rational or intuitive thinking influences the impact of MS on support of massive violent retribution, we not only found that when participants were induced to decide intuitively and emotionally, as previously mentioned, MS led to greater support of a full-fledged attack against Gaza but we also found that when participants were induced to think rationally, MS reduced support of violent retributions.

MOVING BEYOND VIOLENCE

The findings described in the previous section, demonstrating that self-protective concerns may override the need to defend the cultural worldview and may lead to a reduction in violent motivations under MS conditions, are encouraging. But they still suggest that humans are defensive violence-prone creatures in one way or another. In this section of the chapter we demonstrate that focusing on common humanity with others, on compassionate religious values, and on feelings of psychological security enables people to transcend their fear and respond to MS with greater tolerance of others.

In a study examining support of political violence in a sample of Israelis (Hirschberger et al., 2009a), participants were assigned to either an MS condition, a pain salience condition, a "Holocaust as a crime against the Jewish people" condition, or a "Holocaust as a crime against humanity" condition (based on Wohl & Branscombe, 2005). They then answered questions tapping support of violent solutions to conflict. In the MS condition and the "Holocaust as a crime against the Jewish people" condition, support of violence was significantly higher compared with the pain salience condition and the "Holocaust as a crime against humanity" condition. These results suggest that describing the Holocaust as a crime against the Jewish people led to effects similar to MS. However, framing the Holocaust as a crime against humanity reduced support for violent solutions to ethno–political conflict, probably because such portrayal of the Holocaust induced a sense of common humanity.

Another series of studies demonstrated that compassionate religious teachings moderate the impact of MS on support for violence against an adversary among Christian fundamentalists in the United States and Shiite Muslims in Iran (Rothschild, Abdollahi, & Pyszczynski, 2008). In both cases, MS led to greater support of violence against the other after reading a neutral text and even after reading about nonbiblical compassionate values. However, after reading about the compassionate teachings of Jesus or the compassionate teachings from the Koran, MS led participants to significantly reduce their support of violence against the other.

Research has also shown that feelings of security in close relationships reduce support for violence (see Chapters 13 and 14). On this basis, Weise and his colleagues (2008) primed American participants with thoughts of death and then asked them to visualize a warm and accepting personal relationship. Results revealed that the effect of MS on support for harsh counterterrorism measures was reduced after participants thought about close personal relationships. Similarly, in a study conducted on an Israeli sample (Hirschberger, Arias Ben-Tal, Pyszczynski, & Ein-Dor, 2009), participants had to write a brief comment following MS about a sketch of a woman breastfeeding her child (attachment security condition) or about a sketch of a group of women working in a field (neutral condition). They were then asked to rate their approval of military force against the Hamas in Gaza. The effect of MS on support for military force was significant in the neutral condition but not in the attachment security condition.

CONCLUSIONS

The conflict in the Middle East that currently involves Israel, Arab nations, Iran, Europe, and the United States is concerned with disputes over land, water, oil, terrorism, occupation, historical rights, and religious promises. These important reasons notwithstanding, we have suggested in this chapter that human existential concerns also contribute to the perpetuation of this conflict and the inability to reach a peaceful solution. We have reviewed research that sheds light on the underlying mechanisms that transform unobtrusive, brief reminders of personal mortality into powerful motives to subdue an enemy. We demonstrated that perceived consensus, belief in a just cause, and belief that war is inevitable are powerful catalysts that amplify the impact of mortality concerns on support for violent solutions to conflict. However, we also demonstrated that when people focus on the personal price they might pay in a war, when they perceive the adversary as harboring less malevolent intentions, and when they are induced to think rationally MS has a strikingly different effect and leads to reduced motivation for violence. Moreover, when people think of their common humanity with others, focus on compassionate religious teachings, or feel secure in their relationships the effect of MS on support for violence is diminished.

To achieve peace in the Middle East, all involved parties will have to make painful compromises on the concrete issues at stake, but they will also have to change the way they think about their adversaries and transform the symbolic belief structures that contribute to the perpetuation of violence. We have shown here that deep-seated existential concerns lie at the heart of violent conflicts and render them resistant to change. However, our research also suggests that the path to real change and to peace requires that, as people and as nations, we confront our deepest fears with courage rather than denying them. Although many political plans for peace have been proposed over the years, none has been successful. Perhaps in addition to diplomacy and compromises aimed at producing a just resolution of the conflict, policies aimed at changing the psychological forces that promote hatred to those that promote peace are needed to involve in the process of peacemaking people on all sides of the conflict.

REFERENCES

Abdollahi, A., Henthorn, C., & Pyszczynski, T. (2009). Experimental peace psychology: Priming consensus mitigates aggression against out-groups under mortality salience. *Behavioral Sciences of Terrorism and Political Aggression, 2*, 30–37.

Altemeyer, B. (1981). *Right-wing authoritarianism.* Winnipeg, Canada: University of Manitoba Press.

Arndt, J., Greenberg, J., Schimel, J., Pyszczynski, T., & Solomon, S. (2002). To belong or not to belong, that is the question: Terror management and identification with gender and ethnicity. *Journal of Personality and Social Psychology, 83*, 26–43. doi:10.1037/0022-3514.83.1.26

Baumeister, R. F., & Butz, J. (2005). Roots of hate, violence, and evil. In R. J. Sternberg (Ed.), *The psychology of hate* (pp. 87–102). Washington, DC: American Psychological Association. doi:10.1037/10930-005

Bueno de Mesquita, B. (1988). The contribution of expected utility theory to the study of international conflict. *The Journal of Interdisciplinary History, 18*, 629–652. doi:10.2307/204818

Castano, E. (2004). In case of death, cling to the ingroup. *European Journal of Social Psychology, 34*, 375–384. doi:10.1002/ejsp.211

Clausewitz, C. V. (1976). *On war* (M. Howard & P. Paret, Eds. &Trans.). Princeton, NJ: Princeton University Press.

Dechesne, M., Greenberg, J., Arndt, J., & Schimel, J. (2000). Terror management and the vicissitudes of sports fan affiliation: The effects of mortality salience on optimism and fan identification. *European Journal of Social Psychology, 30*, 813–835. doi:10.1002/1099-0992(200011/12)30:6<813::AID-EJSP17>3.0.CO;2-M

Florian, V., & Mikulincer, M. (1998). Terror management in childhood: Does death conceptualization moderate the effects of mortality salience on acceptance of similar and different others? *Personality and Social Psychology Bulletin, 24*, 1104–1112. doi:10.1177/01461672982410007

Greenberg, J., Pyszczynski, T., & Solomon, S. (1997). Terror management theory of self-esteem and cultural worldviews: Empirical assessments and conceptual refinements. In M. P. Zanna (Ed.), *Advances in experimental social psychology* (Vol. 29, pp. 61–139). San Diego, CA: Academic Press.

Greenberg, J., Pyszczynski, T., Solomon, S., Rosenblatt, A., Veeder, M., Kirkland, S., & Lyon, D. (1990). Evidence for terror management theory II: The effects of mortality salience on reactions to those who threaten or bolster the cultural worldview. *Journal of Personality and Social Psychology, 58*, 308–318. doi:10.1037/0022-3514.58.2.308

Greenberg, J., Pyszczynski, T., Solomon, S., Simon, L., & Breus, M. (1994). The role of consciousness and accessibility of death related thoughts in mortality salience effects. *Journal of Personality and Social Psychology, 67*, 627–637. doi:10.1037/0022-3514.67.4.627

Greenberg, J., Schimel, J., Martens, A., Pyszczynski, T., & Solomon, S. (2001). Sympathy for the devil: Evidence that reminding whites of their mortality promotes more favorable reactions to white racists. *Motivation and Emotion, 25*, 113–133. doi:10.1023/A:1010613909207

Greenberg, J., Simon, L., Porteus, J., Pyszczynski, T., & Solomon, S. (1995). Evidence of a terror management function of cultural icons: The effects of mortality salience on the inappropriate use of cherished cultural symbols. *Personality and Social Psychology Bulletin, 21*, 1221–1228. doi:10.1177/01461672952111010

Greenberg, J., Simon, L., Pyszczynski, T., Solomon, S., & Chatel, D. (1992). Terror management and tolerance: Does mortality salience always intensify negative reactions to others who threaten one's worldview? *Journal of Personality and Social Psychology, 63*, 212–220. doi:10.1037/0022-3514.63.2.212

Hirschberger, G. (2006). Terror management and attributions of blame to innocent victims: Reconciling compassionate and defensive responses. *Journal of Personality and Social Psychology, 91*, 832–844. doi:10.1037/0022-3514.91.5.832

Hirschberger, G., Arias Ben-Tal, K., Pyszczynski, T., & Ein-Dor, T. (2009). *Peace and psychological security: Evidence that security primes moderate the impact of mortality salience on violent inclinations.* Unpublished manuscript, Interdisciplinary Center (IDC) Herzliya, Israel.

Hirschberger, G., & Ein-Dor, T. (2006). Defenders of a lost cause: Terror management and violent resistance to the disengagement plan. *Personality and Social Psychology Bulletin, 32*, 761–769. doi:10.1177/0146167206286628

Hirschberger, G., Pyszczynski, T., Canetti, D., & Ein-Dor, T. (2009). *Never again: Evidence that reminders of the holocaust elicit support for violent solutions to contemporary conflicts.* Unpublished manuscript Interdisciplinary Center (IDC) Herzliya, Israel.

Hirschberger, G., Pyszczynski, T., & Ein-Dor, T. (2009a). *The commonalities and differences between group mortality and individual mortality: A terror management perspective on past victimization effects.* Unpublished manuscript, Bar-Ilan University, Ramat-Gan, Israel.

Hirschberger, G., Pyszczynski, T., & Ein-Dor, T. (2009b). *Death and the deliverance of justice: Mortality salience increases support for vindictive yet inefficient violent retributions.* Unpublished manuscript, Interdisciplinary Center (IDC) Herzliya, Israel.

Hirschberger, G., Pyszczynski, T., & Ein-Dor, T. (2009c). Vulnerability and vigilance: Threat awareness and perceived adversary intent moderate the impact of mortality salience on intergroup violence. *Personality and Social Psychology* Bulletin, 35, 597–607. doi:10.1177/0146167208331093

Landau, M. J., Johns, M., Greenberg, J., Pyszczynski, T., Martens, A., Goldenberg, J. L., & Solomon, S. (2004). A function of form: Terror management and structuring the social world. *Journal of Personality and Social Psychology, 87*, 190–210. doi:10.1037/0022-3514.87.2.190

Landau, M. J., Solomon, S., Greenberg, J., Cohen, F., Pyszczynski, T., Arndt, J., . . . Cook, A. (2004). Deliver us from evil: The effects of mortality salience and reminders of 9/11 on support for president George W. Bush. *Personality and Social Psychology Bulletin, 30,* 1136–1150. doi:10.1177/0146167204267988

McGregor, H., Lieberman, J. D., Solomon, S., Greenberg, J., Arndt, J., Simon, L., & Pyszczynski, T. (1998). Terror management and aggression: Evidence that mortality salience motivates aggression against worldview threatening others. *Journal of Personality and Social Psychology, 74,* 590–605. doi:10.1037/0022-3514. 74.3.590

Pyszczynski, T., Abdollahi, A., Solomon, S., Greenberg, J., Cohen, F., & Weise, D. (2006). Mortality salience, martyrdom, and military might: The great Satan versus the axis of evil. *Personality and Social Psychology Bulletin, 32,* 525–537. doi:10.1177/0146167205282157

Pyszczynski, T., Greenberg, J., & Solomon, S. (1999). A dual process model of defense against conscious and unconscious death-related thoughts: An extension of terror management theory. *Psychological Review, 106,* 835–845. doi:10.1037/ 0033-295X.106.4.835

Pyszczynski, T., Solomon, S., & Greenberg, J. (2003). *In the wake of 9/11: The psychology of terror.* Washington, DC: American Psychological Association. doi:10.1037/ 10478-000

Rothschild, Z. K., Abdollahi, A., & Pyszczynski, T. (2008). *Does peace have a prayer? The effect of mortality salience, compassionate values, and religious fundamentalism on hostility toward ourgroups.* Manuscript submitted for publication, University of Colorado at Colorado Springs.

Routledge, C., & Arndt, J. (2008). Self-sacrifice as self-defense: Mortality salience increases efforts to affirm a symbolic immortal self at the expense of the physical self. *European Journal of Social Psychology, 38,* 531–541. doi:10.1002/ejsp.442

Webster, D., & Kruglanski, A. (1994). Individual differences in need for cognitive closure. *Journal of Personality and Social Psychology, 67,* 1049–1062. doi:10.1037 /0022-3514.67.6.1049

Weise, D. R., Pyszczynski, T., Cox, C., Arndt, J., Greenberg, J., Solomon, S., & Kosloff, S. (2008). Interpersonal politics: The role of terror management and attachment processes in shaping political processes. *Psychological Science, 19,* 448–455. doi:10.1111/j.1467-9280.2008.02108.x

Welch, D. (1993). *Justice and the genesis of war.* Cambridge, England: Cambridge University Press. doi:10.1017/CBO9780511521805

Wohl, M. J. A., & Branscombe, N. R. (2005). Forgiveness and collective guilt assignment to historical perpetrator groups depend on level of social category inclusiveness. *Journal of Personality and Social Psychology, 88,* 288–303. doi:10.1037/ 0022-3514.88.2.288

17

THE EMOTIONAL ROOTS
OF INTERGROUP AGGRESSION:
THE DISTINCT ROLES OF ANGER
AND HATRED

ERAN HALPERIN

Prolonged intergroup conflicts are often marked by belligerent actions, provocative statements, and mutual insults. Notable examples are destructive terrorist attacks, the killing of innocent civilians, the kidnapping of citizens or soldiers, offensive maneuvers of military forces, and extremely threatening speeches by political and religious leaders. In most such cases, members of conflicting societies or groups view the conflict through a unidimensional, biased lens and therefore perceive the other group's actions as unjust, unfair, and incompatible with acceptable norms (White, 1970). Often these perceptions are amplified by blindness to the previous wrongdoings of one's own group, which are considered by the opponents to be the reasons for their current actions or statements (Bar-Tal & Halperin, 2010).

Given these biased appraisals, it is not surprising that intergroup anger is a pivotal emotion in every conflict (see Chapters 1 and 9 for cognitive analyses of anger arousal). Think for example of the emotional experiences of U.S. citizens who watched the televised 9/11 terrorist attacks on the World Trade Center almost as they were happening. Surely rage (among other emotions) was central to their experience. Similarly, it is not hard to imagine the rapid heartbeats, the sweaty palms and faces, and the extreme anger felt by Jewish

Israelis who sat down to a Passover dinner on March 27, 2002, and suddenly heard about the destructive suicide bombing at the Park Hotel in Netanya, which resulted in the deaths of 30 citizens dressed in festive holiday clothing. The main issue in this chapter is the role played by public anger in the U.S. decision to invade Iraq or in Israel's decision to initiate a large-scale military action against the Palestinians in March of 2002.

We know that emotions in general, and anger in particular, play a pivotal role in driving people to aggressive behavior (see Chapters 6 and 12). It has long been assumed in social psychology that anger is the most powerful emotional determinant of aggressive behavior (e.g., Berkowitz, 1993). Accordingly, there is evidence that flare-ups of public anger automatically lead to widespread support for vengeful aggression (Huddy, Feldman, & Cassese, 2007; Skitka, Bauman, Aramovich, & Morgan, 2006). In reality, however, despite the prevalence of ingroup anger following an outgroup provocation, public opinion is often divided about the best response (Maoz & McCauley, 2008). Some people clearly advocate an aggressive response, but others counsel self-restraint. These differences in opinion can be explained, at least in part, by differences in rational calculations concerning the costs and benefits of aggressive reactions. But I argue in this chapter that rational analyses are not sufficient to explain public opinion; in addition, a deeper understanding of the emotions involved in prolonged intergroup conflicts is needed.

Specifically, I contend that in the context of prolonged intergroup conflict, short-term anger generates public support for an aggressive response mainly if it is backed by long-term, extremely negative sentiments toward the opposing group. In other words, in the absence of long-term hatred for the outgroup (and especially when a degree of empathy exists), anger will not necessarily lead to support for aggression, and in some cases it may even lead to peaceful outcomes (Fischer & Roseman, 2007; Halperin, 2008b). Similarly, long-term hatred for an opponent will not necessarily cause aggression in the absence of an event that triggers explosive anger. That is, only the combined influences of short-term anger and long-term hatred are likely to produce strong support for large-scale aggression.

The next section provides basic concepts concerning emotions and emotional sentiments within the context of intergroup conflicts. This conceptual foundation is then followed by presentation of an appraisal-based model of emotions in intergroup conflicts. The model highlights relations among long-term emotional sentiments, short-term emotions, and attitudes about intergroup violence. I then review recent findings concerning the roles of anger and hatred in the context of the Middle-East conflict. Finally, I present new data gathered in that context to illustrate the joint effects of anger and hatred on support for intergroup violence.

EMOTIONS, SENTIMENTS, AND AGGRESSION: BASIC CONCEPTS

If we wish to understand the role of *emotion* in generating support for aggressive action in intergroup conflicts, we need a working definition of emotion. For this purpose, I accept William James's (1884) perspective on emotions as response tendencies. According to this view (as elaborated, for example, by Frijda, 1986, and Scherer, 1984), emotions are flexible response sequences evoked when a person evaluates a situation as offering important challenges or opportunities (Tooby & Cosmides, 1990). In other words, emotions transform a substantive event into a motive to respond to it in a particular manner (Zajonc, 1998).

Core components of emotion include subjective feelings, bodily changes, facial expressions, and other physiological reactions (Shaver, Schwartz, Kirson, & O'Connor, 1987). These components help to distinguish emotions from other psychological phenomena, such as attitudes or beliefs (Cacioppo & Gardner, 1999). Following Averill (1994), I view emotions as also comprising stories that help people interpret events and guide their behavioral reactions. This perspective highlights two additional components, cognitive appraisals and emotional goals that guide response tendencies, which I view as central to the links between emotions and support for intergroup aggression.

Extensive research has illuminated the role of cognitive appraisal in the generation of discrete emotions (e.g., Lazarus, 1991; Roseman, 1984; Scherer, 2004; Shaver et al., 1987; Smith & Ellsworth 1985). It is now well established that in most situations, emotions include an evaluation (either conscious or unconscious) of the emotion-eliciting stimulus or event that shapes a person's behavior during and after the event. In other words, a discrete emotion is likely to motivate support for aggressive behavior only if its associated cognitive appraisals correspond with the psychological preconditions for that kind of behavior.

The emotional behavior that one can observe from outside is thought to be the expression of what Frijda (1986; Frijda, Kuipers, & ter Schure, 1989) called "action tendencies." Roseman (1984) more specifically distinguished among actions, action tendencies, and emotional goals. Although actual behavior depends on numerous external factors and cannot usually be predicted by the arousal of specific emotions alone, the action tendencies and emotional goals associated with particular emotions are usually present (Frijda et al., 1989; Roseman, 2002). In this view, a discrete emotion such as anger will cause a person to support aggression against an outgroup only if he or she believes that a violent response will serve the goals activated by the emotion.

Emotions are just one of several kinds of affective responses (Gross, 2007). For the purposes of this chapter, it is important to distinguish between emotions and sentiments. As I have just explained, emotions are multicomponent responses to particular kinds of events. *Sentiments*, by contrast, are enduring configurations of emotions or emotional predispositions (Arnold, 1960; Frijda, 1986; Lazarus, 1994). According to this view, an emotional sentiment is a relatively stable emotional disposition toward a person, group, or symbol (Halperin, 2008a). Emotional sentiments also differ from another kind of affective state, *moods*, in that moods typically do not have well-defined objects (Oatley, Keltner, & Jenkins, 2006), whereas emotional sentiments do. In my view, as I explain in subsequent sections of this chapter, only a combination of a specific long-term sentiment and a momentarily triggered discrete emotion toward an outgroup will lead to support for intergroup aggression.

The emotional sentiments and emotions relevant to the present discussion reflect intergroup and not interpersonal phenomena. In recent years, there has been growing interest in the concept of *intergroup emotions*, emotions that are felt by individuals as a result of their membership in or identification with a certain group or society and are targeted toward another group (Iyer & Leach, 2008; Mackie, Devos, & Smith, 2000; Smith & Mackie, 2008). Research has shown that people may experience emotions not only in response to personal experiences and activities but also in response to events that affect other members of a group with which they identify or in response to activities in which other group members have taken part (Mackie et al., 2000; Smith, Seger, & Mackie, 2007; Wohl, Branscombe, & Klar, 2006; Yzerbyt, Dumont, Wigboldus, & Gordin, 2003). I want to focus here on ways in which events experienced only indirectly (although directly by other group members) elicit intergroup emotions toward an outgroup and thereby arouse support for aggressive political action toward that outgroup.

I adopt a *bottom-up* perspective, according to which emotions, attitudes, and actions of individuals and groups influence the course of a conflict. At least in democratic societies, public support for aggressive retaliation to outgroup provocations can encourage political leaders to initiate military actions. This "psychology of the people" is especially important in the context of intractable conflicts, because such conflicts demand extensive societal investment and are often perceived by both sides as total and zero sum (Bar-Tal, 1998; Kriesberg, 1993).

The nature of these conflicts makes it likely that sentiments will be established that extend way beyond any immediate provocative event. The combination of repeated events over a long period of time and repeated rehashing of these events in the media is likely to result in stable group-related emotional sentiments, such as hatred or despair, toward the opponent and the continuing conflict (Kelman & Fisher, 2003). The interaction between these emotional sentiments and the emotions that arise in response to particular events, as well as their joint influence on support for aggression, can be understood in terms of emotion-related appraisals.

EMOTIONS AND AGGRESSION IN INTERGROUP CONFLICT: AN APPRAISAL-BASED MODEL

The model in Figure 17.1 shows how exposure to a particular conflict-related event is processed and transformed into support for certain political and military actions. The model has been tested among Israeli Jews and found to be valid and analytically useful (Halperin, 2008a). According to the model, the link between exposure to a conflict-related event and a person's attitude concerning the required response to the outgroup is mediated by a discrete emotional response elicited by the event. In turn, this emotional response is influenced by the individual's long-term emotional sentiments toward the outgroup (Halperin, Sharvit, & Gross, 2010). The model is sufficiently general to capture processes initiated by various conflict-related events, including positive events (e.g., a new peace proposal) or negative ones (e.g., a terror attack). In the current chapter, however, I use the model to explain how a

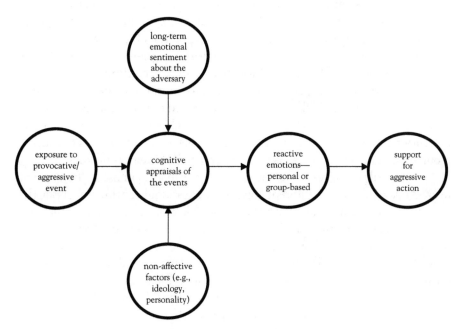

Figure 17.1. An appraisal-based framework for understanding the influence of emotions on support for aggressive action.

discrete emotional reaction to outgroup provocation determines whether a person will support an aggressive response.

The process begins with a particular event or with the arrival of new information related to the conflict. Although events can be experienced personally, in most cases they are experienced directly by only a few group members and transmitted to other group members through leaders, the mass media, or one or more social networks. If a person identifies with the same group as the directly affected individuals, he or she will experience group-based emotions (Mackie et al., 2000; Smith, 1993; Yzerbyt et al., 2003).

Such events will elicit individual and group-based emotions and the ensuing political response tendencies, depending on how the events are appraised. For example, if a violent act committed by outgroup members against one or more members of the ingroup is appraised as unjust and is accompanied by appraisal of the ingroup as strong, it will induce anger (Halperin, 2008b; Huddy et al., 2007; Shaver et al., 1987). Hence, the cognitive appraisal of an event is a crucial factor in determining the kind of emotion that will be evoked by the event.

When an event occurs in the context of a long-term conflict, the appraisal of the event is influenced by three sets of factors: (a) the way in which the event is presented to the public (i.e., the framing of the event by leaders and media reporters); (b) a broad array of nonaffective factors, such as ideology, personality, moral values, and implicit schemas or theories (e.g., Halperin, 2008a; Sharvit, Halperin, & Rosler, 2008); and (c) most important, a set of long-term emotional sentiments that bias the cognitive appraisal of specific events.

The importance of this last set of factors is explained by the *appraisal tendency framework* of Lerner and Keltner (2000), according to which each emotion activates a cognitive predisposition to interpret future events in line with the central appraisal dimensions that triggered the emotion. For example, long-term external threats to one's group are likely to cause bouts of fear and insecurity, and these emotions encourage longer-term sentiments that cause group members to be more sensitive to potentially threatening cues.

This analysis suggests that the same event can be appraised differently by individuals who harbor different long-term emotional sentiments about the opponent. Furthermore, although it is reasonable to assume that a hostile, violent event such as a terror attack or a kidnapping of innocent civilians will elicit strong anger in all members of the victimized society, the nature of that anger as well as its associated political response tendencies will differ depending on the level of long-term hatred felt by an individual toward the opponent (Halperin, Sharvit, et al., 2010). To fully appreciate this analysis, it is necessary to understand the psychological preconditions that support aggressive action and to understand the correspondence between these preconditions and the unique nature of each kind of emotional phenomenon (hatred or anger).

INTERGROUP AGGRESSION: NECESSARY PRECONDITIONS

The most important preconditions for intergroup conflict and intergroup aggression are a perceived conflict of interest between the groups and perception of a long-term threat posed by the outgroup (Maoz & McCauley, 2008; Struch & Schwartz, 1989). Yet in the majority of cases, conflict of interest or even perceived threat alone will not bring about violence in the absence of an immediate provocation.

In terms of the more immediate antecedents of intergroup aggression, it seems that public support for aggression and violence results, in most cases, from a shared belief that the outgroup committed a grievous, unjust action (or made a provocative, unfair statement) aimed at the ingroup (see Chapter 16). To be an adequate trigger of violence, the action or statement must usually be perceived as an extreme deviation from moral norms and a notable deviation from the routine (hence acceptable) reciprocal intergroup hostility.

A second precondition for supporting aggressive action is perceiving the ingroup as strong enough to overpower the outgroup in a future military battle. (See Chapter 3 for a similar analysis at the interpersonal level, and Chapter 16 for a similar analysis at the intergroup level.) This perception of strength and controllability provides the confidence necessary to undertake aggressive action. Similar to the appraised sense of relative power is a sense of willingness or eagerness to accept the risks involved in entering a violent battle. People who have a dispositional tendency to avoid risks are less likely to support a risky military campaign.

Finally, given the high probable costs (in resources, human lives, and international condemnation) of a belligerent campaign, many people will support them only as a last resort (see Chapter 16). In other words, most members who believe that their group is capable of correcting a perceived wrong without resorting to military action (e.g., by relying on diplomacy) will oppose the use of military power, at least for the time being. Moreover, in most cases, public support for an aggressive response to an outgroup's provocation is highly dependent on believing that the outgroup action provocation stemmed from a stable, irreversible, and evil disposition central to the outgroup members' character. If this is not the case, other paths of correction may be perceived as equally beneficial and much less costly than the aggressive one.

INTERGROUP ANGER AND HATRED: SIMILAR BUT DIFFERENT

I turn now to differences in the cognitive appraisals and behavioral tendencies associated with anger and hatred. In a series of studies of the Israeli–Palestinian conflict, I attempted to uncover the unique cognitive and motivational components of each of these two affective phenomena (Halperin, 2008b). In one of the studies (Study 2), 241 Israeli students read about a particular conflict-related event (e.g., a terror attack), followed by a short description of the way the protagonist in each account (an ingroup member) appraised the event. They were then asked to name the emotions experienced by the protagonist in relation to the event.

Both anger and hatred were associated with blaming the outgroup for the conflict-related event and with appraising the outgroup's behavior as unpleasant, hurtful, and contrary to the ingroup's interests and goals. Nevertheless, in line with previous theoretical writings about anger and hatred (e.g., Ben-Zeev, 1992; Royzman, McCauley, & Rozin, 2005; Sternberg, 2003), there was also a clear distinction between the appraisals associated with each of these phenomena. The negative appraisals associated with anger focused solely on unfairness of the outgroup's specific action, whereas the appraisals associated with hatred focused on the nature of the outgroup itself, suggesting that its actions were not aimed at achieving instrumental goals but stemmed from a malevolent disposition to hurt the ingroup.

Important as they may be, cognitive appraisals are just one part of the emotion process. It is well established that the appraisals associated with each emotion underpin the unique content of its corresponding motivational tendencies; these action tendencies are a logical response to the "diagnosis" of the problematic situation inherent in the appraisals (e.g., Frijda et al., 1989). For example, fear aroused by seeing a tiger about to attack leads to running away or hiding behind a barrier of some kind; but fear that one is about to miss the last train home leads to running toward the door of the train. Therefore, in another study (Halperin, 2008b, Study 3) I examined the emotional goals and response tendencies that are associated with anger and hatred in the context of intergroup conflict.

Specifically, I created a simple conflict-related scenario to be presented to 313 Israeli interviewees in a national-representative sample, asking these people to rank the level of each of several emotional reactions (i.e., hatred, anger), emotional goals, and response tendencies as reactions to the scenario. In a subsequent analysis of the data, I regressed each of two reactions (i.e., anger, hatred) on the emotional goals and response tendencies while controlling for sociopolitical variables (e.g., political position, educational level).

As expected, there were interesting dissimilarities between anger and hatred. Hatred was the only emotion associated with the goals of exclusion (i.e., removing outgroup members from one's life) and attack (i.e., hurting the outgroup members). However, anger was associated with the goal of correction (i.e., improving the behavior of outgroup members). Thus, whereas anger causes people to take action to right a specific wrong (see Chapters 4, 13, and 14, for similar analyses of anger), hatred reflects avoidance of any dealings with the outgroup based on having given up on the outgroup's capacity for change.

The findings regarding the response tendencies associated with hatred and anger were complex. Naturally, participants who reported relatively high levels of hatred were more likely to support "denying Palestinians' basic political and social rights" as well as "physical and violent actions toward the Palestinians." It is interesting that although anger was also associated with support for "physical and violent actions toward the Palestinians," it was associated as well with "support for educational channels to create perceptual change among Palestinians." This latter response was obviously a more constructive approach to changing the Palestinians' (perceived) unjust behavior.

It seems, based on my research and previous studies by other researchers, that people who feel angry have one key emotional goal: They wish to correct and redirect behavior that they perceive to have been unfair and unjustified. Researchers have documented that when people feel angry, they believe they have (or at least deserve to have) high control over the situation, are more willing to take risks, and believe they have the ability to create beneficial changes (Lerner, Gonzalez, Small, & Fischhoff, 2003; Lerner & Keltner, 2001; Mackie et al., 2000; see also Chapters 3, 4, and 12, this volume). These components of anger correspond with the first three psychological preconditions required to support aggression, discussed earlier in this chapter. And indeed, previous studies have shown that anger motivates confrontation (Berkowitz, 1993), attack, and even killing the elicitor of anger (Roseman, Wiest, & Swartz, 1994).

Yet observations of the response tendencies associated with anger, as well as findings from a study by Fischer and Roseman (2007), indicate that although some angry people choose aggression and destruction as responses, others choose more constructive responses such as education and efforts to achieve reconciliation. An interesting question, therefore, is what leads some angry individuals to choose aggression and others to choose a constructive response. As I explain in the next section, the most important factor moderating the effect of anger on aggressive behavior is the level of long-term hatred. Viewing an outgroup as inherently evil and unlikely to reform undermines any consideration of seeking constructive change.

THE INTERACTION OF ANGER AND HATRED AND SUPPORT FOR INTERGROUP AGGRESSION

As already mentioned, much of the research literature points to the conclusion that anger is the most important and proximal emotional antecedent of aggressive political action (Cheung-Blunden & Blunden, 2008; Huddy et al.,

2007; Lerner et al., 2003; Skitka et al., 2006). However, the findings I have summarized here suggest that anger interacts with hatred to fuel aggression. This conclusion is supported by recent studies of associations between intergroup emotions and political intolerance. Political intolerance is usually defined as the willingness to deny the political rights of out-group members (Sullivan, Piereson, & Marcus, 1979). This willingness is commonly viewed as a political version of aggressive intentions toward the outgroup, so it is important for understanding the emotional underpinnings of intergroup aggression.

Two studies, one conducted in the post-9/11 period in the United States (Skitka, Bauman, & Mullen, 2004) and the other in the midst of the second Palestinian uprising in the Middle East (Halperin, Canetti-Nisim, & Hirsch-Hoefler, 2009), reveal similar patterns of political intolerance related to anger and hatred. In a two-wave national field study ($N = 550$), Skitka et al. (2004) examined the effects of anger and fear on political intolerance toward Arab Americans, Muslims, and first-generation immigrants 4 months after the terror attacks of 9/11. They found that anger had no direct influence on political intolerance and that most of the indirect effect of anger on intolerance was mediated by moral outrage and outgroup derogation. Unfortunately, hatred of the outgroup was not measured as a separate variable in this study, but arguably, moral outrage and outgroup derogation might be proxies of hatred.

In a more direct examination of the roles played by anger and hatred in political intolerance, my colleagues and I (Halperin, Canetti-Nisim, et al., 2009) conducted four surveys of large representative samples of Israeli Jews. The surveys varied in their design (two panel surveys and two cross sectional surveys), their context (some of the surveys were conducted during war and others at times of relative calm in the conflict between Israelis and Arabs), and the political intolerance measures used ("most disliked group" vs. "Palestinians" as the defined outgroup). The results of the different surveys were essentially the same: Anger toward the outgroup led to political intolerance only if it was supported by hatred. Furthermore, in some cases anger in the absence of hatred was associated with reduced political intolerance.

In search of even more direct support for my growing understanding of the interplay of anger and hatred, I examined survey-based data sets in which explicit measures of support for military action were among the dependent variables. The first analysis was based on a nationwide representative telephone survey conducted among Israeli Jews in March of 2008. The sample consisted of 781 Jewish-Israeli respondents (403 women, 378 men). The reported political affiliation of participants in the survey mirrored the distribution in Israeli society at the time: 37.3% were identified as rightists, 45.2% as centrists, and 17.6% as leftists.

Among other items, the questionnaire included one assessing long-term hatred of Palestinians, two items (i.e., anger and rage) capturing anger about

Palestinian actions, and two items concerning support for aggressive actions against Palestinians (i.e., "In a time of significant Palestinian threat, Israel should use unconventional warfare"; "Only by using force can you achieve anything in the Middle East"). For all of these items, participants used a 6-point response scale ranging from 1 (*not at all*) to 6 (*very much*).

Support for aggressive action toward Palestinians was regressed on hatred, anger, and the interaction of the two while controlling for sociopolitical variables (e.g., political position, educational level). No main effect of anger ($\beta = -.10$) or hatred ($\beta = -.17$) was found, but their interaction was significant ($\beta = .40$, $p < .05$). As shown in Figure 17.2, anger was associated with heightened support for aggressive actions only in the presence of long-term hatred.

Given the provocative nature of the findings, replication of the results was called for. Therefore, I examined data from another nationwide survey conducted in Israel during August and September of 2008. This sample included 500 respondents, of whom 48.4% were men and 51.6% women. The mean age was 45.5 years ($SD = 16.49$), and 41% of the respondents defined themselves as rightists, 28.9% as centrists, and 18.3% as leftists. Socio-demographic measures and scales assessing anger and hatred were similar to the ones used in the previous survey. Support for military action was measured in a slightly different way, with two items: support for initiating a large military operation of the Israeli army and support for using severe military action, even if it meant harming innocent civilians ($\alpha = .74$).

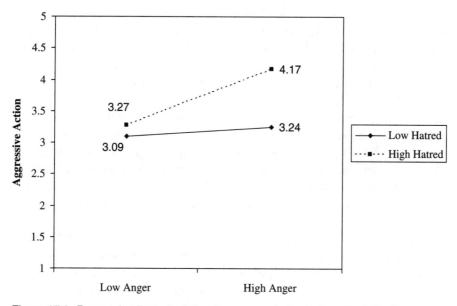

Figure 17.2. Regression lines depicting the anger × hatred interaction affecting support for aggressive action toward Palestinians in the first nationwide survey ($N = 781$).

Again, support for aggressive action against Palestinians was regressed on hatred, anger, and their interaction, while controlling for sociopolitical variables. Except for minor dissimilarities in the effects of sociopolitical variables on support for aggressive action, the findings replicated those of the first survey. There was no main effect of anger ($\beta = -.04$) or hatred ($\beta = -.11$) on support for aggression, but their interaction was significant ($\beta = .45, p < .01$). Again, only the combination of anger and hatred was significantly associated with support for aggressive action.

CONCLUSION

Protracted intergroup conflicts inherently include mutual provocations, violent responses, and diverse transgressions by both parties to the conflict. As a result, members of societies involved in such conflicts experience frequent episodes of anger toward the outgroup, its leaders, and its representatives. This anger, in various degrees, is an inevitable element of every intergroup conflict. The research literature on emotions occurring in the context of conflict shows that anger evoked by an antagonist's behavior is highly associated with support for retaliatory aggression (Huddy et al., 2007; Skitka et al., 2006). In turn, widespread public support for aggression may legitimize and even encourage political decision makers to initiate large-scale military action (Zaller, 1994). This dynamic can easily escalate into a vicious cycle of reciprocal violence that causes a tragic loss of life on both sides of the conflict. However, the theoretical model and the bulk of empirical data presented in this chapter suggest that the seemingly direct link between anger and the cycle of violence is not unavoidable.

The link between anger and support for aggression is dependent on the level of hatred one feels for the outgroup. Anger in the absence of hatred, even though it may have been triggered by appraisals of the outgroup's behavior as painful and unjust, can arouse a desire to correct the wrongdoing without necessarily harming or destroying the outgroup (Fischer & Roseman, 2007). Anger that emerges on top of prolonged hatred, often combined with an appraisal of the outgroup as inherently evil and unlikely to change, is likely to arouse support for aggressive retaliation unchecked by empathy with members of the outgroup.

Another implication of this analysis is that despite prolonged hatred of the outgroup, members of the ingroup may not be motivated to engage in large-scale aggression if their goals are not shifted in that direction by a spike in anger. This is because hatred by itself lacks the anger-related sense of power and self-righteousness that makes aggression seem possible as well as justified.

The analysis of anger's role that I have sketched here suggests a need for studies that identify moderating factors that can reduce the destructive effects of hatred and anger. Possibilities include other emotional sentiments such as despair, empathy, or compassion, but also relevant are personality factors (e.g., authoritarianism, need for structure, attachment security), implicit theories about individuals and groups, adherence to moral values, socioeconomic status, and political ideology.

I hope I have made readers more aware of the role of intergroup emotions as influences on public opinion, political decision making, and intergroup violence. More research is needed on ways to down-regulate "destructive emotions" (Goleman, 2003; Halperin, Sharvit, & Gross, in press), up-regulate more prosocial emotions (Mikulincer & Shaver, 2009), and identify other emotional sentiments and dispositions that might be used to foster more favorable interactions with various emotions. In the long run, basic and applied research along these lines may contribute to a reduction in retaliatory aggression.

REFERENCES

Arnold, M. B. (1960). *Emotion and personality* (Vols. 1 & 2). New York, NY: Columbia University Press.

Averill, J. R. (1994). In the eyes of the beholder. In P. Ekman & R. J. Davidson (Eds.), *The nature of emotion: Fundamental questions* (pp. 7–15). New York, NY: Oxford University Press.

Bar-Tal, D. (1998). Societal beliefs in times of intractable conflict: The Israeli case. *The International Journal of Conflict Management, 9*, 22–50. doi:10.1108/eb022803

Bar-Tal, D., & Halperin, E. (2009). Overcoming psychological barriers to peace making: The influence of mediating beliefs about losses. In M. Mikulincer & P. R. Shaver (Eds.), *Prosocial motives, emotions, and behavior The better angels of our nature* (pp. 431–448). Washington, DC: American Psychological Association.

Bar-Tal, D., & Halperin, E. (2010). Socio-psychological barriers to conflict resolution. In D. Bar-Tal (Ed.), *Intergroup conflicts and their resolution: Social psychological perspective*. New York, NY: Psychology Press.

Ben-Zeev, A. (1992). Anger and hate. *Journal of Social Philosophy, 2*, 85–110. doi:10.1111/j.1467-9833.1992.tb00295.x

Berkowitz, L. (1993). *Aggression: Its causes, consequences, and control*. Philadelphia, PA: Temple University Press.

Cacioppo, J. T., & Gardner, W. L. (1999). Emotion. *Annual Review of Psychology, 50*, 191–214. doi:10.1146/annurev.psych.50.1.191

Cheung-Blunden, V., & Blunden, B. (2008). The emotional construal of war: Anger, fear, and other negative emotions. *Peace and Conflict, 14*, 123–150. doi:10.1080/10781910802017289

Fischer, A. H., & Roseman, I. J. (2007). Beat them or ban them: The characteristics and social functions of anger and contempt. *Journal of Personality and Social Psychology, 93,* 103–115. doi:10.1037/0022-3514.93.1.103

Frijda, N. H. (1986). *The emotions.* Cambridge, England: Cambridge University Press.

Frijda, N. H., Kuipers, P., & ter Schure, E. (1989). Relations among emotion, appraisal, and emotional action readiness. *Journal of Personality and Social Psychology, 57,* 212–228. doi:10.1037/0022-3514.57.2.212

Goleman, D. (2003). *Destructive emotions: How can we overcome them?* New York, NY: Bantam Dell.

Gross, J. J. (Ed.). (2007). *Handbook of emotion regulation.* New York, NY: Guilford Press.

Halperin, E. (2008a). *Emotional barriers to peace: Negative emotions and public opinion about the peace process in the Middle East.* Paper presented at the 31st annual meeting of the International Society of Political Psychology, Paris, France.

Halperin, E. (2008b). Group-based hatred in intractable conflict in Israel. *The Journal of Conflict Resolution, 52,* 713–736. doi:10.1177/0022002708314665

Halperin, E., Canetti-Nisim, D., & Hirsch-Hoefler, S. (2009). Emotional antecedents of political intolerance: The central role of group-based hatred. *Political Psychology, 30,* 93–123. doi:10.1111/j.1467-9221.2008.00682.x

Halperin, E., Sharvit, K., Gross, J. J. (2010). Emotions and emotion regulation in conflicts. In D. Bar-Tal (Ed.), *Intergroup conflicts and their resolution: Social psychological perspective.* New York, NY: Psychology Press.

Huddy, L., Feldman, S., & Cassese, E. (2007). On the distinct political effects of anxiety and anger. In A. Crigler, M. MacKuen, G. Marcus, & W. R. Neuman (Eds.), *The dynamics of emotion in political thinking and behavior* (pp. 202–230). Chicago, IL: Chicago University Press.

Iyer, A., & Leach, C. W. (2008). Emotion in inter-group relations. *European Review of Social Psychology, 19,* 86–125. doi:10.1080/10463280802079738

James, W. (1884). What is an emotion? *Mind, os-IX,* 188–205. doi:10.1093/mind/os-IX.34.188

Kelman, H. C., & Fisher, R. J. (2003). Conflict analysis and resolution. In D. O. Sears, L. Huddy, & R. Jervis (Eds.), *Oxford handbook of political psychology* (pp. 315–353). New York, NY: Oxford University Press.

Kriesberg, L. (1993). Intractable conflict. *Peace Review, 5,* 417–421.

Lazarus, R. S. (1991). *Emotion and adaptation.* New York, NY: Oxford University Press.

Lazarus, R. S. (1994). Universal antecedents of the emotions. In P. Ekman & R. J. Davidson (Eds.), *The nature of emotion: Fundamental questions* (pp. 163–171). New York, NY: Oxford University Press.

Lerner, J. S., Gonzalez, R. M., Small, D. A., & Fischhoff, B. (2003). Effects of fear and anger on perceived risk of terrorism: A national field experiment. *Psychological Science, 14,* 144–150.

Lerner, J. S., & Keltner, D. (2000). Beyond valence: Toward a model of emotion-specific influences on judgment and choice. *Cognition and Emotion, 14*, 473–493. doi:10.1080/026999300402763

Lerner, J. S., & Keltner, D. (2001). Fear, anger, and risk. *Journal of Personality and Social Psychology, 81*, 1 146-1159.

Mackie, D. M., Devos, T., & Smith, E. R. (2000). Intergroup emotions: Explaining offensive actions in an intergroup context. *Journal of Personality and Social Psychology, 79*, 602–616. doi:10.1037/0022-3514.79.4.602

Maoz, I., & McCauley, C. (2008). Threat, dehumanization and support for retaliatory-aggressive policies in asymmetric conflict. *The Journal of Conflict Resolution, 52*, 93–116. doi:10.1177/0022002707308597

Mikulincer, M., & Shaver, P. R. (Eds.). (2009). *Prosocial motives, emotions, and behavior: The better angels of our nature.* Washington, DC: American Psychological Association.

Oatley, K., Keltner, D., & Jenkins, J. M. (2006). *Understanding emotions* (2nd ed.). Maldin, MA: Blackwell.

Roseman, I. J. (1984). Cognitive determinants of emotions: A structural theory. In P. R. Shaver (Ed.), *Review of personality and social psychology* (Vol. 5, pp. 11–36). Beverly Hills, CA: Sage.

Roseman, I. J. (2002). Dislike, anger, and contempt: Interpersonal distancing, attack, and exclusion emotions. *Emotion Researcher, 16*, 5–6.

Roseman, I. J., Wiest, C., & Swartz, T. S. (1994). Phenomenology, behaviors, and goals differentiate discrete emotions. *Journal of Personality and Social Psychology, 67*, 206–221.

Royzman, E. B., McCauley, C., & Rozin, P. (2005). From Plato to Putnam: Four ways to think about hate. In R. J. Sternberg (Ed.), *The psychology of hate* (pp. 3–35). Washington, DC: American Psychological Association. doi:10.1037/10930-001

Scherer, K. R. (1984). Emotion as a multicomponent process: A model and some cross-cultural data. In P. R. Shaver (Ed.), *Review of personality and social psychology* (Vol. 5, pp. 37–63). Beverly Hills, CA: Sage.

Scherer, K. R. (2004). Feelings integrate the central representation of appraisal-driven response organization in emotion. In A. S. R. Manstead, N. Frijda, & A. Fischer (Eds.), *Feeling and emotions: The Amsterdam Symposium* (pp. 136–157). Cambridge, England: Cambridge University Press.

Sharvit, K., Halperin, E., & Rosler, N. (2008). *Forces of stability and change in prolonged occupation: Image threat, emotions, and justifying beliefs.* Paper presented at the 31st annual meeting of the International Society of Political Psychology, Paris, France.

Shaver, P. R., Schwartz, J., Kirson, D., & O'Connor, C. (1987). Emotion knowledge: Further exploration of a prototype approach. *Journal of Personality and Social Psychology, 52*, 1061–1086. doi:10.1037/0022-3514.52.6.1061

Skitka, L. J., Bauman, C. W., Aramovich, N. P., & Morgan, G. C. (2006). Confrontational and preventative policy responses to terrorism: Anger wants a fight and fear wants "them" to go away. *Basic and Applied Social Psychology, 28*, 375–384. doi:10.1207/s15324834basp2804_11

Skitka, L. J., Bauman, C. W., & Mullen, E. (2004). Political tolerance and coming to psychological closure following the September 11, 2001, terrorist attacks: An integrative approach. *Personality and Social Psychology Bulletin, 30*, 743–756. doi:10.1177/0146167204263968

Smith, C. A., & Ellsworth, P. C. (1985). Patterns of cognitive appraisal in emotions. *Journal of Personality and Social Psychology, 48*, 813–838. doi:10.1037/0022-3514. 48.4.813

Smith, E. R. (1993). Social identity and social emotions: Toward a new conceptualization of prejudice. In D. M. Mackie & D. L. Hamilton (Eds.), *Affect, cognition and stereotyping: Interactive processes in group perception* (pp. 297–315). San Diego, CA: Academic Press.

Smith, E. R., & Mackie, D. M. (2008). Intergroup emotions. In M. Lewis, J. M. Haviland-Jones, & L. F. Barrett (Eds.), *Handbook of emotions* (3rd ed., pp. 428–439). New York, NY: Guilford Press.

Smith, E. R., Seger, C. R., & Mackie, D. M. (2007). Can emotions be truly group level? Evidence for four conceptual criteria. *Journal of Personality and Social Psychology, 93*, 431–446. doi:10.1037/0022-3514.93.3.431

Sternberg, R. J. (2003). A duplex theory of hate: Development and application to terrorism, massacres, and genocide. *Review of General Psychology, 7*, 299–328. doi:10.1037/1089-2680.7.3.299

Struch, N., & Schwartz, S. H. (1989). Intergroup aggression: Its predictors and distinctness from in-group bias. *Journal of Personality and Social Psychology, 56*, 364–373. doi:10.1037/0022-3514.56.3.364

Sullivan, J. L., Piereson, J., & Marcus, G. E. (1979). An alternative conceptualization of political tolerance: Illusory increases 1950s–1970s. *The American Political Science Review, 73*, 781–794. doi:10.2307/1955404

Tooby, J., & Cosmides, L. (1990). The past explains the present: Emotional adaptations and the structure of ancestral environments. *Ethology and Sociobiology, 11*, 375–424. doi:10.1016/0162-3095(90)90017-Z

White, R. K. (1970). *Nobody wanted war: Misperception in Vietnam and other wars.* Garden City, NY: Anchor Books.

Wohl, M. J. A., Branscombe, N. R., & Klar, Y. (2006). Collective guilt: Emotional reactions when one's group has done wrong or been wronged. *European Review of Social Psychology, 17*, 1–37. doi:10.1080/10463280600574815

Yzerbyt, V., Dumont, M., Wigboldus, D., & Gordin, E. (2003). I feel for us: The impact of categorization and identification on emotions and action tendencies. *The British Journal of Social Psychology, 42*, 533–549. doi:10.1348/ 014466603322595266

Zajonc, R. B. (1998). Emotions. In D. Gilbert, S. T. Fiske, & G. Lindzey (Eds.), *The handbook of social psychology* (4th ed., Vol. 1, pp. 591–632). Boston, MA: McGraw-Hill.

Zaller, J. (1994). Strategic politicians, public opinion, and the Gulf crisis. In W. L. Bennett & D. L. Paletz (Eds.), *Taken by storm: The media, public opinion, and U.S. foreign policy in the Gulf War* (pp. 250–276). Chicago, IL: University of Chicago Press.

18

TENSION AND HARMONY
IN INTERGROUP RELATIONS

TAMAR SAGUY, NICOLE TAUSCH, JOHN F. DOVIDIO,
FELICIA PRATTO, AND PURNIMA SINGH

Aggression between groups is an extreme manifestation of inter-group tension (see Chapters 16 and 17). This form of tension can result in the killing and displacement of innocent people, the destruction of infra-structure and property, and setback in the process of reconciliation. There-fore, tension between groups has traditionally been viewed as categorically harmful. In sharp contrast, harmony between groups, which encompasses positive perceptions and orientations toward outgroup members, is often viewed as ideal. These categorical views of harmony as "good" and tension as "bad" have guided much thinking in the social sciences, as reflected in research on conflict resolution (Hewstone & Cairns, 2001), prejudice reduction (see Paluck & Green, 2009, for a review), and intergroup contact (Pettigrew, 1998). The primary goal in these areas of research has typically been to eliminate tension between groups and create harmony.

Nevertheless, not all forms of harmony are necessarily beneficial to intergroup relations (Jackman, 1994), and not all forms of intergroup tension

Preparation of this manuscript was supported by NSF Grant # BCS-0613218.

are inevitably destructive (Varshney, 2002). Particularly when the broader social context is taken into account, viewing harmony as good and tension as bad can be an oversimplification of the dynamics of intergroup relations. The context that often characterizes relations between groups is one of systematic inequality (e.g., Jews and Arabs in Israel, Blacks and Whites in the United States or South Africa, Muslims and Hindus in India, Muslims and non-Muslims in the United Kingdom). As exemplified by historical changes, societal tension can be quite constructive in creating pressure for changing unequal structures in the direction of equality. Social struggles such as those initiated by the U.S. civil rights movement or by the African National Congress in South Africa were aimed at disturbing apparent amity in order to "open the eyes of blind prejudice" (King, 1964, p. 35) and incite action for social justice (see Sharp, 2005).

Because the disruption of harmony is often necessary for stimulating change toward social equality, efforts to create harmony between groups may in fact work to undermine these potential changes (see Wright & Lubensky, 2009). Thus, interventions to create societal harmony can potentially have the ironic effect of sustaining negative patterns of intergroup relations, particularly those pertaining to group-based inequality. In the present chapter, we consider research on the effects of harmony-inducing strategies on psychological factors related to changes in group-based inequality.

Our emphasis is on the consequences of intergroup contact, which is psychology's most influential and frequently used strategy for creating harmony, or improving relations, between groups (Dovidio, Gaertner, & Kawakami, 2003; Pettigrew, 1998). In the majority of cases, intergroup contact is implemented to improve relations between members of groups that are unequal in the social system. Although it is well established that intergroup contact relates to improved attitudes toward outgroup members (Pettigrew & Tropp, 2006), little is known about the effect of contact and improved attitudes on factors that relate to social change toward equality. Our central argument is that because harmony undermines tension, and because tension is crucial for social change, a by-product of contact interventions may be the paradoxical stability of unequal social systems that interveners hoped to change.

This chapter is organized into three sections. In the first section, we focus on intergroup tension and discuss factors that can bring about change toward equality. In the second section, we consider how intergroup contact, as a strategy that aims to increase harmony, can work to undermine these factors. Finally, we present empirical evidence that converges on the conclusion that contact may reduce the potential for change. We discuss the implications of these results for intergroup relations in general and for intergroup hostility and aggression more specifically.

PREDICTORS OF SOCIAL CHANGE TOWARD EQUALITY

Our starting point is the assumption that social inequality is likely to remain stable insofar as group members do not oppose it. Therefore, when considering antecedents of social change, we focus on psychological processes that predict group members' motivations to resist the status quo. We begin by explicating who the likely agents of change are in a hierarchical system and then turn to consider the more specific psychological processes involved in the development of social actions that can increase equality.

Who Are the Likely Agents of Change? The Psychologies of Advantaged and Disadvantaged Group Members

Without exception, societies are hierarchically organized such that at least one group controls a greater share of valued resources (e.g., political power, land, economic wealth, educational opportunities, access to health care) than do other groups (Jackman, 2001; Sidanius & Pratto, 1999). Group-based hierarchy is reflected in almost every aspect of social life, from poverty rates and school attrition rates to prison sentences and mortality rates—favoring members of advantaged groups over those in disadvantaged groups (Feagin, 2006; Jackman, 2001; Smooha, 2005; Ulmer & Johnson, 2004). Moreover, members of disadvantaged groups, compared with members of advantaged groups, are subjected to discrimination and social injustice in a wide range of domains, such as interviewing for jobs and being quoted a price for a house or a car (e.g., Ayres, 1991; Bertrand & Mullainathan, 2004).

Group-based disparities accompanied by differential social treatment produce divergent daily realities for members of advantaged and disadvantaged groups. Whereas members of disadvantaged groups find many doors to economic opportunities closed, suffer higher rates of unemployment, have a difficult time climbing the social ladder, and experience legal authorities as a source of violence and intimidation, advantaged group members experience far more economic security, opportunities to advance, and social acceptance. Thus, although the world may seem fair, hospitable, and inviting to members of advantaged groups, it often appears to be unjust, dangerous, and exclusionary to members of disadvantaged groups (Jones, Engelman, Turner, & Campbell, 2009). These different realities and divergent perspectives form the basis for different motives and goals that advantaged and disadvantaged group members often have regarding the status quo, as explained by prominent theories in sociology and social psychology.

In his pioneering work on race relations, for example, Herbert Blumer (1958) proposed that membership in an advantaged group is associated with a need to protect the dominance of one's group, which in turn can account for phenomena such as prejudice, discrimination, and opposition to egalitarian policies (Bobo & Hutchings, 1996). Similarly, according to realistic group-conflict theory (LeVine & Campbell, 1972), motives to advance or protect the interests of one's group are at the root of intergroup processes. Whereas members of advantaged groups are motivated to defend the existing social arrangements that benefit them, members of disadvantaged groups are motivated to gain more resources, and thus to change the status quo so that their groups' position in the social hierarchy can improve. In line with these theories, research on social dominance theory (Pratto, Sidanius, Stallworth, & Malle, 1994; Sidanius & Pratto, 1999) demonstrates that individuals who hold more power in society tend to view the social hierarchy as natural and even necessary, whereas members of disadvantaged groups are more likely to see the hierarchy as in need of change.

Taken together, these views suggest that because members of advantaged groups benefit both practically (Bobo & Hutchings, 1996) and psychologically (Tajfel & Turner, 1979) from hierarchical social arrangements, they are not likely to oppose the status quo. Undoubtedly, because they hold positions of power there is much value in the attempts to reduce potential discriminatory behavior, which can occur in a variety of interpersonal contexts (e.g., in hiring decisions, when shopping in retail stores). Nevertheless, expecting advantaged group members to mobilize for structural-level change fails to consider the psychology associated with their dominant group position. In contrast, because they can benefit from changes toward greater equality, members of disadvantaged groups are generally more likely to be motivated to challenge the status quo and to raise related societal tension so that their group position can improve (Saguy, Dovidio, & Pratto, 2008; Scheepers, Spears, Doosje, & Manstead, 2006; Tajfel & Turner, 1979). Thus, for both practical and psychological reasons, collective action aimed at advancing more equality typically arises from disadvantaged groups.

Broadly speaking, collective action can be either normative or non-normative (Martin, 1986; Wright, Taylor, & Moghaddam, 1990). Normative collective action refers to behaviors such as protesting at legal rallies and organizing or signing a petition to government officials. Nonnormative action refers to more violent types of protest such as destroying property and, in extreme cases, harming innocent individuals. In the current program of research, we built on previous work on collective action, which has largely centered on understanding predictors of normative action (see van Zomeren, Postmes, & Spears, 2008, for a meta-analysis). Whereas there are parallels between predictors of normative and nonnormative action, a fuller account of nonnormative forms of action can be found in research on political violence and terrorism (Lemieux, 2006; Moghaddam & Marsella, 2004). We next consider the conditions that can increase or attenuate tendencies to partake in normative forms of collective action.

Predictors of Collective Action

Although members of disadvantaged groups are likely to desire social change in the direction of greater equality, there are cases in which this motivation is relatively subdued. A large body of research suggests that a key (but not sole) determinant of collective action on the part of disadvantaged group members is their recognition that intergroup inequality exists and that they are unjustly disadvantaged within the hierarchical system (see van Zomeren et al., 2008, for a meta-analysis). This awareness of unjust inequality depends on group members engaging in intergroup comparisons (Tajfel & Turner, 1979; Wright & Lubensky, 2009); that is, they must perceive themselves as members of a group and compare their group's standing with that of other groups. In the context of social inequality, intergroup comparisons are likely to result in a sense of relative disadvantage or unjust deprivation within the social system (Walker & Smith, 2002).

What makes a sense of deprivation a powerful motivator for action is the emotions associated with it, such as anger and resentment (van Zomeren, Spears, Fischer, & Leach, 2004). Beyond the recognition of deprivation that can incite these emotions, members of disadvantaged groups need to perceive an external source as responsible for their situation, typically the privileged outgroup and/or the social system (Simon & Klandermans, 2001; Smith & Walker, 2009). It is unlikely that collective resistance would occur if individuals attributed their own disadvantage to themselves or to their ingroup. Alternatively, when an external, outgroup-related source is identified, negative emotions such as anger can be directed toward it and can also arouse and guide relevant action tendencies.

Because intergroup comparisons are central to the process of recognizing inequality, factors that reduce the tendency to engage in such comparisons can also affect the way group members view their social standing. Research on perceived discrimination is consistent with this idea in showing that factors that reduce the emphasis on group boundaries and on unjust social structures reduce disadvantaged group members' perceptions of discrimination. For example, when primed with beliefs about individual merit, women who were discriminated against were more likely to attribute their disadvantage to their own internal characteristics than to unfair treatment (McCoy & Major, 2007). In another study, participants who were rejected from a desirable position despite their good performance were significantly less likely to act on behalf of their group when the illegitimacy of the decision was not emphasized (compared with when it was emphasized; Wright, 1997). Thus, although relative deprivation is often an objective marker of any social hierarchy (Jackman, 1994, 2001), factors that blur group boundaries can reduce the extent to which disadvantaged group members are aware of the inequality and of their position in it.

Because recognizing ingroup disadvantage and attributing it to external factors (typically related to the outgroup) are crucial for mobilizing members of an oppressed group to act for change, reduced awareness of inequality can have consequences for social hierarchy. Consistent with this idea, group-based hierarchy has been theorized to remain stable insofar as disadvantaged group members deny their disadvantage or make internal attributions for their subordination (Jackman, 1994; Sidanius & Pratto, 1999). As we argue next, the emphasis on commonalities that is part of positive contact can reduce group members' awareness of group-based inequality. Because members of disadvantaged groups are likely agents of social change, their reduced awareness can ultimately stabilize the existing social hierarchy.

INTERGROUP CONTACT AND SOCIAL CHANGE

The fundamental premise of contact theory is that intergroup relations can improve by bringing members of opposing groups together under conditions that involve institutional support, cooperation, equal status, and potential for personal acquaintance (Allport, 1954; Pettigrew & Tropp, 2006). The theory has stimulated a large body of research and has been applied in a wide variety of settings, notably those marked by intergroup aggression (see Brown & Hewstone, 2005, for a review). For example, interventions informed by contact theory were implemented for reducing tension between Catholics and Protestants in Northern Ireland (Hughes, 2001) and between Jews and Palestinians in the Middle East (Maoz, 2004).

Although intergroup contact is the most widely used framework for improving intergroup relations, the association between contact and change toward equality has received surprisingly little research attention. In some cases, researchers have examined the effects of contact on support for egalitarian policies, yet the majority of this work has focused on stated support for such policies on the part of members of advantaged groups, not on actual egalitarian behavior (e.g., Pettigrew, Wagner, & Christ, 2007). Moreover, the way contact affects disadvantaged group members' perceptions of inequality, which is a chief instigator of social change toward equality (Simon & Klandermans, 2001), has rarely been examined.

A fundamental component of positive intergroup contact is the focus on cooperative, commonality-focused aspects. Indeed, contact is typically operationalized as structured intergroup encounters that emphasize commonalities between the groups (e.g., Gaertner, Mann, Murrell, & Dovidio, 1989) or as cross-group friendships (Pettigrew, 1998). Psychologically, then, one of the main ways in which positive intergroup contact operates is by reducing the salience of the psychological distinction between the ingroup and the outgroup

(Gaertner & Dovidio, 2000). In the case of cross-group friendships, a highly personalized form of contact, the goal is to reduce the salience of group boundaries so that people are perceived as individuals and not as representatives of their group (Miller, 2002). In the case of commonality-based encounters, the goal is to redefine original group boundaries so that members of both groups are perceived as part of a single more inclusive category (Gaertner & Dovidio, 2000).

Either way, weakening the salience of original group boundaries is likely to reduce the extent to which group members are focusing on group differences, including those pertaining to differences in resources and power. Thus, the focus on commonalities is likely to reduce awareness of structural inequality, which is a crucial component in motivating disadvantaged group members to advance change toward equality. The fact that this reduced awareness is likely to be coupled with positive attitudes toward the outgroup, makes the reduced motivation for change even more likely, because disadvantaged group members are less likely to attribute unfair or unjust acts to members of the outgroup (see Smith & Walker, 2009). In the next section we present empirical evidence suggesting that intergroup contact can undermine the conditions necessary for social change toward equality (see Wright & Lubensky, 2009, for a similar argument).

RESEARCH SUPPORT

We propose that beyond improving attitudes, the commonality-focused nature of intergroup contact can also affect the way group members view social inequality. Past research has established that forms of contact that are considered "optimal," which are often operationalized as cross-group friendships or as commonality-focused encounters, improve attitudes toward the outgroup (Pettigrew & Tropp, 2006). Because of the blurring of intergroup boundaries, we propose that these forms of contact can also reduce awareness of intergroup inequality. Reduced awareness of inequality along with positive attitudes toward the advantaged group can inflate disadvantaged group members' perceptions of the fairness of the advantaged group, thus encouraging optimism about the prospects of equality between the groups. Because recognition of inequality and external attribution of disadvantage are necessary motivators of collective action, we would expect this optimism ultimately to reduce motivation to advance social change.

To test these ideas we conducted a laboratory experiment and two field studies concerning the effect of intergroup contact on perceptions and motives related to social inequality. In the first study we experimentally manipulated group membership and related power (advantaged vs. disadvantaged) and type of contact (commonality-focused vs. differences-focused). According to our theorizing, a focus on commonalities, compared with differences, should reduce awareness of group-based inequality and can thereby affect the way disadvantaged group members perceive their social standing. Therefore, we were particularly interested in whether, for disadvantaged group members, commonality-focused contact would reduce awareness of inequality in general and of relative disadvantage more specifically. In the subsequent two field studies we examined whether a similar effect would occur among members of naturally occurring disadvantaged groups: Arabs in Israel and Muslims in India. In these field studies, we further tested whether perceptions of group-based inequality predict reduced motivation for social change, our main outcome of interest.

In the laboratory study (Saguy, Tausch, Dovidio, & Pratto, 2009, Study 1), power between two groups to which members were randomly assigned was manipulated by giving the advantaged group the opportunity to assign extra course credits to the two groups. Before the advantaged group members allocated the credits, members of both groups interacted under the influence of instructions to focus on either intergroup commonalities or differences. Consistent with prior research, commonality-focused interactions, compared with differences-focused interactions, produced more positive intergroup attitudes in both advantaged and disadvantaged group members. In addition, however, commonality-focused contact was related to reduced awareness of the inequality between the groups. Moreover, members of the disadvantaged group expected the advantaged group to distribute the credits in a more equitable fashion following commonality-focused rather than differences-focused interactions. Mediation analysis revealed that this expectation was explained by improved attitudes and reduced awareness of inequality. Thus, commonality-focused contact strengthened perceptions of outgroup fairness, reflected in expectations for equality between the groups.

However, when the disadvantaged group members' expectations were compared with the advantaged group's actual allocations, there was a significant discrepancy. As the disadvantaged group members anticipated, advantaged group members were substantially biased against them in the allocation of credits after differences-focused contact. However, although disadvantaged group members expected a more equal distribution of credits after commonality-focused contact, advantaged group members were just as biased in this condition as in the difference-focused interaction. This effect is consistent with extensive research showing that advantaged groups are motivated to maintain their power (Blumer, 1958; Sidanius & Pratto, 1999). Furthermore, as argued by Dixon and colleagues (Durrheim & Dixon, 2004), whereas members of advantaged groups may support equality in principle, which is a likely attitudinal outcome of favorable contact, they may still not act to create equality in practice. Thus, the results from the laboratory experiment support our predictions by showing that for members of disadvantaged groups, commonality-focused contact resulted in inaccurate perception of their social standing.

Although the experimental nature of this study permitted causal analysis, the intergroup relations were situation-based and short-lived. They may therefore not reflect processes that occur in more naturalistic intergroup contexts. For instance, members of disadvantaged groups might initially be overly optimistic regarding outgroup fairness but not show the same effect following repeated intergroup experiences. Our goal in the next set of studies was to examine whether among members of real groups, intergroup contact relates to reduced awareness of inequality and increased perceptions of outgroup fairness. The naturalistic contexts also enabled us to explore whether these outcomes were related to reduced support for social change among members of disadvantaged groups.

Participants in the second study (Saguy et al., 2009, Study 2) were Arabs in Israel, a national minority that suffers notable disadvantage compared with Jews (e.g., in academic achievement, income, political power; Smooha, 2005). We examined the statistical associations among friendships with Jews (a type of positive contact that is particularly likely to involve a focus on commonalities; Aron et al., 2004), attitudes toward Jews, awareness of inequality, and perceptions of Jews as fair. We further measured Arabs' support for social change toward equality (e.g., by asking them the degree to which they support legislation guaranteeing equal work opportunities for Arabs). Drawing on collective action research (Simon & Klandermans, 2001; van Zomeren et al., 2008) we expected that both reduced awareness of inequality and positive outgroup orientations (i.e., improved attitudes toward Jews and viewing Jews as fair) would undermine disadvantaged group members' support for change toward equality.

Consistent with the results of our laboratory experiment, more positive contact with Jews was associated with more positive attitudes toward Jews and with reduced awareness of inequality between Jews and Arabs. In addition, improved attitudes were associated with increased perceptions of Jews as fair. Moreover, and consistent with our theorizing, both perceptions of Jews as fair and reduced awareness of inequality were associated with reduced support for social change. Thus, through its effects on the way disadvantaged group members viewed the social inequality and members of the other group, contact was associated with a decrease in support for social change. The overall model testing the proposed links between variables fit the data well and better than alternative models (see Figure 18.1).

Results of a third study (Tausch, Saguy, & Singh, 2009) replicated these findings, this time among Muslims in India. Muslims in India are disadvantaged compared with other minorities and, most notably, compared with Hindus, the

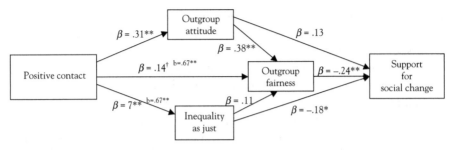

Figure 18.1. Path model examining the mediated relationships among contact and support for social change. The beta value between "positive contact" and "outgroup fairness" = .14†; the beta value between "positive contact" and "inequality as just" = .22**.

*p < .05. **p < .01. †p < .09

dominant majority group. Having more Hindu friends was related to improved attitudes toward Hindus but also to reduced awareness of inequality between Muslims and Hindus. In addition, these outcomes predicted stronger perceptions of Hindus as fair, which in turn were related to weaker collective action tendencies (measured as intentions to participate in various actions that could improve the position of Muslims in India).

Taken together, results from the field studies and the laboratory experiment converge to suggest that experiences of positive, commonality-focused contact can affect the way disadvantaged group members view the social inequality and their own disadvantage. These perceptions, which are parts of an overly optimistic view of intergroup relations, can reduce motivation to challenge existing social inequality. These effects are consistent with our theorizing that the harmony created by contact, reflected in improved attitudes between groups, can paradoxically undermine the potential for social action that might bring about an increase in equality.

More evidence for the connection between intergroup contact and reduced motivation for social change is currently emerging. Wright and Lubensky (2009), who examined data from a survey of African American and Latino/Latina students at a predominantly White university, obtained compatible findings. Positive intergroup contact was associated with more favorable attitudes toward Whites and with less support for collective action. In addition, mediation analyses revealed that the negative effect of contact on collective action was partly a result of reduced ethnic identification. Similarly, Dixon, Durrheim, and Tredoux (2007), in a survey study of Black and White respondents in South Africa, found that more positive intergroup contact was associated with Black South Africans' decreased support for social policies that might enhance racial equality. Black South Africans who reported more positive contact with Whites were less supportive of compensatory policies promoting the interests of Blacks in education and employment. Thus, consistent with our findings from the Arab sample, positive contact predicted less support to legal remedies for inequality offered by institutional authorities.

These recent findings, coupled with our own studies reported here, suggest that the harmony created by intergroup contact can undermine tension that might bring about change toward equality. This suggests that commonality-focused contact can be used as a strategy, or a tool, for maintaining the hierarchy that favors advantaged groups (see Jackman, 1994). If indeed harmony reduces the potential for change, advantaged group members might use it to appease members of disadvantaged groups. An additional implication of the current findings, which is highly relevant to the issue of intergroup aggression, is that in the long term, the effect of commonality-focused contact might not necessarily lead to a reduction in intergroup conflict, particularly if (or when) disadvantaged group members are disillusioned and realize that their expectations of fairness are not met. In the final two sections, we discuss these issues, among others, and offer potential solutions to some of the problems raised by the reported findings.

DISCUSSION AND FUTURE DIRECTIONS

At the beginning of this chapter, we advocated a more refined and less categorical view of intergroup harmony as good and intergroup tension as bad. We proposed that tension can be adaptive for intergroup relations, because it can foster social change that brings about greater equality and justice between groups. For this reason, promoting harmony could be maladaptive because, by reducing potentially constructive tension, it might indirectly reinforce existing inequality.

In general, our research supports this view by showing that the harmony encouraged by contact may not translate into greater equality between groups. The orientations of both disadvantaged and advantaged groups can contribute to this "irony of harmony." For disadvantaged group members, harmony-inducing strategies can turn attention away from social inequities and cause members of the advantaged group to be perceived as fair. Both of these outcomes can lead disadvantaged group members to relax their efforts to promote change toward equality. For members of advantaged groups, improved attitudes as a result of contact do not necessarily translate to more egalitarian intergroup behavior. This finding is consistent with research showing that changes in attitudes produced by contact may reflect mainly a commitment to equality as a principle rather than equality as a reality (Durrheim & Dixon, 2004; but see, Pettigrew et al., 2007).

Future research might fruitfully examine processes related to intergroup harmony that might impede egalitarian actions on the part of advantaged groups members. One possibility is that when intergroup relations are positive, members of advantaged groups feel less urgency to make changes in the social system. Their knowledge that the disadvantaged group members are content can reduce concerns about social inequality and make actual egalitarian behavior seem less necessary. A related possibility is that members of advantaged groups may strategically try to create forms of positive social relations to sustain the status quo (Jackman, 1994). Indeed, the threat of change in the system is reduced if the likely agents of change (i.e., members of the disadvantaged group) see less need for action. Therefore, from the point of view of those who wish to sustain the hierarchy, commonality-focused contact can be functional, if somewhat deceptive.

Future research might also examine the effects of commonality-focused contact over time, especially the effects on members of the disadvantaged group. As we have demonstrated, disadvantaged group members may at first become optimistic, through positive contact, about intergroup relations and the advantaged group's benevolence. In the longer term, however, disadvantaged group members may become "disillusioned," particularly if they are repeatedly appeased without achieving any real change. In addition, their situation might actually get worse rather than improve if members of the advantaged group feel no pressure to be truly egalitarian. This turn of events is likely to produce distrust, disillusionment, and strong resentment, which might fuel more extreme forms of conflict. This possibility points to the potential fragility of harmony created by commonality-focused contact and to the need to develop interventions that would help achieve a more stable and genuine improvement in intergroup relations.

CONCLUSION AND IMPLICATIONS

Harmony-inducing strategies can have obvious and relatively immediate positive consequences for intergroup attitudes. Nevertheless, our work suggests that these benefits can turn out to be superficial and may even impede, in the long run, constructive societal changes. Practical efforts to improve intergroup relations might therefore profit from moving beyond questions about how to create harmony and eliminate tension to studying ways to create harmony without eliminating constructive tension. This requires an approach that views harmony and tension between groups as processes that can coexist. Rather than overlooking the fact that groups operate in a system of asymmetrical power, group-based differences, particularly those pertaining to power, can be acknowledged alongside a focus on commonalities. This can allow the pressure for social change to continue while providing an avenue for communication and exchange (see Halabi, 2004). In addition, to the extent that recognizing both commonality and group-based differences and inequalities helps people to extend moral principles across group lines, advantaged group members may more readily recognize the illegitimacy of group-based disparities and become motivated to respond fairly in a way that supersedes separate group interests.

REFERENCES

Allport, G. W. (1954). *The nature of prejudice*. Reading, MA: Addison-Wesley.

Aron, A., McLaughlin-Volpe, T., Mashek, D., Lewandowski, G., Wright, S. C., & Aron, E. N. (2004). Including others in the self. In W. Stroebe & M. Hewstone (Eds.), *European review of social psychology* (Vol. 15, pp. 101–132). Hove, England: Psychology Press.

Ayres, I. (1991). Fair driving: Gender and race discrimination in retail car negotiations. *Harvard Law Review, 104*, 817–872. doi:10.2307/1341506

Bertrand, M., & Mullainathan, S. (2004). Are Emily and Greg more employable than Lakisha and Jamal? *The American Economic Review, 94*, 991–1013. doi:10.1257/0002828042002561

Blumer, H. (1958). Race prejudice as a sense of group position. *Pacific Sociological Review, 1*, 3–7.

Bobo, L., & Hutchings, V. L. (1996). Perceptions of racial group competition: Extending Blumer's theory of group position to a multiracial social context. *American Sociological Review, 61*, 951–972. doi:10.2307/2096302

Brown, R., & Hewstone, M. (2005). An integrative theory of intergroup contact. In M. P. Zanna (Ed.), *Advances in experimental social psychology* (Vol. 37, pp. 255–343). San Diego, CA: Academic Press.

Dixon, J., Durrheim, K., & Tredoux, C. (2007). Intergroup contact and attitudes toward the principle and practice of racial equality. *Psychological Science, 18*, 867–872. doi:10.1111/j.1467-9280.2007.01993.x

Dovidio, J. F., Gaertner, S. L., & Kawakami, K. (2003). The contact hypothesis: The past, present, and the future. *Group Processes & Intergroup Relations, 6*, 5–21. doi:10.1177/1368430203006001009

Durrheim, K., & Dixon, J. A. (2004). Attitudes in the fiber of everyday life: Desegregation and the discourse of racial evaluation. *American Psychologist, 59*, 626–636. doi:10.1037/0003-066X.59.7.626

Feagin, J. R. (2006). *Systematic racism: A theory of oppression*. New York, NY: Routledge.

Gaertner, S. L., & Dovidio, J. F. (2000). *Reducing intergroup bias: The common ingroup identity model*. Philadelphia, PA: Psychology Press.

Gaertner, S. L., Mann, J., Murrell, A., & Dovidio, J. F. (1989). Reducing intergroup bias: The benefits of recategorization. *Journal of Personality and Social Psychology, 57,* 239–249. doi:10.1037/0022-3514.57.2.239

Halabi, R. (Ed). (2004). *Israeli and Palestinian identities in dialogue: The school for peace approach.* New Brunswick, NJ: Rutgers University Press.

Hewstone, M., & Cairns, E. (2001). Social psychology and intergroup conflict. In D. Chirot & M. E. P. Seligman (Eds.), *Ethnopolitical warfare: Causes, consequences, and possible solutions* (pp. 319–342). Washington, DC: American Psychological Association. doi:10.1037/10396-020

Hughes, J. (2001). Constitutional reform in Northern Ireland: Implications for community relations policy and practice. *The International Journal of Conflict Management, 12,* 154–173. doi:10.1108/eb022854

Jackman, M. R. (1994). *The velvet glove.* Berkeley, CA: University of California Press.

Jackman, M. R. (2001). License to kill: Violence and legitimacy in expropriative social relations. In J. T. Jost & B. Major (Eds.), *The psychology of legitimacy: Emerging perspectives on ideology, justice, and intergroup relations* (pp. 437–467). New York, NY: Cambridge University Press.

Jones, J. M., Engelman, S., Turner, C., & Campbell, S. (2009). Worlds apart: The universality of racism leads to divergent social realities. In S. Demoulin, J. P. Leyens, & J. F. Dovidio (Eds.), *Intergroup misunderstandings: Impact of divergent social realities* (pp. 117–134). Philadelphia, PA: Psychology Press.

King, M. L. (1964). *Why we can't wait.* New York, NY: Penguin Books.

Lemieux, A. F. (2006). Social psychological approaches to understanding and preventing terrorism: Toward an interdisciplinary perspective. *Journal of Security Education, 1,* 75–84. doi:10.1300/J460v01n04_07

LeVine, R. A., & Campbell, D. T. (1972). *Ethnocentrism: Theories of conflict, ethnic attitudes, and group behavior.* New York, NY: Wiley.

Maoz, I. (2004). Coexistence is in the eye of the beholder: Evaluating intergroup encounter interventions between Jews and Arabs in Israel. *Journal of Social Issues, 60,* 437–452. doi:10.1111/j.0022-4537.2004.00119.x

Martin, J. (1986). The tolerance of injustice. In J. M. Olson, C P. Herman, & M. P Zanna (Eds), *Relative deprivation and social comparison: The Ontario Symposium* (Vol. 4, pp. 217–242). Hillsdale, NJ: Erlbaum.

McCoy, S. K., & Major, B. (2007). Priming meritocracy and the psychological justification of inequality. *Journal of Experimental Social Psychology, 43,* 341–351. doi:10.1016/j.jesp.2006.04.009

Miller, N. (2002). Personalization and the promise of contact theory. *Journal of Social Issues, 58,* 387–410. doi:10.1111/1540-4560.00267

Moghaddam, F. M., & Marsella, A. J. (2004). *Understanding terrorism: Psychosocial roots, causes and consequences.* Washington, DC: American Psychological Association. doi:10.1037/10621-000

Paluck, E. L., & Green, D. P. (2009). Prejudice reduction: What works? A critical look at evidence from the field and the laboratory. *Annual Review of Psychology, 60*, 339–367. doi:10.1146/annurev.psych.60.110707.163607

Pettigrew, T. F. (1998). Intergroup contact theory. *Annual Review of Psychology, 49*, 65–85. doi:10.1146/annurev.psych.49.1.65

Pettigrew, T. F., & Tropp, L. (2006). A meta-analytic test of intergroup contact theory. *Journal of Personality and Social Psychology, 90*, 751–783. doi:10.1037/0022-3514.90.5.751

Pettigrew, T. F., Wagner, U., & Christ, O. (2007). Who opposes immigration? Comparing German with North American findings. *Du Bois Review, 4*, 19–39.

Pratto, F., Sidanius, J., Stallworth, L. M., & Malle, B. F. (1994). Social dominance orientation: A personality variable predicting social and political attitudes. *Journal of Personality and Social Psychology, 67*, 741–763. doi:10.1037/0022-3514.67.4.741

Saguy, T., Dovidio, J. F., & Pratto, F. (2008). Beyond contact: Intergroup contact in the context of power relations. *Personality and Social Psychology Bulletin, 34*, 432–445. doi:10.1177/0146167207311200

Saguy, T., Tausch, N., Dovidio, J. F., & Pratto, F. (2009). The irony of harmony: Intergroup contact can produce false expectations for equality. *Psychological Science, 20*, 114–121. doi:10.1111/j.1467-9280.2008.02261.x

Scheepers, D., Spears, R., Doosje, B., & Manstead, A. S. R. (2006). Diversity in in-group bias: Structural factors, situational features, and social functions. *Journal of Personality and Social Psychology, 90*, 944–960. doi:10.1037/0022-3514.90.6.944

Sharp, G. (2005). *Waging nonviolent struggle: 20th century practice and 21st century potential.* Boston, MA: Porter Sargent.

Sidanius, J., & Pratto, F. (1999). *Social dominance: An intergroup theory of social hierarchy and oppression.* New York, NY: Cambridge University Press.

Simon, B., & Klandermans, B. (2001). Politicized collective identity: A social–psychological analysis. *American Psychologist, 56*, 319–331. doi:10.1037/0003-066X.56.4.319

Smith, H. J., & Walker, I. (2009). Feeling relative deprivation: The rocky road from comparisons to actions. In U. Wagner, L. R., Tropp, G. Finchilescu, & C. Tredoux (Eds.), *Improving intergroup relations: Building on the legacy of Thomas F. Pettigrew* (pp.227–243). Malden, MA: Wiley-Blackwell. doi:10.1002/9781444303117.ch15

Smooha, S. (2005). *Index of Arab–Jewish relations in Israel 2004.* Haifa, Israel: The Jewish–Arab Center, University of Haifa.

Tajfel, H., & Turner, J. C. (1979). An integrative theory of intergroup conflict. In W. G. Austin & S. Worchel (Eds.), *The social psychology of intergroup relations* (pp. 33–48). Monterey, CA: Brooks/Cole.

Tausch, N., Saguy, T., & Singh, P. (2009). *Contact between Muslims and Hindus: Benefits and limitations.* Unpublished Manuscript.

Ulmer, J., & Johnson, B. D. (2004). Sentencing in context: A multilevel analysis. *Criminology, 42*, 137–178. doi:10.1111/j.1745-9125.2004.tb00516.x

van Zomeren, M., Postmes, T., & Spears, R. (2008). Toward an integrative social identity model of collective action: A quantitative research synthesis of three sociopsychological perspectives. *Psychological Bulletin, 134*, 504–535. doi:10.1037/0033-2909.134.4.504

van Zomeren, M., Spears, R., Fischer, A. H., & Leach, C. W. (2004). Put your money where your mouth is! Explaining collective action tendencies through group-based anger and group efficacy. *Journal of Personality and Social Psychology, 87*, 649–664. doi:10.1037/0022-3514.87.5.649

Varshney, A. (2002). *Ethnic conflict and civic life: Hindus and Muslims in India.* New Haven, CT: Yale University Press.

Walker, I., & Smith, H. J. (2002). *Relative deprivation: Specification, development, and integration.* Cambridge, England: Cambridge University Press.

Wright, S. C. (1997). Ambiguity, social influence, and collective action: Generating collective protest in response to tokenism. *Personality and Social Psychology Bulletin, 23*, 1277–1290. doi:10.1177/01461672972312005

Wright, S. C., & Lubensky, M. (2009). The struggle for social equality: Collective action versus prejudice reduction. In S. Demoulin, J. P. Leyens, & J. F. Dovidio (Eds.), *Intergroup misunderstandings: Impact of divergent social realities* (pp. 291–310). New York, NY: Psychology Press.

Wright, S. C., Taylor, D. M., & Moghaddam, F. M. (1990). Responding to membership in a disadvantaged group: From acceptance to collective protest. *Journal of Personality and Social Psychology, 58*, 994–1003. doi:10.1037/0022-3514.58.6.994

V

CONSEQUENCES
OF AGGRESSION:
THE VICTIM PERSPECTIVE

19

INFLUENCE OF VIOLENCE AND AGGRESSION ON CHILDREN'S PSYCHOLOGICAL DEVELOPMENT: TRAUMA, ATTACHMENT, AND MEMORY

SHEREE L. TOTH, LATONYA S. HARRIS, GAIL S. GOODMAN, AND DANTE CICCHETTI

The focus of this section of the volume—the consequences of violence and aggression—is particularly relevant to child maltreatment, because aggression and violence directed at children have important implications for their psychosocial development and long-term life outcomes. One issue of particular interest is the effect of aggression and violence on children's memory, a topic that has recently received attention from researchers. Scores of studies spanning several decades of research have shown unequivocally that children traumatized by aggression and violence within their families, including by sexual abuse, physical abuse, or emotional abuse, are at heightened risk of poor mental health outcomes. Only more recently have the implications for children's memory been the focus of study. Understanding the effects of child maltreatment on central psychological processes such as memory is important for clinical, legal, and societal interventions and for basic psychological theory. As Zigler (1998) insisted over a decade ago, it is

This material is based in part on work supported by the National Science Foundation under Grants No. 0545413 and 0851420 to Dr. Gail S. Goodman.

Any opinions, findings, and conclusions or recommendations expressed in this material are those of the author(s) and do not necessarily reflect the views of the National Science Foundation.

important for researchers to recognize their obligations to help formulate policies and practices that benefit the populations they study. Given children's vulnerability and the enduring effects of maltreatment experiences, Zigler's claim is particularly relevant.

In this chapter, we consider how violence can affect children's socioemotional and cognitive development, including their memories. Rather than providing a comprehensive review, we direct our attention to investigations guided by a developmental psychopathology perspective. In so doing, we provide an overview of the sequelae of child maltreatment in relation to emotion regulation, attachment, and psychopathology. We describe how these psychosocial phenomena provide important perspectives from which to understand maltreated individuals' memories for emotional or traumatic events, an issue of special importance to both the field of developmental psychology and the legal system.

PATHOGENIC RELATIONAL ENVIRONMENTS AND CHILD MALTREATMENT

Child maltreatment, in the form of aggression and violence against children, is one of the most profound failures of a social environment to support normal development (Chapter 9). Maltreating families do not provide many of the experiences that theories of normal development view as important for healthy development. Given the cumulative nature of psychological development, early traumatic experiences have implications for psychological functioning and psychopathology across the life span. It is important to note, however, that maltreatment does not automatically doom all children to negative outcomes. In fact, some children are surprisingly resilient even under seemingly overwhelming odds against favorable development. Longitudinal research suggests that resilience is promoted by a child having at least one supportive and security-enhancing attachment relationship; that is, a relationship with a person who believes in the child and offers support when needed (Werner, 1993). This places attachment theory at the heart of theorizing about child maltreatment and its effects.

THE SEQUELAE OF CHILD MALTREATMENT

Research indicates that there are numerous sequelae of child maltreatment. Here we address several of them, specifically emotion regulation, attachment, psychopathology, and memory.

Emotion Regulation and Child Maltreatment

An early issue in infant development is the ability to regulate affective experience. Emotion regulation includes the intra- and extraorganismic factors by which emotional arousal is redirected, controlled, modulated, and modified so that an individual can function adaptively in emotionally challenging situations (Cicchetti, Ganiban, & Barnett, 1991). The ability to regulate emotions develops within the context of early parent–child interactions and relationships (Maughan & Cicchetti, 2002; Thompson, 1999, 1994).

Child maltreatment poses a significant threat to the optimal development of affect regulation. Although there are important individual differences, maltreated children as a group exhibit numerous deficits in the recognition, expression, and understanding of emotions. Even in the early months of life, distortions in affect differentiation can occur in children with a history of maltreatment (Gaensbauer & Hiatt, 1984; Gaensbauer, Mrazek, & Harmon, 1981). Specifically, either excessive amounts of negative affect or blunted affect may be observed in such cases.

Early problems in emotion regulation can lay a foundation for future difficulties in modulating affect. For example, in one study, physically abused preschool boys who witnessed an angry simulated interaction involving their mothers were more behaviorally reactive (e.g., more aggressive) than nonabused boys (Cummings, Hennessy, Rabideau, & Cicchetti, 1994). In a related investigation, physically abused boys (compared with nonabused boys) who viewed videotaped vignettes of angry and friendly interactions reported experiencing more distress in response to angry adult interactions. Physically abused boys also reported greater fear in response to angry interactions between adults, especially when the conflicts were not resolved (Hennessy, Rabideau, Cicchetti, & Cummings, 1994). Finally, in an investigation of 4- to 6-year-old children, approximately 80% of maltreated preschoolers exhibited patterns of emotion dysregulation in response to witnessing an angry interaction between adults (Maughan & Cicchetti, 2002). Findings such as these support a sensitization hypothesis, wherein repeated exposure to anger and familial violence results in greater emotional reactivity.

Difficulties in mentally representing and processing affective information are also observed in children with histories of maltreatment. For example, physically abused children show biased responses to angry emotional expressions (Pollak, Cicchetti, Hornung, & Reed, 2000). Pollak and Sinha (2002) reported that physically abused children required less sensory input than comparison children to accurately identify facial displays of anger (see also Pollak & Kistler, 2002). In an investigation of the attentional mechanisms underlying physically abused children's over-attention to angry expressions, Pollak and Tolley-Schell (2003) discovered that such children notice such expressions readily and find it difficult to disengage attention from them. These results suggest that early adverse experiences influence maltreated children's selective attention to threat-related emotional signals.

Deviations in understanding negative affect and in processing negative affective signals are also evident in children who have experienced forms of abuse other than physical, including sexual abuse, emotional maltreatment, and neglect. Such difficulties are associated with undercontrolled and aggressive behavior in school settings (Rogosch, Cicchetti, & Aber, 1995). In an investigation of attributional processes, Toth, Cicchetti, and Kim (2002) found that children's attributions for positive and negative events moderated externalizing behavior problems (e.g., aggression) and that children's perceptions of their mothers mediated both internalizing and externalizing symptoms. Maltreated children had higher levels of internalizing and externalizing behavior problems than did nonmaltreated children. However, maltreated children with higher positive attribution scores had lower levels of externalizing symptomatology, and those with lower levels of negative attribution scores had lower levels of externalizing behavior problems. These findings suggest that children's positive attributional styles exert a protective force against the damaging effects of child maltreatment. Negative perceptions of mothers served as an independent risk factor for children's internalizing and externalizing behavior problems, regardless of maltreatment status. Finally, maltreated children had less positive perceptions of their mothers. In attachment theory, these perceptions are part of what Bowlby (1982) called internal working models of relationship partners.

Drawing on models of social information processing, Dodge and colleagues (Dodge, Pettit, Bates, & Valente, 1995; see also Chapter 9, this volume) reported that children who were physically abused during the first 5 years of life were later defensively hypervigilant to hostile cues and failed to attend adequately to relevant nonhostile cues. The abused children attributed hostility to others in situations where most people would not make such attributions. In addition, physically abused children acquired large repertoires of highly accessible aggressive responses to interpersonal problems, so that when they were provoked in everyday peer relations, aggressive retaliatory responses were likely.

A number of cross-sectional investigations have examined associations between affect-regulatory problems and behavioral dysregulation among maltreated children. Maltreated preschool and school-age children exhibit a range of dysregulated behaviors that are often characterized by disruptive and aggressive actions. Maltreated toddlers tend to react to peer distress with poorly regulated and situationally inappropriate affect and behavior, including anger, fear, and aggression, as opposed to the more normatively expected responses of empathy and concern (Klimes-Dougan & Kistner, 1990). Shields and Cicchetti

(1998) found that maltreated children were more likely than nonmaltreated children to be aggressive, with physically abused children at heightened risk of reactive aggression (i.e., reacting to perceived provocations). Maltreated children also evidenced attention deficits, and subclinical or nonpathological dissociation was more likely among children with histories of physical or sexual abuse. A history of abuse also predicted emotion dysregulation, affective lability and negativity, and socially inappropriate emotional expressions. In that study, emotion dysregulation was the mechanism whereby maltreatment resulted in reactive aggression (see Chapters 2, 6, and 7, this volume).

Overall, the effects of maltreatment on emotion regulation are profound, and they have important effects on socioemotional development including aggressive behavior. As we describe later, the resulting emotion-regulation difficulties may also have important effects on memories of trauma, which are important clinically and forensically.

Attachment and Child Maltreatment

Establishing a secure attachment relationship between an infant and his or her primary caregiver is an important developmental task during the first year of life (Sroufe, 1979; Thompson, 1999). Attachment theorists have posited that, as development proceeds, a secure attachment relationship provides a secure base from which to explore the environment and, ultimately, contributes to the integration of cognitive, affective, and behavioral capacities that influence ongoing and future relationships as well as self-understanding (Bowlby, 1973, 1980, 1982; Chapters 13, 14, and 18, this volume). Not surprisingly, maltreated children are at heightened risk of developing insecure attachment relationships with their caregivers. Researchers have found that maltreated children are likely to be insecurely attached, with rates of insecurity reaching as high as 95% (Cicchetti, Rogosch, & Toth, 2006; Crittenden, 1988; Lyons-Ruth, Connell, Zoll, & Stahl, 1987). Furthermore, in both cross-sectional and longitudinal studies, maltreated infants and toddlers have elevated rates of *disorganized/disoriented* (Type D) attachment, an atypical form of attachment organization characterized in infancy by behavioral freezing, dazing, stilling, and apprehension of the caregiver; this is characterized later in life by increased risk of serious mental health problems (Barnett, Ganiban, & Cicchetti, 1999; Carlson, Cicchetti, Barnett, & Braunwald, 1989; Cicchetti et al., 2006; Lyons-Ruth et al., 1987).

Although particularly salient during infancy and toddlerhood, attachment continues to be important across the life course, because internal working models (i.e., mental representations) of self, others, and close relationships are carried forward into later stages of development (Chapters 4, 13, and 14). For example, children maltreated in infancy and toddlerhood are more likely than nonmaltreated children to exhibit insecure attachment during all the preschool years (Cicchetti & Barnett, 1991a; Crittenden, 1988), and insecure attachment is common among such children during the school years, when it can be assessed with self-report measures (Lynch & Cicchetti, 1991).

There is evidence (summarized, e.g., in the comprehensive volume edited by Grossmann, Grossmann, & Waters, 2005) that child–parent attachment lays a foundation for later "coherence of mind" with respect to attachment (Hesse, 2008) as well as emotion-regulation strategies relevant to attachment issues (Chapters 13 and 14, this volume). As such, children's attachment security is likely to affect memory and other cognitive processes in ways that are important to close relationships, clinical assessment and intervention, and forensic interviews.

Psychopathology and Child Maltreatment

Although not all maltreated children will have serious mental health problems, disruptions in psychological development during the early years of life can certainly contribute to the emergence of psychopathology later on. In general, the literature on maltreatment reveals a greater preponderance of psychiatric symptoms and diagnoses in maltreated than in nonmaltreated children, and the range of related disorders is broad. Physical abuse and neglect are associated with higher levels of child depressive symptomatology (Cicchetti & Rogosch, 2001; Kaufman, 1991; Manly, Kim, Rogosch, & Cicchetti, 2001; Toth & Cicchetti, 1996; Toth, Manly, & Cicchetti, 1992). In addition, maltreated children have an increased risk of developing depression in adulthood (Widom, DuMont, & Czaja, 2007). Moreover, the risk of adult depression increases even further for adults who were maltreated in the first 5 years of life (Kaplow & Widom, 2007). The same is true for conduct disorder and delinquency (Smith & Thornberry, 1995). Higher rates of attention deficit hyperactivity disorder, oppositional disorder, and posttraumatic stress disorder (PTSD) have also been reported in maltreated children (Famularo, Kinscherff, & Fenton, 1992). Childhood maltreatment is associated with personality disorders, substance abuse, suicidal and self-injurious behavior, somatization, anxiety, and dissociation (Johnson, Cohen, Brown, Smailes, & Bernstein, 1999; Luntz & Widom, 1994; Macfie, Cicchetti, & Toth, 2001a, 2001b; Malinosky-Rummell & Hansen, 1993; McLeer, Callaghan, Henry, & Wallen, 1994; Yates, Carlson, & Egeland, 2008).

Of the various kinds of psychopathology that can develop subsequent to child maltreatment, PTSD is of special interest to memory researchers, because PTSD has sometimes been conceptualized as a memory disorder (involving flashbacks and other troubling and unwanted memories). However, researchers have recently begun to reconceptualize PTSD in terms of normal memory for trauma (Rubin, Berntsen, & Bohni, 2008). These memory issues are addressed in the following section.

Memory and Child Maltreatment

Increasing evidence suggests that being maltreated in childhood not only affects emotion regulation, attachment, and mental health but also affects cognitive functioning (Harris et al., 2008), in particular, memory. In fact, emotion regulation, attachment, psychopathology, and maltreatment all come together to influence memory processes.

Research reviewed earlier in this chapter indicates that victims of maltreatment often overattend to trauma-related information, as in the case, mentioned earlier, of children with histories of physical abuse having difficulty disengaging attention from anger cues while experiencing heightened arousal and emotional dysregulation. One consequence is that many maltreatment victims, especially if they suffer from the trauma-related psychopathology of PTSD, may have unusually accurate memories of childhood traumas (Alexander et al., 2005), because they focused great attention on the events in question and have remembered them in detail ever since. In other words, the oversensitization to trauma cues, mentioned earlier, may make trauma-related memories particularly robust and enduring. However, a subset of maltreatment victims tries to avoid memories and reminders of their traumatic experiences, which may interfere with accurate memory. Such avoidance is due to a need to down-regulate strong emotion as a means of coping.

Attachment theory provides a framework for conceptualizing individual differences in the ways in which aggression and violence toward children may influence memory, especially memory for traumatic childhood experiences (e.g., Alexander, Quas, & Goodman, 2002; Goodman, Quas, Batterman-Faunce, Riddlesberger, & Kuhn, 1996). According to Bowlby (1980; see also Main, 1990), insecure–avoidant children, whose bids for care have been repeatedly rejected or belittled, are theorized to develop a defensive, largely unconscious strategy called "defensive exclusion" (Bowlby, 1980). This strategy limits the processing of stressful information, with the goal of preventing the intense activation of attachment behavior that might remind a person of prior attachment-related rejections, separations, or losses (Chae et al., 2010). Such limits on cognitive processing have important implications for memory.

Relations between patterns of insecure attachment and memory are evident in studies of maltreated samples, especially when participants are asked to recall their abusive experiences. Goodman et al. (1992) first examined the psychosocial effects of testifying against assailants in criminal court. Their study was based on a sample of child victims of sexual abuse (Goodman et al., 1992). About 13 years after their court cases, the victims were interviewed about their abusive experiences (Edelstein et al., 2005; Goodman et al., 2003). The results indicated that victims who scored higher on a measure of avoidant attachment had poorer (i.e., less detailed and less accurate) memories the more severe their assaults had been, a pattern apparently reflecting defensive exclusion. In sharp contrast, victims with lower scores on avoidant attachment were actually more accurate about their more severe abuse experiences.

Coping strategies, which are likely to be affected by child maltreatment, may explain, at least in part, the connection between avoidant attachment, avoidant coping (sometimes called distancing coping), and memory. In a recent study of autobiographical memory, adults and adolescents with or without childhood sexual abuse histories were asked to recount childhood events (Harris et al., 2008). Their accounts were scored for the degree of specificity of the memories (e.g., specificity as to time and place of the incidents described; see Williams, 1996). In line with Bowlby's (1980) conception of defensive avoidance, Harris et al. (2008) predicted that survivors of childhood sexual abuse would adopt a nonspecific memory retrieval style as a way of avoiding unpleasant and intrusive specific memories (e.g., Hermans, Defranc, Raes, Williams, & Eelen, 2005). Harris et al. found that memory nonspecificity was associated with distancing coping processes (i.e., cognitive efforts to detach oneself from and minimize the significance of the situation, as measured by the Ways of Coping Questionnaire; Folkman & Lazarus, 1988), which was expected based on attachment theory and research (Hazan & Shaver, 1987; Mikulincer & Shaver, 2007). The relation between distancing coping and autobiographical-memory nonspecificity was robust; the results held even when measures of PTSD symptomatology and general psychopathology were statistically controlled in regression analyses. The findings support Bowlby's (1980) theory of defensive avoidance.

Overall, the evidence suggests that attachment orientation, emotion-regulation and coping strategies, and psychopathology need to be examined when assessing memories of individuals with maltreatment histories. In some cases, such as with children and adults who suffer from PTSD and overattend to trauma cues, memory for trauma may be robust and accurate. In other cases, such as with children and adults with an avoidant attachment style and who use avoidant emotion-regulation and coping strategies, memory for trauma may be suppressed or weakened, and for that reason may also be less accurate.

METHODOLOGICAL CONSIDERATIONS

Having briefly reviewed research on child maltreatment and some of its effects and moderators, we consider next a few methodological issues in the design and conduct of this research. We are especially interested here in how child maltreatment is defined and in issues of internal validity.

Defining Child Maltreatment

How is child maltreatment defined and operationalized? Historically, research on child maltreatment has been hampered by the lack of clearly articulated approaches to defining maltreatment (Barnett, Manly, & Cicchetti, 1993; National Research Council, 1993) and by a long history of disagreement among researchers, lawmakers, and clinicians (Aber & Zigler, 1981; Barnett et al., 1993). Many researchers have maintained that the definition of maltreatment should focus on specific acts that endanger a child (Barnett et al., 1993; Cicchetti & Barnett, 1991b; Zuravin, 1991). However, because maltreatment is largely determined by legal considerations, it is often identified by social service workers. Yet there is still not a broad consensus among them regarding acceptable disciplinary practices (e.g., spanking) and what counts as child maltreatment (Barnett, Manly, & Cicchetti, 1993; Black & Dubowitz, 1999). There is also a lack of agreement on whether child maltreatment should be defined based on the actions of the perpetrator, the effects on the child, or a combination of the two (Barnett et al., 1993).

Operationalizations of the maltreatment variable have ranged from investigator observations of "poor parenting" through reliance on parent and/or child reports, to utilization of Child Protective Services records. These issues are not easily resolved, but they need to be considered when evaluating studies of the effects of parental aggression on children.

Internal Validity

When conducting research on child maltreatment, clearly, one cannot randomly assign children to abused and nonabused groups. As a result, considerable caution is needed when attempting to draw causal inferences about child maltreatment. There are many co-occurring and intertwined variables to ferret out and statistically control. Nevertheless, carefully designed studies can provide substantial insight into the possible effects of child maltreatment on children's development, including their emotion regulation, attachment, mental health, and memory.

CONCLUSION

Research has demonstrated that multiple psychological processes and outcomes are affected when children experience aggression and violence, particularly in their homes. We have highlighted the importance of examining the influence of maltreatment on several domains of psychological functioning. Many studies, conducted over many years, have implicated maltreatment in disrupting emotion regulation, child–parent attachment, and children's current and later mental health. It is now well documented that violence affects children's emotional memories as well and their feelings and behavior. Further research should examine the extent to which violence adversely affects other cognitive domains such as executive functions, problem solving, planning, and learning. Although research in the area of child maltreatment is not without major challenges and complexities, the potential theoretical, clinical, and social policy implications of such research provide compelling reasons to increase its sophistication and applicability in the future.

REFERENCES

Aber, J. L., & Zigler, E. (1981). Developmental considerations in the definition of child maltreatment. *New Directions for Child Development, 1981*(11), 1–29. doi:10.1002/cd.23219811103

Alexander, K. W., Quas, J. A., & Goodman, G. S. (2002). Theoretical advances in understanding children's memory for distressing events: The role of attachment. *Developmental Review, 22,* 490–519. doi:10.1016/S0273-2297(02)00004-7

Alexander, K. W., Quas, J. A., Goodman, G. S., Ghetti, S., Edelstein, R. S., Redlich, A. D., . . . Jones, D. P. H. (2005). Traumatic impact predicts long-term memory for documented child sexual abuse. *Psychological Science, 16,* 33–40. doi:10.1111/j.0956-7976.2005.00777.x

Barnett, D., Ganiban, J., & Cicchetti, D. (1999). Maltreatment, negative expressivity, and the development of Type D attachments from 12- to 24-months of age. *Monographs of the Society for Research in Child Development, 64,* 97–118. doi:10.1111/1540-5834.00035

Barnett, D., Manly, J. T., & Cicchetti, D. (1993). Defining child maltreatment: The interface between policy and research. In D. Cicchetti & S. L. Toth (Eds.), *Child abuse, child development, and social policy* (pp. 7–74). Norwood, NJ: Ablex.

Black, M. M., & Dubowitz, H. (1999). Child neglect: Research recommendations and future directions. In H. Dubowitz (Ed.), *Neglected children: Research, practice, and policy* (pp. 261–277). Thousand Oaks, CA: Sage.

Bowlby, J. (1973). *Attachment and loss: Vol. 2. Separation: Anxiety and anger.* New York, NY: Basic Books.

Bowlby, J. (1980). *Attachment and loss: Vol. 3. Sadness and depression.* New York, NY: Basic Books.

Bowlby, J. (1982). *Attachment and loss: Vol. 1. Attachment* (2nd ed.). New York, NY: Basic Books.

Carlson, V., Cicchetti, D., Barnett, D., & Braunwald, K. (1989). Disorganized/disoriented attachment relationships in maltreated infants. *Developmental Psychology, 25,* 525–531. doi:10.1037/0012-1649.25.4.525

Chae, Y. (2010). *The influence of child attachment style and parental attachment on memory accuracy and suggestibility on young children.* Manuscript in preparation.

Cicchetti, D., & Barnett, D. (1991a). Attachment organization in preschool-aged maltreated children. *Development and Psychopathology, 3*, 397–411 doi:10.1017/S0954579400007598

Cicchetti, D., & Barnett, D. (1991b). Toward the development of a scientific nosology of child maltreatment. In W. Grove & D. Cicchetti (Eds.), *Thinking clearly about psychology: Essays in honor of Paul E. Meehl: Vol. 2. Personality and psychopathology* (pp. 346–377). Minneapolis, MN: University of Minnesota Press.

Cicchetti, D., Ganiban, J., & Barnett, D. (1991). Contributions from the study of high-risk populations to understanding the development of emotion regulation. In J. Garber & K. A. Dodge (Eds.), *The development of emotion regulation and dysregulation* (pp. 15–48). New York, NY: Cambridge University Press.

Cicchetti, D., & Rogosch, F. A. (2001). The impact of child maltreatment and psychopathology upon neuroendocrine functioning. *Development and Psychopathology, 13*, 783–804.

Cicchetti, D., Rogosch, F. A., & Toth, S. L. (2006). Fostering secure attachment in infants in maltreating families through preventive interventions. *Development and Psychopathology, 18*, 623–649. doi:10.1017/S0954579406060329

Crittenden, P. M. (1988). Relationships at risk. In J. Belsky & T. Nezworski (Eds.), *The clinical implications of attachment* (pp. 136–174). Hillsdale, NJ: Erlbaum.

Cummings, E. M., Hennessy, K. D., Rabideau, G. J., & Cicchetti, D. (1994). Responses of physically abused boys to interadult anger involving their mothers. *Development and Psychopathology, 6*, 31–41.

Dodge, K. A., Pettit, G. S., Bates, J. E., & Valente, E. (1995). Social information-processing patterns partially mediate the effect of early physical abuse on later conduct problems. *Journal of Abnormal Psychology, 104*, 632–643. doi:10.1037/0021-843X.104.4.632

Edelstein, R. S., Ghetti, S., Quas, J. A., Goodman, G. S., Alexander, K. W., Redlich, A. D., & Cordón, I. M. (2005). Individual differences in emotional memory: Adult attachment and long-term memory for child sexual abuse. *Personality and Social Psychology Bulletin, 31*, 1537–1548. doi:10.1177/0146167205277095

Famularo, R., Kinscherff, R. T., & Fenton, T. (1992). Psychiatric diagnoses of maltreated children. *Journal of the American Academy of Child and Adolescent Psychiatry, 31*, 863–867. doi:10.1097/00004583-199209000-00013

Folkman, S., & Lazarus, R. S. (1988). *Manual for the Ways of Coping Questionnaire.* Mountain View, CA: Consulting Psychologists Press.

Gaensbauer, T. J., & Hiatt, S. W. (1984). Facial communication of emotion in early infancy. *Journal of Pediatric Psychology, 9*, 205–217.

Gaensbauer, T. J., Mrazek, D., & Harmon, R. (1981). Emotional expression in abused and/or neglected infants. In N. Frude (Ed.), *Psychological approaches to child abuse* (pp. 120–135). Totowa, NJ: Rowman & Littlefield.

Goodman, G. S., Ghetti, S., Quas, J. A., Edelstein, R. S., Alexander, K. W., Redlich, A. D., . . . Jones, D. P. H. (2003). A prospective study of memory for child sexual abuse: New findings relevant to the repressed-memory controversy. *Psychological Science, 14,* 113–118. doi:10.1111/1467-9280.01428

Goodman, G. S., Quas, J. A., Batterman-Faunce, J. M., Riddlesberger, M. M., & Kuhn, J. (1997). Children's reactions to and memory for a stressful event: Influences of age, anatomical dolls, knowledge, and parental attachment. *Applied Developmental Science, 1,* 54–75. doi:10.1207/s1532480xads0102_1

Goodman, G. S., Taub, E. P., Jones, D., England, P., Port, L., Rudy, L., & Prado, L. (1992). Testifying in court. *Monographs of the Society for Research in Child Development, 57* (Serial no. 229).

Grossmann, K. E., Grossmann, K., & Waters, E. (Eds.). (2005). *Attachment from infancy to adulthood: The major longitudinal studies.* New York, NY: Guilford Press.

Harris, L. S., Block, S. D., Augusti, E. M., Larson, R. P., Culver, M. D., Pineda, R. R., . . . Goodman, G. S. (2008, May). *The relation between coping style and autobiographical memory specificity in maltreated and nonmaltreated adolescents and adults.* Poster session presented at the meeting of the annual convention of the Association for Psychological Science, Chicago, IL.

Hazan, C., & Shaver, P. (1987). Romantic love conceptualized as an attachment process. *Journal of Personality and Social Psychology, 52,* 511–524. doi:10.1037/0022-3514.52.3.511

Hennessy, K. D., Rabideau, G. J., Cicchetti, D., & Cummings, E. M. (1994). Responses of physically abused and nonabused children to different forms of interadult anger. *Child Development, 65,* 815–828. doi:10.2307/1131420

Hermans, D., Defranc, A., Raes, F., Williams, J. M. G., & Eelen, P. (2005). Reduced autobiographical memory specificity as an avoidant coping style. *The British Journal of Clinical Psychology, 44,* 583–589. doi:10.1348/014466505X53461

Hesse, E. (2008). The Adult Attachment Interview: Protocol, method of analysis, and empirical studies. In J. Cassidy & P. R. Shaver (Eds.), *Handbook of attachment: Theory, research, and clinical applications* (pp. 552–598). New York, NY: Guilford Press.

Johnson, J. G., Cohen, P., Brown, J., Smailes, E. M., & Bernstein, D. P. (1999). Childhood maltreatment increases risk for personality disorders during early adulthood. *Archives of General Psychiatry, 56,* 600–606. doi:10.1001/archpsyc.56.7.600

Kaplow, J. B., & Widom, C. S. (2007). Age of onset of child maltreatment predicts long-term mental health outcomes. *Journal of Abnormal Psychology, 116,* 176–187. doi:10.1037/0021-843X.116.1.176

Kaufman, J. (1991). Depressive disorders in maltreated children. *Journal of the American Academy of Child and Adolescent Psychiatry, 30,* 257–265. doi:10.1097/00004583-199103000-00014

Klimes-Dougan, B., & Kistner, J. (1990). Physically abused preschoolers' responses to peers' distress. *Developmental Psychology, 26,* 599–602. doi:10.1037/0012-1649.26.4.599

Luntz, B. K., & Widom, C. S. (1994). Antisocial personality disorder in abused and neglected children grown up. *The American Journal of Psychiatry, 151,* 670–674.

Lynch, M., & Cicchetti, D. (1991). Patterns of relatedness in maltreated and non-maltreated children: Connections among multiple representational models. *Development and Psychopathology, 3,* 207–226. doi:10.1017/S0954579400000080

Lyons-Ruth, K., Connell, D., Zoll, D., & Stahl, J. (1987). Infants at social risk: Relationships among infant maltreatment, maternal behavior, and infant attachment behavior. *Developmental Psychology, 23,* 223–232. doi:10.1037/0012-1649.23.2.223

Macfie, J., Cicchetti, D., & Toth, S. L. (2001a). The development of dissociation in maltreated preschool-aged children. *Development and Psychopathology, 13,* 233–254. doi:10.1017/S0954579401002036

Macfie, J., Cicchetti, D., & Toth, S. L. (2001b). Dissociation in maltreated versus nonmaltreated preschool-aged children. *Child Abuse & Neglect, 25,* 1253–1267. doi:10.1016/S0145-2134(01)00266-6

Main, M. (1990). Cross-cultural studies of attachment organization: Recent studies, changing methodologies, and the concept of conditional strategies. *Human Development, 33,* 48–61. doi:10.1159/000276502

Malinosky-Rummell, R., & Hansen, D. (1993). Long-term consequences of childhood physical abuse. *Psychological Bulletin, 114,* 68–79. doi:10.1037/0033-2909.114.1.68

Manly, J. T., Kim, J. E., Rogosch, F. A., & Cicchetti, D. (2001). Dimensions of child maltreatment and children's adjustment: Contributions of developmental timing and subtype. *Development and Psychopathology, 13,* 759–782.

Maughan, A., & Cicchetti, D. (2002). The impact of child maltreatment and interadult violence on children's emotion regulation abilities. *Child Development, 73,* 1525–1542. doi:10.1111/1467-8624.00488

McLeer, S. V., Callaghan, M., Henry, D., & Wallen, J. (1994). Psychiatric disorders in sexually abused children. *Journal of the American Academy of Child and Adolescent Psychiatry, 33,* 313–319. doi:10.1097/00004583-199403000-00003

Mikulincer, M., & Shaver, P. R. (2007). *Attachment in adulthood: Structure, dynamics, and change.* New York, NY: Guilford Press.

National Research Council. (1993). *Understanding child abuse and neglect.* Washington, DC: National Academy of Sciences.

Pollak, S. D., Cicchetti, D., Hornung, K., & Reed, A. (2000). Recognizing emotion in faces: Developmental effects of child abuse and neglect. *Developmental Psychology, 36,* 679–688. doi:10.1037/0012-1649.36.5.679

Pollak, S. D., & Kistler, D. (2002). Early experience alters the development of categorical representations for facial expressions of emotion. *Proceedings of the National Academy of Sciences of the United States of America, 99,* 9072–9076. doi:10.1073/pnas.142165999

Pollak, S. D., & Sinha, P. (2002). Enhanced perceptual sensitivity for anger among physically abused children. *Developmental Psychology, 38,* 784–791. doi:10.1037/0012-1649.38.5.784

Pollak, S. D., & Tolley-Schell, S. A. (2003). Selective attention to facial emotion in physically abused children. *Journal of Abnormal Psychology, 112,* 323–338. doi:10.1037/0021-843X.112.3.323

Rogosch, F. A., Cicchetti, D., & Aber, J. L. (1995). The role of child maltreatment in early deviations in cognitive and affective processing abilities and later peer relationship problems. *Development and Psychopathology, 7,* 591–609. doi:10.1017/S0954579400006738

Rubin, D., Berntsen, D., & Bohni, M. (2008). A memory based model of posttraumatic stress disorder. *Psychological Review, 115,* 985–1011. doi:10.1037/a0013730

Shields, A., & Cicchetti, D. (1998). Reactive aggression among maltreated children: The contributions of attention and emotion dysregulation. *Journal of Clinical Child Psychology, 27,* 381–395. doi:10.1207/s15374424jccp2704_2

Smith, C. A., & Thornberry, T. P. (1995). The relationship between childhood maltreatment and adolescent involvement in delinquency. *Criminology, 33,* 451–481. doi:10.1111/j.1745-9125.1995.tb01186.x

Sroufe, L. A. (1979). The coherence of individual development: Early care, attachment, and subsequent developmental issues. *American Psychologist, 34,* 834–841. doi:10.1037/0003-066X.34.10.834

Thompson, R. A. (1994). Emotion regulation: A theme in search of a definition. *Monographs of the Society for Research in Child Development, 59,* 25–52. doi:10.2307/1166137

Thompson, R. A. (1999). Early attachment and later development. In J. Cassidy & P. R. Shaver (Eds.), *Handbook of attachment* (pp. 265–286). New York, NY: Guilford Press.

Toth, S. L., & Cicchetti, D. (1996). Patterns of relatedness and depressive symptomatology in maltreated children. *Journal of Consulting and Clinical Psychology, 64,* 32–41. doi:10.1037/0022-006X.64.1.32

Toth, S. L., Cicchetti, D., & Kim, J. E. (2002). Relations among children's perceptions of maternal behavior, attributional styles, and behavioral symptomatology in maltreated children. *Journal of Abnormal Child Psychology, 30,* 487–501. doi:10.1023/A:1019868914685

Toth, S. L., Manly, J. T., & Cicchetti, D. (1992). Child maltreatment and vulnerability to depression. *Development and Psychopathology, 4,* 97–112. doi:10.1017/S0954579400005587

Werner, E. E. (1993). Risk, resilience, and recovery: Perspectives from the Kauai Longitudinal Study. *Development and Psychopathology, 5,* 503–515. doi:10.1017/S095457940000612X

Widom, C. S., DuMont, K., & Czaja, S. J. (2007). A prospective investigation of major depressive disorder and comorbidity in abused and neglected children grown up. *Archives of General Psychiatry, 64,* 49–56. doi:10.1001/archpsyc.64.1.49

Williams, J. M. G. (1996). Depression and the specificity of autobiographical memory. In D. C. Rubin (Ed.), *Remembering our past: Studies in autobiographical memory* (pp. 244–267). New York, NY: Cambridge University Press. doi:10.1017/CBO9780511527913.010

Yates, T. M., Carlson, E. A., & Egeland, B. R. (2008). A prospective study of child maltreatment and self-injurious behavior in a community sample. *Development and Psychopathology, 20,* 651–671. doi:10.1017/S0954579408000321

Zigler, E. (1998). A place of value for applied and policy studies. *Child Development, 69,* 532–542.

Zuravin, S. J. (1991). Research definitions of child physical abuse and neglect: Current problems. In R. H. Starr & D. A. Wolfe (Eds.), *The effects of child abuse and neglect* (pp. 100–128). New York, NY: Guilford Press.

20

THE PARADOX OF PARTNER AGGRESSION: BEING COMMITTED TO AN AGGRESSIVE PARTNER

XIMENA B. ARRIAGA AND NICOLE M. CAPEZZA

Aggression in relationships is a serious problem. In the United States, for example, approximately, 1.3 million women and 835,000 men are physically assaulted by a romantic partner annually, with the majority of reported acts (about 75%) being mild forms of aggression, such as pushing or slapping (Tjaden & Theonnes, 2000). Each year, about 5% of physically abused women (approximately 44,000) suffer serious injuries from being beaten up, choked, or assaulted with a weapon. (Such severe acts are significantly more likely to be perpetrated by men against women than the reverse; Rennison & Welchans, 2000; see also Chapters 2, 13, and 14, this volume.)

Whereas other forms of aggression often occur in contexts where aggression might be expected (e.g., between antagonistic groups), aggression committed by a relationship partner violates most people's fundamental hopes and expectations for a close relationship. Targets of partner aggression who are committed to their relationship are left to make sense of a paradox: The presumed source of love and intimacy is also the source of pain. This paradox often causes outsiders to wonder why the victims of partner aggression remain with their aggressive partner.

In this chapter, we suggest that perceptions or interpretations of the partner's acts play a central role in continuing the relationship, and we consider the possibility that individuals perceive aggressive partner acts as less severe to the extent that they are committed. Victims who downplay their partner's aggression fail to protect themselves and thus run the risk of being hurt further. Moreover, when members of a society fail to recognize that partner aggression has negative consequences and should not be tolerated, partner aggression becomes more likely to continue as perpetrators avoid punishment and targets fail to get needed protection and support.

We begin by defining partner aggression and delineating the different forms it takes. We then review our own and other research on what is known about perceptions of partner aggression in general, and about how victims' perceptions compare with others' perceptions. We then shift the focus from perceptions of partner aggression in general to how victims perceive their own partner's acts. We use concepts from interdependence and consistency theories to suggest that the closer and more committed the victim feels to the perpetrator, the more likely she is to downplay his aggressive acts. We end by discussing how a victim's well-being is affected by continuing a relationship in which she downplays her partner's aggressive acts.

WHAT DO WE MEAN BY PARTNER AGGRESSION?

Our focus is on acts that occur between partners in an intimate relationship and that are intended to inflict harm. These include physically aggressive acts, such as hitting, punching, and kicking. They also include psychologically aggressive acts, such as yelling, derogating, threatening, and otherwise attempting to control and dominate another person (O'Leary, 1999).

For several reasons, we are particularly interested in perceptions of psychological aggression. Severe forms of psychological aggression, such as humiliating, degrading, and threatening a partner, are highly correlated with occurrences of physical aggression (Murphy & Hoover, 1999). Moreover, recent research has revealed, somewhat surprisingly, that a pattern of sustained psychological aggression is as or more damaging to a victim than physical aggression. For instance, over 70% of physically abused women report that emotional abuse had a more damaging effect on their self-esteem and health than physical aggression (Follingstad, Rutledge, Berg, Hause, & Polek, 1990). Psychological aggression not only has a strong, deleterious effect on a victim's mental health (e.g., Arias & Pape, 1999), but it has also been linked to a number of adverse physical health outcomes. Victims of psychological aggression are just as likely as victims of physical aggression to suffer from chronic neck or back pain, migraines, stomach ulcers, spastic colon, and gastrointestinal symptoms, among other health problems (Coker et al., 2002; Coker, Smith,

Bethea, King, & McKeown, 2000). Thus, psychological aggression has clear mental and physical health outcomes for victims.

Yet, as we describe later in this chapter, psychological aggression is not perceived to be as serious as physical aggression, despite the growing literature on the severe consequences of psychological aggression suggesting otherwise. This may make victims themselves and people in general less likely to counter partner psychological aggression than physical aggression.

Much of our analysis focuses on commitment, a strong subjective force that keeps people in relationships (Rusbult, 1983). A victim's feeling tied to a partner, imagining a long-term future with the partner, and intending to remain in the relationship—all of which are aspects of commitment (Arriaga & Agnew, 2001)—create a subjective state that motivates more benign interpretations of negative partner acts (Rusbult, Olsen, Davis, & Hannon, 2001). To date, we have examined commitment and type of aggression (i.e., physical vs. psychological) as important factors predicting perceptions of partner aggression, but there are likely many other personality, relational, and social circumstances that affect perceptions. We begin our analysis by establishing how partner aggression is generally perceived.

HOW IS PARTNER AGGRESSION GENERALLY PERCEIVED?

Perceptions of partner aggression vary. One source of variation is time, in that perceptions are more negative today than they used to be. A second source of variation in perceptions is the specific type of aggression being considered.

General U.S. Norms

In the United States, acts of physical aggression in intimate relationships may have been tolerated 40 years ago, but they are now generally considered unacceptable (Gelles, 1993). Representative U.S. samples have shown that acts of physical aggression (e.g., punch, slap) are considered to be cases of domestic violence and are thus unlawful. For instance, 98.8% of respondents in one study (Carlson & Worden, 2005) reported that a husband punching his wife constitutes domestic violence, and 91.3% considered slapping to be an act of domestic violence.

Although these U.S. norms against physical abuse have become stable parts of American culture, there is an absence of comparable norms against psychological aggression. For instance, only 53.8% of respondents consider a husband insulting his wife by calling her "a stupid slob" to be domestic violence (Carlson & Worden, 2005). Other studies of representative American samples (e.g., Sorenson & Taylor, 2005) have shown that sanctions against a perpetrator (e.g., arrests, restraining orders) are supported more for physically aggressive behaviors (e.g., slapping, punching, beating) than for psychologically aggressive behaviors (e.g., belittling, humiliating, threatening). On one hand, this may not seem surprising given that physical aggression can leave visible injuries whereas psychological aggression leaves no physical marks. But on the other hand, U.S. society's failure to condemn psychological aggression is surprising given that its effects are as or more damaging to the victim's long-term well-being than physical aggression. It is as if American adults adhere to the familiar childhood retort that "Sticks and stones may break my bones, but words will never hurt me." Unfortunately, that long-lived maxim is untrue.

Research that attempts to identify individual characteristics that make a person prone to tolerate domestic violence has yielded mixed findings. For example, several studies examining the sex of the perceiver suggest that women find a perpetrator's aggressive behavior more blameworthy and less acceptable than do men (e.g., Cauffman, Feldman, Jensen, & Arnett, 2000; Pierce & Harris, 1993), but not all studies have found similar sex differences (e.g., Capezza & Arriaga, 2008a). Although there may be some variation among ethnic groups and subcultures, the belief that acts of partner aggression are best avoided seems to be widely held in the United States.

Physical Versus Psychological Aggression

Our own research (Capezza & Arriaga, 2008a, 2008b) suggests that perceptions are strongly influenced by the nature of the partner acts and that not all forms of partner aggression are perceived equally. In one study (Capezza & Arriaga, 2008b), college students who had previously been or were currently in a relationship read a hypothetical scenario in which a marital couple has an argument and the husband becomes aggressive. The levels of physical aggression (i.e., none, low, high) and psychological aggression (i.e., low, high) were crossed in a between-subjects factorial design. After reading the scenario, participants completed measures of their perceptions of (a) the perpetrator's behavior and (b) the conflict.

The results revealed that participants generally held negative perceptions regarding the event, with mean ratings beyond the midpoint and close to the scale anchor indicating negative perceptions. The main effect for physical aggression was strong: Across all dependent variables, participants perceived the perpetrator and conflict in more negative ways with increasing levels of physical aggression, confirming that norms exist among the college students we sampled against using physical force in a relationship. The effect for psychological aggression was not as robust, however: One dependent variable failed to show any effect, one showed a more negative perception for high (vs. low) psychological aggression, and one showed the effect only when physical aggression was absent (i.e., a simple effect within the no physical aggression condition). A similar study (Capezza & Arriaga, 2008a) revealed that participants' perceptions did not vary between a vignette depicting verbal aggression (e.g., yelling and swearing) versus one depicting severe emotional aggression (e.g., ridiculing, degrading, highly threatening behaviors), despite the documented serious consequences of emotional aggression.

People generally see physical partner aggression as negative. Views of psychological aggression, although not positive or neutral, are not uniformly negative. It stands to reason that victims of partner aggression should share these perceptions; that is, they should view their partner's behavior negatively, particularly when the acts qualify as physical aggression. Social psychological theories, however, suggest that this commonsense prediction may be incorrect, as we explain in the next section outlining our theoretical analysis of victim perceptions.

WHY MIGHT VICTIM PERCEPTIONS DIFFER FROM OTHERS' PERCEPTIONS?

At first glance, it seems counterintuitive to suggest that victims of partner aggression might downplay their partner's aggressive acts. One might expect victims to seek help and sympathy and to complain that their partners' acts are severe and damaging. Why and how, then, might victims downplay their partner's aggressive acts? Two social psychological theoretical frameworks are particularly relevant when answering this question.

Consistency Theories

In social psychology, consistency theories suggest that victims who feel particularly tied or committed to their partners would be likely to perceive their partner's aggressive acts less negatively than victims who are less committed to their partners. Heider's (1958) *balance theory*, for example, suggests what he called a positive unit relation between the two partners and a positive unit relation between the perpetrator and his aggressive act. At the outset, the sentiment relation between the victim and the perpetrator's aggressive act would be negative, comprising a state of imbalance among the three relations (i.e., two positive and one negative relation). If the unit relation linking the two partners is strong, that is, if the ties keeping them together are strong and the victim is committed, then this would create pressure to shift the sentiment relation between the victim and the perpetrator's aggressive act from negative to neutral or positive. In short, the victim would adopt a less negative view of the partner's aggressive act.

In addition to commitment, the nature of the aggressive behavior may also make a difference. Overtly aggressive acts (e.g., hitting, punching) are more difficult to reinterpret as being benign than are less physical forms of aggression (e.g., belittling, degrading). Regardless of commitment level, an individual may be more likely to adopt a neutral sentiment relationship toward an act of verbal aggression than toward an act of physical aggression.

Festinger's (1957) *cognitive dissonance theory* would make a similar prediction. The theory suggests that accepting two opposing beliefs results in mental discomfort that motivates a person to change one of the beliefs to be consistent with the other. Less committed individuals faced with an aggressive (and thus negative) partner act might come to feel more negative about the relationship. More committed individuals, however, are motivated to feel positive about the partner and therefore would adopt a less negative perception of the partner act. Similarly, less physical forms of aggression would not create as much dissonance as would overtly physical forms of aggression.

Interdependence Theory

A second theoretical framework that is useful for understanding why victims might downplay partner aggression is *interdependence theory* (Kelley, 1979). This theory provides an analysis of thoughts and actions based on a person's interaction situation (e.g., a partner interaction) and the person's broad goals toward the relationship. Highly committed individuals are strongly affected by what the partner does; they are "dependent" on the partner to the extent that their interaction experience is strongly affected by what the partner does or what the two partners do in unison.

Contentious interpersonal situations, including ones in which a partner is aggressive, trigger in most people an inclination to retaliate with comparable behavior (Kelley, 1979). However, what often redirects the expected reaction and determines the actual response is a person's broader goals for the relationship. Actual behavior reflects any of several broad goals, such as wanting to help the partner, promote the relationship, or be slightly ahead of the partner (McClintock, 1972). When faced with a highly negative interaction—for example, when the partner is aggressive—highly committed individuals will either be motivated to respond in ways that salvage the relationship (e.g., downplay or justify the aggressive act) or reduce their motivation to save the relationship by becoming less committed and dependent. Research has shown that, compared with less committed individuals, more committed individuals respond to a negative partner behavior by redirecting their reaction from retaliation to an attempt to diffuse the contentious situation (Yovetich & Rusbult, 1994).

To the extent that psychological aggression does not have the social taboo attached to physical aggression, situations in which a partner is psychologically aggressive may be perceived as less contentious than physical aggression situations. Victims may find it easier to respond in benign ways toward less rather than more overt forms of aggression, irrespective of their commitment level.

In addition to predicting responses to contentious partner situations, interdependence theory suggests that people become acclimated to events in their relationship by forming expectations of typical behavior, namely a standard of comparison or "comparison level" (Thibaut & Kelley, 1959). Individuals gauge their satisfaction level based on whether events in their relationship exceed their expectations (causing high satisfaction) or fall short of their expectations (causing low satisfaction). As such, victims who repeatedly experience partner aggression may come to expect the occurrence of aggression in their current and future intimate relationships. The more aggression individuals experience, the more likely they are to perceive the acts as normal rather than severely negative.

Taken together, these theoretical frameworks call into question the idea that a target of partner aggression would immediately take a negative stance toward the partner's aggressive actions. It depends on factors such as the individual's level of commitment, the nature of the aggressive acts, and the current comparison level or level of expectations.

REINTERPRETING THE PAST: DO VICTIMS DOWNPLAY THEIR PARTNER'S PAST AGGRESSION?

Earlier we reviewed research examining how people in general view aggression in relationships. Given the theoretical analysis we described, a likely source of systematic variation in perceptions of partner aggression is whether one is currently being victimized. Because current victims are linked to an aggressive partner, they may have a vested interest in holding more tolerant perceptions of partner aggression. Indeed, a recent worldwide study by the World Heath Organization (Garcia-Moreno, Heise, Jansen, Ellsberg, & Watts, 2005) revealed that perceiving a male partner's aggression as normal or justified—specifically, accepting a man's beating of his wife—was more pervasive among women who had experienced such aggression than among those who had not.

Much (but not all) of our own research on this issue has primarily involved female college students. We focus on women mainly to narrow our analysis at the outset, with the intention of expanding it to male victims once the basic processes of entrapment are well understood. By no means do we suggest that men are not victims of partner aggression; in fact, research has shown that they can be at risk with respect to less severe aggression (Johnson & Ferraro, 2000).

We focus on college students for several reasons. From a practical standpoint, it has been convenient to collect data from college samples. More important, however, on theoretical grounds, we have been interested in the forces that keep victims connected to an aggressive partner when there are no legally binding reasons for remaining with the partner (which is the case in marriage), and when victims reside in an environment where there are many other potential partners (which interdependence theory conceptualizes in terms of the comparison level for alternatives; Kelley & Thibaut, 1978). Because the objective circumstances are such that leaving one's abusive partner should not be difficult, it stands to reason that the subjective circumstances keeping victims in the relationship must be strong.

Research Comparing General Perceptions of Current Victims, Past Victims, and Nonvictims

We sought to examine further the link between being victimized and holding tolerant beliefs regarding partner aggression (Arriaga, 2007). We predicted that current or past victims would be more tolerant than nonvictims, based on the idea in interdependence theory that individuals shift their point of reference for expected behavior based on their own experiences. The more aggression one has experienced, the more aggression might come to be expected in relationships, and thus the less likely it would be viewed as grounds for ending a relationship.

Our critical prediction, however, was with respect to differences between current and past victims. If these two groups do not differ in their perceptions of partner aggression, it suggests that these perceptions are not motivated by one's current relationship goals. They are influenced only by the victim's experiences and expectations. Consistency and interdependence theories, however, suggest that current victims should be more tolerant of partner aggression than past victims. Current victims remain involved with their partner and thus have an interest in holding perceptions that are consistent with this involvement. We anticipated support for a motivated cognition process, whereby current victims would be more tolerant in general of partner aggression than past victims, who in turn would be more tolerant than nonvictims.

Across two studies, we recruited female college students who had previously been or currently were in a relationship (Study 1, $n = 186$; Study 2, $n = 156$). Participants completed several measures, including their own relationship status (i.e., currently dating or not), and their victimization status (i.e., current victim, victim in a past relationship, never been victimized) as indicated by a scale modeled after the Conflict Tactics Scale (CTS; Straus & Gelles, 1990). The CTS asks participants to indicate the number of times their current partner has engaged in specific verbally, emotionally, or physically aggressive acts (e.g., partner insulted or swore at you, partner grabbed and shook you).

Participants also completed a scale that asked about the same and additional specific partner aggressive acts; on this scale, they were instructed to indicate the degree to which having a partner commit that act would be grounds for ending a relationship. We also included one nonaggressive conflict act as a comparison point. The scale anchors were *definitely would not end a relationship* versus *definitely would end a relationship*. Responses were recoded and averaged to create three dependent variables, with higher numbers indicating more tolerance for a particular type of act: (a) a nonaggressive act (e.g., refused to talk about an issue with you), (b) psychologically aggressive acts (e.g., insulted or swore at you, intentionally destroyed your belongings), and (c) physically aggressive acts (e.g., grabbed and shook you). Study 2 also assessed the participant's perpetration status and eliminated participants who had been perpetrators more than victims. All analyses controlled for whether the participant was currently in a relationship. Study 1 also controlled for the format of the survey (paper and pencil vs. online). Study 2 exclusively relied on online surveys, but controlled for participant's amount of perpetration.

Generally, both samples perceived physical aggression to be grounds for ending a relationship. Both samples were more tolerant of psychological aggression than physical aggression and were less uniform (i.e., more variable) in their ratings of psychological aggression. Both samples were relatively tolerant of a nonaggressive act. In short, not all aggressive acts are perceived similarly, and there is more tolerance of psychological aggression than of physical aggression.

Despite these general trends, in both studies the participant's victimization status was significantly and positively associated with perceptions of what would be grounds for ending a relationship. This provides evidence that standards shift based on one's experience, consistent with interdependence theory's comparison level construct. Moreover, perceptions of partner aggression were motivated by the amount of connection with a partner. Current victims were more tolerant of psychological aggression than past victims, who were more tolerant than nonvictims. In short, the more connected a victim is, the more motivated the victim may be to tolerate partner aggression.

We now turn to a more direct indicator of connection to a partner: a person's level of commitment. We also focus more specifically on perceptions of acts that have already occurred, rather than perceptions of what might be grounds for ending a relationship if they were to occur. That is, we shift our focus from hypothetical, possible acts to ones that have actually occurred.

Research on Commitment and Partner Aggression

Consistency theories provide a framework for anticipating differences between individuals who are currently involved with an abusive partner and those who are not. However, these theories have not provided precise ways to conceptualize and measure variations in closeness or connection among relationship partners. In that respect, interdependence theory has been useful. Rusbult's concept of relationship commitment (Rusbult, 1983; Rusbult et al., 2001)—thoughts and feelings that reflect wanting to continue the relationship and being attached to the partner, thoughts and feelings that stem from being strongly affected by a partner—is useful for predicting variations in perceptions among current daters. In several lines of work, our basic prediction has been the same: The more committed a victim is to a partner, the more likely the victim will be to avoid maintaining strongly negative views of the partner's aggressive acts.

One study (Arriaga, 2002) testing this basic prediction examined whether victims of partner aggression "spin" (reinterpret) their partner's aggressive acts as "just joking around." Students at a community college and a large university were recruited for a survey study. Of the 82 who reported currently being in a romantic relationship, 54 (18 males and 36 females) reported that their current partner had engaged in at least one aggressive act. Participants completed various relationship measures, including a widely used measure of commitment (Rusbult, Martz, & Agnew, 1998) and the CTS (Straus & Gelles, 1990) to indicate the number of times their current partner had been aggressive, that is, to indicate the amount of conflict-related violence.

Participants also completed a scale modeled after the CTS, listing the same aggressive acts but varying the instructions to elicit instances when the partner was joking around. Some of the acts listed—the same as those used earlier in the survey—might well have occurred when the partner was joking around (e.g., pushing) but other acts were unequivocally aggressive (e.g., kicking, beating up, striking with a weapon). Participants who reported these severely aggressive acts in a joking context were deemed to be reinterpreting unambiguously violent behaviors as being less serious or nonviolent than they really were. The number of times these severe acts occurred provided an indicator of joking violence.

In general, participants who reported more conflict violence also reported more joking violence, $r(54) = .36$, $p < .01$. The association of conflict violence with joking violence was moderated, however, by commitment level, suggesting that highly committed individuals did not share the same pattern of perceptions that characterized less committed individuals. Less committed individuals who reported conflict violence were no more or less likely to report joking violence, $r(22) = -.06$, $p = .79$. In contrast, highly committed individuals were much more likely to have their reports of joking violence associated with their reports of conflict violence, $r(32) = .59$, $p < .01$, suggesting that they reinterpreted their partner's aggression in ways that would make it easier to accept while continuing the relationship.

The highest levels of conflict violence were reported by individuals who were highly committed and who reported joking violence. For highly committed individuals, accepting partner aggression and reinterpreting it go hand in hand. As would be predicted from cognitive dissonance theory, individuals who are strongly tied (i.e., committed) to their partner feel a sense of entrapment (Rusbult & Martz, 1995) and find it difficult to report even particularly difficult instances of aggression (Arriaga, 2002).

PERCEPTIONS OF THE FUTURE: HOW EMOTIONALLY AFFECTED DO VICTIMS ANTICIPATE BEING FROM A BREAKUP?

So far we have focused on victims' motivated perceptions of their partner's past aggressive behaviors. Interdependence theory suggests that victims might suffer from motivated, distorted perceptions of a range of interpersonal situations with their partner, not just those involving aggression. A person who has no overarching goals for interactions with the partner would perceive things differently than a person who is committed to a relationship with the partner (Kelley, 1979). We therefore anticipated that commitment would predict motivated perceptions of how affected one would be if the relationship ended.

Research in the affective forecasting literature (e.g., Wilson & Gilbert, 2003) shows that people overestimate how emotionally affected they are likely to be by positive or negative events. For example, people predict that they would be happier on winning the lottery than lottery winners actually are. Academics predict they would be much less happy if denied tenure than is actually the case among those who actually were denied tenured. In one of several studies discussed by Wilson and Gilbert (2003), Gilbert, Pinel, Wilson, Blumberg, and Wheatley (1998) examined the bias in forecasting future happiness among relationship partners. They found that partners thought they would feel much less happy following a breakup than was actually the case among those who had recently experienced a breakup.

Would victims of partner aggression show the same bias, whereby they overestimate how unhappy they might feel if their relationship with the aggressive partner ended? The commonsense view is that victims should not be as devastated as nonvictims. Victims often are more depressed within their relationships than are nonvictims, and ending the relationship would provide an opportunity to undo the negative consequences of being a victim of partner aggression.

The social psychological prediction, however, goes against this common sense. The same factors that keep a person in a relationship may be the ones that influence biased perceptions of future happiness or unhappiness. Our recent research (including data still being collected at the time this chapter was written) suggests that victims exhibit the same bias as nonvictims in predicting their (un)happiness following a breakup, even though victims report less happiness overall and less satisfaction in their relationships as compared with nonvictims. In an initial cross-sectional survey study ($n = 165$), dating participants were asked to forecast their happiness immediately following, 6 months after, and 1 year after the dissolution of their relationship. Their responses were compared with current happiness ratings of individuals who had been in a past aggressive relationship and who experienced the aggression either within the last month, 6 months, or 1 year.

Several interesting findings emerged for victims of partner aggression. First, current victims forecasted they would feel much less happy if their relationship were to end than was actually the case among past victims (i.e., those whose aggressive relationship had already ended). This was the case for every time frame (i.e., immediately after, 6 months after, and 1 year after the dissolution). Second, current victims reported significantly lower current happiness and relationship satisfaction than individuals whose current partners were not aggressive (i.e., nonvictims). In short, current victims were less happy and less satisfied than their nonvictim counterparts but just as likely to overestimate the negative impact on their well-being of relationship dissolution. This finding contradicts the belief that current unhappiness in an unsatisfying relationship will motivate victims to forecast more happiness if their relationship ends. Instead, victims forecast levels of unhappiness comparable with those predicted by nonvictims.

Third, regardless of current victimization status, level of commitment was strongly related to forecasting future unhappiness were the relationship to end, $r(76) = -.58$, $p < .001$. We are currently collecting longitudinal data to compare with the findings from the cross-sectional study. In short, regardless of whether perceptions concern past partner aggression or the future of a relationship, victims of partner aggression exhibit the same motivated cognitions as nonvictims, cognitions strongly associated with level of commitment.

IMPLICATIONS FOR INTERVENTIONS AND VICTIM WELL-BEING

We have shown that victims of partner aggression find themselves in a very challenging situation: They seek a partner who will love them and yet their partner is capable of harming them. Downplaying partner aggression may help victims manage the paradox that arises from choosing to remain with an aggressive partner (Dunham & Senn, 2000) and is one way of coping with a severely troubling situation. As Dunham and Senn (2000) noted, this coping strategy may have benefits and costs. In the short term, victims can find a "mental space" within which to sustain their relationships. In the long term, however, denying or justifying a partner's aggression may keep a victim from recognizing the acts as aggressive, detecting their negative consequences, and seeking help.

An obvious way to avoid the devastating effects of partner aggression is to prevent it from occurring. Major advances have been made over the last decades in understanding perpetrators of partner aggression (Arriaga & Capezza, 2005; see also Chapters 2 and 14, this volume). Preventing the negative consequences of partner aggression, however, is not limited to ending the violence itself. It also involves helping victims of violence who are at risk of negative mental and/or physical health outcomes (Arriaga & Capezza, 2005).

A major challenge in helping victims is simply finding them. Victims who downplay aggression often do not perceive a problem and thus fail to seek help. Unfortunately, aggressive partners often convince victims that the situation is not so bad, that other relationships would be worse, or that things will get better. At the start of their relationship, the perpetrator may have had qualities to attract the victim, and she may hope that those qualities will prevail and replace the aggressive tendencies. It should come as no surprise, then, that a victim may decline over time—feel more depressed, anxious, and uncertain—and yet not pinpoint a "serious" problem.

Other victims recognize a problem but cannot leave their partner. They may be financially dependent on the partner (Rusbult & Martz, 1995). Alternatively, they may feel increasingly dependent as a result of feeling unworthy of anyone else. Psychologically aggressive partners often convince the victim that she is to blame for the aggression. As she comes to feel increasingly responsible and intent on repairing the relationship, she becomes further exposed to dangerous conditions—isolation from supportive others, coming to feel that she will "never do better"—which may make her less able or motivated to seek help (Ferraro & Johnson, 1983). More psychological aggression triggers a downward spiral of more victim self-blame, self-loathing, and loss of self, which increases dependence and susceptibility to future aggression (Kirkwood, 1993). Many victims accurately fear more violence if they try to leave.

Interventions need to be tailored depending on the specific circumstances of the victim. Financial dependence might best be addressed with immediate and sustained financial assistance (e.g., providing shelter, job training, childcare, and assistance in securing a home and employment). Emotional dependence might best be addressed by (a) redefining what constitutes a healthy, loving, and committed relationship; (b) recognizing highly aggressive partner acts as destructive and understanding how they exert their nefarious effects on the victim; and (c) restoring self-esteem, self-confidence, and a sense that one is capable of happiness alone or in another relationship. Denying aggression might best be addressed by a similar approach, especially by identifying destructive partner acts.

Would reducing commitment and dependence be the basis of an effective intervention? It is violent partners, not commitment or dependence, that causes harm to victims. Commitment and dependence are states that characterize a multitude of close relationships, are crucial to relationship well-being, and predict a vast array of relationship-maintenance behaviors. Indeed, healthy, committed relationships may be a source of physical and emotional well-being (Kiecolt-Glaser & Newton, 2001). It is not commitment per se that needs to change but personal and societal norms that are conducive to the acceptance of violence. As such, interventions might address finding nurturing partners and sustaining a strong commitment to them rather than mistakenly suggesting that commitment or dependence per se is the source of distress.

Reducing the toll of partner aggression on mental and physical health requires changing perceptions of partner aggression. As victims adopt less embellished, more negative perceptions of the partner's behavior, they become more emotionally ready to pursue their own goals with or without the partner. As societies strengthen and articulate negative views of all forms of partner aggression—physical and psychological—they may be more likely to (a) help and, importantly, support victims; (b) ostracize those who engage in partner aggression; and (c) support policies that will eradicate all forms of partner aggression. Eradicating partner aggression will eliminate the paradoxical situations in which victims must choose between sustaining unwarranted partner-enhancing perceptions and sustaining their own well-being.

REFERENCES

Arias, I., & Pape, K. T. (1999). Psychological abuse: Implications for adjustment and commitment to leave violent partners. *Violence and Victims, 14*, 55–67.

Arriaga, X. B. (2002). Joking violence among highly committed individuals. *Journal of Interpersonal Violence, 17*, 591–610. doi:10.1177/0886260502017006001

Arriaga, X. B. (2007, January). *The cognitive entrapment of relationship violence victims.* Invited address at the Relationships Preconference of the annual meeting of the Society for Personality and Social Psychology, Memphis, TN.

Arriaga, X. B., & Agnew, C. R. (2001). Being committed: Affective, cognitive, and conative components of relationship commitment. *Personality and Social Psychology Bulletin, 27*, 1190–1203. doi:10.1177/0146167201279011

Arriaga, X. B., & Capezza, N. M. (2005). Targets of partner violence: The importance of understanding coping trajectories. *Journal of Interpersonal Violence, 20,* 89–99. doi:10.1177/0886260504268600

Capezza, N. M., & Arriaga, X. B. (2008a). Factors associated with acceptance of psychological aggression against women. *Violence Against Women, 14,* 612–633. doi:10.1177/1077801208319004

Capezza, N. M., & Arriaga, X. B. (2008b). You can degrade but you can't hit: Differences in perceptions of psychological versus physical aggression. *Journal of Social and Personal Relationships, 25,* 225–245. doi:10.1177/0265407507087957

Carlson, B. E., & Worden, A. P. (2005). Attitude and beliefs about domestic violence: Results of a public opinion survey: 1. Definitions of domestic violence, criminal domestic violence, and prevalence. *Journal of Interpersonal Violence, 20,* 1197–1218. doi:10.1177/0886260505278530

Cauffman, E., Feldman, S. S., Jensen, L. A., & Arnett, J. J. (2000). The (un)acceptability of violence against peers and dates. *Journal of Adolescent Research, 15,* 652–673. doi:10.1177/0743558400156003

Coker, A. L., Davis, K. E., Arias, I., Desai, S., Sanderson, M., Brandt, H. M., & Smith, P. H. (2002). Physical and mental health effects of intimate partner violence for men and women. *American Journal of Preventive Medicine, 23,* 260–268. doi:10.1016/S0749-3797(02)00514-7

Coker, A. L., Smith, P. H., Bethea, L., King, M. R., & McKeown, R. E. (2000). Physical health consequences of physical and psychological intimate partner violence. *Archives of Family Medicine, 9,* 451–457. doi:10.1001/archfami.9.5.451

Dunham, K., & Senn, C. Y. (2000). Minimizing negative experiences: Women's disclosure of partner abuse. *Journal of Interpersonal Violence, 15,* 251–261. doi:10.1177/088626000015003002

Ferraro, K. J., & Johnson, J. M. (1983). How women experience battering: The process of victimization. *Social Problems, 30,* 325–339. doi:10.1525/sp.1983.30.3.03a00080

Festinger, L. (1957). *A theory of cognitive dissonance.* Stanford, CA: Stanford University Press.

Follingstad, D. R., Rutledge, L. L., Berg, B. J., Hause, E. S., & Polek, D. S. (1990). The role of emotional abuse in physically abusive relationships. *Journal of Family Violence, 5,* 107–120.

Garcia-Moreno, C., Heise, L., Jansen, H. A. F. M., Ellsberg, M., & Watts, C. (2005, November). Violence against women. *Science, 310,* 1282–1283. doi:10.1126/science.1121400

Gelles, R. J. (1993). Through a sociological lens: Social structure and family violence. In R. J. Gelles & D. R. Loseke (Eds.), *Current controversies on family violence* (pp. 31–46). Newbury Park, CA: Sage.

Gilbert, D. T., Pinel, E. C., Wilson, T. D., Blumberg, S. J., & Wheatley, T. (1998). Immune neglect: A source of durability bias in affective forecasting. *Journal of Personality and Social Psychology, 75,* 617–638. doi:10.1037/0022-3514.75.3.617

Heider, F. (1958). *The psychology of interpersonal perception*. New York, NY: Wiley. doi:10.1037/10628-000

Johnson, M. P., & Ferraro, K. P. (2000). Research on domestic violence in the 1990s: Making distinctions. *Journal of Marriage and the Family, 62*, 948–963. doi:10.1111/j.1741-3737.2000.00948.x

Kelley, H. H. (1979). *Personal relationships: Their structures and properties*. Hillsdale, NJ: Erlbaum.

Kelley, H. H., & Thibaut, J. W. (1978). *Interpersonal relations: A theory of interdependence*. New York, NY: Wiley

Kiecolt-Glaser, J. K., & Newton, T. L. (2001). Marriage and health: His and hers. *Psychological Bulletin, 127*, 472–503. doi:10.1037/0033-2909.127.4.472

Kirkwood, C. (1993). *Leaving abusive partners: From the scars of survival to the wisdom for change*. Newbury Park, CA: Sage.

McClintock, C. G. (1972). Social motives: A set of propositions. *Behavioral Science, 17*, 438–454. doi:10.1002/bs.3830170505

Murphy, C. M., & Hoover, S. A. (1999). Measuring emotional abuse in dating relationships as a multifactorial construct. *Violence and Victims, 14*, 39–53.

O'Leary, K. D. (1999). Psychological abuse: A variable deserving critical attention in domestic violence. *Violence and Victims, 14*, 3–23.

Pierce, M. C., & Harris, R. J. (1993). The effect of provocation, race, and injury description on men's and women's perceptions of a wife-battering incident. *Journal of Applied Social Psychology, 23*, 767–790. doi:10.1111/j.1559-1816.1993.tb01006.x

Rennison, C. M., & Welchans, S. (2000). *Intimate partner violence* (Report No. NCJ 178247). Washington, DC: Bureau of Justice Statistics, U.S. Department of Justice.

Rusbult, C. E. (1983). A longitudinal test of the investment model: The development (and deterioration) of satisfaction and commitment in heterosexual involvements. *Journal of Personality and Social Psychology, 45*, 101–117. doi:10.1037/0022-3514.45.1.101

Rusbult, C. E., & Martz, J. M. (1995). Remaining in an abusive relationship: An investment model analysis of nonvoluntary commitment. *Personality and Social Psychology Bulletin, 21*, 558–571. doi:10.1177/0146167295216002

Rusbult, C. E., Martz, J. M., & Agnew, C. R. (1998). The Investment Model Scale: Measuring commitment level, satisfaction level, quality of alternatives, and investment size. *Personal Relationships, 5*, 357–387. doi:10.1111/j.1475-6811.1998.tb00177.x

Rusbult, C. E., Olsen, N., Davis, J. L., & Hannon, P. A. (2001). Commitment and relationship maintenance mechanisms. In J. Harvey & A. Wenzel (Eds.), *Close romantic relationships: Maintenance and enhancement* (pp. 87–113). Mahwah, NJ: Erlbaum.

Sorenson, S. B., & Taylor, C. A. (2005). Female aggression toward male intimate partners: An examination of social norms in a community-based sample. *Psychology of Women Quarterly, 29*, 78–96. doi:10.1111/j.1471-6402.2005.00170.x

Straus, M. A., & Gelles R. J. (1990). *Physical violence in American families: Risk factors and adaptations to violence in 8,145 families.* New Brunswick, NJ: Transaction.

Thibaut, J. W., & Kelley, H. H. (1959). *The social psychology of groups.* New York, NY: Wiley.

Tjaden, P., & Theonnes, N. (2000). *Prevalence, incidence, and consequences of violence against women: Findings from the National Violence Against Women Survey* (Report No. NCJ 183781). Washington, DC: National Institute of Justice, U.S. Department of Justice.

Wilson, T. D., & Gilbert, D. T. (2003). Affective forecasting. In M. Zanna (Ed.), *Advances in experimental social psychology* (Vol. 35, pp. 345–411). San Diego, CA: Academic Press.

Yovetich, N. A., & Rusbult, C. E. (1994). Accommodative behavior in close relationships: Exploring transformation of motivation. *Journal of Experimental Social Psychology, 30*, 138–164. doi:10.1006/jesp.1994.1007

21

THE PSYCHOLOGICAL TOLL OF EXPOSURE TO POLITICAL VIOLENCE: THE ISRAELI EXPERIENCE

ZAHAVA SOLOMON AND KARNI GINZBURG

The proclivity of human beings for aggression, which too often culmi-nates in war, entails a high price in human suffering. Combatants, mostly men, are naturally the ones who suffer most severely. In constant danger themselves, they witness the injury and death of friends and enemies and are repeatedly exposed to the gruesome sights and sounds of slaughter. They struggle with fear and loneliness as well as the more tangible deprivations of food, drink, and sleep. The enormous destructive power of modern weapons and the uncertain-ties of modern guerrilla warfare add to the already massive stress of war.

People have recognized the inevitability of psychological wounds of war since biblical times at least. However, although war-induced psychological disorders receive public attention during and immediately after a war, little attention is devoted to the long-term psychological tolls of war. Hence, until recently, knowledge about this topic has been quite fragmented, and lessons learned in one war have easily been forgotten before the next one begins (Mangelsdorff, 1985).

Life in Israel is characterized by recurrent and prolonged exposure to mil-itary and political violence. After completing 3 years of compulsory military service, all able-bodied men are required to serve in the Israel Defense Forces

(IDF) reserves, which means that they are more or less continually exposed to military violence or training for war. Thus, the postwar experiences of Israeli veterans differ from those of veterans in other countries, where soldiers usually return to a stable civilian society after a war ends. Given that the context of postwar recovery has a substantial effect on traumatized veterans' mental health, one cannot necessarily extrapolate to Israeli veterans from findings of studies conducted in other parts of the world.

In this chapter, we bring together findings from 3 decades of Israeli studies of male combatants designed to shed light on the immediate and long-term effects of recurrent and prolonged exposure to military violence. In particular, the chapter is based on our own prospective longitudinal assessment of two cohorts: (a) veterans of the First Lebanon War (1982) and (b) ex-prisoners of war (POWs) from the Yom Kippur War (1973).

COMBAT-INDUCED STRESS DISORDERS

The most common and conspicuous psychological sequelae of combat are combat stress reaction, an acute response, and posttraumatic stress disorder, a chronic disorder.

On the Battlefield: Combat Stress Reactions

Exposure to battlefield violence is bound to arouse anxiety, which is a perfectly normal response to an imminent threat. The arousal of moderate anxiety seems to be adaptive because it increases concentration and vigilance, which soldiers need on the battlefield. It is perhaps surprising that most combatants manage their anxiety fairly well and remain psychologically immune to the terrible violence of modern warfare. They continue to function as soldiers, do not endanger themselves or their fellow comrades, and do not ask to be evacuated (Solomon, 1993).

Not all combatants are as fortunate, however. A small but important proportion of combatants are overwhelmed by their battlefield anxiety (Solomon, 1993). They perceive the threat as so intense, prolonged, and uncontrollable that they feel totally vulnerable, helpless, and powerless. These are characteristic signs of battlefield-related psychological breakdown, known in various places and eras as *combat stress reaction* (CSR), *shell shock, combat fatigue*, or *war neurosis*, among other terms (Solomon, 1993). CSR occurs when a soldier is stripped of his psychological defenses, feels so overwhelmed by the threat that he becomes powerless to fight, and is inundated by feelings of utter helplessness and anxiety. In such a state, the soldier is a danger to himself and others and is no longer able to perform military duties.

CSR is characterized by polymorphic and labile symptoms (Solomon, 1993). Psychosomatic symptoms, for example, range from loss of bladder and bowel control, trembling, stuttering, and vomiting, to conversion reactions, such as blindness and paralysis without identified organic cause. Cognitive symptoms include confusion, temporal and spatial disorientation, and impaired attention, memory, judgment, and decision making. The main emotional symptoms are alternating states of paralyzing anxiety and deep depression. Behavioral symptoms include manifestations of these emotions: great agitation, on the one hand, and apathy and withdrawal, on the other. Some of the symptoms are quite bizarre, with soldiers tearing off their uniforms and running amok toward the enemy or becoming frozen in their tracks, or clinging to a piece of clothing. These manifestations change as rapidly as the emotional state that underlies them and can be quite perplexing to an observer (Solomon, 1993).

The reported prevalence rates of CSR vary considerably, both within and among wars (Solomon, 1993). The reported rates among World War II's Allied soldiers ranged from 10% to 48% of injured soldiers. In the Vietnam War, rates were significantly lower, with the official figure being 1.2% of the total number of American soldiers wounded on the battlefield. In the Yom Kippur War, the official count was 10% of Israeli soldiers wounded in action, although in some units it was as high as 70%. In the First Lebanon War, the official figure was 23% of Israelis wounded in action, meaning that one of every four war casualties was a psychiatric casualty. More recently, rates of only 3% of CSR casualties were reported among British veterans evacuated from the battle zone in Iraq (Turner et al., 2005). This huge variation seems to reflect differences in identification and counting of CSR casualties as well as differences in the amount and severity of destruction and atrocities to which soldiers are exposed on the battlefield. However, despite this variability, the reported rates clearly indicate that CSR is an inevitable and common consequence of war.

The Aftermath of War: Posttraumatic Stress Disorder and Comorbidities

CSR can be a transient state for some veterans, but for others it marks the beginning of a process of posttraumatic decline. At the end of a war, the debilitating effects of CSR may abate in some cases. In other veterans, however, profound and prolonged psychological sequelae may remain and consolidate into chronic and pervasive psychiatric disorders, such as *posttraumatic stress disorder* (PTSD). PTSD is a constellation of repeated reexperiencing of a traumatic event (e.g., unwanted mental intrusions, memories, images, dreams), reduced involvement with the external world (i.e., trauma-related avoidance), cognitive–affective hyperarousal, and impaired functioning (American Psychiatric Association, 1994).

To understand these individual differences in long-term effects of exposure to war violence, we initiated in 1982 a prospective longitudinal study of all identified Israeli CSR casualties of the First Lebanon War and a matched control group (for details, see Solomon, 1993). Data collection in this unique study commenced during the war itself, and the follow-up study is still continuing. Hundreds of veterans from both study groups have been interviewed at four time points: 1, 2, 3, and 20 years after their active participation in the 1982 war.

Chronic Posttraumatic Stress Disorder

According to currently prevailing psychiatric formulations, PTSD is the most common psychological injury of exposure to war violence (American Psychiatric Association, 1994). Still, few empirical investigations have assessed PTSD in identified CSR casualties. The results of our 20-year follow-up study of all treated Israeli CSR casualties of the First Lebanon War (Solomon & Mikulincer, 2006) revealed that 64% of identified CSR casualties suffered from PTSD symptoms 1 year after the war. At 2 years after the war, the rate of PTSD casualties decreased to 59% and then further to 40% at 3 years. The most interesting and perhaps surprising finding, however, was that the rate of PTSD casualties increased again to 53% 20 years after the war. In other words, the war does not end for many traumatized veterans; instead, CSR marks the beginning of a lifelong psychological vulnerability.

Combat-induced PTSD was also identified among some veterans in our control group who were not identified as CSR casualties on the battlefield. Fourteen percent of them reported suffering from PTSD 1 year after the war, 22% after 2 years, 11% after 3 years, and 27% 20 years later. These figures point to a long-term detrimental effect of war violence even for soldiers who survive the immediate stress of battlefield without any identified psychological breakdown.

It is important to note that the afflicted soldiers in our control group did not seek help. Many of them were probably unaware that they suffered from CSR symptoms or believed that these symptoms were a natural and inevitable outcome of their horrific battlefield experiences. Others probably did realize their plight but were reluctant to seek help. It is likely that these veterans with silent PTSD are a mere fraction of a much larger number of psychiatric casualties of war whose distress is similarly unidentified and untreated. This observation is consistent with studies demonstrating that many traumatized American veterans suffered from PTSD for years without seeking help.

Although we realized that PTSD often goes untreated, it was still surprising and troubling in the Israeli context. Had the PTSD casualties sought help for their war-related disturbances at any IDF mental health clinic, they would have averted the risk of being sent back to the front. In our view, this disinclination to seek help can be explained in part by the finding that PTSD among our control veterans was less severe and less distressing than that of CSR veterans (Solomon, 1993). Earlier studies have shown that the propensity to seek treatment for psychiatric disorders and the propensity to adopt the sick role are closely related to symptom severity (e.g., Nadler, 1983).

Alternatively, it is possible that PTSD casualties in the control group were highly motivated to continue serving in the army and were not interested in obtaining any potential secondary gain. At the time of the study, masculine identity was strongly associated with military service in Israel. Identifying oneself as ill may be costly in terms of both self-esteem and social approval. Veterans who sustained a CSR had to contend with the implications of their breakdown, with the shame and guilt of having let down their buddies and having betrayed the trust placed in them by their family and nation. Considering the great importance attributed to the army in Israel, the silent PTSD sufferers' sense of failure and injured manhood must weigh heavily on them and perhaps contributes to their continuing PTSD.

The high rates of PTSD casualties in both of our study groups are intriguing; they may reflect the recurrent exposure to military and political violence in Israel. All of our study participants, like other Israeli men of their age, have served in the IDF reserves and could have been recalled for active military duty during the first and second intifadas (Palestinian rebellions), the Second Lebanon War, and other military operations in Lebanese and Palestinian territories. Like all other Israeli citizens, they have been repeatedly exposed to Palestinian terror attacks, suicidal bombers, and Iraqi missile attacks during the last 20 years. We believe that such recurrent exposure to war may have impeded the recovery of many of the traumatized veterans.

The unexpected rise in rates of PTSD casualties 20 years after the war may have two main causes. First, 20 years after the war most of our participants were in midlife. This is a particularly high-risk period for either delayed-onset or reactivated PTSD because it often involves some reduction in work and other activities and provides an opportunity, welcome or not, to reminisce and review one's life (Solomon & Mikulincer, 2006). This transition may allow forgotten or suppressed traumatic memories to resurface (Solomon & Prager, 1992). Second, the fourth wave of measurement, 20 years after the war, was carried out in the midst of the second intifada (2003), when the Israeli population was exposed to numerous terror attacks and sights of destruction, injuries, and violent death. This intense exposure of the previously traumatized veterans to harsh political violence may have reactivated the psychological breakdown they had experienced 20 years earlier, during or immediately after the First Lebanon War.

Effects of Repeated Exposure to Combat

Israel's many wars have both obliged and enabled us to study the impact of recurrent combat exposure. Because most countries are fortunate enough not to call up the same soldiers to serve in repeated wars, the available literature on combat stress has little to offer on this issue. However, studies of other adverse experiences provide three alternative theoretical perspectives on the potential effects of recurrent exposure to war violence. First, the *vulnerability perspective* (Coleman, Butcher, & Carson, 1980) considers repeated exposure to stressful events to be a risk factor because it drains a person's coping resources. Second, the *stress inoculation perspective* (Epstein, 1983) holds that repeated exposure to stressful events serves as an "immunizer" because it fosters the development of more effective coping strategies and thereby promotes adaptation. Third, the *stress resolution hypothesis* (Block & Zautra, 1981) proposes that what matters is not so much the person's repeated exposure to a particular stressful event but how he or she coped with it. According to Block and Zautra (1981), successful coping leads to a sense of well-being and to increased coping resources, whereas unsuccessful coping leads to increased vulnerability and distress and an erosion of coping resources.

To examine the effects of recurrent exposure to war violence, we asked our sample of First Lebanon War veterans to indicate whether they had participated as combatants in previous Israeli wars and whether they had sustained a psychological breakdown in each of them (Solomon, Mikulincer, & Jacob, 1987). We found that the highest rate of CSR casualties in the First Lebanon War was among soldiers who had experienced a psychological breakdown in a previous Israeli war (66%); the lowest rate was among soldiers who had fought in previous Israeli wars without experiencing a psychological breakdown (44%). Among soldiers with no prior war experience, the rate of CSR casualties fell in between (57%).

These findings suggest that successful resolution of previous war stress helps soldiers cope with subsequent battles. But they also indicate that novice soldiers are better off than those who had collapsed in a previous war. Although not every soldier who sustains CSR is doomed to a second breakdown under similar circumstances, CSR leaves most casualties more vulnerable the second time around (Coleman et al., 1980). We should note that only a minority of CSR casualties go on to fight in subsequent wars. It is a highly select group, having been deemed fit to return to active duty by the army and having displayed personal motivation to do so. If these veterans still display increased susceptibility, other CSR casualties who were not allowed to return to military duties would presumably be even more vulnerable.

The detrimental impact of recurrent exposure to combat violence becomes more apparent when the number of previous wars is taken into account. Among soldiers with a prior psychological breakdown, CSR rates in the First Lebanon War increased linearly with the number of prior war experiences: 57% after one war, 67% after two, and 83% after three. Among soldiers who had fought without a prior psychological breakdown, CSR rates in the First Lebanon War were curvilinear: Veterans who actively participated in either one or three previous wars had higher CSR rates (50% and 44%, respectively) than did soldiers who participated in two (33%). Taken together, our research findings suggest that exposure to military violence scars an individual and weakens his resistance to future combat-related violence. They also suggest that whatever the possible inoculation benefits of successful stress resolution, repeated trauma may eventually break even the hardiest souls.

Reactivation of Traumatic Reactions

Reactivation of traumatic reactions is a well-known phenomenon. Survivors of many traumatic events, including the Holocaust, combat, and rape, among others, can experience a reactivation of their response to the original trauma when they are reminded of it (Christenson, Walker, Ross, & Malthie, 1981; Lindemann, 1944).

As we have noted, 66% of veterans who suffered from psychological breakdown in the Yom Kippur War showed a recurrent CSR episode in the First Lebanon War. Studying these cases in a deeper and more detailed way, we found that they represented two different types of trauma-related reactivation (e.g., Solomon, Garb, Bleich, & Grupper, 1987). Twenty-three percent of these cases exhibited uncomplicated reactivations or classic reactivations. These veterans seemed to have completely recovered from their previous Yom Kippur War-related psychological breakdown in 1973. They were virtually symptom free between the wars. The first indication that all was not well came with the emergence of CSR during the First Lebanon War, which was generally precipitated by a threatening incident directly reminiscent of their Yom Kippur War experience. The remaining cases (77%) can be more aptly termed *exacerbated PTSD*. Here, the Yom Kippur War-related psychological breakdown in 1973 left more salient scars, and veterans continued to suffer from PTSD symptoms of high (51%), medium (9%), and low severity (17%) between the Yom Kippur War and the First Lebanon War. Symptoms became intensified during reserve duty, and the call-up notice to Lebanon provoked considerable anticipatory anxiety. Moreover, these men were so vulnerable to combat-related violence that their CSR during the First Lebanon War had been triggered by an incident unrelated to their original war trauma and, in many cases, one that did not pose a direct or immediate danger.

All of these casualties had made great efforts to function effectively in the 9 years between the Yom Kippur War and the First Lebanon War, and they had generally been successful. While relying on coping mechanisms such as repression, suppression, denial, and cognitive avoidance, most of them married, started families, and held jobs—and some did well professionally. None were hospitalized. All continued to serve in the reserves, despite the fact that their symptoms were intensified in the presence of military violence. Many hid their symptoms from their friends, families, and army commanders.

Their recurrent CSR during the First Lebanon War revealed the psychological damage that the first breakdown had created and seemed to deepen the damage. In general, there were more symptoms during the recurrent CSR episode in the First Lebanon War than during the first CSR episode in the Yom Kippur War, and the symptoms were more intense and debilitating. Furthermore, even though some soldiers with prior CSR in the Yom Kippur War participated in the First Lebanon War without further breakdown, the detrimental effects of the earlier episode were still detectable a decade later (Solomon, 1993).

LONG-TERM IMPLICATIONS OF WAR CAPTIVITY: LESSONS FROM THE YOM KIPPUR WAR

Participation in active combat exposes soldiers to extreme physical and mental stress that has pathogenic effects. For one group of soldiers, combat is but the first step in a traumatic journey. For these soldiers who fall into enemy hands, the war continues even after the shooting stops. These POWs continue to be exposed to prolonged and often even more extreme traumatic conditions.

Stressors of War Captivity

At time of physical capture, a combatant is engaged directly and at short range with his enemies, and brutal force is typically used to deprive him of his autonomy (e.g., Avnery, 1982). During captivity, the POW is often held in unsanitary and uncomfortable conditions and may be deprived of sufficient amounts of food and water (e.g., Hunter, 1993). The POW may even be subjected to brutal torture and interrogations, as well as humiliation. Mock executions may be carried out, and solitary confinement may be used as well. Deprivation of benevolent human interactions enhances the captive's dependency on his captors. The lack of social support, denial of privacy, and continuous torture and humiliation may cripple a POW's identity and potentially pave the way for a breakdown of psychological defenses.

The trauma of captivity is unique in the sense that it entails recurrent exposure to deliberate infliction of extreme physical and mental violence. These stressors are added on to the extreme conditions and hazards that the

POWs experienced during combat. In addition, although the experience of war may be impersonal, captivity is characterized by personal interactions between captives and captors, and as such it generates a unique form of controlling and coercive relationship (Herman, 1992). Various methods of control and coercion are used to deprive the POWs of their sense of autonomy and replace it with a sense of horror and helplessness.

Captors use various techniques to break a captive's spirit. During the Yom Kippur War, Israeli POWs were repeatedly exposed to anti-Israeli propaganda, misinformed of the death of Israel's leaders, and falsely told about the triumph of Arab states over Israel and the occupation of Israel by Arab armies. At times, captives were informed that their homes had been destroyed and their loved ones and relatives killed (e.g., Avnery, 1982). These were deliberate efforts to exacerbate the POWs' feelings of loneliness, weakness, and isolation.

The trauma of captivity was often made worse by prisoners' feelings that they had failed to meet the heroic standards emphasized by Israeli culture. This ethos requires that prisoners of war refuse to disclose any information, endure the unbearable pain of interrogation without cracking, and even take their own lives if necessary. This code of conduct is entwined with the ideal image of the Israeli combatant who is expected to "fight until the end" and "maintain his honor" during interrogations (Gavriely, 2006). Thus, many Israeli POWs were regarded not only as soldiers who failed in the important role of defending their homeland but also as a threat to national security because they might have disclosed potentially sensitive information. This public notion is mirrored by Israeli military law, which defines surrender to the enemy when not ordered to do so as a severe offense—a betrayal—that may deserve the death penalty. Moreover, disclosure of secrets while in captivity is defined as treason, a despicable behavior (Gavriely, 2006). This intense conflict between personal survival and living up to cultural standards is at the heart of what Avnery (1982) called the *captive's dilemma:* staying alive and sustaining criticism and condemnation versus complying with the norm at the cost of losing one's life. For many ex-POWs, this dilemma produced feelings of utter failure and unbearable weakness.

During the 1973 Yom Kippur War, several hundred Israeli soldiers were captured on the Syrian and Egyptian fronts. POWs held in Egypt were released relatively quickly, within 4 to 6 weeks. POWs in Syria were held for 8 months. During captivity in Egypt, the prisoners were held in separate cells, whereas in Syria, after a rigorous interrogation period, POWs were held in groups, each in a large common room. In both states of captivity, Israeli soldiers were subjected to interrogation and torture designed to break them down mentally.

To study the psychological consequences of war captivity, we followed-up ex-POWs from the Israeli army land forces who were taken captive on either the Egyptian or the Syrian front during the Yom Kippur War, and we compared them with a control group of combat veterans who fought on the same fronts as the ex-POWs during the same war but were not taken captive. Controls were matched with the ex-POWs in terms of personal and military background. Participants in the two groups (i.e., ex-POWs, controls) were interviewed twice: 18 and 30 years after the war (see Solomon & Dekel, 2005, for details).

Long-Term Psychological Sequelae of War Captivity

Findings from our study reveal that 3 decades after their release from captivity, 23% of former Israeli POWs still met symptom criteria from the *Diagnostic and Statistical Manual of Mental Disorders* (4th ed.; American Psychiatric Association, 1994) for PTSD, as compared with 5% of non-POW controls (Solomon & Dekel, 2005). This figure points to both the resilience of the 77% of former POWs who did not meet PTSD criteria and to the long-lasting psychological damage of captivity to the remaining 23%. The question is why the psychological damage of captivity should be so much more enduring than that of combat, which is itself pathogenic.

Several explanations may be offered. The simplest is based on the special hardships of captivity: the torture, humiliation, and isolation that are part and parcel of war captivity (Mollica et al., 1990). In addition, these hardships are personal (Herman, 1992). That is, the threat of combat to the life and physical integrity of the soldier is a relatively impersonal threat; it is directed toward whomever is in the line of fire and not at any particular soldier. Thus, there is no affront to the soldier's personhood, even if he is injured. The trauma of captivity, however, occurs within a personal relationship between the captive and his captors. The special torments of captivity are part of a planned and concerted effort to "break" a particular person and are intentionally inflicted on him by persons he gets to know and on whom he is dependent for physical survival.

Another explanation for higher PTSD levels among POWs has to do with the uniqueness of the social context of combat captivity. Combatants are equipped with weapons and protective devices, and they fight alongside commanders and comrades. The powerful stress-reducing effect of unit cohesion and social support derived from comrades and commanders is a well-documented sustaining force for combatants (e.g., Solomon, Mikulincer, & Hobfoll, 1987). However, captivity renders the POW totally isolated and deprived of any human compassion or support. The severity of captivity may thus be compounded by isolation and loneliness, leaving a more profound and enduring traumatic imprint.

Still another possible explanation is that POWs adopt strategies that are useful in captivity, such as suspiciousness and hyperalertness, and then apply them in civilian life later on, where they are often counterproductive. Eberly,

Harkness, and Engdahl (1991) suggested that traumatized POWs can be viewed as survivors who continue to exhibit patterns of thought, emotion, and behavior that were adaptive during their period of traumatization.

A fourth possible explanation focuses on the compounding of traumatic experiences. For most POWs, the trauma of captivity follows on the heels of the trauma of combat. Captivity thus extends the duration of the traumatic experience, further drawing on the soldier's already depleted coping resources (Ursano et al., 1996). As is well known, the longer a traumatic experience lasts, the more severe the ensuing psychiatric disorders are likely to be (Hunter, 1993). The cumulative damage of multiple traumas is known to be more severe than the damage of a single trauma (Herman, 1992).

Trajectories of Posttraumatic Stress Disorder: Changes Over Time

The theoretical literature on the longitudinal effects of trauma offers three alternative views on the temporal course of postcaptivity symptomatology. One view is that time is a healer and that ex-POWs will recover partially or completely with the passage of time (e.g., Engdahl, Speed, Eberly, & Schwartz, 1991; Potts, 1994). A second, different view is that PTSD is a chronic ailment that will intensify over time because of a natural decline in resilience, perhaps especially in midlife (e.g., Maercker, 1999). This view gains some support from a study that documented increased rates of PTSD symptoms over a period of 4 years in a group of community-dwelling former American POWs from World War II and the Korean War (Port, Engdahl, & Frazier, 2001). The third view is that, barring an initial decline in psychological distress soon after a POW is released from captivity, no clear temporal trajectory is discernable (Zeiss & Dickman, 1989). In this view, time can either heal or intensify the psychological wounds of captivity, depending on an ex-POW's personality and life experiences after release. This view stresses the liability of PTSD symptomatology and the possibility that life events and psychological changes or developments can cause the symptoms to intensify or decline (Buffum & Wolfe, 1995).

Trauma researchers have not yet established which of these three views best describes the long-term effects of war captivity. Too few studies tracing the longitudinal effects of captivity have been carried out, and most have assessed recovery and other changes in PTSD symptomatology only through retrospective self-reports. In addition, the observed variability in the aftermath of captivity, both between and within groups, is not well understood.

In our longitudinal two-wave study conducted 18 and 30 years after the Yom Kippur War (Solomon & Dekel, 2005), we found that PTSD followed a different course among ex-POWs and combat controls. Ex-POWs were 10 times more likely than controls to experience deterioration in their psychological condition in the 12-year interval between the two assessments. Almost 20% of ex-POWs who did not meet PTSD criteria 18 years after their release did meet them at the 30-year assessment. This deterioration occurred in less than 1% of combat controls. Given the study design, it is impossible to know whether this 20% rise in ex-POWs' PTSD rates reflects reactivation or delayed onset of PTSD. Previous studies reported delayed-onset PTSD in 11% (Green et al., 1990) and 20% (Wolfe, Erickson, Sharkansky, King, & King, 1999) of various traumatized groups.

POWs also showed a statistically significant increase in endorsement of each of the PTSD symptom clusters (i.e., intrusion, avoidance, hyperarousal). Among controls, in contrast, there was no change in endorsement of the three symptom clusters, along with a downward trend in the endorsement of most PTSD symptoms. These findings indicate that time exacerbates the detrimental effects of war captivity. This increase in PTSD among ex-POWs is consistent with findings of increased PTSD rates and symptom levels over a 4-year measurement interval among American ex-POWs (Port et al., 2001) but differs from findings of decreased PTSD symptoms over time (Engdahl et al., 1991). The differences are probably related to the times of measurement in the research studies.

A previous study (Port et al., 2001) found a U-shaped pattern, with high PTSD rates immediately after captivity, followed by a gradual decline, and then, from midlife onward, a rise in PTSD rates. It is possible that our first assessment, taken 18 years after prisoners' release, fell within the lower part of the curve, and our second assessment, 12 years later, reflected the rising rates as men aged. It is interesting to note that ex-POWs' heightened PTSD is similar to increases in PTSD rates observed among First Lebanon War veterans (reported earlier in this chapter). In our view, both of them can be explained either by aging or by the unremitting threat of war and terror in Israel.

Along with the vulnerabilities of ex-POWs found in this study, we should mention the resilience of the non-POW veterans, who had low rates of PTSD both 18 and 30 years after the war (3.8% and 4.8%, respectively). Even though all of them had seen combat and, as noted, most continued to serve in active reserve and were exposed to the ongoing threat of terror, they did not show any sign of psychopathology. Among ex-POWs, the PTSD rates were considerably higher, but the majority did not meet PTSD criteria at either time of assessment. This high level of resilience in both groups lends further support to the contention that resilience in the face of trauma is more common than psychopathology (American Psychiatric Association, 1994).

Posttraumatic Stress Disorder and Changes in Attachment Orientation

Studies of individuals who were subject to repeated abuse in which they were helpless captives under control of their captors suggest that survivors

tend to develop not only PTSD but also a unique form of posttraumatic sequelae that penetrates and alters their personality, often referred to as *complex
PTSD* or *disorder of extreme stress not otherwise specified* (DESNOS; Herman,
1992; Terr, 1991; van der Kolk, 2002). Herman (1992) suggested that prolonged captivity disrupts captives' personal relationships, which may result in
long-lasting attachment injuries and may be manifested in either anxious or
avoidant attachment. Whereas *anxious attachment* characterizes individuals
who are concerned that their significant others will not be available in times
of need and who wish intensely for proximity to and care from others, *avoidant
attachment* characterizes individuals who cannot trust others and who withdraw from intimacy and interdependence (Mikulincer & Shaver, 2007).

To test Herman's (1992) ideas, we assessed attachment orientations
among former POWs and controls 18 and 30 years after the Yom Kippur War,
and we examined reciprocal associations between PTSD and attachment orientations over time (Solomon, Dekel, & Mikulincer, 2008). Paralleling the
increase in PTSD rates among ex-POWs between the two waves of assessment,
there were increased levels of self-reported anxious and avoidant attachment
among ex-POWs during the same period. This trend was evident only in the
ex-POW group; levels of anxious and avoidant attachment were quite stable
in the control group. In addition, increases in both anxious and avoidant
attachment were positively associated with increases in PTSD symptoms.
These findings further highlight the pervasive impact of captivity. In line with
previous studies (van der Kolk, Roth, Pelcovitz, Sunday, & Spinazzola, 2005),
they suggest that exposure to repeated interpersonal trauma inflicts long-term
psychological injuries that are not captured by the PTSD diagnosis alone.

Clinical observations have suggested that repeated and prolonged trauma
may lead to major personality changes, including significant changes in one's
identity and one's behavior in close relationships (Herman, 1992; Terr, 1991).
Similarly, harsh and dramatic experiences, such as war captivity, may alter a
person's basic trust in others in a way that undermines the ability to maintain
secure attachments. Hence, even ex-POWs who have had secure attachments
may become more anxious and may defensively avoid interpersonal contact following exposure to trauma. The fact that changes in attachment orientations
were found so many years after the war ended demonstrates the pervasive and
dramatic effects of intentional, human-inflicted victimization.

Need for Professional Help and Help Seeking

Finally, our findings indicate that about twice as many ex-POWs as combat controls felt that they needed psychotherapy, and about five times as many
ex-POWs as combat controls actually sought and obtained it. The observed
rates of seeking psychotherapy and being willing to admit a need for help

among the ex-POW group were high relative to norms in Israel. They are testimony to the intensity of the distress from which ex-POWs suffer and to the increasing acceptance in Israeli society of seeking help following traumatic military experiences (Gavriely, 2006).

The higher rates of both reported need for help and actual help seeking among ex-POWs may be explained by their greater trauma-related and general distress and their lower recovery rates. Even those who received treatment were less prone to recover than combat controls who were treated. The complex and prolonged stressors to which they were exposed may have contributed to their intensive, pervasive, and widespread distress (Herman, 1992). The lower rate of recovery among treated POWs than among untreated controls is further evidence not only of the difficulties in treating trauma but also of the fact that the more massive the trauma, the more damage it causes and the more difficult it is to ameliorate with professional intervention.

CONCLUSIONS

The studies discussed in this chapter were conducted among Israeli combatants and ex-POWs. They were based on longitudinal designs, with assessments conducted 20 and 30 years after exposure to war-related violence. Findings showed that for many combatants and former POWs, exposure to war violence, atrocities, and massive acts of destruction can cause severe, long-lasting psychological disorders. Although the war ended and the prison doors opened years ago, many of the combatants and ex-POWs are still faced on a daily basis with the pathogenic effects of political aggression. Moreover, for many of these veterans, the picture has become even bleaker with time, as their mental and physical state has deteriorated.

Although our studies shed light on the enduring toll of political aggression, they also testify to the amazing resilience of many veterans. Further research is needed to determine what differentiates resilient from nonresilient war casualties and to devise more effective therapeutic interventions and preventive measures.

PTSD is the only psychiatric disorder that directly follows exposure to a recognized traumatic stressor. Thus, the best way to prevent combat-induced psychopathology is to stop making war. We have not yet been able to do that in all of recorded history, so we must continue to rely on our ability to learn more about causes of psychopathological disorders following traumatic experiences and ways to reduce their prevalence and severity. More thorough and systematic research on PTSD can increase our understanding of effective ways to help traumatized individuals. Increased awareness of their plight may open our hearts to these men and chip away at the denial that generally blinds us to their suffering.

REFERENCES

American Psychiatric Association. (1994). *Diagnostic and statistical manual of mental disorders* (4th ed.). Washington, DC: Author.

Avnery, A. (1982). *Coping and adjustment to war captivity* (Unpublished master's thesis). Hebrew University, Jerusalem, Israel.

Block, M., & Zautra, A. J. (1981). Satisfaction and distress in the community: A test of the effects of life events. *American Journal of Community Psychology, 9*, 165–180. doi:10.1007/BF00896365

Buffum, M. D., & Wolfe, N. S. (1995). Posttraumatic stress disorder and the World War II veteran: Elderly patients who were in combat or were prisoners of war may have special health care needs that may not be obvious. *Geriatric Nursing, 16*, 264–270. doi:10.1016/S0197-4572(95)80006-9

Christenson, R. M., Walker, J. L., Ross, D. R., & Malthie, A. A. (1981). Reactivation of traumatic conflicts. *The American Journal of Psychiatry, 138*, 984–985.

Coleman, J. C., Butcher, J. N., & Carson, R. C. (1980). *Abnormal psychology and modern life*. Glenview, IL: Scott Foresman.

Eberly, R. E., Harkness, A. R., & Engdahl, B. E. (1991). An adaptational view of trauma response as illustrated by the prisoner of war experience. *Journal of Traumatic Stress, 4*, 363–380. doi:10.1002/jts.2490040305

Engdahl, B. E., Speed, N., Eberly, R. E., & Schwartz, J. (1991). Comorbidity of psychiatric disorders and personality profiles of American World War II prisoners of war. *Journal of Nervous and Mental Disease, 179*, 181–187. doi:10.1097/00005053-199104000-00001

Epstein, S. (1983). Natural healing processes of the mind: II. Graded stress inoculation as an inherent coping mechanism. In D. Meichenbaum & M. Jaremko (Eds.), *Stress prevention and management: A cognitive behavioral approach* (pp. 39–66). New York, NY: Plenum Press.

Gavriely, D. (2006). Israel's cultural code of captivity and the personal stories of Yom Kippur War ex-POWs. *Armed Forces and Society, 33*, 94–105. doi:10.1177/0095327X05282531

Green, B. L., Lindy, J. D., Grace, M. C., Gleser, G. C., Leonard, A. C., Korol, M., & Winget, C. (1990). Buffalo Creek survivors in the second decade: Stability of stress symptoms. *American Journal of Orthopsychiatry, 60*, 43–54. doi:10.1037/h0079168

Herman, J. L. (1992). *Trauma and recovery*. New York, NY: Basic Books.

Hunter, E. J. (1993). The Vietnam prisoner of war experience. In J. P. Wilson & B. Raphael (Eds.), *International handbook of traumatic stress syndromes* (pp. 297–303). New York, NY: Plenum Press.

Lindemann, E. (1944). Symptomatology and management of acute grief. *The American Journal of Psychiatry, 101*, 141–148.

Maercker, A. (1999). Lifespan psychological aspects of trauma and PTSD: Symptoms and psychosocial impairments. In A. Maercker, M. Schutzwohl, & Z. Solomon

(Eds.), *Posttraumatic stress disorder: A lifespan developmental perspective* (pp. 7–42). Seattle, WA: Hogrefe & Huber.

Mangelsdorff, A. D. (1985). Lessons learned and forgotten: The need for prevention and mental health interventions in disaster preparedness. *Journal of Community Psychology, 13,* 239–257. doi:10.1002/1520-6629(198507)13:3<239::AID-JCOP2290130302>3.0.CO;2-T

Mikulincer, M., & Shaver, P. R. (2007). *Attachment in adulthood: Structure, dynamics, and change.* New York, NY: Guilford Press.

Mollica, R. F., Wyshak, G., Lavelle, J., Truong, T., Tor, S., & Yang, T. (1990). Assessing symptom change in Southeast Asian refugee survivors of mass violence and torture. *The American Journal of Psychiatry, 147,* 83–88.

Nadler, A. (1983). Personal characteristics and help-seeking. In J. D. Fisher, A. Nadler, & B. M. DePaulo (Eds.), *New directions in helping: Help-seeking* (Vol. 2, pp. 124–151). New York, NY: Academic Press.

Port, C. L., Engdahl, B., & Frazier, P. (2001). A longitudinal and retrospective study of PTSD among older prisoners of war. *The American Journal of Psychiatry, 158,* 1474–1479. doi:10.1176/appi.ajp.158.9.1474

Potts, M. K. (1994). Long-term effects of trauma: Posttraumatic stress among civilian internees of the Japanese during WW2. *Journal of Clinical Psychology, 50,* 681–698. doi:10.1002/1097-4679(199409)50:5<681::AID-JCLP2270500504>3.0.CO;2-3

Solomon, Z. (1993). *Combat stress reaction: The enduring toll of war.* New York, NY: Plenum Press.

Solomon, Z., & Dekel, R. (2005). Posttraumatic stress disorder among Israeli ex-prisoners of war 18 and 30 years after release. *The Journal of Clinical Psychiatry, 66,* 1031–1037. doi:10.4088/JCP.v66n0811

Solomon, Z., Dekel, R., & Mikulincer, M. (2008). Complex trauma of war captivity: A prospective study of attachment and PTSD. *Psychological Medicine, 38,* 1427–1434. doi:10.1017/S0033291708002808

Solomon, Z., Garb, R., Bleich, A., & Grupper, D. (1987). Reactivation of combat-related posttraumatic stress disorder. *The American Journal of Psychiatry, 144,* 51–55.

Solomon, Z., & Mikulincer, M. (2006). Trajectories of PTSD: A 20-year longitudinal study. *The American Journal of Psychiatry, 163,* 659–666. doi:10.1176/appi.ajp.163.4.659

Solomon, Z., Mikulincer, M., & Hobfoll, S. (1987). Objective versus subjective measurement of stress and social support: The case of combat-related reactions. *Journal of Consulting and Clinical Psychology, 55,* 577–583. doi:10.1037/0022-006X.55.4.577

Solomon, Z., Mikulincer, M., & Jacob, B. R. (1987). Exposure to recurrent combat stress: Combat stress reactions among Israeli soldiers in the Lebanon War. *Psychological Medicine, 17,* 433–440. doi:10.1017/S0033291700024995

Solomon, Z., & Prager, E. (1992). Elderly Israeli Holocaust survivors during the Persian Gulf War: A study of psychological distress. *The American Journal of Psychiatry, 149*, 1707–1710.

Terr, L. C. (1991). Childhood traumas: An outline and overview. *The American Journal of Psychiatry, 148*, 10–20.

Turner, M. A., Kiernan, M. D., McKechanie, A. G., Finch, P. J. C., McManus, F. B., & Neal, L. A. (2005). Acute military psychiatric casualties from the war in Iraq. *The British Journal of Psychiatry, 186*, 476–479. doi:10.1192/bjp.186.6.476

Ursano, R. J., Rundell, J. R., Fragala, M. R., Larson, S. G., Jaccard, J. T., Wain, H. J., . . . Beach, B. L. (1996). The prisoner of war. In R. J. Ursano & A. E. Norwood (Eds.), *Emotional aftermath of the Persian Gulf War* (pp. 443–476). Washington, DC: American Psychiatric Press.

van der Kolk, B. A. (2002). The assessment and treatment of complex PTSD. In R. Yehuda (Ed.), *Treating trauma survivors with PTSD* (pp. 127–156). Washington, DC: American Psychiatric Press.

van der Kolk, B. A., Roth, S. H., Pelcovitz, D., Sunday, S., & Spinazzola, J. (2005). Disorders of extreme stress: The empirical foundation of a complex adaptation to trauma. *Journal of Traumatic Stress, 18*, 389–399. doi:10.1002/jts.20047

Wolfe, J., Erickson, D. J., Sharkansky, E. J., King, D. W., & King, L. A. (1999). Course and predictors of posttraumatic stress disorder among Gulf War veterans: A prospective analysis. *Journal of Consulting and Clinical Psychology, 67*, 520–528. doi:10.1037/0022-006X.67.4.520

Zeiss, R. A., & Dickman, H. R. (1989). PTSD 40 years later: Incidence and person-situation correlates in former POWs. *Journal of Clinical Psychology, 45*, 80–87. doi:10.1002/1097-4679(198901)45:1<80::AID-JCLP2270450112>3.0.CO;2-V

INDEX

Anderson, C. A., 4, 24
Anger, 53–67
    in aggressive retaliation, 316–321
    and apologies, 61, 64
    and arguments, 62
    and attachment, 244–246, 260
    behavioral responses to, 59–60,
        62–63
    brain regions for, 109–114
    cognitive model of, 57
    control of, 262
    and cost imposition, 60–61, 63
    and evolutionary biology of conflict,
        54–57
    and face, 64
    features of, 60–64
    functional, 245
    and hatred, 322–324
    insults as cause of, 62, 64–65
    and intent, 61, 63–64
    in intergroup aggression, 315–316,
        320–326
    neurophysiological locality of, 63
    in power-system activation, 76
    recalibrational theory of, 58–60,
        63–66
    short-term, 316
    in social neuroscience perspective,
        109–110
    and status, 64
    welfare tradeoff ratios of, 57–58
"Anger of despair," 245, 246
"Anger of hope," 245, 246
Angry rumination, 109–110
Antisocial behavior
    in adolescents, 125–126
    aggressive, 153–155
    attachment insecurity in, 247–248
    candidate genes for, 157–158
    defined, 17
    familial influences on, 143–144
    nonaggressive, 153–155
Anxiety
    attachment-related, 242, 243,
        245–246
    battlefield, 386
Anxious attachment, 247
Apologies, 61, 64
Appraisal-based model, 319–320

Appraisal tendency framework,
    320–321
Approach/inhibition theory of power,
    250–251
Approach orientation, 250–252
Arguments, 62, 65
Armageddon, 268
Arousal, 21
Arousal routes, 36
Arriaga, X. B., 376
Assertion behavioral system. *See* Power
    system
Assertiveness Questionnaire, 78
Attachment, 241–254, 259–270
    and abusive personalities, 264–265
    in adulthood, 243–244
    and aggression, 246–249
    and anger, 244–246
    in approach/inhibition theory of
        power, 250–251
    attachment threat, 266–269
    in children's psychological
        development, 355–356
    dyadic processes in, 265–266
    empirical studies on, 262–264
    neurobiology of, 261–262
    neuropsychological aspect of, 261
    and power, 249–253
    "primitive" attachment threat,
        260–261
    religion as symbolic form of, 268
    theory of, 242–243
Attachment and Loss (J. Bowlby), 72, 76
Attachment anxiety, 245–247, 262–263
Attachment avoidance, 252–253,
    262–263, 358
Attachment behavioral system, 242
    activation of, 73
    in combat, 267
    fear-based activation of, 260
Attachment disruption, 266
Attachment figures
    and anger, 260
    in attachment theory, 242
    in behavioral systems, 73
    perceived unavailability of, 243–244
Attachment insecurity
    and anger, 246
    in antisocial behavior, 247–248
    and attachment figure unavailability,
        243–244

and death, 269
forms of, 261–262
in intergroup aggression, 248–249
in intimate partner abuse, 247,
263–264
and memory, 357–358
with primary caregivers, 355–356
severe and early, 265
Attachment orientation, 396–397
Attachment relationships, 355–356
Attachment security
and attachment styles, 242–243
broaden-and-build cycle in, 243
and parent–child respectfulness,
283–285
and power, 75–76
Attachment style
in adults, 262–263
and attachment theory, 242–243
in intimate relationships, 265–266
and mortality salience, 269
power in, 251
security in, 242–243
Attachment theory
application of, 241
attachment style in, 242–243
behavioral systems in, 71–72
Attachment threat, 266–269
Attention, 166–167
Attention-deficit hyperactivity disorder
(ADHD), 157
Attitudes
and behavior changes, 343–344
and intergroup contact, 341–342
and mortality salience, 300
and respect, 278, 288–289
supportive of violence, 26
toward advantaged group, 338
Automatic systems, 21
Automatization, of complex
judgments, 19
Autonomy-inhibiting behaviors, 285
Avoidance, 242–243
Avoidant attachment. See Attachment
avoidance
Avoidant individuals, 247, 248
Awareness, of inequality, 338, 340, 341
Axelrod, R., 231
Ayers, E., 190

Baer, B. A., 78
Baker, L. A., 152
Balance theory, 371–372
Baldwin, Stanley, 297
Bartels, M., 156
Bartholomew, K., 265
Battlefield violence, 386
Baumeister, R. F., 204, 207
Behavior(s)
aggressive. See Aggressive behavior
antisocial. See Antisocial behavior
autonomy-inhibiting, 285
changes in, 343–344
conditioning of, 132–133
disrespectful, 289
effects of combat stress reaction on,
387
externalizing. See Externalizing
behaviors
functional definitions of, 223–224
hyperactivated power-oriented, 77–78
measurement of, 210
normal ranges of, 107–108
of parents, 131–137
and personality traits, 89–90, 94–96
relatedness-inhibiting, 285
resource-holding power, 76
social factors in, 206–207
stability of, 156–157
Behavioral dysregulation, 354–355
Behavioral economics, 226–227
Behavioral phenotypes, 129–130
Behavioral responses, 59–60, 62–63
Behavioral scripts, 111
Behavioral signatures
and culture, 189
in CuPS approach, 188–189
in different cultures, 191–192
and ideals of culture, 191
Behavioral systems perspective, 72–74
Behavior genetic studies, 145–151
of aggression, 146–147
models for, 149–150
Beliefs
normative, 128
supportive of violence, 26
Berkowitz, L., 111
Bias
of advantaged group members, 340
in intergenerational aggression
studies, 126–127

Bifactor model, 92–93
Biological factors, 134. *See also* Genetic
    and environmental influences
Block, M., 390
Blumer, H., 335
Boden, J. M., 206
Boivin, M., 151
Boomsma, D. I., 156
Borderline personality, 264–265
Boundaries, group, 339
Bowlby, J., 71–73, 76, 241–242,
    244–245, 260
Brain activity
    with anger, 63
    effects of environmental variables
        on, 176
    in social information processing, 172
Brain anatomy, 106
Brain lesions, 107
Brain regions, 105, 109–114. *See also*
    Prefrontal cortex (PFC)
Branden, Nathaniel, 204
Brendgen, M., 151, 152
Broaden-and-build cycle, 243
Buckley, K. E., 24
Bugental, D. B., 284
Bullying, 286
Bushman, B. J., 4, 207
Buss, A. H., 78

Callous–unemotional traits, 95
Candidate genes, 157–158
Canetti-Nisim, D., 324
Captive's dilemma, 393
Caring, 288–289
Carnagey, N. L., 24
Carpenter, J. P., 229
Carver, C. S., 250
Caspi, A., 98
Cassidy, J., 265
Causal direction, 168
Change, agents of, 335
Changes over time, 395–396
Chicchetti, D., 354
Childhood development
    and aggressive parenting, 133–137
    contextual influences in, 130–133
    information processing, 168–169
    in maltreated children, 173–174
    neurological, 260–261
    and peer social rejection, 174–175

power system in, 77
psychological development. *See* Psy-
    chological development in
    children
respect in, 282–285
and transmission of aggression,
    126–127
Child maltreatment
    in children's psychological develop-
        ment, 352–358
    and coping strategies, 358
    and externalizing/internalizing
        behaviors, 354
    operationalization of, 359
    and posttraumatic stress disorder,
        356–357
    and resilience, 351
    sexual abuse, 357–358
    and social information processing,
        173–174
Children
    aggression continuity in, 125
    aggression prevention/intervention
        strategies for, 212
    conditioning of, 132–133
    externalizing spectrum in, 93–95
    fostering respect in, 289–290
    lower order traits in, 94–95
    memory in, 351, 357–358
    narcissism in, 208
    physical abuse of, 353–354
    respect for parents in, 282
    self-esteem as cause of aggression in,
        206–207
CHRM2, 97
Chronic posttraumatic stress disorder,
    388–389
Cicchetti, D., 354–355
Clausewitz, C. V., 297, 303
Climate, school, 285–286
Clutton-Brock, T. H., 225
Cognition, 18–19, 21, 223
Cognitive appraisal, 316, 321–322
Cognitive dissonance theory, 372
Cognitive effects
    of child maltreatment, 357–358
    of combat stress reaction, 387
Cognitive-information processes, 128
Cognitive model of anger, 57
Cognitive neoassociationistic model of
    aggression, 111

Horowitz, L. M., 78
Horwood, L., 206
Hostile attribution, 165
Hostile cues, 354
Hostile intent, 167
Hudziak, J. J., 156
Huesmann, L. R., 128
Humiliation, 208
Humility, 191
Hyperactivated power-oriented behavior, 77–78
Hyperactivating strategies, 73, 244
Hyperactivation (power system), 79–84

I^3 Theory, 35–48
    components of, 35–36
    future research, directions for, 46–48
    impelling forces in, 39–40
    inhibiting forces in, 40–41
    instigating triggers in, 37–39
    interaction effects of, 43–46
    main effects in, 41–43
    risk factors, 46–47
Iacono, W. G., 98
IDF (Israel Defense Forces), 385–386
Imitation, of parent behavior, 131–132
Immediate appraisal processes, 21–22
Impelling forces, 35, 36
    in I^3 Theory, 39–40
    and inhibiting forces, 45–46
    and instigating triggers, 43–44
Impellors, 40
Impulsivity, 114, 265
Incentives (revenge systems), 222–224
Individual differences, 187–189
Individual emotion, 320
Infant development, 260–261
Information-processing model, 128–133
Information processing patterns, 170
Ingroup, 321
Inhibiting forces, 35, 36
    in I^3 Theory, 40–41
    and impelling forces, 45–46
    and instigating forces, 45–46
    and instigating triggers, 44–45
Inputs, 36
Insecure attachment. See Attachment insecurity
Instigating forces, 45–46

Instigating triggers, 35, 36
    in I^3 Theory, 37–39
    and impelling forces, 43–46
    and inhibiting forces, 44–45
Institutionalized violence, 25
Insults, 62, 64–65
Integrity, 194–196
Intent
    of adversary, 308–309
    as feature of anger, 63–64
    and forgiveness, 233
    interpretation of, 167
    and likelihood of anger, 61
Intentional action, 61
Interaction effects, 43–46
Interdependence theory, 372–373
Intergenerational aggression, 126–127.
    See also Continuity of aggression
Intergroup aggression, 315–327
    anger and hatred in, 315–316, 320–326
    appraisal-based model for, 319–320
    attachment insecurity in, 248–249
    emotions and sentiments in, 316–319
    and general aggression model, 26–27
    necessary preconditions for, 320
Intergroup attitudes, 300
Intergroup comparisons, 337
Intergroup conflict, 299–300
Intergroup contact
    and attitudes, 341–342
    and change for equality, 338–339
    research on, 339–343
Intergroup relations, 333–345
    future directions for, 343–344
    intergroup contact research, 339–343
    and social change, 338–339
    and social inequality, 334–339
    tension and harmony in, 333–334
Internalizing behaviors, 354
Internal states, 21, 22
Internal working models, 73, 242
Interventions
    effective strategies for, 212–213
    as experimental evidence, 169–170
    general aggression model for, 29
    I^3 theory in, 47
    for partner aggression, 378–379

Masculine identity, 389
Mathews, V. P., 115
Matthews, P. H., 229
Mauricio, A. M., 263
Mawson, A. W., 267
McGue, M., 98
Medial prefrontal cortex (mPFC), 106,
    110, 113
Mediational approach, 188
Media violence
    in social neuroscience perspective,
        111–112
    and top-down control mechanisms,
        115–116
Memory, 351, 357–358
Men
    abusive, 260, 264–265
    abusive personality in, 262–263
    attempts to save face by, 61–62
    socialization of, 125
Mental disorders, 90–91
Mental processes, 105
Mental representation, 167
Middle East conflict, 311
Mikulincer, M., 243, 248–249, 262, 269,
    388
Military violence
    and attachment, 266–267
    in Israeli experience, 385–386
Miller, D. T., 281
Model-fitting analyses, 149–150
Molecular genetic studies, 97–98
Monitored welfare trade ratios, 58
Monoamine oxidase-A (MAO-A), 98,
    172, 175, 177–178
Moods, 318
Moral righteousness, 299–300
Mortality, 298–301, 304, 307–308
Mortality salience (MS)
    and adversary intent, 308–309
    and attachment style, 269
    and consensus, 302–303
    impact of, 304–305
    and inevitability of violence, 307
    and perceived vulnerability,
        308–309
    in support for violence, 301
    in terror management research, 299,
        300
Motives, 303–305

MPFC. *See* Medial prefrontal cortex
MS. *See* Mortality salience
Mullen, B., 148
My Lai massacre, 267

Narcissism
    in children, 208
    developmental origins of, 213–214
    and ego threat, 43–44
    as self-view, 207–209
Narcissistic Personality Inventory
    (NPI), 207
Natural selection, 54, 66. *See also*
    Evolutionary perspective
Neale, M. C., 156
Negative affect, 266, 354
Negative emotional states, 111
Negative outcome expectancies, 45
Neoassociation theory, 4, 111–112
Neural alarm system, 115
Neural processes, 171–173
Neurobiology, 261–262
Neurophysiology, 63, 261
Neuroticism, 90
Neurotransmitters, 106, 172
Nonadditive genetic influences, 149
Nonaggressive antisocial behavior,
    153–155
Noncontingent punishment, 226
Nondemocratic societies, 302
Nonnormative collective action, 336
Normal behavior, 107–108
Normal narcissism, 207
Normative beliefs, 128
Normative collective action, 336
Normative parameters (power system),
    74–77
Norms
    with intimate relationship aggression,
        369–370
    violation of, 196–197
NPI (Narcissistic Personality Inventory),
    207

Objectification, 252–253
Observational learning processes,
    131–132
Openness to experience, 90
Organized violence, 301–303
Outcome expectancies, 45

Power
  of advantaged groups, 340
  and aggression, 4
  in approach orientation, 251–252
  and attachment, 75–76, 249–253
  defined, 75
  as goal, 250–251
  and objectification, 252–253
  in parent–child relationship, 284
  sense of, 75
Power behavioral system. *See* Power
  system
Power Behavioral System Scale (PBSS),
  79–84
Powerless individuals, 78
Power-oriented behavior, 77–78
Power system, 71–85
  activation and functioning of,
    77–79
  and behavioral systems perspective,
    72–74
  hyperactivation and deactivation of,
    79–84
  normative parameters of, 74–77
POWs (prisoners of war), 392–398
Pratto, F., 340
Precursor genes, 158
Predictive validity, 84
Preemptive violence, 308
Prefrontal cortex (PFC)
  importance of, 106
  in information processing, 172
  in self-control, 114–115
Prevention orientation, 250
Primary caregivers, 243, 355–356
Primary strategy, 73
"Primitive" attachment threat, 260–261
Prisoner's dilemma, 226
Prisoners of war (POWs), 392–398
Proactive aggression, 151–152
Procedural justice, 281
Process dissociation paradigms, 47
Prolonged trauma, 397
Promoting Alternative Thinking
  Strategies program, 212
Promotion focus, 77
Promotion orientation, 250
Provocation, 44, 45, 109
Psychobiology, 96

Psychological aggression
  in intimate relationships, 368–369,
    375
  perceptions of, 373
  physical aggression vs., 370–371
  and victim well-being, 379
Psychological breakdown, 390–391
Psychological control, 284
Psychological development in children,
  351–360
  attachment in, 355–356
  emotion regulation in, 353–355
  and maltreatment, 352–358
  memory in, 357–358
  methodological considerations with,
    358–359
  in pathogenic relational environ-
    ments, 352
  and psychopathology, 356–357
Psychological processes, 128–133
Psychological sequelae, 394–395
Psychology of revenge, 223
Psychopathology, 91, 356–357
Psychophysiology, 171–173
Psychosomatic effects, 387
Psychotherapy, 397–398
P300 component, 112
PTSD. *See* Posttraumatic stress disorder
Public goods games, 228–229
Public support
  for aggressive retaliation, 316–317,
    321
  for intergroup aggression, 323–326
  for military action, 324–326
  for organized violence, 301–303
Punishment, 225–227, 229
Pyszczynski, T., 304

Race relations, 335–336
Raine, A., 152
Rathus, S. A., 78
Rational decision making, 305
Reactivation, of traumatic reactions,
  391–392
Reactive aggression, 151–152
Realistic group-conflict theory, 336
Reappraisal processes, 21–22
Recalibrational theory, 53–54
Receptor genes, 158
Reciprocal altruism, 231–232

Stability
    of aggressive behavior, 156–157,
        211–212
    of PBSS instrument, 80
    in personality, 95–96
Status, 64
Steinberg, L., 282
Strength model of self-regulation, 42
Stress, 386–392
Stress inoculation perspective, 390
Stressors, 392–394
Stress resolution hypothesis, 390
Structural inequality, 335–339
Substance-dependence syndromes, 97
Suicidal terrorism, 15, 302
Suicide, 266
Support, public. *See* Public support
Symbolic immortality, 269
Syndromes (CuPS approach), 188–189

Tausch, N., 340
Taylor, S. P., 113
Teachers, 286–287
Tedeschi, J., 61
Tein, J. Y., 263
Tension, 333–334, 343
Terrorism, 15, 25, 301, 302, 306–307.
    See also Political violence
Terror management theory (TMT)
    attachment security in, 268–269
    and political violence, 298–300
Testosterone, 42
Third-party deterrence, 228
Third-party triggers, 37, 39
Threatened egotism, 207–208, 212–213
TMT. *See* Terror management theory
Toth, S. L., 354
Traits. *See* Personality traits
Transient criminality, 267
Transporter genes, 158
Trauma. *See also* Posttraumatic stress
        disorder
    of captivity, 391–394
    repeated and prolonged, 397
Tredoux, C., 342
Triggering events, 23
Trust, 233
Trust game, 227
Trustworthiness, 194–196
Turning points, 131

Twin studies
    on genetic and environmental
        influences, 144–145
    on heritability of aggression,
        176–177
Type D (disorganized/disoriented)
        attachment, 261–262, 355

Ubeida, Marwan Abu, 15
Ultimatum game (UG), 227
Unconditional respect, 278–282
Universalism, 287
Universality, of anger, 66
Ureno, G., 78
U.S. War on Terrorism, 28
Utility motives, 304–305, 309

Vagal tone, 246
van Beijsterveldt, C. E., 156
van der Valk, J. C., 156
Vengeance, 232–234
Ventral prefrontal cortex, 106
Verhulst, F. C., 156
Veterans, 388, 389, 395–396
Victimization, peer, 286
Victim perceptions
    of breakup aftermath, 377–378
    and commitment level to relation-
        ship, 376–377
    of partner aggression, 371–375
Video games, 112
Villasenor, L., 78
Violence
    and aggression, 4
    beliefs, attitudes, and expectations
        supportive of, 26
    defined, 18
    inevitability of, 306–307
    influence of government actions on,
        27–29
    institutionalized, 25
    intimate partner, 175, 247, 260,
        262–266
    media, 111–112, 115–116
    military, 266–267, 385–386
    motives for, 303–305
    moving beyond, 310–311
    organized, 301–303
    perpetrators of, 25–26
    political. *See* Political violence

ABOUT THE EDITORS

Phillip R. Shaver, PhD, a social and personality psychologist, is Distinguished Professor of Psychology at the University of California, Davis. Before moving there, he served on the faculties of Columbia University, New York University, University of Denver, and State University of New York at Buffalo. He has coauthored and coedited numerous books, including *In Search of Intimacy; Measures of Personality and Social Psychological Attitudes; Measures of Political Attitudes; Handbook of Attachment: Theory, Research, and Clinical Applications;* and *Attachment in Adulthood: Structure, Dynamics, and Change,* and has published over 200 scholarly journal articles and book chapters. Dr. Shaver's research focuses on attachment, human motivation and emotion, close relationships, personality development, and the effects of meditation on behavior and the brain. He is a member of the editorial boards of *Attachment and Human Development, Personal Relationships,* the *Journal of Personality and Social Psychology,* and *Emotion,* and has served on grant review panels for the National Institutes of Health and the National Science Foundation. He has been executive officer of the Society of Experimental Social Psychology and is a fellow of both the American Psychological Association and the Association for Psychological Science. Dr. Shaver received a Distinguished Career Award from the International Association for Relationship Research and has served as president of that organization.

Mario Mikulincer, PhD, is professor of psychology and dean of the New School of Psychology at the Interdisciplinary Center in Herzliya, Israel. He has published three books—*Human Helplessness: A Coping Perspective; Dynamics of Romantic Love: Attachment, Caregiving, and Sex;* and *Attachment in Adulthood: Structure, Dynamics, and Change*—and over 280 scholarly journal articles and book chapters. Dr. Mikulincer's main research interests are attachment theory, terror management theory, personality processes in interpersonal relationships, coping with stress and trauma, grief-related processes, and prosocial motives and behavior. He is a member of the editorial boards of several scientific journals, including the *Journal of Personality and Social Psychology, Psychological Inquiry,* and *Personality and Social Psychology Review,* and has served as associate editor of two journals, the *Journal of Personality and Social Psychology* and *Personal Relationships.* Recently, he was elected to serve as chief editor of the *Journal of Social and Personal Relationships.* He is a fellow of the Society for Personality and Social Psychology and the Association for Psychological Sciences. He received the EMET Prize in Social Science for his contributions to psychology and the Berscheid–Hatfield Award for Distinguished Mid-Career Achievement from the International Association for Relationship Research.